THE PSYCHOLOGY
OF AGGRESSION

THE PSYCHOLOGY OF AGGRESSION

ARNOLD H. BUSS

Associate Professor of Psychology, University of Pittsburgh

John Wiley and Sons, Inc., New York and London

to Harry and Esta

Preface

The literature on aggression is scattered, and researchers in one area may be unaware of what has been happening elsewhere. This isolation prevents researchers from sharing promising methods of investigation, and it tends to make theoretical formulations too narrow. It is hoped that this book will meet the need for communication; the aim is to accomplish this in three ways. First, there is a systematic presentation of what is known about aggression, thereby revealing gaps in knowledge. Second, theoretical formulations are compared, and their assumptions and implications are examined. Third, there is a delineation of the problems of investigating aggression in the laboratory and the field, as well as a presentation of methods of solving these problems.

The original goal was comprehensive coverage, but the amount of material proved to be too great for a single volume, especially in the areas of projective techniques, psychopathology, psychosomatics, prejudice, and development. Therefore the review has been selective, especially in the areas just noted. There is an emphasis on previously unpublished material (doctoral dissertations, papers presented at meetings) because of the relative unavailability of such material.

The book is divided into three parts, although the division is at best a rough one. Part 1 deals with aggression as it is studied in the laboratory, with an emphasis on discrete aggressive responses and reactions to hostile stimuli. Part 2 is concerned with aggressiveness, i.e., aggression as an enduring response tendency; this section deals with methods of measuring aggressiveness, theories of aggressiveness, and aggressiveness and hostility in psychopathology. Part 3 concerns developmental and social aspects of aggression, with the social aspects limited to prejudice.

I am indebted to the following companies for permission to reproduce copyrighted material: American Heart Association, American Journal of Orthopsychiatry, American Psychological Association, Columbia University Press, Free Press, Harper, Journal of Clinical Psychology, Journal Press, Macmillan, McGraw-Hill, National Psychological Association for Psychoanalysis, W. W. Norton, Oxford University Press, Random House, University of Minnesota Press, Yale University Press.

It is a pleasure to acknowledge those who were of help during the writing of this book. Frederick Kanfer, Peter Lang, and Charles Windle offered valuable criticisms of early drafts, and Merle Moskowitz and Arthur Orgel were of great help with the final draft. Oakley Ray sharpened issues and made useful suggestions about several drafts, and Terry Miller tried to improve style and clarity. The following colleagues and friends had expert advice in their fields of specialization: Alan Fisher, Harry Fowler, David Lazovik, Bernard Mausner, William Meyer, William Shipman, Larry Stein, Thurlow Wilson, and George Wischner.

Several secretaries converted cluttered pages into readable manuscript: Sharon Brock, Patricia Driscoll, Betty Pavlovich, Margaret Ross, and Ann Shaw. Jean McCulla and Nancy Hartmann aided in indexing. Of greatest help was my wife, Edith, whose encouragement and common sense facilitated the writing of this book from its inception.

ARNOLD H. BUSS

Pittsburgh, Pennsylvania
June, 1961

Contents

PART ONE

1

Aggression, anger, and hostility

This chapter defines terms and discusses the consequences of these definitions. There are three sections, one each for aggression, anger, and hostility. These three terms refer to three different aspects of behavior: instrumental response, emotional reaction, and attitude. Aggression is an instrumental response that administers punishment; anger is an emotional reaction with prominent autonomic and skeletal-facial components; hostility is a negative attitude, with attitude defined in terms of implicit verbal responses. Although these three aspects of behavior often cluster together, it is necessary for expositional purposes to treat them separately.

AGGRESSION

The term *aggression* subsumes a large number of responses that vary in topography, energy expenditure, and consequences. All aggressive responses share two characteristics: (1) the delivery of noxious stimuli and (2) an interpersonal context. Thus aggression is defined as *a response that delivers noxious stimuli to another organism;* the term *attack* will be used as a synonym.

In some definitions of aggression the central concept is "intent" to do harm. There are definitions that appear to use this concept with-

1

out actually employing the term "intent." For example, Dollard et al. define aggression as "an act whose goal response is injury to another organism . . . " (1939, p. 11). In their context goal response appears equivalent to aim or intent, despite their avoidance of these words.

There are two reasons for excluding the concept of intent from the definition of aggression. First, it implies teleology, a purposive act directed toward a future goal, and this view is inconsistent with the behavioral approach adopted in this book. Second, and more important, is the difficulty of applying this term to behavioral events. Intent is a private event that may or may not be capable of verbalization, may or may not be accurately reflected in a verbal statement. One might be led to accept intent as an inference from the reinforcement history of the organism. If an aggressive response has been systematically reinforced by a specific consequence, such as flight of the victim, the recurrence of the aggressive response might be said to involve an "intent to cause flight." However, this kind of inference is superfluous in the analysis of behavior; it is more fruitful to examine directly the relation between reinforcement history of an aggressive response and the immediate situation eliciting the response.

In summary, *intent* is both awkward and unnecessary in the analysis of aggressive behavior; rather, the crucial issue is the nature of the reinforcing consequences that affect the occurrence and strength of aggressive responses. In other words, what are the classes of reinforcers that affect aggressive behavior?

Reinforcers of Aggression

There are two major classes of reinforcers of aggression: (1) the stimulus of the victim suffering injury or being in pain and (2) extrinsic rewards. Pain and injury to the victim are the usual consequences of physical aggression, and since they are closely associated with aggression, it is not surprising that they serve as reinforcers.

Some psychologists have defined aggression as a response that causes injury, implying that pain or injury is the sole reinforcer of aggression. Underlying this definition is the assumption that aggression occurs only in the presence of anger. This definition was popularized by *Frustration and Aggression* (Dollard et al., 1939) and a generation of textbooks.

The Dollard et al. approach emphasizes *angry aggression,* which is usually reinforced by the victim's pain, but it neglects an entire class of aggressive responses. These are *instrumentally aggressive* responses, which are reinforced by the same reinforcers that follow any instrumental responses: food, water, sex, money, approval, dominance, and the removal or escape from aversive stimuli. The thug who beats his victim and steals his money is reinforced by the acquisition of money; the son who wins a street fight with a peer is likely to be rewarded by the approval of his father ("He's a real boy, some fighter!"). When the barrier between the individual and a reward is another organism, the "intent" of the aggression is to achieve the reward, not to cause pain or injury, i.e., the reinforcer is the reward, not the victim's pain.

For expositional purposes it is necessary to separate these two classes of reinforcers, but it must be acknowledged that there are many situations in which both are operating. This is especially true when the aggressive response is triggered by noxious stimulation, such as an attack. When an individual is attacked, the aggression, if successful, is reinforced not only by his victim's pain but also by termination of the noxious stimulus (the attack on himself). When both types of reinforcer are present, it may be difficult to decide whether one or the other is responsible for strengthening the aggressive response.

On the other hand, there are many situations in which the reinforcer is clearly the acquisition of some reward (such as money), not causing the victim injury. The emphasis in prevalent definitions of aggression on victim's injury as the sole reinforcer (in fact, the basic part of the definition) of aggression has unfortunately led to a neglect of instrumental aggression. It may well be that angry aggression and instrumental aggression should be kept separate as subclasses of aggression, but both belong under the heading of aggression. Thus aggression consists of delivering noxious stimuli, but the victim's emotional or physiological reaction may not be the crucial consequence. In instrumental aggression the acquisition of some extrinsic reinforcer or the cessation of aversive stimuli are the crucial consequences, not the victim's discomfort.

There are certain behaviors that are ordinarily not labelled as aggressive, though they do involve the delivery of noxious stimuli. These are behaviors whose reinforcer is a socially acceptable goal; e.g., a dentist may hurt his patient when repairing a tooth, a doctor may cause pain when giving an injection, a parent may hurt a child when punishing him. To the extent that the child's pain or discomfort is a source of satisfaction to the parent, the parent's punishing response is aggressive.

It is important to understand the basis for excluding such behavior from the class of aggressive responses: it is generally recognized (by society) that the administration of noxious stimuli is carried out temporarily in the hope of greater good resulting in the long run. The individual who administers the painful stimuli does so in a clearly recognized *social role* (a parent who needs to discipline his child, a physician who must inject drugs into a patient). So long as the noxious stimuli are delivered within the context of a recognized social role and with socially desirable, long-run consequences, the behavior is not considered aggressive. On the other hand, when noxious stimuli are delivered in the context of an interpersonal situation and/or with no long-range social good as a likely consequence, the response is aggressive.

Finally, the *accidental* delivery of noxious stimuli does not fall under the heading of aggression. If the attack is accidental, an examination of the reinforcement history of the response in the context of the two people involved (aggressor and victim) should reveal no consistent relationship. There are, of course, "accidents" that are not accidents. The individual who harms others and claims it is accidental should show a consistent history of attacking others. Were the delivery of noxious stimuli truly accidental, there should be no consistency in the history. Accidents are by definition random occurrences, manifesting no pattern of consistent behavior.

Older children and adults are capable of disguising aggression behind a façade of accidents. An individual may reach to pick up a belonging and bump another person. It may be difficult to establish whether the jostling was accidental or not. Therefore the individual who does seek to cause pain may use this and similar situations to disguise his aggression. So long as these exceptions to the response class of aggression exist (and they are clearly recognized by most people), some individuals will use them as a means of escaping punishment. Since aggressive responses usually occur in a social matrix, occasional misclassification is inevitable.

Noxious stimuli may be delivered in the context of different kinds of aggressive responses, and the various responses may be classified in two ways. The first is on the basis of the organ systems involved: physical versus verbal aggression. The second is on the basis of the interpersonal relationship: active versus passive aggression, direct versus indirect aggression.

Physical Aggression

Physical aggression may be defined as an assault against an organism by means of body parts (limb, teeth) or weapons (knife, club, gun). Assault may have two kinds of consequences. The first includes overcoming or removing a barrier and eliminating the source of noxious stimulation. The definition of aggression specifies that the victim must be an organism, which means that the barrier or the source of aversive stimulation must be (directly or indirectly) another organism. If the barrier is inanimate, removing it by force is not that aggressive,[1] e.g., breaking a window to enter one's own house.

Assault is only one of several instrumental responses that may overcome an organismic barrier. If one's path is blocked by another person, the barrier may be removed by a polite request to move, which is nonaggressive. If this response fails, aggression may be attempted. Because of the inhibitions associated with aggression (the lessons of socialization), the milder, nonaggressive responses are likely to be tried first. If these do not succeed, there may be recourse to assault, which is likely to be more successful in removing the organismic barrier than nonaggressive responses. The potential aggressor needs only to discriminate between those weaker and those stronger than himself.

The second kind of consequence of physical aggression is pain or injury to another organism. *Pain* is the more inclusive term; physical aggression, when successful, inevitably leads to pain but not necessarily to injury. Certain kinds of pain are not accompanied by tissue damage, e.g., electric shock, pinching, twisting the arm (without breaking it). On the other hand, injury that results from assault is virtually always accompanied by pain.

Earlier, accidental injury was classified as nonaggressive; now consider accidental noninjury. An aggressive response may miss its mark and not lead to pain or injury, e.g., a gun is fired but the bullet misses, a punch is thrown but the victim ducks. The pain or injury that would ordinarily ensue, does not occur. When the aggressor attempts to deliver noxious stimuli, the attempt may fail either because of his own ineptitude or because of the skill of his victim; the response is aggressive whether or not pain or injury ensues. The definition of aggression is predicated on the *attempt* to deliver noxious stimuli, not on whether the attempt is successful in every instance.

Accidental noninjury represents the exception, not the rule; assault is usually successful in causing at least some pain. Concerning intensity, it is injury and not pain that appears to be crucial. The association between assault and injury seems to be sufficiently close for the intensity of physical aggression to be graded on the basis of

[1] However, destroying another's property may be aggressive; see the section on indirect aggression.

seriousness of injury. Firing a gun is more aggressive than kicking, which is more aggressive than slapping. Since weapons can accomplish more damage than limbs or teeth, intensity of aggression cannot be gauged solely by the force of the blow, and therefore the only criterion is probability of serious injury. There is legal recognition of the greater injury potential of weapons, the penalties for armed crimes being more severe than for unarmed crimes. Most adults have learned at least an implicit intensity hierarchy of physically aggressive responses, and this hierarchy is undoubtedly amenable to psychological scaling.

Verbal Aggression

Seriousness of injury may be used as a basis for grading the intensity of physical aggression, but probability of serious injury cannot be used as a basis for grading or defining verbal aggression. Threats, criticism, and verbal abuse leave no scars and draw no blood. Some psychologists have used the notion of injury to define not only physical aggression but also verbal aggression; they refer vaguely to "psychic injury." Injury in the usual biological sense is a clear term. Since adding the adjective *psychic* to it renders the term fuzzy and imprecise, it is preferable to avoid the notion of a bruised or wounded ego.

Rather, verbal aggression is defined as a vocal response that delivers noxious stimuli to another organism. The noxious stimuli delivered in physical aggression are pain and injury; the noxious stimuli delivered in verbal aggression are rejection and threat.

Rejection. A rejecting response labels the victim as aversive, bad, and unwanted. Rejection may be nonverbal (shunning of an individual by avoiding his presence or escaping from it, making gestures of disgust, ejecting him forcibly from the group), but it is most frequently verbal. There are three types of verbal rejection. The first is direct and unvarnished dismissal; "You must leave," "Go away," or "Get out." The second type is a hostile remark; "I do not like you," "Your presence annoys me," or "I hate you." In this second type the aggressor indicates by his negative affective reaction that the victim is aversive; the target organism is attacked by the feeling response of the responder.

The third type of rejection includes three subcategories; in order of increasing intensity they are criticism, derogation, and cursing. Criticism is the mildest of the three subcategories because it is the most substantive. The essence of rejection is an attack on the individual himself, rather than on his behavior or his products. Criticism attacks the victim indirectly by negatively evaluating his *who* work, clothes, home, and so forth. When criticism is substantive *decides?* and the individual himself is not attacked, the response is not aggressive, e.g., a teacher grading an essay is not making an aggressive response when he points out the mistakes and bad features of the student's work. Criticism is aggressive only when the critique goes beyond the work and extends to the victim himself.

As criticism becomes more personal, it shades into the second subcategory, derogation. Derogation extends beyond criticism of the victim's work, the negative comments being applied to the victim himself. "This work is no good" is critical; "This poor work shows how stupid you are" is derogatory. Derogation implies that the recipient is personally aversive. Derogation, being directed at the individual, is therefore more aggressive than criticism, which is directed toward the individual's products or possessions.

The third subcategory, cursing, represents the most intense verbal aggression. Through cursing, the victim is attacked directly with strong, tabooed words that are typically delivered with considerable vocal force. Cursing represents an extreme form of derogation that is set off from it by the social unacceptability (and therefore the greater intensity) of the verbal labels employed.

Threat. Verbal threat is defined as a response that symbolizes, substitutes for, or is anticipatory of subsequent attack. Threat acquires its aggressive connotations by association with responses that are already aggressive. The recipient learns that threats are noxious stimuli by a process of classical conditioning. The unconditioned stimulus is physical or verbal aggression; the conditioned stimulus is the threat "I am going to hit you." The unconditioned stimulus of being attacked usually elicits an emotional response (fear or anger). The threat initially does not produce an emotional response, but after pairing with the unconditioned stimulus of attack, the threat comes to elicit the same or a similar emotional response. Eventually the victim makes similar responses to both the threat and the attack.

The aggressor learns that threat is an aggressive response principally by imitation. He sees threat used on others or on himself, and learns from his own response or from the emotional response of others that threat has virtually the same noxious properties as the attacking behavior it symbolizes. Once he makes a threatening response and discovers the victim responds as though he is attacked, the threat response becomes functionally equivalent to other attacking responses.

Direct versus Indirect Aggression

Most of the examples mentioned so far have been of direct aggression. From the aggressor's vantage point, the best mode of aggression is one that avoids counterattack. Indirect aggression solves the problem by rendering it difficult to identify the aggressor. Indirect aggression may be verbal (spreading nasty gossip) or physical (a man sets fire to his neighbor's home). These examples illustrate the two ways in which aggression can be indirect. Gossip is indirect in that the victim is not present, and the noxious stimuli are delivered via the negative reactions of others; the victim gets into trouble at the end of a chain of mediating events and people. Damaging a person's possessions is indirect in that the victim is not hurt or injured, but objects associated with and valued by him are destroyed.

Because damage to one's possessions or harm to one's loved ones is in part a substitute for damage to oneself, the definition of aggression as the delivery of noxious stimuli to another organism must be expanded to include "organism-surrogate." Thus it is possible to attack the victim via the objects that are closely associated with him. Such indirect aggression requires mediating responses that serve to relate an attack on a substitute or symbol of the victim to attack against the victim himself.

Indirect aggression may shade over into nonaggressive destruction. If the object being damaged clearly belongs to someone and the destructive act is reinforced by the victim's loss and discomfort, the response is aggressive. If the object belongs to no one (or possession is in doubt) and the destructive act is not reinforced by another's loss or discomfort, the act is not aggressive. If a given response results in noxious stimuli being delivered to another organism, no matter how deviously, the response is aggressive. So long as the response does not lead to the eventual delivery of noxious stimuli, it is not aggressive, whether or not destruction of material is involved.

The distinction between aggression and destruction may be unnecessary, i.e., if it can be demonstrated empirically that the two kinds of responses are equivalent (made in response to similar stimuli, reinforced by similar reinforcers). Until such a demonstration occurs, it seems best to separate attacks against organisms from destruction of objects.

Active versus Passive Aggression

Most aggressive responses are active; the aggressor makes an instrumental response that delivers noxious stimuli to the victim.

However, noxious stimuli may also be delivered in the absence of an active response by the aggressor; he may aggress by preventing the victim from achieving a goal. Blocking of another's path is aggressive in that noxious stimuli are presented to the victim, despite the aggressor's lack of activity.

Most passive aggression is direct, the aggressor blocking the ongoing behavior of the victim. Passive, indirect aggression is rare, but it does occur, e.g., the hunger strikes by Ghandi against the British in India, the "sit-ins" by Negro students in the South. Such acts are aggressive only via a complex chain of events, the aggressor delivering noxious stimuli merely by his presence or by self-denial. In passive, indirect aggression the ongoing behavior of the victim is not immediately and directly blocked, but the refusal of the passive aggressor to act for himself constitutes an aversive stimulus. This kind of aggression differs considerably from the active, direct aggression of assault or cursing, and perhaps it constitutes the borderline of aggression.

Passive aggression is a subordinate's best weapon against his superior. Active attack invites retaliation. When the attack is passive, however, it is usually difficult for the victim to establish blame or to determine whether aggression has occurred.

ANGER

Anger is a response with facial-skeletal and autonomic components. It may be conceptualized as a drive state, and for some psychologists it does have this dual nature: as behavior with salient autonomic aspects and as a concept related to aggression. In this respect anger is like anxiety, which is a response with strong autonomic components and which some psychologists conceptualize as a drive state.

Anger as an Emotional Response

The study of the postural and facial aspects of anger dates back many years, and there is still controversy over whether anger can be separated from fear on the basis of physiognomy alone. The interested reader is referred to Coleman (1949), Reymert (1950), and Young (1943) for expositions of facts and issues concerning identification of anger. This brief section is concerned with the impact of socialization on the anger reaction; physiological aspects are mentioned only in passing and are discussed in Chapter 6.

Because the expressions characteristic of anger undergo modification during socialization, the skeletal and facial aspects of anger are best seen in children. Children are taught to modulate both aggression and expression of anger; a scowling mien and a threatening position of the limbs are punished, and with continued punishment these expressions of anger are inhibited. For some individuals the inhibition is so severe that at maturity only the physiological aspects remain, the facial and skeletal aspects of anger having been suppressed.

While the postural features of anger may be suppressed, the physiological aspects are unaffected by socialization. Society is concerned mainly with responses that have interpersonal consequences, and both overt anger and attacking responses are shaped and inhibited by society. However, the heightened level of physiological activity in anger is less public, and there are no taboos concerning such physiological arousal. Furthermore, it is difficult to control autonomic responses; though they may be conditioned in the laboratory, it is extremely difficult to modulate or inhibit them in everyday situations. Thus the autonomic aspects of anger remain intact while the postural and facial aspects are modulated and inhibited.

The salient characteristics of anger are: diffuseness, energizing properties, and tension.

Diffuseness. Autonomic activation during anger produces widespread changes in blood pressure, pulse rate, respiration rate, blood sugar mobilization, and so forth, which will be discussed in Chapter 6. The postural reactions are not activated by the autonomic nervous system, but when they occur (prior to complete socialization or when there is incomplete socialization), they are also widespread. The temper tantrum of a child involves such actions as kicking, screaming, beating of the hands, thrashing, distorted facial features, and crying. Thus a rage reaction involves the entire body.

Energizing aspects. Anger typically intensifies aggression; a playful tap becomes a harmful blow, a minor scuffle becomes a full-fledged brawl. The physiological arousal seems to energize the attacking response.

On the other hand, when the response that occurs is nonaggressive, anger may disorganize it. An angry person finds it difficult to concentrate, to show skill in a task requiring attention and control. Worchel (1957) showed that angry subjects scored lower on a digit symbol task than did subjects who had been allowed to dissipate their anger.

Tension and tension reduction. The pattern of autonomic arousal that occurs in anger constitutes a physiological tension state. The individual is aware of this tension state because interoceptors are sensitive to these internal stimuli, but it is difficult to verbalize precisely what the tension state is like. The subject typically reports being stirred up, aroused, tense, excited, tight, etc. The tension state is sufficiently different from the resting state to be discriminated but too diffuse to be described in detail.

A similar tension state exists when anxiety occurs, but in anxiety the tension state is clearly aversive; escape responses diminish the tension of anxiety, and such reduction of tension is reinforcing. Is the tension state of anger also aversive? When the tension state is at high levels, as in rage, it is probably aversive, and a sudden drop in rage is reinforcing. Violent aggression (perhaps any violent activity) appears to diminish anger level. The phrase "blowing off steam" connotes both the drop in tension level and the feeling of satisfaction at having done so. Thus intense tension appears to be aversive, and a sudden drop in tension appears to be reinforcing.

When the tension state is at lower levels, as in mild anger, it does not seem to be aversive; some individuals are even reinforced by increments in the tension state when the initial level of anger is low. Thus the tension state may be reinforcing when anger level is low and aversive when anger level is high.

Anger as a Drive

Anger is an emotional reaction, and emotions have drive properties; therefore, anger may be regarded as a drive state. But is anger *the* drive for aggression; must anger be present for aggression to occur? Anger is certainly present in "angry aggression," but in the other kind, instrumental aggression, anger need not be present. Instrumental attack, like any instrumental response, may occur in the absence of an identifiable stimulus or antecedent. The attacking response is reinforced by acquisition of a reward, and anger need not occur.

Since instrumental aggression can occur in the absence of anger, it follows that anger is not *the* drive for aggression. Rather, anger may be regarded as *one* of the drives that lead to aggression. The other drives are ostensibly related to the reinforcers that follow any instrumental response: food, water, dominance, etc. If anger is not *the* drive for aggression, is it fruitful to regard it as a drive? The position adopted here is that it is not fruitful. Regarding anger as an emotional response accounts for all its properties (tension level, energizing of aggression) without the encumbering assumption that aggression must be preceded by a drive state (anger or some other drive). The nondrive approach is adopted here because it is more parsimonious and because it emphasizes stimulus operations and internal responses.

HOSTILITY

The instrumental response of aggression and the emotional response of anger each occupy brief temporal intervals. The attack is made and is over; anger rises to a pitch and then subsides. Hostility is an attitudinal response that endures: *an implicit verbal response involving negative feelings (ill will) and negative evaluations of people and events.* The hostile response is neither instrumental nor autonomic. Rather, it involves the interpretation and evaluation of stimuli, and the negative evaluations have no impact on others unless they are verbalized.

When they are verbalized, hostile responses take the form of negative labels of the kind that are used in derogatory (aggressive) comments or feeling statements, such as "I hate you," "I despise you." This does not mean that hostility and aggression are identical, but rather that aggression may have hostile components. Just as anger may be part of an aggressive response in that it adds autonomic and certain postural features to an attacking response, hostility may be part of an aggressive response in that there is strong resentment of and negative evaluation of the victim of the attack.

Hostility is usually not verbalized openly as part of an aggressive response. Typically it is implicit, consisting of the mulling over of past attacks on oneself, rejections, and deprivations. If the hostile response is verbalized as part of an aggressive response (the victim is told directly that he is disliked or resented), it is easy to identify the presence of hostility and to gauge its intensity. But if the negative labels are made implicitly, hostility must be inferred from other aggressive behavior. Hostility may be inferred when the attack is reinforced more by injury than by attaining an extrinsic reinforcer, i.e., whenever the aggression has connotations of vengeance.

Hostility may be regarded as a conditioned anger response that has none of the autonomic or postural aspects of anger. When an anger stimulus is presented to a recipient, it elicits an anger reaction and a tendency to counterattack. The anger stimulus not only elicits an anger response but also the passive response of observing and labeling the stimulus. Such observing responses occur whether or not an instrumental or emotional response is made, so long as the organism is aware of the presence of the stimuli. These implicit responses of perceiving, catagorizing, and evaluating stimuli may be called observing-labeling responses;[2] when they are associated with anger reactions, they become hostile responses.

An anger stimulus consists of a noxious stimulus presented to the individual, usually by another individual. The stimulus and the originator of the stimulus are labeled with negative terms at the same time the anger response occurs. The longer the anger persists, the greater is the association in time between the autonomic aspects of anger and the implicit, negative language responses. After the anger subsides, there remain negative language responses, consisting of resentment, jealousy, belief that others are threatening, etc. These responses have been conditioned to anger, but they persist after anger dissipates; they are the residuals called hostility. They determine how negative the feeling reaction will be to the same or similar stimuli the next time they are presented. Once such observing-labeling responses have been conditioned to anger stimuli, they are more or less substitute anger responses. The conditioned anger response (hostility) resembles anger in its orientation toward injury and punishment but differs in that it lacks the autonomic and postural components of anger. The enduring or persisting quality of hostility may be attributed to the language (mediational) responses that constitute hostility.

Since hostility develops on the basis of the verbal labels that identify and categorize stimuli and since language responses exist only in humans, hostility occurs only in humans. Animals and prelanguage human beings do not hate. They become enraged and they attack, but since they do not possess the mechanisms necessary for symbolic responses, they are not capable of resentment, grudges, and revenge.

The pairing of *observing* with *labeling* in the observing-labeling response indicates that the two occur more or less simultaneously. The process of observing is so closely allied to the process of categorizing that the two cannot be separated. It is impossible to observe punishment being inflicted upon oneself without making a negative labeling response. The negative term becomes part of the observation and of the memory of the stimulus, and this merged observation-label is what constitutes the hostile response.

[2] For an exposition of observing response in animals, see Wyckoff (1952). The present account owes more to Osgood's mediational concept (1953).

In the conditioning of hostility it is not necessary for the anger stimulus to be delivered firsthand. Viewing motion pictures or reading about crimes against others may induce anger. The anger is accompanied by negative labels, and after the anger has subsided there is a residual of ill will toward the culprits. The enduring nature of this second-hand hostility may be seen in those Americans who still hate Germany and Germans because of their atrocities during World War II.

For some individuals hostility is not limited to one group or one nation but pervades their outlook toward everyone. If presented with a standard series of stimuli, they see more hostile connotations than do most people. In a study described in Chapter 7 a number of words were presented to college students, who were instructed to rate them for hostility. The term *plain-spoken* received an average rating of 2.0 on a nine-point scale, connoting little hostility. However, several subjects gave this term a rating of 6.0, which was the mean rating for such words as *insulting, curse, maddened,* and *embittered.* These extreme subjects tend to see the world as a cold, threatening place and attribute more hostility to stimuli than do most people.

Hostility and Aggression

Since hostility may be inferred from certain kinds of aggression, the two may be confused. The response "I hate you" is both hostile and aggressive. The victim is attacked with the aggressor's own negative feelings. However, not all hostile responses are necessarily aggressive, since at times responses are not verbalized in the presence of the victim. Thus saying "I hate him" to oneself is a hostile response, but since the noxious stimulus is not delivered to the victim, it is not aggressive. On the other hand, not all verbal aggression implies the presence of hostility. The attack that is contained in a string of oaths and curses is usually associated with rage but not with the more enduring ill will of hostility. The person who "blows off steam" by cursing at his victim is less likely to harbor resentment in the future. Most instrumental aggression has no hostile component; the victim is not hated. Thus hostility can occur in the absence of aggression, and aggression can occur without hostility.

As an enduring response with both feeling and labeling aspects, hostility is by implication a dispositional response; i.e., it may lead to aggression. The dispositional nature of hostility has been mentioned in connection with vengeful aggression. Man has the symbolic language responses necessary to maintain stimuli years after the actual stimuli have disappeared. He can mull over rejections, attacks, and disappointments for long periods; when the opportunity presents itself, such hostility may erupt into violent revenge. Whether aggression occurs is related not only to the intensity of the hostile response but also to the habit strength of aggression and the potency of inhibitors of aggression.

When hostility is learned secondhand, usually it will not lead to aggression. As noted earlier, the media of mass communication (motion pictures, books, radio, television, newspapers) detail behavior of individuals who come to be hated at a distance. Since aggression is physically impossible during the learning of such hostile attitudes, the two are not associated. If the hated individual does become available at a later date, an attacking response would probably not occur because there would have been no pairing of a tendency to aggress with the hostile attitude. Thus the relationship between hostility and aggression depends in large part on whether they are initially elicited by the same stimulus.

Summarizing, when an attack from another organism leads to both hostility and aggression, the mulling over of the attack (hostility) may subsequently lead to an aggressive response. On the other hand, hostility rarely accompanies instrumental aggression. When hostility is learned secondhand, it does not lead to aggression.

Hostility and Anger

Though the evidence is by no means conclusive, an attacking response appears to react back on the autonomic components of anger, reducing the state of tension. Aggression has no similar effect on hostility. Unlike anger, hostility is an enduring response that builds up slowly and changes slowly. There is no tension state in hostility comparable to the physiological arousal of anger, and, therefore, aggression cannot have the same precipitous effect on hostility that it does on anger.

Hostility may lead to anger. Initially the same stimulus that elicits an anger reaction also calls forth an observing-labeling response. The longer the anger reaction endures, the more anger and hostility will be associated. The greater such association, the more likely that a hostile response (mulling over past attacks, etc.) in the future will tend to elicit a rage reaction. For some individuals the association between anger and hostility is close, and they have only to recall past humiliations and resentments in order to become angry.

The implicit verbal responses of hostility have become cues for the anger response, substituting for the stimuli that originally elicited anger.

REFERENCES

Coleman, J. C. Facial expression of emotion. *Psychol. Monogr.*, 1949, No. 296.

Dollard, J., Doob, L. W., Miller, N. E., Mowrer, O. H., & Sears, R. R. *Frustration and aggression.* New Haven: Yale University Press, 1939.

Osgood, C. E. *Method and theory in experimental psychology.* New York: Oxford University Press, 1953.

Reymert, M. D. (Ed.), *Feelings and emotions.* New York: McGraw-Hill, 1950.

Worchel, P. Catharsis and the relief of hostility. *J. abnorm. soc. Psychol.*, 1957, **55**, 238–243.

Wyckoff, L. B. The role of observing responses in discrimination learning. *Psychol. Rev.*, 1952, **59**, 431–442.

Young, P. T. *Emotion in man and animal.* New York: Wiley, 1943.

2

Antecedents of aggression

When an individual is engaged in instrumental behavior that typically leads to a reinforcer and this behavior is blocked, aggression may be successful in overcoming this interference. When an individual is confronted with noxious stimuli, one way of getting rid of the stimuli is to attack the responsible person. These two classes of situations, frustration and noxious stimuli, are the antecedents of aggression. In the following discussion, frustration will receive more attention because of the considerable literature about it and because of the importance of the frustration-aggression hypothesis.

FRUSTRATION

Varieties of Frustration

The typical behavioral sequence may be divided into three segments: (1) instrumental response, (2) presentation of the reinforcer, and (3) consummatory response. The sequence may be blocked in any of these three segments, and frustration operations may be grouped on the basis of which segment they block.

Instrumental response. There are four ways to interfere with a chain of instrumental responses: barriers, failure, distractors, and conflict.

BARRIERS. Barriers have been used to study the learning process rather than aggression, and there are few experiments on aggression as a consequence of instrumental blocking. An interesting study of instrumental blocking is one of the OSS experiments (OSS Assess-

17

ment Staff, 1948). The subject was to direct two subordinates in a building task, but the subordinates (experimental accomplices) never allowed him to attain the goal of completing the small structure. Some subjects became sufficiently enraged to strike the subordinates.

Traffic jams illustrate one kind of barrier, namely delay. Delay is a frequent frustration whose consequences have not been investigated. It has been used to irritate subjects, but it has always been confounded with other irritating procedures (blocking of consummatory responses, insult, presentation of annoying stimuli, etc.). Another kind of barrier is a permanent block to an instrumental response, but permanent barriers have been used experimentally only to block consummatory responses.

FAILURE. This operation consists of telling the subject that he has not met a criterion of performance and that he will not receive a reward. There are two kinds of failure manipulations. In the first, the subject is stopped before he can complete the task, e.g., the task is timed, and the subject is stopped when the (insufficient) time is up. Thus the subject is not allowed to complete his instrumental response. In the second kind of failure, the subject is allowed to complete his instrumental response and then failed; this kind is discussed below.

DISTRACTORS. These are stimuli that interfere with instrumental activity by diverting the subject's attention from the task at hand; studying for an examination may be blocked by the excessive noise of a nearby party. Distractors have been studied only in terms of their effect on work efficiency. There appear to be no laboratory data on the effect of distractors on subsequent aggression, but casual observation of everyday situations indicates that distractors may lead to aggression.

CONFLICT. The fourth way to block an instrumental response is by means of conflict (Brown & Farber, 1951). There may be two incompatible responses leading to the same goal, one canceling out the other; or there may be both approach and avoidance aspects associated with a given instrumental response, the avoidance aspects canceling out the tendency to make the response. Approach-avoidance conflicts occur very frequently in everyday life because the consequences of most responses are usually both positive and negative. Fortunately, conflict is rarely followed by aggression.

Presentation of the reinforcer. The behavioral sequence may also be blocked by omitting the reward; in fact, Amsel (1958) has defined frustration in terms of extinction, or in his terms, "frustrative nonreward." The reward may be omitted on some trials, as in partial reinforcement. Studies of partial reinforcement now number in the hundreds, but none of them has attempted to relate this operation to aggression.

A variant of omission of reward is failure, but this kind of failure differs from interrupting an instrumental response, as described above. In this second kind of failure, the subject is allowed to complete the task and is then told that he has failed. The manipulation is similar to negative reinforcement (the subject is told *wrong* or *no good*), and it is less likely to lead to aggression than the first kind (blocking of an instrumental response).

Consummatory response. Finally, when the reinforcer is available, the individual may be prevented from making the appropriate consummatory response. Kimbrell & Blake (1958) had college students eat crackers coated with Mexican hot sauce and then wait near a water fountain. The tendency to drink was strong, but at least some subjects were prevented from doing so by a printed sign that forbade drinking. Unfortunately, there was no measure of tendency to aggress, but the experiment does illustrate how a consummatory response may be frustrated.

It is clear from the preceding account that frustration includes a variety of operations: barriers, failure, distractors, conflict, omission of reward, with some of these manipulations occurring at different places in the behavioral sequence. The inclusion of these different operations under one heading means that frustration is not only a very large class of manipulations but also an ever-present one in everyday life. More important, it is difficult to see how such divergent operations could all lead to the same class of responses —aggression.

Some of the manipulations that fall under the heading of frustration clearly do not elicit aggression: extinction, partial reinforcement, and conflict. Others would seem to lead to aggression only under special conditions, e.g., when the barrier or the failure is clearly associated with one or several individuals, an attack against whom might succeed in overcoming the frustration. This issue will be discussed below.

In summary, the varieties of frustration raise two important issues. First, the operations subsumed under frustration are so different that one may question whether they belong together. Second, in light of this variety it is not fruitful merely to list frustration as an antecedent of aggression; it is necessary, in addition, to specify what kind of frustration, in which segment of the behavioral sequence it occurs, and the conditions under which it occurs.

An attempt may be made to reconcile the divergent operations subsumed under frustration by treating frustration as a drive state. Brown & Farber (1951) have made the clearest statement of frustration as a drive, their assumption being that the diverse antecedent operations all lead to incompatible response tendencies. This approach to frustration has led to fruitful research on extinction (Amsel, 1958; Lawson & Marx, 1958), but it has been of little value in stimulating research on aggression.

Brown & Farber are necessarily vague about the consequences of the drive state of frustration:

It will be apparent from this treatment of frustration as a determinant of behavior that no attempt has been made to specify which responses will appear in thwarting situations. . . . there is nothing in the theory itself to imply that aggression, for instance, will occur more frequently than withdrawal, or withdrawal more frequently than, say, primitivation. (1951, p. 490)

Thus the drive concept of frustration adds little to the study of aggression. Different manipulations are lumped under one heading (as antecedents of a drive state), and the drive state is followed by a variety of behaviors. Frustration appears more likely to lead to nonaggressive than to aggressive behavior. In the present context (the study of aggression) it seems best to define frustration as a set of blocking operations, taking care to specify the kind of blocking and where it occurs in the behavioral sequence.

Conditions under which Frustration Leads to Aggression

Frustration sometimes leads to aggression and other times to nonaggressive behavior; this section discusses the variables that determine whether aggression follows frustration.

Strength of frustration. It has been suggested (Dollard et al., 1939) that the intensity and/or frequency of aggression covaries with the strength of frustration. Strength of frustration is ostensibly determined by the strength of the response tendency being blocked, the degree of interference, and the number of frustration sequences. Strength of the blocked response tendency has been investigated in two questionnaire studies separated by 20 years. Doob & Sears (1939) had college men rate the strength of various instigations and then report on their typical response when these instigations were blocked. It was found that the frequency of aggression covaried with the rated strength of the frustrated instigations. Since the same subjects rated the instigations and also supplied the reactions to frustration, there may have been a built-in relationship. To correct for this possible artifact Allison & Hunt (1959) presented college students with frustrated instigations that had already been rated by judges as being weakly motivated or strongly motivated. The subjects indicated the probability that they would become angry (which is ostensibly related to the probability that they would aggress), and it was found that frustration of the strongly motivated behaviors led to a higher probability of being angry than frustration of weakly motivated behaviors. Taken together, the two questionnaire studies offer support for the relationship between strength of frustration and tendency toward aggression.

The closer an individual is to a goal, the stronger will be his tendency to reach the goal (the goal-gradient hypothesis), and, therefore, blocking a response when it is close to the goal should be more frustrating than blocking it far from the goal. This was the reasoning of Haner & Brown (1955), who used children as subjects. The task was placing marbles in holes until all the holes were filled, and when the task was completed, a reward was given. The experimenter signaled the end of a trial (whether or not all the holes were filled) by sounding a loud buzzer, which the subject terminated by pushing a plunger. Groups of subjects were failed at varying distances from the goal (varying numbers of holes filled), and it was found that the closer to the goal they were frustrated, the greater was the pressure on the plunger. This finding has been interpreted (Berkowitz, 1958; McNeil, 1959) as evidence for a relationship between intensity of frustration and strength of aggression, an interpretation that rests on the assumption that depressing a plunger is an aggressive response. However, depressing a plunger is not an aggressive response; it does not even fall under the heading of destruction (attacking an object). Therefore, the Haner & Brown results cannot be used to support the hypothesized relationship between intensity of frustration and strength of aggression.

Parenthetically, the Haner & Brown findings have not been substantiated by subsequent experiments. McDonough (1958) used a similar task, including marbles to fill holes and a plunger to be depressed by child subjects. She found no change in amplitude of the plunger-pressing response from before to after frustration. Roehl (1959) studied a similar response in adults and found that frustration tended to *decrease* the amplitude of the response.

The second variable affecting strength of frustration is the extent to which the response tendency is blocked. Hovland & Sears (1940) reasoned that lowered prices for cotton, etc., would lead to economic privation: the lower the prices, the more would a variety of response tendencies (all requiring money) be blocked. They reported a correlation of —.67 between an economic index and the number of lynchings in the South over a period of approximately 50 years. Mintz (1946) reanalyzed their data and discovered statistical artifacts; appropriate statistical procedures led to substantially lower correlations. On the basis of the lower correlations and data from English studies, Mintz concluded that there was no relationship between physical violence and economic privation.

The third variable affecting intensity of frustration is the number of frustrated response-sequences, but there is only one relevant study. Otis & McCandless (1955) mildly frustrated preschool children. The experimenter and the child started down opposite ends of a single play road with toy cars. The cars met in the middle, and only one could pass; the child could either insist that his car go through or allow the experimenter's car to go through, the former being "dominant-aggressive" and the latter "complaisant-submissive." There were eight trials, and dominant-aggressive behavior increased in frequency from the first four to the last four trials. There are two alternative explanations for these results. First, they may be interpreted as confirming the hypothesis that frequency of aggression is a function of the number of frustrations. Second, they may be interpreted in reinforcement-learning terms. Pushing past the experimenter's car leads to the child's winning the game, and the reinforcement of winning may be expected to increase the tendency to make this response. It should also be added that pushing past the experimenter's car would seem to be more of a dominant than an aggressive response. Since the results may be explained in terms other than frustration-aggression (and the reinforcement view is more parsimonious), this experiment does not offer unequivocal support for the hypothesized relationship between intensity of frustration and strength of aggression.

There have been several other studies that attempted to relate aggression to frustration (Cox, 1952; Funkenstein et al., 1957; Weiss & Fine, 1956; Zuckerman, 1955), but in all of them frustration was combined with verbal attack (insult). Therefore these studies cannot be used to evaluate the hypothesized relationship between intensity of frustration and strength of aggression. In summary, the

Instrumental value of aggression.   When the barrier to continuation
of a behavior sequence is another person, an aggressive response is
often successful in removing this barrier.   Thus aggression may have
instrumental value in that it allows the individual to overcome the
organismic barrier that blocks his path to the reinforcer.

Dollard et al. (1939) tended to neglect the instrumental value of
aggression as a response to frustration; rather, they emphasized the
pain-inducing aspects of aggression—as an emotional reaction to
frustration.   Maier (1949) has taken a more extreme position on
aggression as emotional reaction to frustration.   He believes that the
emotional reaction to frustration is so great that the organism strikes
out against any object in the environment; not only does such aggression have no instrumental value, but the occurrence of injury is
more or less accidental.   Thus Maier denies that intent to injure is
a consequence of frustration; the only consequence he sees is an
emotional flailing that has no direction, no goal.

In Maier's experimental situation aggression was instrumentally
valueless.   In fact, aggression rarely follows conflict (Maier's situation) because it leaves the conflict unresolved.   However, frustration that involves blocking by another organism will often lead to
aggression, such attacking behavior often being successful in removing the barrier.   Aggression is certainly not the only means of
overcoming organismic barriers, but it is a major means that has a
high probability of doing so.   It appears that Maier's views are
overgeneralizations from the particular conflict situation he studied.

There is no laboratory study that compares instrumentally valuable
aggression with instrumentally valueless aggression, but there are
data in the Doob & Sears questionnaire study (1939) that bear on
this issue.   Of the 16 situations presented to the subjects, six were
clearly frustrating, the others containing elements of attack or non-
frustrating annoyance.   The six clearly frustrating situations are
presented in Table 2.1.   (Including the other 10 situations would
not substantially affect the difference between the situations calling
for instrumentally valuable aggression and those that do not.)

The first two situations in Table 2.1 involve frustration by another
person in which verbal aggression would be instrumentally valuable.
In both instances a verbal attack on the frustrator might well end
the distraction.   In the remaining four situations, aggression would
have little instrumental value.   In the third and fourth there is no
frustrator to attack.   In the fifth an attack on the frustrator might
lead to rejection by the attractive partner (aggression is not gentle-
manly); but verbal aggression might have some utility, and we may

frustration-aggression hypothesis has been confirmed in qu
studies but not in the laboratory. It may be speculate
paucity of laboratory studies in this area is due to the
eliciting aggression in a laboratory setting, an issue that i
in detail in the next chapter.

Arbitrariness of frustration. When one person block
ongoing behavior, the frustration may be arbitrary (rela
whimsy or petulance of the frustrator) or nonarbitrary
in terms of conditions beyond control). In analyzing the
presented by Doob & Sears (1939) to their college subje
(1952) noted the arbitrary nature of several of the frustr
"You desired to board a boat . . . . The guard forba
what seemed to be entirely unnecessary technicalities
such as "entirely unnecessary technicalities" tend to mak
tration unreasonable. Pastore believed that nonarbitrary
would tend to elicit less aggression, and he devised t
situations to test this hypothesis. One set was arbitra
waiting on the right corner for a bus, and the driver i
passes you by"; the other set was nonarbitrary; "You're
the right corner for a bus. You notice that it is a special
to the garage." The two sets were administered to colleg
who wrote their responses to the situations. It was foun
nificantly more aggressive responses would have been mad
the arbitrary frustrations than following the nonarbitrary f

Allison & Hunt (1959) presented college students wi
tionnaire that included three kinds of frustrating situation
unjustified, and unspecified. The students rated their pro
becoming angry, and it was found that the justified situati
a lower probability of anger than either the unjustified or
situations. Cohen (1955) also confirmed the importance
trary—nonarbitrary dimension in a questionnaire study w
women.

Arbitrariness of frustration is an important variable in
frustration as well as in questionnaire studies of frustr
(1955) studied the effect of a teacher's acting in opposi
desires of a small class, with the teacher giving as a ratio
behavior either the good of the students (nonarbitrary)
desires (arbitrary). The arbitrary frustration led to s
more aggressive verbalizations by the students than dic
arbitrary frustration.

TABLE 2.1. FREQUENCY OF AGGRESSION FOR THE SIX
FRUSTRATING SITUATIONS IN THE DOOB & SEARS STUDY

1. Someone in a seat near you in a theater or concert wriggled and squirmed about in a totally unnecessary way.	51%
2. A guest of yours whom you know only slightly persisted in telling you how to drive and in general pestered you with back seat criticism.	72%
3. You were bored stiff by a conversation of friends, but the social situation was such that you had to endure it for several minutes at least.	6%
4. In an informal gathering of people with whom you were not well acquainted, you found you couldn't solve what everyone else considered a very simple parlor trick.	9%
5. When you finally managed to dance with a particularly attractive girl, a good friend of yours cuts in.	36%
6. You desired to board a boat or train to see a friend off or to enter an examination or park; the guard forbade you on what seemed to be entirely unnecessary technicalities.	17%

note that this has the highest percentage of aggression of the last four situations. In the sixth there would be little to gain from attack on the guard. The last four situations lead to a substantially lower percentage of aggression than the first two situations, and the main difference between the two sets of stimulus conditions is that aggression is appropriate in the first two and inappropriate in the last four. Thus the questionnaire data are clear in showing a relationship between the instrumental value of aggression and its frequency.

Frustration tolerance. Developmentally, the earliest reaction to frustration is generalized excitement, a combination of anger, anxiety, and bewilderment (Bridges, 1932). By the time the child is capable of displaying discreet emotional reactions, he is also capable of making instrumental responses oriented toward coping with the obstacles to reinforcers. As the child matures he learns to inhibit and modulate emotional reactions, not only to frustration but to a variety of stimulus situations. The very young child is often unable to tolerate waiting, whereas the older child can tolerate at least a moderate period of delay, long enough for potentially successful instrumental responses to occur. The older child has also learned, at least in part, to bow to the inevitable, to give up in the face of insurmountable obstacles.

Of course, it is not simply the passage of time that produces such maturity but learning on the part of the child. Since children differ in their rates of learning and since differential methods of child rearing may be expected to hasten or retard emotional control, children of the same age should vary considerably in their response to frustration. Some children may have failed to learn control over their emotional reactions in the face of frustration, whereas other children may have overlearned inhibition of emotional or spontaneous response. These two extremes (overcontrollers and undercontrollers) were studied by Block & Martin (1955). Observers first rated children for control on the basis of their play in several situations. Then children were observed in the Barker, Dembo, & Levin paradigm (1941): children played with very attractive toys and were then removed from the toys and prevented from returning. It was found that the undercontrollers tended to react to this frustration with violent attacks on the wire mesh screen and were unable to play constructively with the less desirable toys. The overcontrollers played patiently and constructively with the less desirable toys and tended not to attack the barrier.

Presumably the difference between undercontrollers and overcontrollers may be attributed both to enduring reaction tendencies in the face of emotional situations and to specific learning concerning aggression. Davitz (1952) demonstrated the importance of both personality and training in determining reactions to frustration. One group of children was encouraged to aggress in several kinds of games; in each game the winner was the most aggressive child (who broke the most ping pong balls of his neighbor, who shoved harder than anyone else). A second group of children was reinforced for playing quiet games like drawing and puzzles, with aggressive behavior being discouraged. Subsequently, both groups were frustrated. They were told that they would see five reels of movies that appeared to be especially interesting from their titles. The first reel was shown, and the children were given candy. At the climax of the second reel the experimenter stepped in front of the screen, took away the candy, and brought the children out of the projection room. He told them there would be no more candy or movies but that they could play with anything in the playroom. The children could still see the projector running but could neither see the movie nor return to the projection room.

The free play of the children was then observed and compared with similar free play prior to the start of the experiment; aggressiveness was rated from protocols by judges who did not know whether the play session was pre- or postfrustration. It was found that the aggressively trained subjects showed a significantly greater increase in aggression than did the peacefully trained subjects. However, one third of the peacefully trained subjects were more aggressive after than before frustration, and one fourth of the aggressively trained subjects were less aggressive after than before frustration. These reversals may be attributed to enduring response trends; some children in each group resisted the training given in the experimental situation because of overriding tendencies to aggress or to submit. Thus Davitz' study demonstrated the importance of both aggression training and of personality dispositions in reactions to frustration.

Adults also differ in frustration tolerance. This variable should be taken into account in experiments on frustration; else it contributes to the error term. Overcontrollers may be expected to remain passive and inhibited, and undercontrollers may be expected to become angry and possibly aggressive as a consequence of severe frustration. When both extremes of subjects are lumped into a single treatment group, they may cancel each other out.

It was noted earlier that arbitrariness of frustration was an important variable in determining response to frustration. It should be added that arbitrariness would seem to be important for adults but not for children. It is only as the child matures that he begins to understand the inevitability of barriers and delays; when he attains maturity, he can easily distinguish between justifiable and arbitrary frustration. This distinction probably has little meaning for a child, and it would be interesting to have developmental data concerning the arbitrariness of frustration.

The Frustration-Aggression Hypothesis

Having discussed the nature of frustration and the conditions under which frustration is likely to lead to aggression, it is now possible to evaluate the frustration-aggression hypothesis. This hypothesis originated in *Frustration and Aggression,* and it is stated clearly on the first page of this book: "This study takes as its point of departure the assumption that *aggression is always a consequence of frustration.* More specifically the proposition is that the occurrence of aggressive behavior always presupposes the existence of frustration and, contrariwise, the existence of frustration always leads to some form of aggression." (Dollard et al., 1939, p. 1) The immediate reaction to this sweeping generalization was negative, and one of the authors quickly amended the hypothesis to read, "Frustration produces instigations to a number of different types of response, one of which is an instigation to aggression." (Miller, 1941, p. 338) This new version of the hypothesis does not retain the sweep and generality of the original, and it is certainly more in line with the facts concerning frustration and aggression.

In denying that frustration always leads to aggression, Miller did not retract the other half of the hypothesis, namely that aggression is always caused by frustration: " . . . the assertion that the occurrence of aggression always presupposes frustration, is in our opinion defensible and useful as a first approximation, or working hypothesis." (1940, p. 338) This notion, that the only antecedent of aggression is frustration, has been accepted by most psychologists who have dealt with this issue. There have been two outstanding exceptions. Maslow (1941) denied that simple frustration would lead to aggression, which he believed would be caused only by attack or threat. Rosenzweig (1944) also emphasized that nonthreatening stimuli would not lead to aggression but that threatening, frustrative stimuli would lead to aggression. Except for these two writers, most psychologists appear to have accepted the frustration-aggression hypothesis, denying any antecedent to aggression other than frustration. For example, in the two most recent comprehensive reviews by psychologists (Berkowitz, 1958; McNeil, 1959) the frustration-aggression hypothesis is fully accepted. Berkowitz goes so far as to state that frustration includes attack and insult, arguing that frustration and attack cannot be distinguished operationally; this issue will be discussed in the next chapter, where attack and frustration operations will be clearly distinguished.

The frustration-aggression hypothesis may have been a useful working hypothesis 20 years ago, but it has limited utility today. Concerning the antecedents of aggression, the next section will show that both attack and annoyers clearly lead to aggression; neither attack nor annoyers constitute a frustration operation. Furthermore, like many other learned responses, aggression does not necessarily have identifiable antecedents. An attacking response may occur simply because it has led to a reward in the past and not because it is provoked by an immediate noxious or frustrating situation. On the basis of these considerations the frustration-aggression hypothesis should be discarded. It may be argued that the hypothesis has heuristic value, that it has led to a body of research. However, the emphasis on frustration has led to an unfortunate neglect of the other large class of antecedents (noxious stimuli), as well as a neglect of aggression as an instrumental response. Frustration is only *one* antecedent of aggression, and it is not the most potent one.

As the next chapter will show, when experimenters wish to elicit aggression in the laboratory, they rely more on attack (insult) than on frustration.

NOXIOUS STIMULI

The noxious stimuli that lead to aggression include attack and annoyers. Attack, as defined previously, involves the delivery of noxious stimuli to the victim, the reinforcement being the victim's pain or the acquisition of a reinforcer. Annoyers are stimuli that in some way irritate or are aversive (the smell of garlic on another's breath); but these stimuli are not focused toward a victim or group of victims, and there is no reinforcement. The distinction between attack and annoyers will become clearer as they are discussed.

Attack

It is important to distinguish active from passive attack as antecedents of aggression. Passive attack includes some kinds of frustration; when the barrier to an instrumental or consummatory response is another person or the barrier has obviously been placed there by another person, it is appropriate to label this passive attack. (Note, however, that a barrier need not be a person or an object associated with a person; also note that other kinds of frustration, not involving barriers, do not fall under the heading of passive attack.) Since passive attack as an antecedent of aggression has been discussed under Frustration, this section will deal only with active attack.

When the individual is attacked, he can either flee or fight back. There are several variables determining whether the response will be flight or fight (habit strength of each, position of attacker and victim on a dominance hierarchy, which includes strength, prestige, etc.), but only one variable will be considered here. Assuming equal habit strength for both flight and fight, and assuming that the attacker and the victim are of equal status, the tendency to counterattack should vary curvilinearly with the intensity of the attack. This relationship is especially apparent when the attack consists of physical aggression. If the physical attack is mild, it serves as only a weak stimulus for counteraggression, and there should be little tendency to fight back. As the physical aggression becomes more intense, it is a stronger stimulus for counteraggression; fighting back thus becomes more probable and more intense as the attacking stimulus increases through the middle range of intensity. At the upper levels of intensity, physical attack may be so strong as to induce a flight response rather than a fight response.

For obvious ethical and practical reasons there are no laboratory data bearing on the comments just made concerning physical aggression, but there is an experiment that varied verbal attack on subjects through the middle range of intensity. McClelland & Apicella (1945) had an experimenter use two degrees of insult (one mildly derogatory and the other more intense, including cursing), with the experimenter and the subjects being peers. It was found that the more intense verbal attacks elicited more frequent and more intense verbal counteraggression than the less intense attacks. Though this was the only study to vary intensity of attack, there are a number of other studies of attack as an antecedent of aggression. These (laboratory) studies will be reviewed in the next chapter.

Annoyers

There is a large class of aversive stimuli that may be called annoyers or irritants. These stimuli have been discovered by systematic exploration in the laboratory and by casual observations of everyday life. They are often simple sensory stimuli: a bright light shining directly at the eyes, the smell of a skunk, radio static, or laboratory "white" noise. One way to escape such noxious stimuli is to leave the situation; another way is to attack the source of the irritant in an attempt to remove the annoying stimulus.

The annoyer may be somewhat more complex than a simple sensory stimulus. For example, Doob & Sears (1939) included this item in their study: "You were behaving decorously at a party and a drunk spilled some food, his drink or cigarette ashes all over you." Note that neither this annoyer nor the previous simple sensory stimuli necessarily involved blocking of ongoing instrumental or consummatory behavior. Thus annoyers do not fall under the heading of frustration.

Cason (1930) collected a fairly complete list of stimuli that annoy college students. The list included both simple, sensory stimuli (someone chewing gum loudly) and complex social stimuli (a person bragging about himself, an effeminate man). The majority of the annoyers referred to the behavior of others, and another 27% of the list referred to clothes, dress, or physical characteristics. Thus the large majority of annoyers was not frustrating stimuli.

While annoyers are not in themselves frustrating stimuli, they may become frustrating in some situations. If the irritating stimulus occurs during the performance of ongoing instrumental behavior, it may interfere with that behavior. Thus street noises may in themselves be only an irritant, but if they interfere with the problem-solving behavior of a student doing homework, they are also a frustrator.

FRUSTRATION AND AGGRESSION AS ANTECEDENTS

In an early draft of this book an attempt was made to order the various antecedents in terms of their potency in eliciting aggression. It was suggested that attack would be more potent than frustration; in attack the noxious stimuli are delivered directly and cannot be avoided, whereas in frustration the indirectly delivered noxious stimuli can be avoided by withdrawal or noninvolvement. At the time there were no data bearing on this hypothesis, but subsequently an experiment was conducted that compared frustration with verbal attack (Gillespie, 1961).

Gillespie's experiment was conducted in classroom settings and the subjects were college men and women. There were three groups: frustration, attack, and control. All groups were administered an "Abstract Ability Test" and told that the test correlated highly with IQ. They were also told that the test could easily be completed in the time allotted. In the frustration group insufficient time was allowed: subjects were stopped after five minutes, with no one able to complete the test. The attack group was allowed to complete the test but insulted immediately afterward. The experimenter derogated their performance, ability, and maturity level, using the kind of insult technique that has previously proved to be effective (Feshbach, 1955). The control group was allowed sufficient time to complete the test but was not insulted afterward.

Subsequently, all groups were administered three measures designed to assess aggressiveness. The first was a word association task devised by Gellerman (1956), consisting of several neutral and several aggressive words; the score was the number of aggressive associations to the aggressive stimulus words. The second measure was a Scrambled Sentences task (see Chapter 7), in which words could be rearranged to form a neutral or an aggressive sentence; the score was the number of aggressive sentences. The third measure was an attitude questionnaire, adapted from Feshbach (1955), which contained items involving attitudes toward the experimenter and the experiment.

The results were analyzed in terms of whether the two experimental groups were significantly more aggressive than the control group, with men and women kept separate:

1. *Word association*—for both men and women, both the frustration and attack groups were more aggressive than the control group.

2. *Scrambled sentences*—for men, the attack group was more aggressive than the control group, but the frustration group was not, and there was no difference between the attack and frustration groups; for women, the attack group was more aggressive than both the control group and frustration groups, with no difference between the latter two.

3. *Questionnaire*—for men, both the frustration and attack groups were more aggressive than the control group; for women, the attack group was more aggressive than both the control and frustration groups, with no difference between the latter two.

Summarizing, attack yielded significantly more aggression than a control condition in all six comparisons—three measures, two sexes; whereas frustration yielded significantly more aggression than a control in only three of six comparisons. Furthermore, in two instances attack yielded significantly more aggression than frustration. These results are clear in indicating that verbal attack is a more potent antecedent of aggression than frustration.

The findings also revealed interesting sex differences. In the last two measures, (Scrambled Sentences and the questionnaire), there were sex differences in relation to frustration: frustration led to more aggression than the control for men but not for women. Perhaps men are more susceptible to frustration or more angered by frustration than are women. It will be interesting to discover whether this possibility also occurs in other studies in which both sexes are used as subjects, especially since virtually all aggression experiments have employed only men as subjects.

REFERENCES

Allison, J. & Hunt, D. E. Social desirability and expression of aggression under varying conditions of frustration. *J. consult. Psychol.*, 1959, **23**, 528–532.

Amsel, A. The role of frustrative nonreward in noncontinuous reward situations. *Psychol. Bull.*, 1958, **55**, 102–119.

Barker, R. G., Dembo, Tamara, & Lewin, K.   Frustration and regression: an experiment with young children.   *Univ. Iowa Stud. Child Welf.*, 1941, **18**, 1–314.

Berkowitz, L.   The expression and reduction of hostility.   *Psychol. Bull.*, 1958, **55**, 257–283.

Block, Jeanne & Martin, B.   Predicting the behavior of children under frustration.   *J. abnorm. soc. Psychol.*, 1955, **51**, 281–285.

Bridges, K. M. B.   Emotional development in early infancy.   *Child Develpm.*, 1932, **3**, 324–341.

Brown, J. S. & Farber, I. E.   Emotions conceptualized as intervening variables —with suggestions toward the theory of frustration.   *Psychol. Bull.*, 1951, **48**, 465–495.

Cason, H.   Common annoyances: a psychological study of everyday aversions and annoyances.   *Psychol. Monogr.*, 1930, **40**, No. 182.

Cohen, A. R.   Social norms, arbitrariness of frustration and status of the agent of frustration in the frustration-aggression hypothesis.   *J. abnorm. soc. Psychol.*, 1955, **51**, 222–226.

Cox, E. N.   Some effects of frustration: I. a methodological programme.   *Austral. J. Psychol.*, 1952, **4**, 94–106.

Davitz, J. R.   The effects of previous training on postfrustration behavior.   *J. abnorm. soc. Psychol.*, 1952, **47**, 309–315.

Dollard, J., Doob, L. W., Miller, N. E., Mowrer, O. H., & Sears, R. R.   *Frustration and aggression*.   New Haven: Yale University Press, 1939.

Doob, L. W. & Sears, R. R.   Factors determining substitute behavior and the overt expression of aggression   *J. abnorm. soc. Psychol.*, 1939, **34**, 293–313.

Feshbach, S.   The drive-reducing function of fantasy behavior.   *J. abnorm. soc. Psychol.*, 1955, **50**, 3–11.

Funkenstein, S. H., King, S. H., & Drolette, Margaret E.   *Mastery of stress*.   Cambridge: Harvard University Press, 1957.

Gellerman, S.   The effects of experimentally induced aggression and inhibition on word-association response sequences.   Unpublished doctor's dissertation, University of Pennsylvania, 1956.

Gillespie, J.   Aggression in relation to frustration, attack, and inhibition.   Unpublished doctor's dissertation, University of Pittsburgh, 1961.

Haner, C. F. & Brown, Patricia A.   Clarification of the instigation to action concept in the frustration-aggression hypothesis.   *J. abnorm. soc. Psychol.*, 1955, **51**, 204–206.

Hovland, C. I. & Sears, R. R.   Minor studies of aggression: VI. correlation of lynchings with economic indices.   *J. Psychol.*, 1940, **9**, 301–310.

Kimbrell, D. L. & Blake, R. R.   Motivational factors in the violation of a prohibition.   *J. abnorm. soc. Psychol.*, 1958, **56**, 132–133.

Lawson, R. & Marx, M. H.   Frustration: theory and experiment.   *Genet. psychol., Monogr.*, 1958, **57**, 393–464.

Lee, F. J.   Frustration and hostility: the effects of differential reduction in power over decision-making.   Unpublished doctor's dissertation, Boston University, 1955.

McDonough, Leah B.   A developmental study of motivation and reactions to frustration.   Unpublished doctor's dissertation, Michigan State University, 1958.

Maier, N. R. F.   *Frustration*.   New York: McGraw-Hill, 1949.

Maslow, A. H. Deprivation, threat and frustration. *Psychol. Rev.*, 1941, **48**, 364–366.

McClelland, D. C. & Apicella, F. S. A functional classification of verbal reactions to experimentally induced failure. *J. abnorm. soc. Psychol.*, 1945, **40**, 376–390.

McNeil, E. B. Psychology and aggression. *J. conflict. Res.*, 1959, **3**, 195–293.

Miller, N. E. The frustration-aggression hypothesis. *Psychol. Rev.*, 1941, **48**, 337–342.

Mintz, A. A re-examination of correlations between lynchings and economic indices. *J. abnorm. soc. Psychol.*, 1946, **41**, 159–160.

OSS Assessment Staff. *Assessment of Men.* New York: Rinehart, 1948.

Otis, Nancy B. & McCandless, B. Responses to repeated frustrations of young children differentiated according to need area. *J. abnorm. soc. Psychol.*, 1955, **50**, 349–353.

Pastore, N. The role of arbitrariness in the frustration-aggression hypothesis. *J. abnorm. soc. Psychol.*, 1952, **47**, 728–731.

Roehl, A. C. The effects of frustration on the amplitude of a simple motor response. Unpublished doctor's dissertation, University of Minnesota, 1959.

Rosenzweig, S. An outline of frustration theory. In J. McV. Hunt (Ed.), *Personality and the Behavior Disorders.* New York: Ronald Press, 1944.

Weiss, W. & Fine, B. J. The effect of induced aggressiveness on opinion change. *J. abnorm. soc. Psychol.*, 1956, **52**, 109–114.

Zuckerman, M. The effect of frustration on the perception of neutral and aggressive words. *J. Pers.*, 1955, **23**, 407–422.

3

Investigating aggression in the laboratory

This chapter deals with the problems that arise when aggression is studied in the laboratory. The laboratory study of anger, especially its physiological aspects, is discussed in Chapter 6.

The initial problem facing the investigator of aggression is the subject's orientation toward the laboratory. The subject enters the laboratory with several possible sets (self-instructions) that may be inimical to his responding aggressively.

1. *Company manners.* The subject knows that the experimenter has status as a professional person, and as such is entitled to at least a minimum of respect and politeness. The subject may also be somewhat guarded in his responses.

2. *Desire to please.* Subjects often seek the experimenter's approval, and their behavior may be largely determined by what they believe the experimenter wishes from them. Were the experimenter to indicate in some way that he expected his subject to aggress against him, the subject would be involved in an intense approach-avoidance conflict.

3. *Artificiality.* Most important of all, the subject is aware that his behavior is being studied in the laboratory, and there is a tendency to manifest "as if" behavior, which may differ markedly from the same individual's behavior outside the laboratory.

These sets of the subject must be overcome if aggression is to be studied meaningfully in the laboratory. The first part of the chapter discusses different means of overcoming these sets and of eliciting aggression. The second part discusses problems of measuring aggression.

35

TECHNIQUES OF ELICITING AGGRESSION

There are two different approaches to eliciting aggression in the laboratory. In the first, an attempt is made to duplicate an everyday situation but with experimental controls; the independent variables are the two classes of antecedents discussed in the last chapter —frustration and noxious stimuli. In the second approach, the situation is presented to the subject as unreal and artificial. The subject may be instructed to play the role of an individual who is aggressing, or he may be hypnotized and given the suggestion that he is angry and about to attack. These two approaches will be discussed in turn.

"Realistic" Laboratory Situations

Since the antecedents of aggression have already been discussed, there is no need to repeat the contents of the last chapter. Rather, this section will include details about the manipulations that often lead to aggression in the laboratory.

Frustration. As noted in the last chapter, the behavior sequence may be blocked at one of three points: instrumental response, presentation of the reinforcer, consummatory response. The blocking of instrumental behavior is best illustrated by an OSS study (1948), which occurred in a semilaboratory context. The task was to construct a four-cornered enclosure, with the subject acting as a boss who was to direct two helpers.   The helpers were experimental accomplices who sabotaged the job: one dawdled or did meaningless work, and the other pestered the subject with irrelevant questions and comments. The two helpers so completely blocked the efforts of the subject that the task could not be completed within the allotted time. Since the subject was always motivated to succeed in this assessment situation, the frustration was severe; since the barriers were other individuals, it is not surprising that some subjects were goaded into physical violence.

The OSS study involves one type of failure; the other type consists of allowing the instrumental sequence to run to completion and then failing the subject. Lindzey & Riecken (1951) described a paradigm for this kind of failure. In a group situation in which the other "subjects" were experimental accomplices, the real subject was given a card-sorting problem. Each subject in the group would receive five dollars if every subject completed the task without error and within the time limit. The task was rigged so that the real subject always performed more poorly than the rest, and on several trials he was the sole cause of group failure. This situation was successful in eliciting anger from subjects, but unfortunately the tendency to aggress was often directed against the self because of a belief that the group had been let down. A possible modification would have only two people in the group, with the experimental accomplice being the one responsible for group failure; the subject would then have a suitable target for the aggressive tendencies elicited by failure.

In addition to failure, the presentation of the reinforcer may simply be omitted, which also blocks the behavioral sequence at the second point. Extinction has not been used in studying aggression because aggression has no instrumental value in extinction. There is usually no target when a reinforcer is omitted. It may be that omission of a reinforcer elicits aggression in everyday situations (for example, when a payroll is not met), but such situations have not yet been duplicated in the laboratory.

The behavioral sequence may also be blocked at the third point—consummatory responses. Sears, Hovland, & Miller (1940) kept male college students awake all night, permitting neither smoking nor eating. The subjects could not make any of three possible consummatory responses (sleeping, smoking, or eating), all of which were probably strongly motivated. There were several manifestations of indirect aggression toward the frustrating experimenters, but the aggression was probably contaminated with tendencies toward making the blocked responses, such tendencies competing with the tendency to aggress.

The last comment points up a deficiency in attempting to elicit aggression by preventing a consummatory response that is related to a basic need, such as sleep or water. The individual's motivation is so strongly directed toward relief of the need state that any tendency toward aggression may be overshadowed by tendencies toward the necessary reinforcer, e.g. water. It is better to block consummatory responses that are oriented toward non-need reinforcers. For example, in the Barker, Dembo, & Lewin experiment (1940) the children's attempts to get to the toys were not contaminated with tendencies to respond in any other direction because of the absence of a need state, and a number of children had violent temper outbursts. The only fault to be found in this experimental situation is in the nature of the barrier, which was a physical object rather than another person. Frustration is most likely to lead to aggression when the barrier is another individual because both the consummatory response and the aggressive response are oriented in the same direction, i.e., the aggression is instrumentally valuable in overcoming the barrier. Thus when a response is being blocked in order to elicit aggression in the laboratory, it is best to have another person as the frustrator in order to present the possible aggressor with a suitable target.

Noxious stimuli. The presentation of noxious stimuli includes both attack and annoyers. The latter, because they are not directed toward any particular victim, are less likely to elicit aggression than is attack. Therefore it is not surprising that a search of the literature revealed no experiment in which annoyers were used to incite aggression, and this section deals only with attack.

As noted in the last chapter, the antecedent event most likely to elicit aggression is an attack. The victim is confronted with noxious stimuli that cannot be ignored, and he must counterattack or escape. While flight is often successful in reducing the noxious stimulation, escape is not always possible; the only recourse is to attempt putting an end to the aversive stimuli by attacking the person responsible for them. This is especially true in the laboratory, where there is strong social pressure to remain until the experiment has been completed.

ATTACK BY THE EXPERIMENTER. In most studies it is the experimenter who attacks the subject, either individually or in a group; individual attack will be discussed first.

Several investigators have conducted "frustration" experiments but perhaps because frustration alone did not elicit aggression, they added attack. Thus Weiss & Fine (1956) failed subjects but also derided their ability. Zuckerman (1955) failed subjects and went on to insult their intelligence. Funkenstein et al. (1957) gave subjects successively harder tasks; as they began to fail, the experimenter criticized them in a sneering, exasperated manner. Cox (1952) gave his subjects a box to carry across the room and "accidently" knocked it to the floor as he handed it over. He berated the subjects for being so clumsy and demanded that they pick up the tiny contents. Then the experimenter scored the subject's TAT protocols, laughing at the stories in a derogatory fashion. Occasionally he stopped to tell the subject to hurry with his inconsequential task.

While these investigators seemed to believe that the independent variable was frustration, it is clear that frustration was confounded with attack. On the basis of the previous discussion of frustrating procedures, it seems reasonable to conclude that it was the attack of the experimenter that led to anger, not the frustrating task. Any anger that was initiated by frustration was surely overshadowed by the anger caused by the experimenter's verbal attack.

A frustrating task may be used simply as a basis for allowing the experimenter to aggress against a subject. This technique was used by McClelland & Apicella (1945). The experimenter was a student who knew all his male subjects at least casually. After failing them on a task, he initiated a campaign of vituperation, as follows: "Not too good, you screwed up that one . . . . You're the worst I've had yet . . . . You're ruining my whole experiment." This was followed by cursing and more intense derogation. It was found that 40% of the subjects' responses fell into a combined anger-aggression category that included undirected oaths and cursing, as well as intense verbal attacks and cursing at the experimenter. The subjects' intense verbal aggression may be attributed not only to the provocation but also to the experimenter's being a peer and an acquaintance of the subjects.

Concerning the attack of subjects in a group, the only technique that has been reported is that of insulting students in a classroom situation. Feshbach's procedure will serve to illustrate it:

The E was briefly introduced to the class by its instructor . . . . After the instructor left the classroom, E in an authoritarian, arrogant manner made several derogatory remarks about the motivation, ability, and level of maturity of the student body of the college. For example, he made such comments as "Now I realize that you _____ College students, or should I say _____ College grinds have few academic interests outside of your concern for your grades . . . if you will try to look beyond your limited horizons, your cooperation will be useful. In others words, I'd like you to act like adults rather than adolescents. (1955, p. 4)

An inherent limitation of arousal of anger in groups is the difficulty of obtaining a direct measure of anger level or aggression. The dependent variable must be assessed indirectly by means of group tests, tasks, or questionnaires. This difficulty is not important during the early phase of investigating the antecedents of aggression because it is important to identify in a gross way the important functional relationships between insult and verbal aggression. Furthermore, the technique is effective in that it solves the problem of the artificiality of the laboratory situation. However, the greatest need at present is for more precise information concerning the antecedents of aggression, and such information is more likely to come from studies in which aggression is elicited individually rather than in a group of subjects.

ATTACK BY AN ACCOMPLICE OF THE EXPERIMENTER. When the experimenter is the attacking agent, he has the dual burden of interacting with the subject and recording responses. An accomplice can better play the provocative role, because he can more easily assume a peer role which is more conducive to aggression than an authoritarian role. Ax (1953) used the technique of having two experimenters, one of whom was a polygraph operator supposedly in some disrepute:

He was described to the subject as not the regular operator but one who had been fired for incompetence and arrogance, but due to the sickness of the regular operator he had to be employed for that day. Thus he was labelled as a suitable target for hostility by the subject. At the beginning of the anger stimulus, the operator entered the room stating that he must check the wiring because some calibration might be off. The experimenter objected but agreed to go into the other room and operate the polygraph. The operator shut off the music, criticized the nurse, and told the subject sarcastically that it would have helped if he had been on time. He checked the electrodes, roughly adjusted the subject, and criticized him for moving, noncooperation, and other behavior. After five minutes of abuse, the operator left and the experimenter returned, apologizing for this rude behavior. (p. 435)

In this situation the target for aggression was clearly marked, and there was considerable verbal aggression.

In Ax's experiment the accomplice served as experimenter. There are advantages to having the accomplice pose not as an experimenter but as a fellow subject, because an attack from a fellow subject is unexpected and "real." Thibaut & Coules (1952) set up a note-passing situation between a real subject and a bogus subject. A second accomplice delivered notes back and forth in which each subject was to describe such items as his personality, ambitions, preferences. The ostensible task was for each subject to diagnose the other's personality. In the eight notes delivered, the bogus subject first described himself as being arrogant, opinionated, weak. His final note attacked the real subject as follows:

You know, you are so full of bull _____, that I'm not going to talk about myself anymore. You're the most egotistical, deceitful *liar* I've ever seen. How anybody can fake about his own abilities as much as you have I'll never know. I don't think you're the type of guy I'd care to associate with. Why don't you play it straight, fellow? (1952, p. 771)

The provocation is made even more intense by the instigator's pose as the very kind of person he claims the real subject is. As measured by the personality evaluations, the subjects' aggression rose sharply from before to after the note-passing session.

Margolin (1954) used a similar procedure, varying it to include provocation from the messenger who delivered notes. This messenger became increasingly aggressive as the session proceeded and accused the subject of being stupid, slow, sloppy, immature, etc. At one point he "accidently" knocked over the subject's books and then glared at him.

While most attacks by accomplices have been direct and active, it is also of interest to investigate the effect of subtle and passive attack. Pepitone & Wilpizeski (1960) assembled three-man groups each consisting of a subject and two experimental accomplices. The subject first stated his views on a topic, and the accomplices then adopted an opposite view. Then the accomplices ignored the subject or met his approach responses with curt answers and unfriendly looks. Subjects responded to this rejection with both hostility and avoidance behavior.

COMMENTS ON ATTACK. The artificiality of the laboratory is a major obstacle to inducing anger and aggression. The subject knows that he is engaging in an experiment and responds with one of the sets mentioned earlier. An attack from the experimenter or from another subject is an excellent solution to this problem. The subject's relationship with the experimenter or with other subjects is real in the sense that it transcends the laboratory situation. His response to them is determined not so much by a laboratory set as by previous learning with authority figures and peers. When they attack the subject, he is more likely to respond as he would outside the laboratory.

Of course, the subject may be constrained by the presence of an authority figure, and for this reason paradigms that employ a peer as the attacking agent have been more successful in eliciting aggression than those that employ an authority figure as the attacker. When it is not possible to present the attacker as a peer of the subject, the discrepancy between the status of subject and experimenter should be minimized, e.g., the experimenter presents himself to college students as a graduate student rather than as a faculty member.

The content of the attack also offers problems. A number of investigators have used failure on the experimental task as a springboard for criticizing subjects. To the extent that the criticism is valid, the subject may react with a sense of chagrin and inferiority rather than with aggression. It seems best not to emphasize the task at hand nor to justify the attack. The attacking agent should simply insult the subject with a minimum of rationale and a maximum of anger and indignation.

Variations in the content of the experimenter's attack have made it difficult to compare different experiments. The term *insult* has included criticism, derogation, sarcasm, and even cursing at the subject. Two kinds of verbal attack have yet to be used but are inevitable: threats and hostile attitudes ("I hate you"). A reasonable next step in this area would be a study comparing the effects of these different kinds of verbal attack. If the resultant aggression were similar in intensity regardless of the kind of verbal attack, then the different contents could be used interchangeably. This possibility seems unlikely because some kinds of attack appear to be more provocative than others, at least in extra-laboratory situations; cursing and threats tend to provoke more intense aggression than do criticism and sarcasm. What is needed is a "calibration" of the different kinds of verbal attack.

This methodological issue leads to another one. Within each kind of verbal attack there are variations in intensity. It was mentioned above that criticism with some basis in fact seemed to be milder than criticism that had no rationale. The more personalized the criticism, the more provocative it is. One way of checking on these statements would be to scale various kinds of verbal aggression. This has been done with a few critical remarks in an unpublished study. The following three items were rated on a nine-point scale of intensity of aggression:

1. Your work does not meet our standards. (2.2)
2. Your sloppy work does not meet our standards. (5.1)
3. Your sloppy work shows your lack of intelligence. (7.3)

The numbers in parentheses are scale values; the larger the number, the more intense the aggression. Criticism based on an objective standard is rated low in aggression. The word *sloppy*, which adds some personalization, increases the intensity of aggression of the comment. The attack on intelligence represents more personalization, and it receives the highest rating for intensity of aggression. When additional data of this kind are available, the next step would be to have an experimenter use each kind of insult on a different group of subjects in order to discover functional relationships between intensity of attack and intensity of anger and aggression.

A final comment concerning attack is in order. It is necessary to inform the subject at the conclusion of the experiment that the attack on him was part of the study and have him ventilate any feelings he may have about being tricked. This postexperimental session is especially important when verbal attack is used because attack is more threatening and more interpersonal than frustration. Attack is a riskier procedure than frustration, and the experimenter must be prepared to deal with more intense reactions from his subjects.

"Artificial" Laboratory Situations

Role playing. The technique of insult attempts to solve the artificiality problem by making the attack appear to be an incidental, unrelated aspect of the laboratory situation. The role playing approach, on the other hand, accepts the artificiality, admitting openly that the situation is unreal. The expectation is that the subject will become caught up in the situation, so that his play acting will have elements of realistic, nonlaboratory behavior embedded in it. To the extent that this assumption is true (and it seems to hold in the therapeutic use of psychodrama), role playing is an effective means of studying aggression in the laboratory. Two studies will illustrate the technique. Harris et al. (1953) had college women act out two situations:

The subject was instructed that she was a college student, that she was going to a dance that evening, and that she was to pick up an evening gown that she had left at the dry cleaner's. In the experimental room, on a slightly raised platform, she was met by a staff member who played the role of the proprieter. He informed her that her gown was not ready, that it was not even in the shop. He met her every question or demand with stubborn indifference. In the second psychodrama the subject was instructed that a number of fellow students had asked her to call on the dean of women of the college to request that an examination be postponed. She was also told that the dean was an old friend of her mother. The dean was played by a professional actress with considerable skill and versatility. She met the student initially with warm acceptance, and then became critical and personally attacking and rejecting. (1953, p. 876)

In both situations there was considerable verbal aggression.

Buss & Foliart (1959) had college men and women act out the following situation:

We are two acquaintances. I have been gossiping about you, talking behind your back. I called you a hothead and a cheat and said that you were completely dishonest and utterly unreliable. You heard about this, and since of course it is not true, you are very angry. Now you are confronting me.

Both techniques have advantages. The technique used by Harris et al. guarantees more involvement by the subject because he is attacked or frustrated during the course of the role playing. On the other hand, the subject might recognize that the attack or frustration is deliberate and part of the experiment. The technique used by Buss & Foliart does not involve the subject as much because his role playing of anger is based solely on instructions, but there is no problem of the subject discovering any artifacts. Both techniques have one obvious limitation. To the extent that the subject can divorce the role playing situation from real life, he will simply follow another laboratory set and go through the motions of verbal aggression. If the number of subjects who remain uninvolved can be held down, role playing will be a useful technique for studying verbal aggression.

Hypnosis. Hypnosis has been used to induce a variety of behaviors. In the few studies that have attempted to induce subjects to commit antisocial acts of violence, insufficient attention was paid to measurement of the dependent variable. The two studies to be mentioned here both assessed posthypnotic aggressiveness by means of the Rorschach. Counts & Mensh (1950) hypnotized college subjects and then read the following instructions (note the similarity to those used by Buss & Foliart in setting up role playing):

"I am now going to recall something that happened to you several weeks ago. It is now very vague in your mind and consciously you don't remember it. However, as I recall it to you, you will picture it in your mind's eye—how it happened, and how you felt at the time. You were just getting out of your psychology class. As you were walking down the hall, Dr. Mensh came rushing out of one of the rooms. He bumped into you. It was obviously his fault as he was not looking where he was going. He was walking so fast that you were almost knocked down. As you were recovering your balance and dignity, he said very sarcastically that you were very clumsy to bump into him, that if you didn't watch what you were doing he would make trouble for you. You immediately felt very angry but realized that you could say nothing. As you walked away you felt more and more angry and thought of many sarcastic things that you might have said but didn't. Now when you awaken you will not remember this event consciously, but it will be preying on your unconscious mind. During the Rorschach test you are about to take with Dr. Mensh you will feel very uncomfortable and quite angry with him but you will not know why. Nevertheless, you will be able to complete the series of ten cards. You will dislike him very much during the procedure but you will not know why. You will feel angry with me and you will be hypnotized after the procedure as readily as you have just been. (1950, p. 326)

Posthypnotic Rorschachs were compared with prehypnotic Rorschachs, but only a few changes were evident. Pattie (1954) first hypnotized college students and told them that after coming out of the trance they would be in a "calm, normal frame of mind" and would forget the responses they gave on the test. Afterward they were again hypnotized and this time told that after coming out of the trance they would be extremely hostile and aggressive toward the person administering the ink blot test. This suggestion was evidently effective because after it the majority of subjects increased the number of aggressive responses on the Rorschach or became uncooperative (card criticism and rejection).

There are possible dangers in using hypnotism to induce aggression, but these are minimal when the hypnotist is experienced. The main disadvantage lies in the possibility of artifacts associated with suggestion, especially when the trance is not a deep one. In addition, many subjects cannot be hypnotized, which leads to a sampling bias; but many subjects cannot be angered in the laboratory with the techniques described earlier, so that this limitation is not unique to hypnotism.

MEASURING AGGRESSION

It seems clear from the preceding account that the problems listed at the beginning of the chapter may be solved by the techniques described in the preceding section. The remaining challenge is to measure the frequency and intensity of aggression. Assessment of the dependent variable is one of the more serious problems in the study of behavior, and the study of aggression is no exception.

Because of the difficulties associated with allowing physical aggression to occur in the laboratory and of assessing the intensity of verbal aggression, many psychologists have turned to indirect measurement of aggression—via tests, projective techniques (see Chapter 8), and learning tasks (see Chapter 7). Others have continued to wrestle with the problems of measuring aggression directly. The two approaches, indirect and direct measurement, will be discussed in turn.

Indirect Measurement

One means of assessing aggression is to ask the subject about his aggressive tendencies in a questionnaire. For example, after insulting students, Feshbach (1955) administered a questionnaire that inquired about the subject's opinion of the experiment and of the experimenter's competence, his dislike of the experimenter, and his feelings about volunteering for another experiment. The disadvantage of this kind of questionnaire is that it has little generality. Each experimenter constructs his own questionnaire that taps aggressiveness within a specific experimental context, and it may be hazardous to compare the results of studies using different questionnaires.

Questionnaires are also subject to faking. The items inquire in a fairly obvious manner about the subject's aggressive tendencies toward the experimenter, and at least some inhibition of report is inevitable. Faking and inhibition may be dealt with in two ways. First, the items can be made more subtle, and the form of the item can be manipulated to control for social desirability (see Chapter 9). Second, response sets (faking, acquiescence) may be controlled by the use of scoring keys (Jackson & Messick, 1958). Both solutions require considerable pretesting of questionnaires, which involves more work than most investigators are willing to do in developing a measure of aggression.

Projective techniques avoid most of the problems of response sets but fall heir to other kinds of problems; standardization of stimuli, influence of the examiner, scoring. Aside from these technological problems, which may be solved by research, there is the issue of what is measured by projective techniques. While these instruments are affected by transient experimental situations, they tend to reflect the individual's enduring response tendencies rather than transient changes. To the extent that projective techniques do reflect aggressiveness as a personality variable, they are of limited use as measures of aggression in the laboratory.

Direct Measurement

When aggression is allowed to occur in the laboratory, it may be observed and measured directly. The most common method of assessing the intensity or strength of aggression is to rate it. It may be helpful to borrow from techniques used to evaluate interview material in clinical situations. For example, Buss, Durkee, & Baer (1956) interviewed psychiatric patients in an attempt to evaluate their aggressiveness and hostility. One category was verbal aggression, which included yelling, cursing, screaming, arguing, and being caustic, ironic, or teasing. Three observers rated the material for intensity, the ratings correlating from .83 to .87. The good interobserver agreement was obtained both by pretraining and by detailed instructions concerning the behavior to be rated.

As instructions became more detailed, the rating procedure approaches the check list method, in which an observer merely checks the occurrence of particular responses or tendencies. Harris et al.

(1953) used an adjective check list to evaluate a number of behaviors, including aggression, in their study of role playing. Unfortunately, such check lists do not lead to a measure of the strength or intensity of aggression. What seems to be needed is a list of aggressive responses that has been scaled in advance for intensity of aggression in the same way that aggressive verbal stimuli have been scaled for intensity (see Table 7.1, Chapter 7).

It is necessary to resort to ratings because of the difficulty of discovering an intensity dimension of aggression that can easily be quantified. The practical and ethical problems associated with the occurrence of physical aggression in the laboratory must also be solved. What is needed is an aggressive response that varies in intensity along an easily quantified dimension. The subject must be placed in a situation in which aggression has some instrumental value and is allowed and unpunished. There is, of course, the restriction that no serious harm befall the victim. The remainder of this section describes an apparatus designed to meet these criteria—an "aggression machine."

The mode of aggression is the delivery of electric shock. The subject is instructed to play the role of an experimenter in a learning experiment: he is to administer shock whenever the subject of the

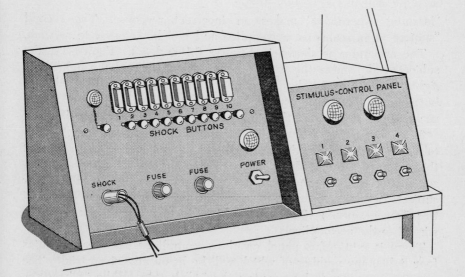

Fig. 3.1. Aggression machine, subject's side.

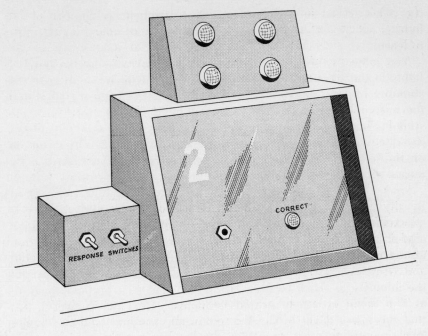

FIG. 3.2. Aggression machine, accomplice's side.

"learning experiment" makes an incorrect response. The second "subject" is in reality an accomplice and will be referred to as such.

The apparatus is shown in Figures 3.1 and 3.2. Figure 3.1, the subject's side, shows the stimulus control buttons and the lights that signal which response has been made. It also depicts the "correct" button and the shock control buttons and lights. Figure 3.2, the accomplice's side, shows the stimulus lights and the response buttons.

At the beginning of the experiment the subject is seen alone. He is told that he will train the accomplice in a conceptual task and that the purpose of the study is to investigate the effect of sex and personality of the experimenter on conceptual learning. (Only a few subjects require further explanation, and they receive more details of this "cover story.") Then the subject is told how to present the stimuli to the accomplice.

There is a stimulus panel on the accomplice's side that contains four lights, any number of which will be lit on any given trial. The accomplice responds by pressing the "A" button or the "B" button, with the "A" button being correct whenever the upper left light on the panel is lit; the "B" button is correct whenever the upper left light is not lit. This is the concept that the accomplice is ostensibly to learn.

The subject is given a sequence that randomly presents patterns of lights to the accomplice. The stimulus panel is lit by depressing the stimulus buttons marked 1, 2, 3, and 4 on the subject's side, and the accomplice's response is indicated by the lights just above the stimulus buttons. Upon noting the accomplice's response, the subject decides whether it is correct or not and presses the "correct" button on the left or one of the shock buttons. The shock is delivered by means of electrodes fastened to the third finger.

Since the subject should discover how much shock is represented by the 10 buttons, the electrodes are attached to him, and he is shocked. He is administered shock from buttons 1, 2, 3, and 5 and is told that the intensity of the shock continues to increase to button 10. The shock level is set so that 1 is slightly above touch threshold and is essentially only a signal that the response was incorrect. As the intensity of shock increases through 2 and 3, it becomes painful; at 5 it is an extremely noxious stimulus. Thus the subject learns that the lowest level of shock is essentially a signal, and the higher levels are painful.

He is then ready to run the ostensible subject (accomplice). The accomplice is brought into the room, and the real experimenter leaves. After the accomplice is instructed about the task and the shock electrodes attached to him, the experiment proper begins. The subject sets up the pattern of lights indicated for the first trial, notes the accomplice's responses and then presses the "correct" button or delivers a shock of whatever intensity he choses. The shock never reaches the accomplice, who has surreptitiously reached down and disconnected it by moving a mercury switch placed out of sight under the table. The accomplice must know what level of shock is ostensibly being delivered to him because it is his job to record this level (the dependent variable). He receives this information from the translucent plastic screen, which lights up with a number corresponding to the number of the shock button pressed by the subject. Since the subject and the accomplice are shielded from each other's sight by a wooden barrier, the subject sees neither these numbers nor the accomplice, who is recording the level of shock.

Several pilot studies have been conducted with the following "learning series." There are two series of 30 trials each, and in both series the accomplice has a programmed pattern of responses such that there are 6 incorrect responses in the first 10 trials, 4 incorrect in the second 10 trials, and 2 incorrect in the third 10 trials. The first 30 trials are followed by 10 trials with shock on every trial, the subject being instructed to do this in order to confuse the accomplice. After the accomplice has been "confused," the second series of 10 trials is initiated. Thus each subject shocks the accomplice 12 times during each of the learning series and 10 times during the "confusion" series, a total of 34 times.

In order to mask the real purpose of the experiment, the concept learning task is carried through to completion: the accomplice is asked to verbalize the concept and responds with a rough approximation of the correct concept. It is crucial that the subject believe the accomplice is receiving shock, and to foster this belief conditions remain constant whether shock is delivered or not: when a shock button is depressed, there is a clicking sound and the light above the button flashes. Of the approximately 100 subjects who have been run, only a few suspected that the accomplice was not receiving shock.

It might be argued that shocking the accomplice should not be considered an aggressive response because the subject is instructed to do it. This argument holds so long as the shock level is kept below 3; shock levels of 1 and 2 are sufficiently mild to serve merely as cues without being noxious stimuli. Shocks of 3 and higher, however, are clearly above the pain threshold and are therefore noxious stimuli. When a subject delivers a painful stimulus in a situation that calls for only a cue, he is making an aggressive response; the higher the shock level, the more intense the aggression.

If the subject is not angry, why should he use any but the lowest shock levels? There are two alternative answers. First, the subject might believe that higher shock levels for incorrect responses would tend to facilitate learning. If this were true, he would lower the shock level during the "confusion series," when the accomplice is shocked regardless of the correctness of his response. The results of pilot studies reveal that, with occasional exceptions, subjects do not decrease shock level during the middle 10 nonlearning trials.

The alternative answer is that the intensity of shock is an index of aggressiveness, with more aggressive subjects using the higher levels of shock. It should be remembered that the subject's aggression is unpunished, and the administration of shock can be rationalized as being part of the experiment. Thus the subject has a rare opportunity to aggress without concern for ethics or counterattack. Pilot data are consistent with this second answer if it is assumed that men are more aggressive than women. Men's shock levels clearly exceed women's. There is an interesting sex difference in the intensity of shock administered to men and women accomplices. When men are aggressing, they use higher levels of shock with male accomplices than with female accomplices. When women are aggressing, there is virtually no difference in the shock levels administered to male and female accomplices.

In a study not yet completed there was "feedback" for the higher shock levels: the accomplice gasped audibly or groaned whenever the shock exceeded 5. This feedback was effective in reducing the intensity of shock in some subjects but not in others. The following protocols illustrate an effect and no effect, respectively (gasps marked with an asterisk):

4—1—2—4—8*—2—4—7*—3—5* (accident)—2—1—4—6*—2—6*
　—3—4—1—3—8*—4—1—2—2—2—6*—2—3—2—8*—4
1—2—3—4—4—6*—6*—7*—7*—8*—4—4—5—6*—6*—7*—7*—8*
　—8*—8*—5—5—6*—5—6*—5—6*—5—6*—6*—7*—7*—7*

These protocols represent two different effects of the victim's pain on the aggressor's continuing attacks, and an attempt is being made to discover possible relationships between the effects of feedback and personality variables (aggressiveness, guilt, etc.).

The feedback paradigm is only one of several that are possible with the "aggression machine." The apparatus appears to be a potentially fruitful solution to the ethical, practical, and measurement problems that are associated with studying aggression in the laboratory. The same subject can be used to run several accomplices, which makes possible repeated measures of aggression. Such repeated measures should prove valuable in studying effects of frustration, attack, and catharsis on aggression.

REFERENCES

Ax, A. F. The physiological differentiation between fear and anger in humans. *Psychosom. Med.*, 1953, **15**, 433–442.

Barker, R. G., Dembo, Tamara, & Lewin, K. Frustration and regression: an experiment with young children. *Univ. Iowa Stud. Child Welf.*, 1941, **18**, No. 1.

Buss, A. H., Durkee, Ann & Baer, M. The measurement of hostility in clinical situations. *J. abnorm. & soc. Psychol.*, 1956, **52**, 84–86.

Buss, A. H. & Foliart, R. Role-playing aggression and the catharsis hypothesis. Unpublished research, 1958.

Buss, A. H. & Shipman, Virginia. The scaling of verbally aggressive statements. Unpublished research, 1958.

52   THE PSYCHOLOGY OF AGGRESSION

Counts, M. & Mensh, I. N.   Personality characteristics in hypnotically induced
    hostility. *J. clin. Psychol.,* 1950, **6**, 325–330.
Cox, E. N.   Some effects of frustration: I. a methodological programme. *Austral. J. Psychol.,* 1952, **4**, 94–106.
Feshbach, S.   The drive-reducing function of fantasy behavior. *J. abnorm. soc. Psychol.,* 1955, **50**, 3–11.
Funkenstein, D. H., King, S. H., & Drolette, Margaret E.   *Mastery of stress.*
    Cambridge: Harvard University Press, 1957.
Harris, R. E., Sokolow, M., Carpenter, L. G., Freedman, M., & Hunt, S. P.
    Response to psychological stress in persons who are potentially hypertensive. *Circulation,* 1953, **7**, 874–879.
Jackson, D. N. & Messick, S.   Content and style in personality assessment.
    Psychol. Bull., 1958, **55**, 243–252.
Lindzey, G. & Riecken, H. U.   Inducing frustration in adult subjects. *J. consult. Psychol.,* 1951, **15**, 18–23.
McClelland, D. C. & Apicella, F. S.   A functional classification of verbal reactions to experimentally induced failure. *J. abnorm. soc. Psychol.,* 1945, **40**, 376–390.
Margolin, J. B.   The effect of perceived cooperation or competition on the
    transfer of hostility. Unpublished doctor's dissertation, New York University, 1954.
OSS Assessment Staff.   *Assessment of Men.* New York: Rinehart, 1948.
Pattie, F. A.   The effect of hypnotically induced hostility on Rorschach responses. *J. clin. Psychol.,* 1954, **10**, 161–164.
Pepitone, A. & Wilpizeski, C.   Some consequences of experimental rejection.
    J. abnorm. soc. Psychol., 1960, **60**, 359–364.
Sears, R. R., Hovland, I., & Miller, N. E.   Minor studies of aggression: I.
    measurement of aggressive behavior. *J. Psychol.,* 1940, **9**, 275–295.
Thibaut, J. U. & Coules, J.   The role of communication in the reduction of
    interpersonal hostility. *J. abnorm. soc. Psychol.,* 1952, **47**, 770–777.
Weiss, W. & Fine, B. J.   The effect of induced aggressiveness on opinion
    change. *J. abnorm. soc. Psychol.,* 1956, **52**, 109–114.
Zuckerman, M.   The effect of frustration on the perception of neutral and
    aggressive words. *J. Pers.,* 1955, **23**, 407–422.

4

Punishment, displacement, and conflict

In Chapter 2 various antecedents of aggression were discussed; this chapter considers variables that inhibit aggression or alter its direction. The major inhibitor of aggression is punishment. When both punishment and reward follow an aggressive response, there is an approach-avoidance conflict. The result of such conflict may be displacement of aggression.

PUNISHMENT

Punishment consists of the delivery of a noxious or aversive stimulus to an organism, and, as noted earlier, the aversive character of punishing stimuli is known from the attempts of subjects to escape when presented with such stimuli. Though there have been numerous studies of punishment with human subjects, there has been no laboratory study in which aggressive *behavior* has been punished. There are few studies in which fantasy aggression has been punished or in which there is the *threat* of punishment for behavioral aggression. These few will be reviewed briefly.

Studies of Punishment and Threat of Punishment

The single laboratory study that punished aggression used as its dependent variable, not behavioral aggression, but the fantasy aggression that occurs in doll play. This was the study by Hollenberg & Sperry (1951) undertaken at Iowa under the general direction of R. R. Sears. Two groups of children were run through four doll play sessions. In the first session both groups were treated alike, the experimenter being permissive toward all activities, including aggression. In the second session the control group was allowed to continue in this fashion, but in the experimental group, each time there was doll play aggression the child was punished verbally, for example, "No John, don't you know that nice boys shouldn't do a thing like that?" It was found that the control group increased its doll play aggression from one session to the next, a finding that is typical of the doll play situation (see Chapter 14). In the experimental group, doll play aggression did not increase from the first to the second session, and in the third session it dropped off sharply. The inhibition was only temporary, and when the experimenter returned to being permissive (in the third and fourth sessions), aggression was found to rise again in the fourth session.

Laboratory data may be supplemented by data from questionnaire studies. Doob & Sears (1939) had college men rate the amount of punishment they believed would ensue from various aggressive acts, and they also indicated whether they would make these aggressive responses. The amount of aggression was found to be inversely related to the amount of punishment anticipated; the more punishment expected, the less likely the occurrence of aggression. The same students who rated expectancy of punishment also indicated whether they would aggress. They might simply have been indicating a logical course of action, and it is not known if they would have behaved so rationally in actual situations.

The anticipation of punishment is obviously related to the probability that the victim of the attacking response will retaliate. If the victim's status is known, the aggressor can make a rough guess about the probability of counterattack. Thus authority figures will, in general, punish aggression, which inhibits the aggressive tendencies of subordinates. The authority may be institutionalized legally, as in the case of a judge who metes out prison terms for violence; or it may be an integral part of enduring social or economic relationships, (parents or bosses). In general, the higher the status of the target of aggression, the greater is the probability (and severity) of punishment. The more likely the punishment, the weaker the aggressive response, whether it is measured in terms of frequency or intensity. There is both laboratory and questionnaire evidence confirming this generalization (note that in these studies the independent variable is threat of punishment, not punishment itself).

Worchel (1957) frustrated college students and subjected them to severe verbal attack in a group situation. After being insulted, the students were allowed to express verbal aggression to the experimenter, one group to a faculty member and another group to a student assistant. There was considerably more aggression toward the student assistant than to the faculty member. Reiser et al. (1955) kept two groups of enlisted army men in suspense for half an hour concerning the nature of the experiment. All subjects were then seen individually and told the nature of the study. One group talked to a captain and the other to a private. The latter group verbalized much hostility toward the army and engaged in a great deal of griping; the former group did not gripe, and there were no signs of hostility toward the army.

McClelland & Apicella (1945) employed a student experimenter to insult subjects. The aggression thereby elicited from the subjects was of greater intensity and frequency than that seen in comparable experiments in which the experimenter was a faculty member or doctoral candidate. This finding, taken together with other laboratory results, provides a firm experimental basis for the generalization that aggression is inversely related to the status of the target organism.

Further corroboration comes from questionnaire studies. Cohen (1955) presented situations in which half the frustrating agents were authority figures (professors, executives, administrators) and half were peers (fellow students, roommates). The subjects (college women) reported that they would respond with significantly more aggression to the peer frustrators than to the authority frustrators.

Graham et al. (1951) varied both the target and the strength of the instigations. The instigations were attacks; "When John's mother hit him, he . . . ." The subjects, adolescents of both sexes, were instructed to complete 50 such statements. There were five kinds of attacking agents: inferior, sibling, friend, parent, and authority (teacher or policeman). There were also five intensities of attack: hitting, criticizing, carrying tales, giving nasty looks, and not liking. Intensity of counterattack was determined by ratings of the investigators. Both intensity and frequency of aggressive responses were found to be related to the status of the attacking agent. Aggression was greatest when the attacker was a friend, sibling, or inferior and least in response to attack by parents or authority. Strength of attack and status of the attacker were found to interact: for siblings, friends, and inferiors, intensity of aggression increased with intensity of instigation; for authority this relationship was attenuated; and for parents there was no relationship between intensity of attack and intensity of aggressive response.

Effects of Punishment on Aggression

Aggression versus competing responses.   When aggression is one of
several possible responses leading to reward, the aggressive response
is in competition with other responses in the hierarchy.   However,
there are some situations in which aggression is the only response
that achieves the reinforcer, e.g., Miller's displacement study (1948).
So long as punishment is administered after an aggressive response,
the tendency to make the response is suppressed.   As soon as punishment no longer follows the aggressive response, it should return to a
frequency (and intensity) consistent with the reinforcement that is
following it.   Thus when aggression is the sole response that leads
to the reward, i.e., there are no competing responses, punishment
will lead to only a temporary decrement in frequency of aggression.

Fortunately, aggression is rarely the sole response that leads to
reward, and when there are competing responses, punishment may
be expected to have a stronger and more lasting effect on aggression.
For example, if two small children are playing together, the stronger
child may wish to play with the toy that the other child possesses.
Probably the strongest initial response is aggression; he forcibly
seizes the toy and beats off any verbal or physical objections by the
weaker child.   The aggression is rewarded by acquisition of the
toy.   At this point an adult may step in and punish the aggressing
child by verbal or physical means.   If the stronger child does not
have in his repertoire any alternative responses for acquiring the
toy, then aggression is the only response that leads to the reward.
Punishment would prevent further aggression only so long as the
adult were available to mete out the punishment.   In the absence
of the adult the aggressive response would return to its previous rate.
However, if the child has an alternative response in his repertoire or
if the adult teaches him one, then the effects of punishment would
be more enduring.   The adult must set up a situation in which the
stronger child asks for the toy and the weaker child yields it.   If the
aggressive response is punished and the nonaggressive response is
reinforced (by acquisition of the toy), the two responses may trade
places in the hierarchy of habit strength.   Successive punishments
of the aggressive response and reinforcements of the nonaggressive
response should lead to a weakening of the aggressive response, not
only in the presence of the adult (punishing agent) but also when
there is no threat of punishment.   Stated another way, punishment
of the incorrect response and reinforcement of the correct response

should lead to faster and more enduring learning than merely punishment of the incorrect response. Thus, in attempting to secure a lasting inhibition of aggression, it is of crucial importance to have the individual make nonaggressive responses that lead to the same reward as does the aggressive response.

Extrinsic versus intrinsic reinforcement. Reinforcers may be divided into two kinds. One may be termed *extrinsic* or external because it represents a stimulus that impinges on the responding organism. This is the usual kind of reward or positive reinforcement that tends to build up habit strength. However, there are certain classes of responses that may be reinforced by *intrinsic* or internal reinforcers, and aggression falls in this category. When an attacking response is made in the presence of anger, there is a drop in the level of anger. A sudden drop in physiological tension is often reinforcing; the everyday phenomenon of "blowing off steam." Thus, when an aggressive response occurs in the context of anger, there are two possible sources of reinforcement—one extrinsic and one intrinsic. The attacking organism may acquire a reward (extrinsic) or he may have a sudden drop in his anger level (intrinsic) as a consequence of the aggressive response.

The fact that a sudden drop in anger does occur as a consequence of aggression and is somehow reinforcing or satisfying to the organism, complicates the control of aggression. While aggression can often be inhibited by means of differential reinforcement (punishing aggression and rewarding a nonaggressive alternative response), the problem arises of internal reinforcement, over which there can be no direct experimental control. The aggressive response can be punished and a competing response rewarded, but if anger is present when aggression occurs, the sudden drop in anger level will reinforce the aggressive response. Thus an individual may attack another person without hope of achieving an extrinsic reward and with punishment as a likely consequence of the aggressive act, but the aggressive response still occurs because it dissipates the tension of the anger state.

Although there can be no direct control of this intrinsic reinforcement, there can be indirect control: the shaping up of a nonaggressive response that leads to a drop in physiological tension. The possibilities of accomplishing this are discussed in the next chapter. Parenthetically, aggression is not the only kind of behavior that is difficult to control because of intrinsic reinforcement. The difficulties of inhibiting such diverse behaviors as masturbation and drug addiction may also be attributed to powerful intrinsic reinforcement.

Impersonal versus personal punishment. The consequences of the punishing stimuli depend upon the context in which they are delivered. Punishment may be impersonal (undirected) or personal (direct). One kind of punishment for aggression is impersonal in the sense that it is not a directed attack against the aggressor. For example, the aggressor may hurt himself while attempting to strike his victim. Certain aggressive responses have an element of danger, not because the victim may retaliate, but because the act itself may cause injury to the responder; punching someone in the mouth may lead to a bruised and bleeding fist.

On the other hand, most punishment for aggression is personal. The victim counterattacks either directly or indirectly, inflicting noxious stimuli on the individual who initiated the aggression. The victim of an insult often answers back with his own verbal attack, and the person who is struck may use his own fists in return. Personal punishment constitutes an attack, and the noxious stimuli impinging on the original aggressor make him angry and instigate further attack or flight. Thus personal punishment is more likely to lead to further aggression than is impersonal punishment. The less personal the punishment, the less it is a direct attack and therefore the less intense it is as a stimulus for aggression.

Aggression as a consequence of punishment. Punishment may act in one fashion on the aggressive response that has preceded it and have an opposite effect on subsequent responses. When punishment follows a response, it weakens the tendency to make the response on subsequent occasions, but the immediate effect may be to incite an aggressive response.

Punishment will elicit aggression only if it is sufficiently intense. If the punishment is too weak, it will not breach the threshold of the attacking response. On the other hand, if punishment is too strong, it will elicit anxiety and flight rather than anger and aggression. Punishment must be in the middle range of intensity in order to maintain an aggression-punishment-aggression sequence, the relationship between intensity of punishment for the preceding aggressive response and the occurrence of a subsequent aggressive response being curvilinear.

The initial aggressive response may be followed not only by punishment but also, eventually, by reinforcement, as follows: aggression-punishment-aggression-reward. For example, a hoodlum attacks his victim, and the victim fights back; then the hoodlum counterattacks and succeeds in overpowering the victim, running off with his money. The hoodlum has acquired the reward but has also been punished. Since money is probably a stronger positive reinforcer than cuts and bruises are negative reinforcers, the net effect on habit strength of aggression would be to increase it. In the long run, it is the reinforcement history of the response that is important and not the particular stimuli that elicited the response. The effect of punishment as an instigator of further aggression is transient, being limited only to the immediate situation, but it exerts a more enduring effect as a negative reinforcer of the aggressive response that preceded it.

Anger as a consequence of punishment. When aggression is followed by personal punishment, the aggressor usually becomes angry. Punishment from an authority figure generally does not lead to aggression because aggression against authority is rarely successful and leads to more punishment. The anger engendered by punishment may persist after the threat of punishment has passed, i.e., after the punishing agent leaves the scene. Anger tends to lower the threshold for aggressive responses, and in the absence of imminent punishment, a stimulus that would ordinarily not elicit an aggressive response, would lead to aggression. The aggressor would probably learn that it is safe to aggress while the adult is absent but not while he is present—the "cop on the corner" approach.

When such discriminations are learned, the effect of punishment is limited to those situations in which punishment closely follows aggression and in which the punishing agent is present. Initially the inhibiting effects of punishment may generalize to situations other than the immediate one, the inhibiting effects becoming weaker as the stimulus situation is more disparate from the punishing situation. Discrimination learning steepens the gradient of stimulus generalization and tends to limit the inhibiting effects of punishment to situations very similar to the ones in which punishment is delivered. The way to insure a generalized inhibition of aggression is to punish it in a variety of situations so that the individual learns that aggression is associated with so many stimuli that it is simply not safe to aggress. Such training leads to the behavior seen in overinhibited patients encountered in clinics, who are incapable of even the mildest aggression, no matter what the provocation.

DISPLACEMENT

Two Kinds of Displacement

The psychoanalytic mechanism of displacement is an extremely broad concept: "The energy of the forces behind the mental phenomena is displaceable." (Fenichel, 1945, p. 13) This notion is intended to explain paradoxical behavior in which the intensity of a response is in excess of what is ordinarily elicited by the stimulus. The usual anecdote that is told in connection with displacement of aggression is as follows. A man is berated or insulted by his boss, against whom he cannot retaliate for fear of losing his job. He arrives home sometime later, still fuming over the maltreatment and proceeds to kick the dog and beat his wife on the merest provocation. According to the psychoanalytic explanation, the energy that was suppressed in the presence of the boss was displaced to the dog and the wife, in whose presence the energy was manifested freely.

This explanation appears to be reasonable, but it needs translation into more behavioral terms. Anger tends to energize aggressive behavior, and one aspect of this energizing function is a lowering of the threshold for the occurrence of aggressive responses. The angry man did not kick his dog merely because the dog was present. The dog must have done something, perhaps something as trivial as blocking the man's path or jumping on him and getting him dirty. If the man were not angry, the dog's behavior would not be sufficient to elicit an aggressive response. But, in the presence of anger, the threshold for aggression would be lower, and these responses of the dog, which would ordinarily not elicit aggression, now lead to severe attack.

The man who failed to discriminate situations involving his boss from those involving his family would tend to aggress equally in both situations. Bindra assumes that this is the usual case:

> Thus, a man in whom aggressive acts are not prepotent is less likely to act aggressive in *any* situation than one in whom aggressive acts have reached a high level of habit strength. This statement implies that the man who, on being reprimanded and, thus, provoked by his boss, does not act aggressively in the office situation is not likely to act aggressively even when he sees his wife or children. But the man who does act aggressively in the office situation is also likely to act aggressively in the home situation, provided his arousal level remains high. (1959, p. 266)

Bindra notes that his predictions are opposed to the one usually made on the basis of the traditional interpretation of displacement.

What leads him to different predictions is his assumption that aggressive habit strength is generalized, being the same regardless of the situation or target. This assumption may hold true for some individuals, but most people are forced to make discriminations because of the noxious consequences of aggression when it is directed against targets capable of retaliation. Most men would probably make a clear discrimination between aggressing against the boss and aggressing against the wife. The threat of punishment effectively counteracts any aggressive tendencies toward the boss, but punishment is not as effective in inhibiting aggression against the wife.

It is necessary to distinguish between the target of aggression and the stimulus for aggression. Aggression does not occur merely because a target is present; a stimulus is required. The stimulus may be very mild, but in presence of anger it might be sufficient to elicit an attack. However, the stimulus for aggression must be present, else the attack will not occur. Ordinarily a victim evokes a number of tendencies that are based on past experiences with him. The tendency to become angry and aggress against him is usually only one of several possible tendencies; others include such approach tendencies as friendship and love. The mere presence of another person thus evokes many tendencies, and aggression is generally low in the hierarchy of potential responses. It takes some action by the person to induce anger and elicit an attack against himself, and without this stimulus for an aggressive response there is no attack.

The notion of displacement as it applies to aggression was given its major impetus by the Yale group in *Frustration and Aggression* (1939), and they cited two kinds of evidence. The first line of evidence involved experiments in which a subject was angered, and then his attitude toward minority groups was measured. Ostensibly he would displace aggression from those who angered him to the minority groups, who could not retaliate. The evidence for such displacement is at best equivocal (see Chapter 13). The other line of evidence consists of an experiment by Miller (1948), who related displacement to stimulus generalization. Pairs of rats were placed in an enclosure and given sufficient shock to keep them active. They were trained to make vigorous striking responses at each other, this behavior being reinforced by termination of the shock. Then a white celluloid doll was added to the enclosure, but the rats continued to strike only at each other. Finally, the animals were placed singly in the enclosure in the presence of the doll, and it was found that half the animals commenced to strike the doll. Thus half the animals generalized from the partner animal to the doll, the attacking response being made to the doll when the partner was absent; the other half did not generalize. This interesting demonstration has been widely quoted and is now regarded as a classic experiment. The findings on displacement of aggression would have been more conclusive if there had been a control group that had not been trained to attack a partner rat.

Miller's animals were not angry, and their aggressive response was instrumental in escaping from the noxious stimulation of shock. In the example of the man who beats his wife, the presence of anger (which lowers the threshold of aggressive responses) accounts for the superficially puzzling behavior. In Miller's study it is stimulus similarity (a white, upright object as the target of attack) that accounts for the spread of aggression.

The lowering of threshold that occurs in anger is obviously not the same as the spread of aggression to similar targets, yet both fall under the heading of displacement. Apparently the psychoanalytic notion "energy is displaceable" includes two disparate processes. When anger is present, the thresholds for *all* aggressive responses are lowered, and the shift in targets is not based on their similarity. When anger is absent, the shift in targets depends upon some dimension of similarity, there being no basis for the displacement other than stimulus generalization. This distinction is an important one because the two kinds of displacement underlie very different phenomena.

Certainly stimulus generalization cannot account for the behavior of the man who, angered by his boss, beats his wife. The wife is surely quite dissimilar from the boss, unlike the situation in Miller's experiment, in which there was some similarity between an upright rat and an upright white doll. Nor would there be any verbal labels that might lead to mediated generalization, linking the boss with the wife. The man's behavior is understandable only in terms of a lowering of the threshold of aggression, and this process (the energizing function of anger) is clearly different from stimulus generalization.

Stimulus Generalization

The two kinds of stimulus generalization, primary and mediated, are well known. Briefly, primary stimulus generalization involves the spread of a response to stimuli that are in some way similar to the original training stimulus. The further away the stimuli are from the training stimulus, the weaker is the tendency to make the response. The dimensions of similarity are physical: loudness, pitch, brightness, color.

Mediated stimulus generalization does not involve physical similarity of stimuli. Rather, stimuli are linked by a common response. The mediating response is usually a verbal label such as "dog." The child who learns to avoid dogs might be confronted with a new animal that is different from any dog he has previously encountered. If he labels this new animal with the word "dog," he would probably avoid this stimulus. The avoidance response would have generalized to a new stimulus, not because of any physical similarity (after all, dogs vary from Chihuahuas to great Danes) but because of the mediated verbal response. Since mediated stimulus generalization has received attention only in recent years and little is known about it, especially in quantitative terms, the emphasis in the following discussion will be on primary stimulus generalization.

Earlier a distinction was made between the target of aggression and the stimuli that incite aggression, a distinction that has relevance for the slope of generalization gradients. The stimuli that lead to aggression include frustration, attack, and annoyers. Any of these stimuli can elicit aggression, and it is expected that stimuli similar to them will also elicit aggression. The gradients of generalization around such stimuli may be expected to be relatively flat because of the absence of discrimination training.

On the other hand, the generalization gradients around targets of aggression may be expected to be steep. When a particular individual incites anger and becomes a target of aggression, there will be a tendency to attack persons who resemble this original target, but this tendency will fall off very sharply with only slight degrees of dissimilarity. There are two reasons to expect steeper gradients. First, the person becomes an anger stimulus only by virtue of his association with certain of his responses, i.e., those noxious to the individual who attacks him. The presence of a person constitutes an anger stimulus only insofar as the other responding organism redintegrates the entire pattern of stimulus cues, both physical presence and the delivery of noxious stimuli. Since a target is an aggressive stimulus only by association, the gradient of generalization around targets should be steeper; the aggressive response does not generalize to other *targets* as much as it does to other *stimuli*, which, because they are noxious, tend to elicit aggression directly.

The second reason for steeper gradients of generalization around targets is the extensive cultural training in distinguishing between people as targets not only of aggression but also of other responses. There is considerable training in distinguishing between sex objects: at first making such gross discriminations as girl-boy and man-woman, and then moving on to finer distinctions, such as single woman versus married woman. Perhaps the discriminations with respect to targets of aggression are not so fine, but there is extensive training in distinguishing between boys and girls with respect to physical aggression, and between authority and peers and peers and subordinates, insofar as these figures may be objects of aggression. The maintenance of these discriminations is facilitated by verbal labels, the mediation of such verbal responses helping to steepen the gradient of stimulus generalization. Thus aggression does not spread between targets as much as it does between the stimuli that incite it.

Response Generalization

The last section dealt with the spread of an aggressive response to stimuli other than the one to which it was originally conditioned; the response remained the same, but the stimuli changed. This section deals with response generalization, which involves a change in the response, with the stimulus remaining essentially the same. For example, the man being angered by his boss, instead of suppressing all aggressive responses, might express his aggression indirectly. The Yale group were the first to point out directness of aggression as a major dimension along which response generalization might occur.

It is likely that response generalization is more common than displacement of anger. It was noted in Chapter 1 that aggression varies in both directness and activity. When the target of aggression is authority, direct and active aggressive responses are punished and thereby inhibited. Less direct and less active attacking responses (negativism, malicious gossip) are likely to be substituted. When a boss angers his subordinate, the latter would probably gripe to his office mates, complaining bitterly about the boss' behavior. In this fashion he discharges the physiological tension of his anger state but escapes punishment because of the indirect nature of his attack. He is less likely to suppress all aggression, including very passive and indirect forms, and allow his anger level to remain high; he is more likely to utilize a roundabout means of aggressing and thereby secure at least some release of the physiological tension of anger.

Activity-passivity and directness are two obvious dimensions along which aggressive responses might generalize, but there is perhaps a less obvious dimension of generalization. When the strongest response in the hierarchy cannot be made, there may be a shift to another subclass of aggression, e.g., a shift from physical aggression to verbal aggression. Furthermore, generalization may be entirely unrelated to the characteristics of the response; it may be more closely related to the hierarchy of habit strength of the various aggressive responses in the individual's repertoire.

When the strongest response in the hierarchy is prevented from occurring, response generalization is affected by the manner of prevention. The initial response may be prevented solely by the absence of the appropriate target. Since a direct aggressive response cannot occur in the absence of a victim, the attack that does occur must be indirect. The substituted indirect response will not necessarily be more passive; it may well become more active and possibly shift from verbal to physical aggression, e.g., a shift from derogating and cursing (impossible because the victim is absent) to destroying personal property of the victim. What does diminish (by definition) is the directness of the attack.

The situation is quite different when the target is available, but because of the high probability of retaliation, the strongest response in the aggression hierarchy is inhibited. Here there is likely to be a diminution in activity, assuming an aggressive response does occur. The substitute aggressive response will usually be more passive, negativism and delaying tactics being more probable than active verbal or physical attack. All substitute responses that are made in the presence of the victim are direct by definition, although the aggressor may suppress all aggression until the target is no longer present and then aggress indirectly.

CONFLICT

The man most responsible for the model of conflict in terms of approach and avoidance gradients is Neal Miller. His model was originally designed to account for the behavior of animals under conditions of conflicting tendencies (e.g., approach for food but avoid because of shock) toward the same goal object. Miller stated the basis for extending the model to dimensions other than a goal gradient and, together with Dollard, employed the approach-avoidance paradigm as a means of explaining some of the events in psychotherapy (1950). The model has been applied to the study of aggressive behavior, which involves assumptions concerning the dimension of generalization. The plan for this section is to present the conflict model, then questions that arise in applying it to aggressive behavior, and, finally, an examination of studies that have attempted such extrapolation.

The Conflict Model

The conflict model in its simplest form is a graphic representation of approach and avoidance gradients of response strength, such as is shown in Figure 4.1. The following assumptions are necessary: the closer the subject is to the goal, the stronger are both approach and avoidance tendencies; the avoidance gradient is steeper than the approach gradient; increased motivation (e.g., drive) increases the height of an entire gradient; and the response that occurs is the one with the greater response strength. These assumptions have all been confirmed by research with animals (Brown, 1942; Brown, 1948; Miller & Kraeling, 1952; Miller & Murray, 1952). One further assumption was made only because it was the simplest—that the gradients of approach and avoidance are linear—and this assumption has never been verified.

In all the animal studies on approach and avoidance tendencies, the dimension plotted on the abscissa of graphs like Figure 4.1 was spatial distance from the goal, a clear-cut dimension that is relatively easy to measure. It is well known that the effects of reward weaken as the distance increases between the reward and the organism—the

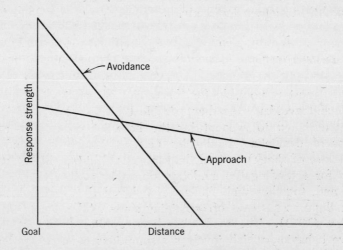

FIG. 4.1. Approach and avoidance gradients (after Miller, 1944).

familiar goal gradient hypothesis, which has been amply confirmed. If the dimension measured on the abscissa were restricted to spatial distance from the goal, the conflict model would be useful but would not possess the generality that it might if other dimensions could also be plotted on the abscissa. Miller has recognized this point:

The definition of nearness is extended to apply to any situation in which the subject can be said to be coming nearer to a goal in space, time or some dimension of qualitatively or culturally defined similarity of cues. (1959, p. 226)

Such a dimension might consist of targets of aggression. For example, when a mother scolds her son, his tendency to counteraggress is inhibited by the incompatible tendency to escape or avoid the stimuli associated with an angry mother; this inhibitory tendency would stem from past punishment for aggression toward the mother. It may be expected that both the approach tendency (aggression) and the avoidance tendency (inhibition) generalize to targets that are similar in some way to the mother. In order of diminishing strength of such tendencies there would be: the boy's aunt, his female music teacher, the female librarian, and women in general. According to the conflict model, aggressive tendencies generalize to more distant targets than inhibitory tendencies (based on the relative slopes of the two gradients).

Applying the Conflict Model to Aggression

In extrapolating from a runway situation with animals to an aggressive situation with humans (in which the generalization dimension may be culturally defined), two conditions need to be met. First, there must be some means of assessing nearness, the dimension that is plotted on the abscissa. There must be a dimension of generalization that is comparable to distance from the goal, and measurements must be available at various points on the dimension. Preferably, the dimension should be established by research on stimulus generalization, but dimensions of generalization in the area of interpersonal behavior (such as aggression) have not been investigated with this purpose in mind, and it is difficult to find appropriate data. An alternative is to use *a priori* dimensions, such as the one stated above (mother, aunt, teacher, librarian, women in general). However, the use of such qualitatively defined dimensions may result in the conflict model being used *post hoc* to "explain" results that could not have been predicted in advance. If there are no quantitative data concerning the dimension of generalization, then it is not possible to locate experimental conditions on the abscissa in advance. An examination of Figure 4.1 shows what the problem is. Locating a group to the right of the intersection of the gradients means that there will be some evidence of aggression; locating to the left of the intersection means there will be no evidence of aggression. Inability to locate experimental groups on the abscissa until after the study has been completed may then lead to a neat "explanation" of the results simply by *post hoc* placement of groups on the abscissa.

The second condition that should be met in employing the conflict model in the study of aggression is the use of separate measures of approach and avoidance tendencies. In most studies all that is available is a measure of the tendency to aggress, probably because it is difficult to measure inhibition tendencies outside of a spatial situation like the alleys used in rat research. However, if the model is to be used in its entirety, it is necessary to have an avoidance measure. Consider what happens if there is a measure of the tendency to aggress but not of the tendency to inhibit, again referring to Figure 4.1. The tendency to aggress (frequency or amplitude of response) will decrease as the subject moves closer to the goal or prime target (or whatever is to the left on the abscissa). Eventually there will be no aggressive response, which occurs at the intersection of the aggression (approach) and inhibition (avoidance) gradients. Beyond the intersection as the individual moves closer to the goal there will still be no aggression, but there is no way of knowing how much stronger the inhibition tendency is than the aggression tendency. Thus it is not possible to draw in anything to the left of the intersection of the gradients. Furthermore, all there would be to the right of the intersection is a measure of the *net* aggressive tendency, i.e., the total tendency to aggress minus the tendency to avoid or inhibit.

The notion of net strength suggests an alternative to separate measures of the tendencies to approach and to avoid. This would be to obtain two measures of aggression: the first in the absence of any competing responses to avoid and the second in the presence of such inhibition tendencies. The first measure would yield the approach (aggression) gradient in its entirety, from the most distant point to the goal. The second measure would yield the avoidance gradient by subtraction. Under the condition of the aggressive response's being punished, the tendency to aggress must be weaker than under the condition of its not being punished. The net drop in tendency to aggress must therefore be equal to the strength of inhibition tendencies. This would yield a graph of the avoidance gradient up to the point where it intersects (attains equal strength with) the aggression gradient. To the left of the point of intersection the avoidance gradient might be extrapolated on the assumption that it continues to become stronger in linear fashion. This solution avoids the thorny problem of obtaining direct measures of avoidance.

The Conflict Model and Studies of Aggression

Murray (1954) analyzed the protocols of a psychotherapy case by means of the conflict model. The client verbalized hostility[1] toward his mother, then toward his aunt (with whom he was living), then other people in general, and, finally, more intense hostility toward his mother. The dimension of distance from the mother is a meaningful *a priori* dimension along which generalization might occur, and Murray correctly identified the shifts in target as a displacement phenomenon. In a subsequent paper (Murray & Berkun, 1955) the analysis of this same case became considerably more complex. The dimension of similarity of targets was retained, but another dimension was added—nearness to the goal—with the goal being defined as the expression of strong hostility toward the mother. These two dimensions were combined with the usual ordinate (response strength) to form a three-dimensional model of conflict and displacement, and the explanation of the client's behavior was as follows. His goal was the expression of intense hostility toward his mother, but when he came near to this goal, anxiety prevented him from going further toward it. He then displaced his hostility to a target somewhat removed from the original one (from mother to aunt), which, therefore, was associated with less anxiety. Hostility against this target eventually led to anxiety, and another displacement occurred (from aunt to other people), again in the direction of less anxiety being associated with the expression of hostility. Once hostility was expressed openly toward other people with little fear of punishment, some of the anxiety extinguished, lowering the entire avoidance gradient. Then the client was able to verbalize more intense hostility toward his mother, which was closer to the goal.

Although this line of reasoning is plausible, is it necessary to add

[1] It may be assumed that *hostility*, as reported by the client, refers not only to hatred and resentment but also to aggressive tendencies.

a dimension of nearness to the goal and assume it was to express strong hostility toward the mother? Since the client was living with his aunt, there must have been sufficient interaction for him to have developed hostility toward her as well as toward his mother, and this is probably true to a lesser extent of people in general. It cannot be assumed that the mother was the sole aggressor or frustrator of the client, his hostility toward others being a matter of generalization from this single source. No doubt the client harbored stronger hatred and aggressive tendencies toward his mother than toward less central figures in his life, but this does not mean that verbalizing intense hostility toward her was his only goal, to the exclusion of verbalizing hostility toward others. The point here is that the data of the psychotherapy case can be handled without the addition of this extra dimension of nearness to the goal, with the goal being defined as strong hostility toward the mother. There is no clear need for three-dimensional model when a two-dimensional model (response strength on the ordinate and targets on the abscissa) is sufficient.

In contrast to the three-dimensional model, Murray, in his original paper (1954), indicated the dimension of targets and stated that generalization along this dimension could explain the displacement of that was occurring during the process of psychotherapy. His account requires fewer assumptions and appears to stay closer to the data. During the course of psychotherapy, the total number of hostile statements per session tended to rise. Murray's explanation was that expressing hostility toward displaced targets was accompanied by very little anxiety, which means that the anxiety response was extinguished. Such extinction would tend to generalize back up the dimension of targets, thus lowering the strength of the entire avoidance gradient and leading to more hostility being verbalized. Although this version in terms of the conflict model does account for the data, it is only fair to state an alternative explanation that is consistent with the results of investigations of interpersonal behavior. There have been a number of studies in which a subject's verbal output has been manipulated by the experimenter's verbal reinforcement, and Buss & Durkee (1958) have shown that hostile verbalizations can be increased by means of such reinforcement in a two-person situation. The client's therapist believed that one of the client's major problems was the inhibition of hostility and aggression; it seems reasonable to believe that he tended to reinforce any hostile statements. Such reinforcement would lead to an increased number of hostile statements as therapy progressed. Furthermore, more intense hostility is usually taken as a sign of progress, assuming the central problem to be repression of such responses. The therapist would also tend to furnish more reinforcement for the stronger hostile responses, which would then start occurring more often. Since the client could not talk about his mother for an unlimited number of sessions and since the therapist would want him to talk about his feelings toward other people, it is reasonable for there to be a shift in the topic of conversation and, therefore, of the target of hostility. This alternative account in no way implies criticism of the conflict model that Murray applied as an explanation of the therapy protocols. However, what it does illustrate is: (a) there may be several good ways to interpret the same data, which negates the argument that the conflict model is necessary because it is the only plausible explanation and (b) psychotherapy is perhaps not an optimal situation for employing the model because of the powerful variable of therapist intervention—after all, the therapist is supposed to be doing something to alter his client's behavior.

Sears et al. (1953) attempted to apply the conflict model to the aggressive behavior and doll play aggression of preschool children. They assumed that aggression learned in the home would generalize to other situations, " . . . the preschool situation, with its teachercum-mother and its inevitably at-times-frustrating social relationships, is in some degree similar to but not identical with the home." (1953, p. 217) It was further assumed that punishment for aggression would produce aggression-anxiety, which would also generalize. Finally, doll play was thought to have some element in common with both the nursery and home situations, since it takes place in the nursery and involves toy home furniture, symbolic family figures, etc. These assumptions gave rise to a conflict model of displaced aggression, which is discussed in detail in Chapter 14.

Briefly, in their study they attempted to relate maternal punitiveness to both aggressive behavior in the preschool nursery and doll play aggression. For some of the children at least, the conflict model could handle the data, stronger punishment being associated with greater displacement of aggression; but for other children the model was not sufficient to account for the relationships.

Ferson (1958) investigated the displacement of hostility[2] along a dimension of academic authority: professor, teacher assistant, exam grader, student. In the experimental group a professor came to class and insulted the students, thereby generating anger. The con-

[2] Again, the term *hostility* refers to both dislike and the tendency to aggress verbally.

trol group was not angered. Both groups were administered an inventory that tapped attitudes toward the four figures mentioned above. The scores were derived from the subjects' ranking of the four academic figures, with high scores indicating more hostility.

The results are shown in Table 4.1. Examination of the scores

TABLE 4.1. MEAN HOSTILITY SCORES FOR VARIOUS
ACADEMIC FIGURES*

	Professor	Teaching Assistant	Exam Grader	Student
Experimental	69	80	81	70
Control	68	75	83	74

* From Ferson, 1958.

of only the experimental group suggests that displacement had indeed occurred. Ostensibly the angry students could express only part of their hostility toward the professor who angered them and displaced some of it onto less threatening figures. However, the means for the control group were similar to those of the experimental group, and the control group had not been angered. They had no anger to displace, yet they manifested less hostility toward the professor than toward the other three figures. The only significant difference between groups was for the hostility scores on teaching assistants. Because other variables were manipulated, Ferson ran 12 F tests, and only this one was significant at the .05 level, which suggests that it might not be a reliable difference. This difference is also clouded by the fact that the scores were ranks rather than independent evaluations of the four figures separately. In brief, the only evidence of displacement is equivocal.

The most unusual modification of the conflict model is that of Hokanson & Gordon (1958). They employed two abscissa (nearness) dimensions, arousal and cue relevance. Locating the arousal dimension on the abscissa would appear to be a misreading of the conflict model. Miller (1944) is explicit concerning the effect of such arousal as occurs in drive states; the effect is to elevate the entire approach gradient. This assumption has been confirmed by Brown (1948) and others. Increased arousal in the Miller model is unrelated to nearness and cannot be plotted on the abscissa.

It is also questionable to place cue relevance on the abscissa, especially when it is defined (as Hokanson & Gordon do) in terms of frequency of aggressive themes elicited by TAT cards. They assume that as cue relevance increases, inhibition (avoidance) will increase faster than expression (approach) of aggression. This prediction may be correct or incorrect, depending upon where the stimuli are located on the abscissa.

An adequate exposition and critique of the Hokanson & Gordon study would require too much space; their interesting paper should be read in full. In passing, it should be noted that they appear to have fallen into the error of using qualitative dimensions as substitutes for the abscissa dimension of nearness to the goal. Not only are their assumptions concerning these dimensions questionable, but it is impossible to test their predictions. Location of experimental groups to the right of the intersection[3] of expression and inhibition gradients yields one set of predictions (i.e., would be consistent with one set of results), and locating experimental groups to the left of the intersection would yield an opposite set of predictions. Thus increasing arousal (anger) leads to more expression of aggression to the right of the intersection but to less aggression to the left of the intersection.

This examination of attempts to use the conflict model in the study of aggression reveals varying degrees of success. The model does appear to have heuristic value as a propagator of experiments. However, its ultimate utility would seem to depend upon efforts in the direction of quantification of the nearness dimension. In the absence of quantified dimensions of nearness or similarity, the conflict model has an unfortunate flexibility that makes difficult a rigorous test of its worth.

REFERENCES

Bindra, D. An interpretation of the "displacement" phenomenon. *Brit. J. Psychol.*, 1959, **50**, 263–268.

Brown, J. S. Gradients of approach and avoidance and their relation to level of motivation. *J. comp. physiol. Psychol.*, 1948, **41**, 450–465.

Brown, J. S. The generalization of approach responses as a function of stimulus intensity and strength of motivation. *J. comp. Psychol.*, 1942, **33**, 209–226.

Buss, A. H. & Durkee, A. Conditioning of hostile verbalizations in a situation resembling a clinical interview. *J. consult. Psychol.*, 1958, **22**, 415–418.

Cohen, A. R. Social norms, arbitrariness of frustration, and status of the agent of frustration in the frustration-aggression hypothesis. *J. abnorm. soc. Psychol.*, 1955, **51**, 222–226.

Dollard, J., Doob, L. W., Miller, N. E., Mowrer, O. H., & Sears, R. R. *Frustration and aggression.* New Haven: Yale University Press, 1939.

[3] Reference to Figure 4.1 will make these comments more meaningful.

Dollard, J. & Miller, N. E. *Personality and psychotherapy.* New York: Mc-Graw-Hill, 1950.

Doob, L. W. & Sears, R. R. Factors determining substitute behavior and the overt expression of aggression. *J. abnorm. soc. Psychol.,* 1939, **34,** 293–313.

Fenichel, O. *The psychonanalytic theory of neuroses.* New York: Norton, 1945.

Ferson, Jean E. The displacement of hostility. Unpublished doctor's dissertation, University of Texas, 1958.

Graham, Frances K., Charwat, Wanda A., Honig, Alice S., & Weltz, Paula C. Aggression as a function of the attack and the attacker. Barnard College, Columbia University, 1950, *J. abnorm. soc. Psychol.,* 1951, **46,** 512–520.

Hokanson, J. E. & Gordon, J. E. The expression and inhibition of imaginative and overt behavior. *J. abnorm. soc. Psychol.,* 1958, **57,** 327–333.

Hollenberg, Eleanor & Sperry, Margaret. Some antecedents of aggression and effects of frustration in doll play. *Personality,* 1951, **1,** 34–43.

McClelland, D. C. & Apicella, F. S. A functional classification of verbal reactions to experimentally induced failure. *J. abnorm. soc. Psychol.,* 1945, **40,** 376–390.

Miller, N. E. Liberalization of basic SOR concepts: extension to conflict behavior, motivation and social learning. In vol. II, Sigmund Koch (Ed.), *Psychology: A study of a science.* New York: McGraw-Hill, 1959.

Miller, N. E. Theory and experiment relating psychoanalytic displacement to stimulus-response generalization. *J. abnorm. soc. Psychol.,* 1948, **43,** 155–178.

Miller, N. E. Experimental studies of conflict. In J. McV. Hunt (Ed.), *Personality and the behavior disorders.* New York: Ronald Press, 1944.

Miller, N. E. & Kraeling, Doris. Displacement: greater generalization of approach then avoidance in a generalized approach avoidance conflict. *J. exp. Psychol.,* 1952, **93,** 217–221.

Miller, N. E. & Murray, E. J. Displacement and conflict: learnable drive as a basis for the steeper gradient of avoidance than of approach. *J. exp. Psychol.,* 1952, **43,** 227–231.

Murray, E. J. A case study in the behavioral analysis of psychotherapy. *J. abnorm. soc. Psychol.,* 1954, **49,** 305–310.

Murray, E. J. & Berkun, M. M. Displacement as a function of conflict. *J. abnorm. soc. Psychol.,* 1955, **51,** 47–56.

Reiser, M. F., Reeves, R. B., & Armington, J. Effect of variations in laboratory procedure and experiments upon ballistocardiogram, blood pressure, and heart rate in healthy young men. *Psychosom. Med.,* 1955, **17,** 185–199.

Sears, R. R., Whiting, J. W. M., Nowlis, V., & Sears, Pauline S. Some child-rearing antecedents of aggression and dependency in young children. *Genet. Psychol. Monogr.,* 1953, **47,** 135–234.

Worchel, P. Catharsis and the relief of hostility. *J. abnorm. soc. Psychol.,* 1957, **55,** 238–243.

5

Catharsis

The concept of catharsis has emerged from psychoanalytic theory. It is similar to *abreaction,* a more commonly used psychoanalytic term that refers to a sudden expression of previously repressed affect. Catharsis is defined in broader terms, and it includes the expression of any emotional impulses—the idea of a "release" being a crucial part of the concept. The concept of catharsis is part of the "hydraulic" model of personality, which is based on the analogy to a liquid held under pressure in a container or reservoir (Hendricks, 1948). Additions to the liquid increase pressure on the walls. There are regular channels for drainage, which operate when the liquid places sufficient pressure on the container. In the absence of adequate drainage, the pressure builds up until there is a leak in the walls of the reservoir. Each increase in the liquid adds pressure for release of the liquid; each time there is drainage, there is at least a temporary decrement in pressure for release.

The pressure is analogous to impulses, in the present context—aggressive impulses. The reservoir is fed by incitements to aggression, and the walls of the reservoir represent inhibitions against expressing aggressive impulses. The inhibitions may be normal and adjustive, such as the delays that must often be endured by mature individuals; or the inhibitions may be neurotic and maladjustive, such as the rigid tendency to block all direct expression of aggressive impulses until there is either an overflow or a breakthrough of defenses. The expression of aggression represents a draining of the reservoir; the more drained, the less that remains in the reservoir. The less that remains in the reservoir, the less pressure is exerted by impulses seeking release. The expression of aggression is called *catharsis,* and the diminution in the tendency to aggress as a consequence of such expression of aggression is called the *cathartic effect.*

75

This concept was taken over and translated by the Yale group, as follows: "The expression of any act of aggression is a catharsis that reduces the instigation to all other acts of aggression. From this and the principle of displacement it follows that, with level of original frustration held constant, there should be an inverse relationship between the expression of various forms of aggression." (Dollard et al., 1939, pp. 53–54) Their hypothesis is sweeping in nature, and the Yale group felt compelled to qualify it by suggesting that both time and learning variables might be important; the disclaimers were contained in a footnote that has received little attention.

The variable of time is important. Assuming there is a cathartic effect, how long does it endure? Surely the reservoir must refill and the pressure for release again mount. The drop in tendency to aggress probably does not last more than a few hours, a day at most, and measures of the cathartic effect that are taken subsequently will probably not show any diminution in strength of aggression.

The Yale group did not distinguish between the instigation to aggression (drive) and the emotional reaction of anger, the assumption being that anger is part of aggressive drive. In their view, any act of aggression presupposes an instigation to aggression, and there is no need for assuming a separate anger reaction. Nevertheless, as was shown in Chapter 1, aggressive responses may occur with or without anger, and the distinction between angry aggression and instrumental aggression is crucial to an understanding of catharsis.

In anger there is a temporarily heightened physiological state, a preparedness for aggressive action. If no aggressive response ensues, this tension state will gradually subside. If there is an aggressive response, the tension state will dissipate faster. Thus when an attacking response occurs in the presence of anger, there is a cathartic effect that drops tension back to its resting level. When an aggressive response occurs in the absence of anger, there is no drop in tension level; since tension (anger) level is at its low point, it cannot be lowered. Hence, when an aggressive response occurs in the absence of anger, there is no cathartic effect.[1]

In contrast, the Yale group predicts that there is a cathartic effect whenever an aggressive response has been made. They did not mention anger, nor were they concerned with the physiological tension state of the organism. Therefore, in their view the level in the reservoir is reduced after each aggressive response, regardless of the presence or absence of anger, and the cathartic effect is a consequence of any aggressive act.

[1] This is also the psychoanalytic position, which insists that a cathartic effect requires the expression of affect.

In studying the catharsis effect, several experimental designs are available, and there are different kinds of laboratory measures of aggression. The occurrence of a cathartic effect depends upon reinforcement, inhibition, and fatigue. A discussion of these issues is essential to an understanding of the catharsis experiments that follow.

Experimental Designs and Measures of Aggression

In the absence of anger the basic design should include two measures of aggression:

experimental   measure #1—catharsis—measure #2
control   measure #1—neutral activity—measure #2

The experimental group is allowed to aggress, and the effect is assessed by comparing the first measure with the second. Since it is possible that any activity occurring between measurements may affect the tendency to aggress, it is necessary to have a control group that is engaged in a "neutral" activity.

In the presence of anger the basic design should include three measures of aggression:

experimental—measure #1—anger arousal—measure #2—catharsis
            —measure #3
control   —measure #1—anger arousal—measure #2—neutral activity—measure #3

The first measure is necessary to insure that both groups are equated for pre-experimental level of tendency to aggress, and the second measure is needed to insure that both groups have been equally affected by anger arousal. The third measure assesses the cathartic effect.

These paradigms depend upon measures of aggression that can be repeated during a fairly short interval. Since it is difficult to obtain such measures, some investigators have resorted to a substitute paradigm:

experimental   anger arousal—catharsis—measure #1
control   anger arousal—neutral activity—measure #1

This design assumes that randomly selected subjects will not differ in either initial tendency to aggress or in the effect of anger arousal. It is further assumed that the control activity occurring between anger arousal and the measurement of aggression will have no effect. To the extent that these assumptions are correct, this design may be substituted for the own-control design mentioned above. Unfortunately, little is known about the effects of various methods of arousing anger, and slight variations may produce large differences in anger level. The control activity may increase aggressive tendencies rather than leave them unaffected. There is insufficient knowledge about anger arousal, about the effect of various activities on aggressive tendencies, and about measures of aggressive tendencies. The only way to avoid artifacts in a catharsis study is to employ both pre- and postcatharsis measures.

Ideally, the same instrument should be used to measure aggression repeatedly. If the measurement involves the expression of aggression, it may serve as a means of catharsis. The "aggression machine" described in Chapter 3 would probably be a useful tool for this purpose. The real subject could punish the accomplice, then be angered, again punish (the catharsis), and punish a third time (the final measurement). The measure of aggression could be used repeatedly, with only the target of aggression being changed.

The two major kinds of instruments that have been used to assess aggression in catharsis experiments are brief attitude questionnaires and projective tasks. Such measures may be affected by three variables: anger, hostility, and aggressive habit strength.

Anger level is a determiner of the aggression score; angry subjects tend to tell more aggressive TAT stories and to direct more verbal aggression and blame toward experimental figures on questionnaires. After the expression of aggression, anger level should drop—the cathartic effect; but hostility may remain at a high level. When the subject learns negative labels and dislike of another person in an experimental situation, this hostility may remain after anger subsides. Even if he is allowed to aggress verbally against his attacker, the subject may still dislike him. This dislike shows up in attitude questionnaires, which tap attitudes and feelings toward specific individuals and groups. Thus after catharsis has occurred, an attitude questionnaire may not show a drop in the aggression score. This prediction is predicated on the assumption that there is no change in the attacking individual or in the group that is doing the attacking, or frustrating. If the experimenter first attacks a subject and then allows the subject to counterattack, the change in the experimenter's attitude from punitiveness to permissiveness may be reflected in a lowered aggression score on an attitude questionnaire. Here the cathartic effect would be confounded with a real change in the stimulus object (the experimenter) being evaluated on the questionnaire.

The more diffuse measures of aggression, such as the TAT, word associations, and scrambled sentences, would seem to be the preferred measures of aggression in a catharsis experiment. It is possible to devise alternate forms of these tasks so that they may be administered both before and after catharsis. Unlike questionnaires, they are not focused on individuals, and they measure anger more than hostility. Unfortunately, no studies could be found in which these measures were used for both pre- and postcatharsis measurement of aggression.

Finally, most measures are affected by the subject's habit strength of aggression, i.e., the pre-anger measure is a measure of the subject's enduring tendency to aggress. However, if the measure taps *only* enduring response tendencies, it will be useless in the investigation of the cathartic effect. It must be susceptible to changes in aggression that occur when the subject is angry. Fortunately, the measures noted above (TAT, scrambled sentences, word association, and the aggression machine) are sufficiently susceptible to transient changes in aggression to be used in the laboratory.

Variables Affecting Catharsis

In the catharsis paradigm the subject is encouraged to aggress; this encouragement may be viewed as either reinforcement for aggression or as a signal that aggression need not be inhibited. If the subject continues to aggress, there may be built-in inhibitions to further aggression. These variables have different effects on catharsis.

Reinforcement. After the subject has been angered, it is necessary for the experimenter to get him to cathart. This is accomplished by urging the subject to vent his anger and by reinforcing either implicitly (increased attention, permissiveness) or explicitly (verbal reinforcers like "good"). Another source of reinforcement is internal: the sudden drop in anger level that usually accompanies an attack. The release of tension and the production of relaxation may be a powerful reward.

These reinforcements should increase the habit strength of aggression, i.e., an increase in the frequency or intensity of aggression, or both. While the effects of such reinforcement may be expected to be long-range, there may also be a short-range effect: an *increase* in aggression after catharsis rather than a decrease.

Inhibition. The experimenter's permissiveness and encouragement may be regarded as a signal for decreased inhibition of aggressiveness. During the acculturation process, children are punished for their attacking responses; such punishment leading to avoidance of aggression and to approach-avoidance conflicts. Inhibition or avoidance of aggression is particularly strong in laboratory and classroom situations, the usual experimental contexts. If inhibition is decreased by signals from the experimenter, the subject is free to express more aggression. The lowered inhibition may be expected to carry over from the catharsis period to the period of postcatharsis measurement, and the final measure might reflect an *increase* not a decrease in aggression. Note that both reinforcement and decreased inhibition lead to the same result; in the absence of anger, catharsis increases aggression.

Reactive and conditioned inhibition. During the catharsis period, the subject may make a number of attacking responses, some of them very intense. When aggression is prolonged or intense, there may be a build-up of two kinds of "internal inhibition." The first kind is reactive inhibition or fatigue; the second is conditioned inhibition, a mechanism that is believed to prevent the organism from continuing to make the same response indefinitely. Thus in satiation tasks, subjects may become bored and quit, and if conditioned inhibition does not stop them from responding, fatigue eventually will.

The effect of these two kinds of inhibition on the postcatharsis measure is to *decrease* the aggression score. Note that the effect is temporary, and after a period of rest the tendency to aggress should return to full strength. Parenthetically, the notion that aggressive tendencies may be reduced by means of violent play is based in part on reactive inhibition—getting the aggressor too tired to attack.

Studies of Catharsis

The catharsis paradigm has been outlined and the major variables discussed. Of the variables just mentioned, reactive and conditioned inhibition play minor roles in the typical catharsis experiment because there is usually insufficient intensity or duration of aggression. The other variables are important. In the absence of anger, reinforcement (or a drop in inhibition) should lead to an increase in the tendency to aggress. In the presence of anger, catharsis should temporarily decrease the tendency to aggress because of the lowering of anger level.

Catharsis without anger. Kenny (1952) used as his pre- and postcatharsis tasks an incomplete stories task that was scored for aggres-

sion. In the experimental group, children were given two interpolated sessions; they played with dolls in a sibling rivalry situation,
and engaged in hitting, slapping, and verbally attacking the dolls.
The interpolated sessions of the control group were permissive; the
children engaged in nonaggressive play on swings and with jigsaw
puzzles. Five aggression scores were derived from the incomplete
stories task. It was found that the experimental group manifested
no significant change from pre- to postcatharsis on any of the five
scores, and the control group showed significant *decreases* in two of
the scores. Kenny concluded that the catharsis hypothesis is not
valid.

This conclusion seems hasty. There is evidence that the catharsis
hypothesis holds, but only when anger is present. Concerning
Kenny's experiment, several features are worthy of note. First, the
control group showed a significant change in aggression on two of
the measures, illustrating both the unpredictability of control activities and the need for pre- and postcatharsis measures. Second, the
interval between pre- and postcatharsis measures ranged from 5 to
25 days, and it is doubtful that any cathartic effect could last more
than a few hours. Third, Kenny's measure of aggression (incomplete stories) may be unreliable.

Feshbach (1956) used play as the mode of catharsis. The experimental group had toys that would ordinarily lead to aggressive play:
cowboys, Indians, soldiers, and pirates. The control group played
with neutral toys: trains, circus, farm, stories. Play activities were
observed and rated for thematic aggression (attacks occurring in
play, as between cowboys and Indians) and for inappropriate aggression (verbal attacks or blows struck at another child outside of
play). It was found that the experimental group showed significantly more inappropriate aggression than the control group, suggesting that the aggressive toys tended to elicit aggressive behavior.

Teachers rated the children for classroom aggression before and
after the cathartic play sessions. There was no significant change for
either group and no significant difference between the experimental
and the control group. The absence of a change cannot be attributed
to a lack of aggressive catharsis because the experimental group
manifested significantly more inappropriate (interpersonal) aggression than the control group during the catharsis sessions.

In accounting for his results, Feshbach suggested that there may
have been insufficient generalization from the play activities to the
classroom. Of possibly greater importance are the variables of time
and anger. Feshbach's procedures extended through a period of
4 weeks, during which time any cathartic effect should have dis-

sipated. Since his subjects were not angered, the aggressive play sessions could involve no drop in anger. In the absence of anger, the pattern of reinforcement and permissiveness (diminishing inhibition of aggression) succeeded in increasing the tendency of some of the children to aggress in both the experimental and control groups.

A television or motion picture audience often participates vicariously in the events that transpire on the screen, and this phenomenon has been used to study the effect of vicarious aggression on the tendency to aggress subsequently. Siegel (1956) had nursery school children watch aggressive and neutral films, with sequence effects controlled. The children's play was rated for aggression after each film. A cathartic effect would lead to less aggression after the aggressive film than after the neutral film. The results were in the opposite direction but not significantly so; there was more play aggression after the aggressive film than after the neutral film. In the absence of anger, it is possible that the presence of aggressive stimulation might incite aggression, a notion that receives partial corroboration from two studies with college students.

Buss & Foliart (1958) had college students play different roles. Subjects in the experimental group played the role of someone who had been severely maligned and was now confronting the person who had gossiped about him. The role of the gossiper was played by a college-age experimenter, who did nothing further to incite anger in the acting situation. Subjects in the control group played the role of someone meeting an old friend, again played by the college-age experimenter. Four TAT cards were administered before role playing and another four afterward, with sequence controlled. The TAT was scored for violence. Themes of knifing, raping, shooting, strangling, and murdering received twice the weight of themes of fighting and robbing. The results are presented in Table 5.1.

TABLE 5.1. MEAN TAT VIOLENCE SCORES BEFORE AND AFTER
ROLE PLAYING

	Experimental		Control	
	Men	Women	Men	Women
Before	2.7	3.3	2.8	2.6
After	4.0	3.4	2.3	2.4

The *Before* scores show some variability between groups, but the differences are statistically insignificant. The only large before-after change is that of the men in the experimental group, and this increase is statistically significant. The slight changes in the other groups are not significant. Thus the effect of role playing catharsis is to increase the aggression scores of men and to leave unaffected the aggression scores of women.

The increase of aggression in the men may be explained in reinforcement terms. During role playing, the subject was encouraged to be verbally aggressive and his efforts were commended by the experimenter, and this encouragement would tend to reinforce aggression. The reinforcement should increase the habit strength of all verbally aggressive responses via stimulus generalization, i.e., there should be an increase in aggression in the TAT protocols. In the absence of anger arousal, there was no drop in anger level after role playing of aggression. Since the session was short (less than 5 minutes of role playing), there was no opportunity for either reactive or conditioned inhibition to build up. Therefore, the only variable acting on the tendency to aggress in this catharsis situation was reinforcement, which should increase subsequent aggression. This explanation fits the men's data, but it fails to account for the women's data. Perhaps women are more reluctant to be verbally aggressive, especially toward a male experimenter, despite the make-believe (role playing) situation. There is some evidence (see Chapter 7) that women have a lower operant rate of verbal aggression than men, and perhaps in this situation they simply could not be induced to increase this rate.

The last study in this section involves catharsis with and without anger. Feshbach (1958) investigated the effect of vicarious aggression (watching a prize fight film) on subsequent tendency to aggress in college students. Two groups were angered by means of insult, and two groups were not. Then one angry and one non-angry group watched the prize fight film; the other angry and non-angry groups watched a neutral film. Two measures of aggression were used, both administered after the films. One was a word association task that included aggressive and nonaggressive stimulus words, and the other was a questionnaire that tapped attitudes toward the experimenter and the experiment.

The attitude questionnaire yielded no statistically significant findings, but there was a significant interaction on the word association task. The angry group that catharted vicariously (watched the prize fight film) gave significantly *fewer* aggressive word associations than the angry group that did not cathart (watched the neutral film). The non-angry group that catharted gave significantly *more* aggressive associations than the non-angry group that did not cathart. This study clearly reveals the effect of anger on catharsis. In the absence of anger, vicarious catharsis of aggression increased the tendency to aggress, the film acting as a stimulant to aggression. In the presence of anger, vicarious aggression decreased the tendency to aggress, the film acting to lower anger level.

Catharsis with anger. The best known study of catharsis with anger is that of Feshbach (1955) with college students. He ran his subjects in groups and used insult to anger them. The experimental group (Insult Fantasy) was first angered and then allowed to take a group TAT, which served as both the means of catharsis and the measure of aggression after anger. One control group (Insult Control) was angered, but instead of taking the TAT, they engaged in several neutral intellectual tasks. A second control group (Non-insult Fantasy) was not angered, but took the TAT. Finally, all groups were administered a sentence completion task and a questionnaire tapping attitudes toward the experimenter and the experiment.

The insulting procedure proved to be effective in angering subjects, the TAT aggression scores of the Insult Fantasy group being significantly higher than those of the Non-insult Fantasy group. The sentence completion task yielded equivocal results concerning catharsis, the various aggression scores on it being either statistically nonsignificant or significant but self-contradictory. The attitude questionnaire yielded significant results, the aggression scores of the Insult Fantasy (catharsis) group being lower than those of the Insult Control group. Thus the effect of vicarious aggression (the telling of aggressive stories) in the presence of anger is to lower the tendency to aggress.

Hornberger (1959) attempted to replicate and extend Feshbach's study, using the same group insult procedure and measures of post-catharsis aggression. Of the subjects who were angered, one group was administered two TAT cards (Insult Fantasy), one group engaged in an intellectual task (Insult Control), and one group pounded nails in a board for 10 minutes (Insult Physical Activity). There were three comparable non-angered groups. The subjects were insulted by being told that they had done poorly on an arithmetic task. This procedure did not result in as much anger as Feshbach was able to arouse, and only the attitude questionnaire yielded significant differences between the angered and non-angered groups. However, there was no other statistically significant finding for the attitude questionnaire; neither fantasy nor physical catharsis served to reduce aggression.

Note that Feshbach was more successful in angering his subjects, which should have led to a higher level of aggression. If Hornberger had angered his subjects more, the Insult Control group would probably have had a higher aggression score; this might have led to a significant difference between this control group and the Insult Fantasy group. Furthermore, Feshbach used four TAT cards and Hornberger only two cards; the additional catharsis available to Feshbach's subjects might account for his significant findings. Assuming that the differences in procedure between the two experiments were important, Feshbach's subjects would have been angrier before catharsis and had more opportunity to cathart than Hornberger's subjects. Had these studies measured aggression both before and after catharsis, there would be no need to speculate; the data would have been available.

Thibaut & Coules (1952) used a different means of angering their male college subjects. Pairs of subjects communicated with each other via written notes, the ostensible purpose being to discover how well they could assess each other's personality. They could see each other, but communication was otherwise blocked by a glass screen. One member of the pair was an experimental accomplice, who used the last note to insult and derogate the real subject. The experimental group was permitted to cathart by writing one note answering the attack, while the control group was allowed no further notes. Prior to the note writing there was a very brief interaction between the accomplice and the real subject. The subjects wrote two personality sketches, one before and one after the note passing, and these sketches were scored for aggression and friendliness. Thus there were two measures of aggression, one before anger arousal and one after catharsis, but no measure after anger arousal but before catharsis.

In both groups, the aggression score rose and the friendliness score dropped from the first personality sketch to the second. The changes were greater in the catharsis group than in the control group, but the differences between groups did not attain statistical significance. In evaluating the failure to find a significant cathartic effect, two features should be mentioned. First, during the preliminary note passing (before the insulting note) the accomplice wrote about himself as a weak, unpleasant person, and it is probable that subjects in both groups came to dislike him *before* they were insulted. This dislike would probably endure whether or not there was an opportunity for catharsis, thus diminishing the difference between experimental and control groups. Second, the experimental subjects were given only a minimal opportunity to cathart; one note seems insufficient to ventilate anger, and perhaps several notes are needed.

Rosenbaum & DeCharms (1960) suggest that self-esteem is important in catharsis. They followed up the Thibaut & Coules study, this time attacking subjects vocally; otherwise the procedure was similar. Subjects were instructed to describe themselves, and they listened to a tape recording of the other "subject's" self-report (again this fake subject described himself so as to give the impression of egotism). Then the real subject was attacked verbally. In addition to the usual catharsis group, there was a vicarious group, which listened to a third "subject" verbally aggress against the attacker. The control group was not allowed to reply to the attacker and had no expectation of doing so because of prior instructions. Finally, all subjects wrote a personality sketch about the attacker, which was scored for aggression.

The aggression scores of the three groups were not significantly different. Subjects were divided into high and low self-esteem groups on the basis of a questionnaire taken previously. For the low self-esteem subjects, the catharsis group was significantly lower in aggression than the control group. For the high self-esteem subjects, the differences between the three groups were small and statistically nonsignificant. Thus high self-esteem subjects manifested no reduction in aggression after being allowed to cathart, whereas low self-esteem subjects showed a clear cathartic effect. There is no obvious explanation for this difference, though Rosenbaum & DeCharms suggest that high self-esteem subjects are less threatened by verbal attack and are simply not angered by it; in the absence of anger there is nothing to cathart.

A study by Worchel (1957) is relevant if it is assumed that anger interferes with efficient performance on a task that calls for concentration. Three groups of subjects were insulted and thereby angered in a classroom situation. The catharsis group was allowed to gripe in group fashion about the procedure; one control group was allowed to talk but only about neutral topics; the second control group remained silent. A digit symbol task was administered to all subjects both before and after these procedures, the pre-insult scores being used to control for individual differences in this task. It was found that the catharsis group scored significantly higher on the second digit symbol administration than did the control groups. Thus, assuming that anger interferes with the task, the subjects who were allowed verbal aggression showed a decrease in anger that allowed them to do better in the task.

An extension of this study may be found in a doctoral dissertation by Pirojnikoff (1958), under the direction of Worchel. Subjects were given a group intelligence test and told that the scores would become part of their permanent records. The examiner badgered and insulted them, and then he left, to be replaced by the experimenter. The catharsis group was then encouraged to gripe about the procedure, and the control group engaged in a discussion concerning the place of Sociology in a college program. The digit symbol task was administered both before the anger arousal and after the discussion period. Also administered after the discussion period was a questionnaire tapping attitudes toward the experiment and the insulting examiner.

The entire experiment was replicated with the same insulting examiner but with a new experimenter and a new sample of subjects. The replication yielded quite different results from the first experiment. Combining the two experiments yielded equivocal results. Contrary to the results of Worchel's study, the digit symbol scores showed no systematic effects in relation to catharsis. The one significant finding was that the catharsis group had a *higher* aggression score on the attitude questionnaire than the control group. This result is contrary to the findings of experiments on catharsis with anger (Feshbach, 1955; Thibaut & Coules, 1952; Rosenbaum & De-Charms, 1960); even Hornberger (1959) found no difference between groups, rather than an increase in aggression in the catharsis group.

Pirojnikoff's procedure differed from previous ones in that the subjects catharted in a group, and, in attempting to reconcile his findings with previous results, he offered the following explanation. The subjects had been classmates for most of a semester, and there must have been at least some group cohesiveness. Once the griping began, it was reinforced by the presence of the group; one student's complaint might easily have incited another student to complain. There may have been a build-up of aggression within the catharsis group that would carry over into the subsequent taking of the attitude questionnaire. Thus the process of listening to each other's gripes may have initiated more anger rather than serving to dissipate the anger already present.

It follows from this explanation that more verbal aggression might be expected in such a group situation because of the facilitating effect of one student's complaining upon another's. This assumption may hold for large groups, but Pepitone & Reichling (1955) have shown that it does not hold for a two-person group. Half their subjects were told that they had been matched for personality traits with someone who was desirable and compatible (high cohesive group). The other half were told that it had been impossible to obtain a good match and that they would probably not get along well with the partner (low cohesive group). Then they were insulted in groups of two by an "instructor," who subsequently left them alone for 6 minutes. During this time the subjects were observed and rated for verbally aggressive behavior. Finally, they filled out a questionnaire that assessed liking or disliking of the insulting instructor and the partner in the two-person group.

The 6 minutes were divided into one minute segments, and it was found that the high cohesive group spent more of the time (more segments) being verbally aggressive than did the low cohesive group. During the course of the 6 minutes, both groups showed less and less verbal aggression; the high cohesive group started out at a higher level of aggression and dropped more sharply than the low cohesive group. Thus there were differential amounts of catharsis. On the questionnaire the high cohesive group showed better liking for both the partner and the insulting instructor than did the low cohesive group. Assuming that both groups had been equally angered by the insulting procedure, the group that catharted more (high cohesive) ended up with less aggression (as measured by the questionnaire), which is evidence for a cathartic effect.

Berkowitz (1960) investigated the effects of filling out a self-report check list versus taking the TAT on subsequent evaluations of another "subject" (an experimental accomplice) in a two-person situation. The procedure was in some ways similar to that of Thibaut & Coules (1952), except that the subject was not attacked directly; rather the accomplice was presented as being pleasant or unpleasant at first, and later he rated the subject either high or low. The subject first evaluated the accomplice before knowing much about him, again after discovering whether he was pleasant or not, and finally after receiving a good or bad rating from him and then filling out the check list or taking the TAT.[2]

When the accomplice was initially pleasant and then rated the subject low, the group that filled out the check list increased in dislike of the accomplice, whereas the group that took the TAT showed no increase in dislike. When the accomplice was initially unpleasant

_____

[2] It is difficult to summarize the complex design and procedure of this study, which should be read in its entirety.

and then rated the subject high, all subjects showed a decrease in dislike of the accomplice. The results were quite different for the subjects toward whom the accomplice was initially pleasant. All subjects later given a low rating increased their dislike score, while all subjects later given a high rating showed no difference in their dislike of the accomplice. When the accomplice was initially pleasant, it made no difference whether the subject filled out a check list or took the TAT. Berkowitz noted that a catharsis interpretation would account for at least some of his data, but he preferred to explain them in terms of guilt. However, the results appear to be too complicated to be explained by any existing formulation.

CONCLUSIONS

When aggression occurs in the absence of anger, there is an *increase* in the tendency to aggress. When aggression occurs in the presence of anger, there is a cathartic effect, i.e., a decrease in the tendency to aggress. Thus the most important determiner of the cathartic effect is the presence or absence of anger.

Other variables also influence catharsis. Encouragement of aggression serves as a reinforcer (or alternatively as a reducer of inhibition) of aggression, thereby increasing the tendency to aggress. Reactive and conditioned inhibition, which reduce the tendency to aggress, appear to be relatively minor variables in the laboratory, where aggression is neither intense nor prolonged.

Since anger is only a transient reaction, time is an important variable in catharsis. Anger slowly dissipates whether or not aggression occurs, and as the tension state of anger diminishes, the tendency to aggress also diminishes. There is a cathartic effect only so long as anger is present; and when sufficient time has elapsed for anger to subside, there is no longer a cathartic effect.

Since anger is an emotional response, the cathartic effect must involve a lowering of physiological tension. No study has measured the effect of an aggressive response on the subject's physiological state, and such a study would seem to be an important next step in the investigation of catharsis.

Because aggression may take many forms, there are many modes of catharsis. In the studies reviewed in this chapter, aggression was expressed in thematic fantasy, play, note writing, griping, evaluating another subject, and by several vicarious means. Surely these various modes of aggression do not reduce the tendency to aggress equally;

there must be a hierarchy of cathartic effectiveness. The most direct and active forms of aggression should have the greatest cathartic effect and the least direct and active forms, the least cathartic effect.

Finally, a relatively neglected issue in this area is that of sex differences. Men, for the most part, aggress more than women, but it is not known whether their aggression has a greater cathartic effect. Perhaps very little aggression is needed in order to reduce anger level, and the less intense aggression of women yields as great a cathartic effect as the more intense aggression of men.

REFERENCES

Berkowitz, L. Some factors affecting the reduction of hostility. *J. abnorm. soc. Psychol.*, 1960, **60**, 14–21.

Buss, A. H., & Foliart, R. Role-playing aggression and the catharsis hypothesis. Unpublished research, 1958.

Dollard, J., Doob, L. W., Miller, N. E., Mowrer, O. H., & Sears, R. R. *Frustration and aggression.* New Haven: Yale University Press, 1939.

Feshbach, S. The stimulating versus cathartic effects of a vicarious aggressive activity. Paper read at Eastern Psychological Assn. meetings, 1958.

Feshbach, S. The catharsis hypothesis and some consequences of interaction with aggressive and neutral play objects. *J. Pers.*, 1956, **24**, 449–462.

Feshbach, S. The drive-reducing function of fantasy behavior. *J. abnorm. soc. Psychol.*, 1955, **50**, 3–11.

Hendricks, I. *Facts and theories of psychoanalysis.* New York: Knopf, 1948.

Hornberger, R. The differential reduction of aggressive responses as a function of interpolated activities. Paper read at American Psychological Assn. meetings, 1959.

Kenny, D. T. An experimental test of the catharsis theory of aggression. Unpublished doctor's dissertation, University of Washington, 1952.

Pepitone, A. and Reichling, G. Group cohesiveness and the expression of hostility. *Hum. Rel.*, 1955, **8**, 327–337.

Pirojnikoff, L. A. Catharsis and the role of perceptual change in the reduction of hostility. Unpublished doctor's dissertation, University of Texas, 1958.

Rosenbaum, M. & DeCharms, R. Direct and vicarious reduction of hostility. *J. abnorm. soc. Psychol.*, 1960, **60**, 105–111.

Siegel, Alberta E. Film-mediated fantasy aggression and strength of aggressive drive. *Child Develpm.*, 1956, **27**, 365–378.

Thibaut, J. & Coules, J. The role of communication in the reduction of interpersonal hostility. *J. abnorm. soc. Psychol.*, 1952, **47**, 770–778.

Worchel, P. Catharsis and the relief of hostility. *J. abnorm. soc. Psychol.*, 1957, **55**, 238–243.

6

The physiology of anger

The bodily changes that occur in anger have been studied principally in animals. Studies on humans have in the main used only "peripheral" measures like reactions of the vascular system and the viscera; measures of central nervous system activity have been limited to animal subjects. Since the emphasis here is on human anger, considerably more space will be devoted to the autonomic components of anger than to the central neural mechanisms of anger.

PHYSIOLOGY

Until recently the physiological components of anger and fear were believed to be the same and were treated under the heading of *emotion*. This usage may be attributed to Cannon (1929), who emphasized the bodily preparations for "flight or fight"—the twin responses to danger. In the face of danger the organism must prepare itself for sustained, violent activity: to run long enough to out-distance a pursuer or to attack with sufficient force to overcome the source of the danger. Cannon listed the following changes that occur in anger or rage:

Slowing or stopping of processes in the digestive tract
Shift of blood from the abdominal organs to skeletal muscles
More vigorous contraction of the heart
Deeper respiration
Dilatation of the bronchioles
Mobilization of sugar in the circulation.

These physiological reactions, which prepare the organism for violent, sustained activity, are ostensibly set in motion by discharges of the sympathetic nervous system.

91

Cannon thought that sympathetic nervous system activity was mediated by a substance called *sympathin,* which contained both inhibitory and excitatory components. The excitatory component was thought to be adrenaline, but more recent research has established that adrenaline is not a mediator of sympathetic activity. The sympathetic mediator is noradrenaline, which is identical in molecular composition to adrenaline except for the absence of a methyl group (the absence leading to the use of the prefix *nor-*).

In recent years adrenaline and noradrenaline have been assigned central roles in attempts to account for physiological changes in fear and anger. Adrenaline is secreted by the adrenal medulla, and there is suggestive evidence that noradrenaline may be a precursor in the line of chemical transformations that end in adrenaline. Adrenaline has widespread autonomic effects of the kind that were listed above as Cannon's list of reactions to danger. Goldenberg et al. (1948) found the following reactions to adrenaline by normal subjects:

Striking increase in cardiac output
Significant rise in systolic blood pressure
Insignificant rise in diastolic blood pressure
Slight rise in mean arterial pressure
Sharp drop in peripheral blood vessel resistance
Moderate rise in pulse rate.

The response of subjects to noradrenaline was somewhat different:

No change or moderate increase in cardiac output
Significant rise in systolic blood pressure
Significant rise in diastolic blood pressure
Significant rise in mean arterial pressure
Striking increase in peripheral resistance
Significant increase in pulse rate.

Examination of these lists reveals two main differences. Adrenaline elevates cardiac output so that more blood is delivered; and it acts as a vasodilator, allowing the blood to reach skeletal muscles and decreasing peripheral resistance. Noradrenaline has little or no effect on cardiac output; and it acts as a vasoconstrictor, cutting off blood to the peripheral blood vessels that supply muscles. Thus adrenaline is an emergency stimulant with widespread and differentiated action, while noradrenaline is useful in the everyday vegetative process of blood pressure homeostasis (von Euler, 1955). Noradrenaline is produced at sympathetic nerve endings, and there is evidence that it may also be produced by the adrenal medulla. Whether the adrenal medulla secretes adrenaline or noradrenaline or both in varying proportions appears to be determined by stimulation from the central nervous system. von Euler has also demonstrated that when the hypothalamus of a cat is stimulated, there is a selective release of adrenaline and noradrenaline.

Research on Cardiovascular Changes

The discovery of noradrenaline was facilitated by the development of refined separation techniques, such as paper chromatography; investigation of physiological reactions in anger was facilitated by an experiment on anger and fear that is a landmark in this area (Ax, 1953). The anger situation (described in detail in an earlier chapter) consisted of jostling, verbal abuse, and general nastiness from a technician supposedly in disrepute but hired for the day only.

The fear stimulus consisted of a gradually intermittent Shock stimulus to the little finger which never reached an intensity sufficient to cause pain. When the subject reported the sensation, the experimenter expressed surprise, checked the wiring, pressed a key which caused sparks to jump near the subjects, then exclaimed with alarm that this was a dangerous high voltage short circuit.
The experimenter created an atmosphere of alarm and confusion. After five minutes from the time the subject reported the shock, the experimenter removed the shock wire, assuring the subject that all danger was past, that the short circuit had been found and repaired. (Ax, 1953, p. 35)

The same subjects were used in both the anger and fear situations.
There were 14 physiological measures, but Ax's dependent variable was *frequency* rather than *amplitude* of response. He noted whether the measures rose, fell, remained the same, and in some instances what the peaks were. Seven of the 14 frequency measures were found to show significant differences between anger and fear. Anger was higher than fear in number of diastolic blood pressure rises, heart rate falls, galvanic skin responses, and muscle tension increases; fear was higher than anger in skin conductance increases, muscle tension peaks, and respiration rate increases. These physiological differences between anger and fear refute the notion that the "flight or fight reflex" stems from a single pattern of physiological changes.
Ax attempted to relate his findings to the actions of adrenaline and noradrenaline. He suggested that the anger pattern resembles the changes that occur when both adrenaline and noradrenaline are

injected, and the fear pattern resembles the changes that occur when adrenaline is injected.

Schachter (1957) performed an experiment identical to that of Ax. He used 15 of Ax's subjects and added 35 more subjects, who varied considerably in the height of their blood pressure. He reported both his results and those of Ax in terms of amplitude of change. The third study to offer comparable data (Funkenstein et al., 1954) used only college men as subjects, and it is possible that the absence of women is a source of systematic difference between the studies. Funkenstein et al. used two kinds of frustrating tasks in an attempt to induce anger. The first was a difficult digit span test in which the experimenter sarcastically criticized the subject's efforts. The second task required the subject to speak as rapidly as possible while an acoustical feedback so confused his speech that he stuttered and had to speak slowly. Whenever the subject spoke slowly, he was given a mild electric shock. The subjects were subsequently interviewed and divided into "anger out," anxiety, and "anger in" groups, but only the first two groups are of interest in the present context.

Goldenberg et al. (1948) demonstrated that there are six cardiovascular changes distinguishing the action of adrenaline from noradrenaline. In the three studies just mentioned, five of the six cardiovascular measures are available in two studies and three in the third study. Thus the three studies may be compared with respect to how closely the patterns in anger and fear resembled the actions of noradrenaline and adrenaline.[1] The anger reactions are presented in Table 6.1.

TABLE 6.1. MEAN CARDIOVASCULAR CHANGES DURING ANGER

	Systolic b.p.*	Diastolic b.p.	Heart Rate	Cardiac Output	Peripheral Resistance
Ax	22	20	30		
Schachter	21	15	11	22%	1%
Funkenstein et al.	13	23	7	−3%	33%

* All blood pressure changes are in mm. of mercury.

[1] The noradrenaline changes reported by Goldenberg et al. (1948) included a significant rise in heart rate, but many investigators believe that noradrenaline affects pulse rate very little. Where Goldenberg et al. found only a moderate rise in heart rate after injection of adrenaline, most investigators believe that adrenaline leads to a steep increase in heart rate. In this instance it seems best to accept the weight of numbers and agree that a steep increase in heart rate is an adrenaline effect, not a noradrenaline effect.

There were no data available on Ax's subjects for cardiac output or peripheral resistance. Inspection of the table reveals a lack of consistency from one study to the next. The failure of Ax and Schachter to agree is especially perplexing because they used identical procedures, yet managed to find heart rate changes that differed by 29 beats per minute.

Ax's results are consistent with the noradrenaline pattern in that both systolic and diastolic blood pressure rose markedly, but the data are inconsistent with the noradrenaline pattern because of the steep increase in heart rate. Schachter's data also reveal a mixed pattern. Consistent with the noradrenaline pattern are the rises in systolic and diastolic blood pressure and the moderate rise in heart rate; inconsistent are the large jump in cardiac output and the absence of change in peripheral resistance, both of which are adrenaline phenomena. The most consistent findings with respect to the noradrenaline pattern are those of Funkenstein et al. Both systolic and diastolic blood pressure rose sharply, but heart rate rose only moderately; cardiac output was down very slightly, and peripheral resistance increased markedly. The whole picture fits the pattern associated with noradrenaline, i.e., reflex vasoconstriction.

The three studies may also be compared with respect to the adrenaline pattern in fear, and the appropriate data are presented in Table 6.2.

TABLE 6.2. MEAN CARDIOVASCULAR CHANGES DURING FEAR

	Systolic b.p.	Diastolic b.p.	Heart Rate	Cardiac Output	Peripheral Resistance
Ax	23	18	32		
Schachter	23	14	19	48%	−12%
Funkenstein et al.	20	10	33	62%	−19%

Concerning Ax's data, the jumps in systolic blood pressure and heart rate are consistent with the adrenaline pattern, but the diastolic pressure should not have increased so much. Schachter's findings are more in line with the adrenaline pattern: a rise in systolic blood pressure and heart rate and a smaller increase in diastolic blood pressure. The increase in cardiac output and decrease in peripheral resistance are entirely consistent with the adrenaline pattern. The results of Funkenstein et al. fit the pattern even better because the rise in diastolic blood pressure was only moderate, and the changes in cardiac output and peripheral resistance were larger than Schachter's comparable data. Thus all three sets of data support the adrenaline pattern but with varying degrees of consistency.

Schachter also used the cold pressor test, which consists of having the subject submerge his hand in a bucket of ice water for one minute. This produces a reflex vasoconstriction similar to that produced by noradrenaline. He compared the cardiovascular reactions to cold, fear, and anger, using his own criteria for adrenaline and noradrenaline patterns. He used a five-point scale whose ends were +2 for noradrenaline effect and —2 for adrenaline effect:

+2	—2
a. Marked rise in peripheral resistance	a. Marked drop in peripheral resistance
b. Drop in at least two of the following: cardiac output, stroke volume, heart rate	b. Marked rises in at least two of the following: cardiac output, stroke volume, heart rate
c. Marked rise in diastolic blood pressure.	c. Marked rise in systolic blood pressure.

Between these extremes were +1 (moderate noradrenaline effect), 0 (mixed effect), and —1 (moderate adrenaline effect). The mean scale values for the three induced states were:

cold pressor	+0.9
anger	—0.1
fear	—1.1

Thus the cold pressor test yielded a moderate noradrenaline effect; anger a mixed effect; and fear a moderate adrenaline effect. In terms of the frequencies that made up the above means, in the cold pressor test most subjects were adrenaline-like; in anger half were adrenaline-like and half noradrenaline-like; and in fear most subjects were adrenaline-like. Thus Schachter confirmed the results of Ax: the fear pattern resembles the action of adrenaline, and the anger pattern resembles the action of adrenaline and noradrenaline combined.

The presence of two kinds of patterns within the anger situation raises a question concerning the comparability of the three studies just reviewed. Ax and Schachter both induced fear and anger, and the experimental manipulations determined the reaction. Funkenstein et al. used a different method, allowing the reaction of the subjects (as determined by observers) determine whether they were placed in the fear or the anger group. It is possible that in Schachter's experiment half the subjects in the anger situation reacted predominantly with fear and the other half predominantly with anger. If this were true, it would account for his equivocal findings.

One other difference between the studies should be noted. Ax and Schachter both used men and women as subjects, while Funkenstein et al. used only men. The data on sex differences in anger are certainly not conclusive, but there is evidence (see Chapter 5) that men tend to become angrier than women and tend to ventilate their anger more. Perhaps the more unequivocal pattern of adrenaline-like action that Funkenstein et al., found in anger is due to their using only men; the use of women may tend to obscure otherwise consistent physiological patterns. Men and women may have different physiological patterns in anger.

It seems likely that if there is a relationship between noradrenaline and anger, the best chance of demonstrating it will occur in a study that uses only men as subjects and in which the presence of anger is determined by observers rather than by operational definition (the presence of an anger-inducing situation). This inference receives support from a report of several studies by Cohen & Silverman (1959). They used air force men as subjects, and their procedures included stress tolerance tests in a centrifuge apparatus, harassment from the experimenters, interviews, and injections of mecholyl. The centrifuge apparatus rotated each subject until he blacked out, and the measure used was the number of g's (pressure of gravity) he could endure before blacking out. Urine samples were taken before and after this stress, and it was found that the higher the noradrenaline in the urine (both before and after stress), the higher was the g level that could be withstood.

Subjects were interviewed by a psychiatrist and rated for both aggression and anxiety. They were then divided into those with anxiety rated higher than aggression (anxiety/aggression) and those with aggression being rated higher than anxiety (aggression/anxiety). It was found that the aggression/anxiety subjects could withstand higher g levels than the anxiety/aggression subjects. Then attempts were made to raise the amount of stress (g level) tolerance either by lowering anxiety level or by making the subjects angry. Both reducing anxiety and arousing anger increased the amount of stress tolerance in the centrifuge.

Next, subjects were angered by harassment, injected with mecholyl, and their blood pressure and urine noradrenaline measured. Anxiety/aggression subjects showed a drop in systolic blood pressure after mecholyl, while aggression/anxiety subjects showed a rise in systolic blood pressure. Anxiety-aggression subjects had higher pre-experimental adrenaline levels (in the urine) and lower pre-experimental noradrenaline levels than did the aggression/anxiety subjects. The more aggressive subjects manifested a marked increase in noradrenaline level from before to after the anger stimulus, while the anxious subjects showed little or no change or a decrease in noradrenaline level. When anxious subjects were subsequently angered, there was an *increase* in systolic blood pressure after mecholyl injections. When aggressive subjects were made more anxious, there was a *decrease* in the systolic blood pressure response to mecholyl. Thus the systolic blood pressure response to mecholyl was reversed by making anxious subjects angry and by making aggressive subjects anxious.

These results indicate a close link between anger and noradrenaline level. Cohen & Silverman attempted to tie in developmental considerations in their explanation of the results; their hypotheses conclude this section.

The relationship of specific affective constellations and catechol amine levels may have its basis on the association of certain infantile emotional responses and their physiological concomitants. An infant's reaction to unpleasant inner sensations associated with deprivation, frustration or pain can be perhaps characterized as a massive dedifferentiated discharge phenomena. A propros of this is West's (1951) study which showed that neonates have high levels of noradrenaline and low levels of adrenaline. The high noradrenaline levels may in part be the result of this diffuse muscular activity. As infants develop their first attempts to cope with their increased tension may be defined as primitive aggression. Hence, it is postulated that the affect of rage or anger or the carrying out of aggressive behavior might re-excite these circuits and lead to the release of noradrenaline even in the absence of the diffuse muscular activity which was the original stimulus calling forth the noradrenaline release. As muscular coordination increases, this ability might be used in the service of goal directed activity. The amount of activity might become considerably less than the diffuse uncoordinated activity of the infant, but the association of more specific aggressive behavior and feelings with the original primitive reaction patterns may lead to the reexcitement of the original circuits. Although the manifest behavior may be culturally determined modification of aggressive behavior, the circuits associated with primitive rage may be aroused. Thus, the hormonal reaction may be similar to that of the infant in a primitive rage state although the affect perceived is far less intense, and the muscular activity less diffuse. (Cohen & Silverman, 1959, pp. 206–207)

Research on Gastric Changes

There have been two approaches to the study of gastric changes in anger. The first lacks experimental rigor but offers leads to further experimentation; it is exemplified by Wolf & Wolff (1947), who studied in detail the gastric reactions of a man with a gastric fistula. They reported differences between fear and anger, as follows:

> . . . emotions involving an attitude of fearsome shrinking or a desire for escape were accompanied by a depression of gastric function in terms of vascularity, acid production and motor activity.
> Emotions involving an aggressive attitude, on the other hand, were found accompanied by an increase in vascularity, secretion and motility such as would be found as a prelude to ingestion of food.   (p. 148)

The second approach is to induce an emotional response by means of hypnosis and study its effect on gastric reactivity. This was attempted by Tracktir (1954), who used male graduate students as subjects. Each subject was hypnotized, and states of anger, fear, and contentment were suggested. For the total sample of subjects it was found that anger and fear had similar effects on gastric reactivity, both inhibiting secretion. Then the subjects were divided into high and low anxious groups on the basis of Manifest Anxiety Scale scores. The high anxious subjects secreted more acid in fear than in anger, whereas the low anxious subjects secreted more acid in anger than in fear. Evidently fear and anger do have different effects on gastric reactivity, but the difference emerges only when anxiety level is taken into account.

These findings are consistent with those of Wolf & Wolff (1947) if it is assumed that their subject was low anxious. Like the low anxious subjects in Tractir's study, he secreted more acid in anger then in fear. It would be of considerable interest to discover if there is a similar interaction between strength of aggressive tendencies and secretion of acid in the stomach.

The Tracktir study illustrates what seems to be a consistent relation between fear and anger. The physiological changes accompanying these emotional reactions are for the most part similar, but there are small differences in the *patterns*. Sometimes the differences between fear and anger interact with other variables, as in Tracktir's study, and examination of main effects yields no significant differences. Anger and fear do differ physiologically, but the differences are complicated and difficult to measure.

Variables Affecting the Physiology of Anger

Time relations. When adrenaline or noradrenaline is injected into the body, there is a lapse of time before the substance can be circulated throughout the body to target sites. The same is true when either substance is secreted by the adrenal medulla into the blood stream. Schachter (1957) reported that in many subjects heart rate and galvanic skin response attained their peak changes within 3 seconds of the onset of the anger stimulus. While the action of chemicals circulating in the blood would require a longer interval than 3 seconds, neural mediation could easily occur in less time. Therefore, it would seem that the *first* changes in fear and anger are mediated by sympathetic nervous system activity and not by the direct chemical action of noradrenaline or adrenaline circulating in the blood stream.

At this point it is necessary to distinguish two modes of operation of noradrenaline. First, it is the mediator of sympathetic neural discharge, operating to pass along a nervous impulse. Second, as a chemical agent in the blood stream it acts in the fashion described earlier, as a vasoconstrictor substance. It is this second action that is important in this discussion.

Returning to the issue of time relations, it can be seen that the action of the two catechol amines as chemical agents in circulation can account for only those changes in anger and fear that occur after 15 or 20 seconds. Changes occurring within, say, 10 seconds must be mediated by neural action.

With the passage of time the physiological picture becomes complicated by the action of homeostatic mechanisms. Initial vasoconstriction that leads to higher blood pressure will activate reflex vasodilator mechanisms, which lower blood pressure. There are mechanisms like the carotid sinus reflex, which insures that blood flow to the brain does not become excessive. Thus, even if the physiological response to anger were initially uncomplicated, it would appear complicated as soon as homeostatic mechanisms began to operate.

Intensity of anger. Another complicating variable is the intensity of anger. It seems reasonable that the relationship between anger stimuli and physiological reactions should be quantitative, but Schachter (1957) reported data that suggest a qualitative relationship. He had judges rate intensity of anger, dividing subjects into high, middle, and low angry groups. It was found that "high and low intensities of anger tended to be associated with epinephrine-like (adrenaline-like) effects, whereas moderate intensities of anger were associated with nor-epinephrine-like (noradrenaline-like) effects." (Schachter, 1957, p. 25) This conclusion must be tempered by the fact that the F value was significant at only the .10 level of confidence. However, if these results stand up, it means that there is a quantitative relationship between intensity of anger and physiological reaction.

Perhaps the relationship is simpler than Schachter found it to be. In laboratory experiments like those of Ax and Schachter, the intensity of fear is greater than the intensity of rage. The nasty technician of these experiments may induce considerable anger, but its intensity is mild compared to the intensity of the fear that occurs when the subject learns that 5000 volts are loose in a machine to which he is wired. If subjects could be sufficiently enraged, the physiological reaction might resemble that of fear, i.e., adrenaline-like. It may be assumed that at the moderate levels of anger there is less arousal of the "emergency mechanisms," and surely there is less arousal than in the enraged cats studied by Cannon. Thus at the moderate levels of fear and anger, it is possible to distinguish between adrenaline-like and noradrenaline-like patterns. However, when both anger and fear attain peak levels of intensity, the differences between them may disappear because the massive physiological response of the organism overshadows smaller differences in emotional reactions.

Individual differences. Another variable that must be taken into account in evaluating physiological patterns in anger is individual differences. First, there is wide variability in *resting level* of blood pressure, pulse rate, gastric reactivity, etc. This variability is typically handled by using measures of change in which each subject is in effect his own control. Thus the studies reviewed above reported mean rise in diastolic blood pressure, mean rise in pulse rate, mean drop in gastric acid, and so on.

A second kind of variability involves differences in *extent of change*. It is well known that individuals differ in physiological reactivity, some having somewhat more labile visceral reactions than others (Lacey, 1950). This kind of variability often constitutes error variance, producing a spread of scores within groups that may obscure differences between groups.

A third kind of variability, emphasized by Lacey (1950), involves individual differences not in resting level or lability but in the *pattern* of physiological response elicited by a given stimulus. For example, some individuals react to anger stimuli with a marked circulatory change and little change in galvanic skin response, whereas others reverse this pattern in response to anger stimuli. Such patterns are consistent within the individual over a period of time.

It is possible that these differences in resting level, lability, and pattern of physiological response are related to enduring response modes. Perhaps an individual's response to an anger stimulus is determined not only by the intensity of the stimulus but also by enduring response trends relating to anger and aggression. For example, the quick-tempered, explosive individual may have a quick, labile physiological response to anger stimuli.

The function of anger in man. It has been noted that many of the physiological changes occurring in anger serve to prepare the organism for violent activity. In the cat a massive discharge of the sympathetic nervous system not only triggers off visceral reactions but also observable changes, such as piloerection, arching of the back, and hissing. These reactions are part of a pattern of preparedness for attack or counterattack. In uncivilized man, living as a predator, similar physiological reactions were probably of considerable utility; but the modern, acculturated adult has little need of these bodily preparations for violent action. His aggression is accomplished mainly by mechanical or verbal means. Man has developed a variety of weapons that require not brute strength over time but rather fine motor coordination. He has also learned to attack others with his speech mechanism. Physiological preparation for attack is therefore unnecessary.

Furthermore, the physiological reactions in anger may be harmful. If the organism responds with "emergency mechanisms" that have little utility, it is possible that there will be an overtaxing of the capacity to respond to stress. The continued use of emergency reactions during the course of everyday living often leads to irreversible tissue changes, e.g., the chronically angry person may eventually have a permanently elevated blood pressure (essential hypertension).

NEURAL MECHANISMS

Previous sections have dealt with visceral changes; this section deals with the action of the central nervous system in anger. Virtually all the research has been conducted with infra-human subjects, with the findings being applied to man by analogy. Since this book focuses on anger and aggression in man, the section here on neural mechanisms will be brief.

Research on the neural aspects of rage has shown that parts of both the brain stem and the cerebral cortex are important. The early work of Cannon (1929) pointed to the thalamus as a center involved in rage reactions. Refinements in technique by Bard (1928)

THE PHYSIOLOGY OF ANGER

suggested that the hypothalamus, rather than the thalamus, is crucial for the rage response in cats. He showed that decorticated cats had a lowered threshold for "sham rage," and this effect lasted only so long as the hypothalamus remained intact. When the hypothalamus was removed, some of the feline rage pattern disappeared, e.g., the cat no longer attacked with claws and teeth.

The importance of the hypothalamus, established by ablation experiments, has been corroborated by electrical stimulation studies. Ranson (1934) stimulated the hypothalamus of cats with intact brains and elicited the full rage pattern; stimulation of other parts of the brain stem did not evoke such a reaction. Similar results have been obtained by Hess & Akert (1955), who also found that other areas of the midbrain yielded a rage reaction upon electrical stimulation.

Taken together, the ablation and stimulation findings suggest that the hypothalamus is the major center for the expression and patterning of the rage response. In light of evidence that other parts of the brain stem are involved in sham rage (e.g., Bard & Macht, 1958), older notions about the hypothalamus as the "seat of the emotions" have been discarded. Rather, it is regarded as an integrator of the action of lower neural mechanisms in the elicitation of a full-fledged rage reaction.

The role of the cerebral cortex in rage has been thought to be inhibitory. Bard's (1928) decorticated cats had a lowered threshold for the rage reaction. If the cortex were suppressing action of the hypothalamus, removal of the cortex should free the hypothalamus and lower the rage threshold. This notion was supported by the systematic studies of Bard & Mountcastle (1947), who removed different parts of the cerebral cortex of cats.

There is conflicting evidence regarding the role of the amygdaloid complex. Its removal should result in a ferocious animal, but Kluver & Bucy (1939) were the first of several investigators to demonstrate that removal of the amygdala (and parts of the temporal lobes) produces a placid animal, relatively unresponsive to noxious stimuli. Their findings with monkeys have been fully corroborated by Bard (1950), and partially confirmed by Rosvold et al. (1954). The definitive study in this area was conducted by Schreiner & Kling (1956), who used animals varying in ferocity. Their animals were the lynx, which is savage; the agouti and the monkey, which tend to attack but are not as ferocious as the lynx; and the domestic cat, which is tame. Their lesions were in the rhinencephalon, primarily restricted to the amygdaloid complex; the diencephalon and cerebral cortex were untouched. The lynxes, which preoperatively were so vicous that they had to be anesthetized in order to be transferred from shipping crate to cage, postoperatively were so tame that they could be roughly handled without retaliation. The agoutis, monkeys, and cats manifested the same kind of postoperative placidity.

The finding that cats are placid after removal of the amygdala conflicts with the results of Bard & Mountcastle (1947), whose cats became ferocious. A plausible hypothesis is that the structures removed by Bard & Mountcastle are not completely analogous to those removed by other investigators. The production of placidity by removal of the amygdaloid complex in animals varying in aggressiveness suggests that the amygdala is necessary for a full rage reaction to occur.

If this hypothesis is correct, electrical stimulation of the amygdala should yield a rage reaction. This is precisely what occurred in experiments by Shealy & Peele (1957) and Molina & Hunsperger (1957). In addition to these animal studies, there are two lines of evidence from studies with humans. Heath et al. (1955) stimulated the amygdala, producing rage and fear reactions. Chapman et al. (1954) elicited a fear reaction with similar stimulation of four humans. Fear reactions have also been elicited by stimulation of the amygdala in monkeys. Thus in primates the amygdala is important for both rage and fear.

The second line of evidence comes from a report by Terzian & Ore (1955) of a patient with the Kluver-Bucy syndrome. Preoperatively the patient was aggressive and ill-tempered; after removal of both temporal lobes and the amygdaloid complex, he lost his fear and rage reactions.

Summarizing, the amygdaloid complex and possibly related structures in the rhinencephalon tend to facilitate rage, which can be elicited by electrical stimulation of these structures. The cerebral cortex must have a suppressor effect on rage because decorticate preparations tend to show "sham rage"; the neocortex may possibly have this suppressor function. The hypothalamus seems to be necessary for an integrated rage reaction.

CONCLUSIONS

The physiology of anger has been studied mainly in infrahuman organisms, and there is a paucity of knowledge about bodily changes in human anger. The following account of human anger is based on the meager knowledge that is available.

An anger stimulus impinges on a receptor, which initiates an afferent neural impulse to the cerebral cortex. The cortex in turn stimulates the hypothalamus, the amygdala, and related structures in the rhinencephalon (which are evidently necessary for an integrated rage pattern). The hypothalamus relays impulses in two directions. First, as the "head ganglion" of the autonomic nervous system, it initiates or relays impulses to the sympathetic nervous system. The action of the sympathetic nervous system is only moderate in anger, there being only slight increases in heart rate, galvanic skin response, etc. The hypothalamus also stimulates the adrenal medulla to secrete both noradrenaline and adrenaline, with the major component being noradrenaline. Noradrenaline in overflow quantities may also be produced at sympathetic nerve endings, and its effect is a large increase in peripheral vascular resistance, a rise in both systolic and diastolic blood pressure, and a diminution in the activity of the stomach and intestines. These changes are different from those in fear, but there is an overlap in the physiology of fear and anger.

REFERENCES

Ax, A. F. The physiological differentiation between fear and anger in humans. *Psychosom. Med.*, 1953, **15**, 433–442.

Bard, P. Central nervous mechanisms for the expression of anger in animals. In M. L. Reymert, (Ed.), *Feelings and emotions.* New York: McGraw-Hill, 1950.

Bard, P. A diencephalic mechanism for the expression of rage with special reference to the sympathetic nervous system. *Amer. J. Physiol.*, 1928, **84**, 480–515.

Bard, P. & Macht, M. B. The behavior of chronically decerebrate cats. In Wolstenholme, G. E. W., & O'Connor, Cecilia M. (Eds.), *Neurological basis of behavior.* Boston: Little, Brown, 1958.

Bard, P. & Mountcastle, V. B. Some forebrain mechanisms involved in expression of rage with special reference to suppression of angry behavior. *Proc. Assn. Res. Nerv. Ment. Disease*, 1947, **27**, 362–404.

Cannon, W. B. *Bodily changes in pain, hunger, fear, and rage.* New York: Appleton, 1929.

Chapman, W. P., Schroeder, H. R., Geyer, G., Brazier, Mary A. B., Poppen, J. L., Solomon, H. C., & Yakovlev, P. I. Physiological evidence concerning the importance of amygdaloid nuclear region in the integration of circulatory function and emotion in man. *Science*, 1954, **120**, 949–950.

Cohen, S. I. & Silverman, A. J. Psychophysiological investigations of vascular response variability. *J. psychosom. Res.*, 1959, **3**, 185–210.

von Euler, U. S. Noradrenaline in adrenergic nerves. In Elliot, K. A. C., Page, I. H., & Quastel, J. H. (Eds.), *Neurochemistry.* Springfield, Ill.: Thomas, 1955.

von Euler, U. S. Autonomic neuroeffecter transmission. In John Field (Ed.), *Handbook of physiology: Section 1, Neurophysiology.* Washington, D.C.: American Physiological Society, 1959.

Funkenstein, D., King, S. H., and Drolette, Margaret. The direction of anger during a laboratory stress-inducing situation. *Psychosom. Med.,* 1954, **16**, 404–413.

Goldenberg, M., Pines, K. L., Baldwin, Eleana de E., Green, D. G., & Roh, C. E. The hemodynamic response of man to norepinephrine and epinephrine and its relation to the problem of hypertension. *Amer. J. Med.,* 1948, **5**, 792.

Heath, R. G., Monroe, R. R., & Mickle, W. A. Stimulation of the amygdaloid nucleus in a schizophrenic patient. *Amer. J. Psychiat.,* 1955, **11**, 862–863.

Hess, W. R. & Akert, K. Experimental data on role of hypothalamus in mechanisms of emotional behavior. *Arch. Neurol. Psychiat.,* 1955, **73**, 127–129.

Kluver, H. & Bucy, P. C. Preliminary analysis of the functions of the temporal lobes in monkeys. *Arch. Neural. Psychiat.,* 1939, **42**, 979–1000.

Lacey, J. I. Individual differences in somatic response patterns. *J. comp. physiol. Psychol.,* 1950, **43**, 338–350.

Molina, A. F. & Hunsperger, R. U. Affective reactions obtained by electrical stimulation of the amygdala. *J. Physiol.,* 1957, **138**, 29–30.

Ranson, S. W. Autonomic reactions induced by electrical stimulation of the hypothalamus. *Amer. J. Physiol.,* 1934, **109**, 185.

Rosvold, H. E., Mirsky, A. F., & Pribram, K. H. Influence of amygdalectomy on social behavior in monkeys. *J. comp. physiol. Psychol.,* 1954, **47**, 173–178.

Schachter, J. Pain, fear, and anger in hypertensives and normotensives: a psychophysiological study. *Psychosom. Med.,* 1957, **29**, 17–29.

Schreiner, L. & Kling, A. Rhinencephalon and behavior. *Amer. J. Physiol.,* 1956, **184**, 486–490.

Shealy, C. N. & Peele, T. L. Studies on the amygdaloid neuclus of the cat. *J. Neurophysiol.,* 1957, **20**, 125–139.

Terzian, H. & Ore, G. O. Syndrome of Kluver and Bucy reproduced in man by bilateral removal of the temporal lobes. *Neurology,* 1955, **5**, 373–380.

Tracktir, J. The relationship between anxiety, hypnotically induced emotions, and gastric secretion. Unpublished doctor's dissertation, University of Houston, 1954.

West, G. B., Shepherd, D. M., & Hunter, R. B. Adrenaline and noradrenaline concentrations in adrenaline glands at different ages in some diseases. *Lancet,* 1951, **261**, 966–969.

Wolf, S. & Wolff, H. G. *Human gastric function.* New York: Oxford University Press, 1957.

7

The learning of hostile materials

This chapter deals with the learning of stimuli that symbolize aggressive events and weapons, hostile attitudes, and anger. Since they have negative emotional connotations, the stimuli are called hostile. In this respect they differ from "neutral" stimuli, which have none of the connotations of hostile stimuli: punishment of aggression, the learning of complex discriminations concerning aggression, guilt or anxiety associated with aggression, pleasure (direct or vicarious) in aggression. Hostile stimuli should be more vivid or intense than neutral stimuli, and the aggressiveness or hostility of the learner should affect learning of hostile stimuli.

Hostile verbal stimuli have been investigated by means of a variety of tasks. These may be grouped under the headings of rote learning, operant verbal conditioning, galvanic skin response situations, and stimulus generalization.

Rote Learning

Learning may be measured by the number of trials it takes to reach the criterion or by the amount of material recalled. The hostile connotations of the stimuli should retard learning because of associative interference, effects of anxiety, guilt, and so forth. Once the material has been learned, however, the hostile connotations should have little effect on memory. Thus the measure of learning is an important variable, and studies have been divided into those using number of trials to criterion as the measure and those using recall or savings as the measure.

Trials to criterion. In this group of experiments all but one used paired associates, and the subjects were for the most part college students. Williams (1951) had college men learn the following lists of paired associates:

Neutral	Hostile
cold-bird	dark-blow
swift-tree	square-harm
soft-room	slow-fight
high-book	blue-rage
green-cliff	short-hate
light-read	white-threat
loud-height	deep-curse
long-stone	hard-death

The neutral list was learned first and the hostile list 24 hours later; for one group the hostile words were the stimuli, and for the other group the hostile words were the responses. It was found that it did not matter whether the hostile words were stimuli or responses; both groups learned the neutral list significantly faster than the hostile list.

Wolf (1954) also used college men as subjects, having them learn hostile and neutral lists by the serial anticipation method. The Rorschach was used to divide subjects into high and low aggressive groups. All subjects learned the neutral list faster than the hostile list, corroborating Williams' findings. The hostile-neutral difference in learning was significantly greater for the high aggressive than for the low aggressive subjects, suggesting that, while hostile material retards learning, the retardation is greater for aggressive subjects.

A study by Smith (1954) tends to corroborate Wolf's results. Smith selected high and low aggressive subjects from a sample of college men and women, using the Iowa Hostility Inventory and certain scales of the MMPI (Minnesota Multiphasic Personality Inventory). Hostile and neutral word lists were learned by the paired associates method. The low aggressive subjects showed no significant difference in the learning of hostile and neutral materials, but the high aggressive subjects learned the neutral list significantly faster than the hostile list. This finding is in line with Wolf's in that the high aggressive subjects showed a greater neutral-hostile difference than low aggressive subjects, but it differs in that there was no neutral-hostile difference for low aggressive subjects. The discrepancy may be attributed to differences in selecting the extremes of aggressiveness or to differences between serial anticipation and paired associates.

The last study to use trials to a criterion as the measure of learning is that of Holzberg et al. (1955). The subjects were male psychiatric patients, and the method was paired associates. The stimulus words were either hostile or neutral, and the responses were numbers. High, average, and low aggressive groups were selected by means of the Thematic Apperception Test. There was no neutral-hostile difference for the average aggressive group, but both high and low aggressive subjects learned the hostile words *faster* than neutral words. This finding is contrary to those of the previous three studies. Since this study differs from the others in several different ways, it is not clear which variables underlie the discrepancy in results. This is a recurring phenomenon in this area: it is often difficult to reconcile conflicting findings because experiments differ in such factors as subjects, tasks, kind of learning, and nature of the learning measure.

On the basis of these four studies it may be concluded that college students learn hostile material slower than neutral material. The results are clearer when only men are used as subjects, and the relationship may hold only for men; sex differences appear to be the rule rather than the exception in the area of aggression. The slower learning of hostile lists indicates that the connotations of the hostile words are disrupting learning. The aggressiveness of the learner is a relevant variable; aggressive college students learn hostile material even slower with respect to neutral material than do nonaggressive students.

Savings and recall. Only one study in this group used normals as subjects. Riggs (1956) had college men and women memorize 40 nouns, 10 each from the categories of violence, proper names, animals, and schemata. The violent words had three degrees of emphasis: plain, underlined, and underlined plus an exclamation mark. It was found that increasing emphasis yielded better recall. Approximately one fourth of all the words recalled were violent words, but since 10 out of the 40 were violent, this finding would be expected by chance alone. Thus hostile words were not recalled any better or worse than neutral words.

The remaining retention experiments all used psychiatric patients as subjects. Soffer (1956) had 30 neurotic inpatients and 30 normal veterans, all men, learn either an aggressive or a neutral list of words. Learning of neutral material followed the original learning, and the subjects were then required to relearn the original list (the usual retroactive inhibition paradigm). A recall measure yielded no significant differences between either materials or subjects. A savings measure revealed that normals manifested less retroactive inhibition than patients for both neutral and hostile materials. Both normals and patients manifested more retroactive inhibition for the hostile list than for the neutral list, with the greatest amount of retroactive inhibition being shown by the neurotics for hostile materials.

Normals and neurotics offer few difficulties in experimentation, in contrast to psychotics. Psychotics tend to lack motivation and the ability to make a sustained effort; some cannot remain in contact over an entire experimental session. These issues should be considered in evaluating the remaining studies of recall, all of which employed psychotic patients as subjects. The Holzberg et al. study (1955), mentioned above, had a recall task as well as paired associates. Most subjects could recall nothing, the task evidently being too difficult for them. This result suggests that it may be important to control for difficulty level. If the task is too hard, as in this instance, too few subjects learn for any treatment differences to emerge. On the other hand, if the task is too easy, virtually all the subjects learn, and again there are no treatment differences. It is possible that negative findings concerning hostile-neutral differences may be determined in part by too-easy or too-hard tasks.

Robinson (1954) had schizophrenic subjects read evaluative statements that ostensibly referred to the work of discharged mental patients. There were both favorable and unfavorable statements. Recall was tested after varying intervals, but the intervals had no effect on the ratio of favorable to unfavorable statements recalled. A larger proportion of favorable statements was recalled than unfavorable statements, perhaps because the anxiety associated with hostile material inhibits its retention.

Most experiments in this area do not specify varieties of hostile content; the target of hostility may be a pertinent variable. Mallet (1956) had stories in which a boy is aggressive toward his mother and other stories in which a boy is hostile toward peers. Recall of these stories was compared with recall of neutral stories. The subjects were schizophrenics and nonpsychiatric medical patients, all males. There were no significant differences in recall between groups of subjects, hostile versus neutral stories, or direction of hostility.

It is customary to select high and low aggressive groups on the basis of a test, but Gofstein (1956) selected on the basis of psychiatric diagnosis. One group consisted of brain-damaged patients, who ostensibly manifest considerable irritability and have no inhibitions about expressing aggression. The other group consisted of catatonic schizophrenics, who supposedly have conflict over aggressive urges and tend to act out less. Thus the two groups are presented as being approximately equal in intensity of aggressive urges, but one has conflict over expressing aggression and the other does not. The stimuli were two stories, one hostile and one neutral. They were equated for length and grammatical complexity, and were judged equal in familiarity and concreteness, but the hostile story was judged to be more vivid than the neutral story. Thus in the absence of conflict, the hostile story should be recalled better than the neutral story.

The catatonics and brain-damaged patients did not differ significantly in recall of the neutral story. The catatonics recalled significantly more of the neutral story than of the hostile story, while the brain-damaged patients recalled significantly more of the hostile story than of the neutral story. These results confirm Gofstein's prediction that subjects having no conflict over expressing aggression would recall more of the vivid material. For subjects with conflicts over expressing aggression, the anxiety associated with hostile material inhibits its recall, despite its increased vividness.

Unlike the first group of experiments, no unequivocal conclusion emerges from retention studies. While the subject's aggressiveness is a pertinent variable, Gofstein's study suggests that its effects are complex. In addition to assessing aggressiveness, it may be necessary to evaluate the strength of inhibitions against expressing aggression. Both difficulty level and vividness of the materials appear to be important variables.

A comparison of learning studies with recall studies is revealing. Hostile material is *learned* slower than neutral material, but there is predominantly negative evidence concerning a difference in *recall* between hostile and neutral materials. The simplest hypothesis is the one stated at the beginning of the first section: the associational or anxiety-producing features of hostile words that tend to retard learning are effective during learning but relatively ineffective once the material has been learned.

Operant Verbal Conditioning

Operant verbal conditioning differs from rote learning in that the subject is reinforced for making a response when the response falls within the class that has been selected for reinforcement. There have been two major techniques of operant conditioning of hostile materials, both involving the construction of sentences. The first is a modification of Taffel's procedure of having the subject select a word and use it in a sentence (1955). The second stems from the scrambled sentences technique of Watson et al. (1955), in which the subject must omit one of four words and rearrange the remaining three to form a meaningful sentence. Several other tasks have been developed recently, reflecting the increasing popularity of operant verbal conditioning.

Making up sentences. The first study to attempt operant conditioning of hostile material was that of Buss & Durkee (1958). On each trial the subject was presented with three verbs in the past tense: neutral, mildly hostile, and intensely hostile. He was to use *one* verb in making up a sentence. During the first 10 trials the subject made up sentences by using one of the three words, and he was not reinforced; this free operant period established his initial rate of using each kind of word. During the next 50 trials the experimenter said *Right* or *Wrong* after each sentence was spoken. For one group, using the intensely hostile verb was correct, and for the other group, using the neutral verb was correct. The subjects were college students of both sexes.

It was found that the hostile words conditioned faster (frequency of usage rose more steeply) than the neutral words, a result that may be attributed to sampling differences in the two kinds of materials. The hostile verbs were sampled from a population of hundreds of words, but the neutral verbs were sampled from a population of many thousands of words. Since the hostile words used in the experiment constitute a larger sample of the population of hostile words, they were more discriminable and easier to condition than the comparatively smaller sample of neutral words.

There were significant sex differences. First, the women conditioned faster than the men. Second, in the free operant period the women emitted significantly fewer intensely hostile responses (lynched, mauled, smashed, stabbed, strangled, tortured) than the men. The words symbolized violent physical aggression, which is more taboo for women than for men. Thus the difference in sex role may account for the difference in operant level of intensely hostile words. However, the inhibition that depressed the women's operant level evidently did not retard their learning, for they conditioned faster than the men. While inhibition affected the initial *level* of responding in women, it did not affect the *rate* of conditioning. Perhaps some of the discrepant results in this area are due to one investigator's using level, while another uses rate.

This experiment was followed up by Binder et al. (1957), who varied the role of the experimenter. The subjects were college men and women, who were divided into two groups in a way that precluded discovering any sex differences. One group's experimenter was a large, powerfully built man, whose personality was evidently aggressive in appearance. The other group's experimenter was a diminutive, youthful woman, who was quiet and nonassertive. The stimuli were those used by Buss & Durkee, except that only mildly hostile and neutral verbs were used. Only the mildly hostile alternative was reinforced.

The group run by the aggressive man manifested virtually no conditioning, but the group run by the nonassertive woman did condition. Thus the conditioning of hostile verbs was retarded by the presence of the aggressive male experimenter.

In order to establish whether it was gender or aggressiveness that affects learning, Ferguson & Buss (1960) replicated the study; this time both the male and female experimenters played neutral and aggressive roles. These two experimenters were husband and wife, and unlike the experimenters in the Binder et al. study, they differed only slightly in size. There were four groups of subjects. Each experimenter ran two groups, playing a neutral role with one group and an aggressive role with the other group. The neutral experimenter role was patient, calm, and courteous; the aggressive experimenter role was brusque, unfriendly, and impatient, with a tendency to sneer and scowl. Reports from subjects at the termination of the experiment revealed that the two roles were enacted appropriately. The stimuli and procedure were in all other respects identical to those of Binder et al.

There were no significant differences between male and female subjects in conditioning of the mildly hostile words, nor were there significant differences in conditioning between the male and female experimenters. The one significant difference in learning rate was between the aggressive experimenter role and the neutral experimenter role. The two neutral experimenter groups learned significantly faster than the two aggressive experimenter groups.

There are two possible explanations of the retarding effect of an aggressive experimenter on the learning of the hostile material. First, the angry, overassertive experimenter may threaten the subject, who tends to suppress the verbalization of hostile material. The subject would have little trouble in using the hostile alternative if the experimenter acted in a friendly fashion, but he inhibits use of the hostile verbs in the presence of a threatening experimenter.

The second explanation emphasizes reinforcement. The experimenter delivers the reinforcer *Good,* which increases the tendency to make the response that preceded it, in this instance a hostile response. When the experimenter is friendly, *Good* acts like any reinforcer, leading to an increment in the frequency of hostile responses. When the experimenter is unfriendly, *Good* is no longer an effective reinforcer, i.e., the subject is reluctant to make a response that the experimenter feels is a "good" one. This explanation applies to *any* verbal content, not just hostile content.

One way of testing these alternative hypotheses is to compare friendly and unfriendly experimenters in an operant conditioning situation in which the content is neutral. If the unfriendly experimenter retards learning, the effect is not limited to hostile content, and the second explanation is the better one.

A study by Sapolsky (1960) is relevant here. His subjects were college women, and the task was to make up sentences using one of six pronouns on a card. First person pronouns were reinforced by the experimenter's saying "mmm-hmmm." One group of subjects was told that their experimenter had been especially selected because the two of them would be congenial; this was the high attraction group. In the second (low attraction) group the subjects were told that it was not possible to match them with a congenial experimenter and that the experimenter might irritate them. There were two series, one for acquisition and one for extinction. It was found that during acquisition the high attraction group conditioned (frequency of first person responses increased), but the low attraction group did not. During extinction the high attraction group tended to give fewer first person responses, despite the absence of any reinforcement. Evidently, there had been some learning in the low attraction group during acquisition, but it had been suppressed. During extinction, when the experimenter was absent, this learning manifested itself.

There was a second experiment in which the two groups differed in the compatibility between experimenter and subject. The low compatible group tended not to condition during acquisition but increased the frequency of first person responses during extinction (when the experimenter left the room). The results of both experiments clearly support the reinforcement interpretation given above. When the experimenter is friendly or congenial or compatible, his verbalizations (*Good* or mmm-hmmm) serve to reinforce the responses that precede it. Since the experimenter's verbalizations may serve as cues or "information," it is possible for a subject to learn, but such learning will not become manifest so long as the subject is under the guidance of the aversive experimenter. It is not fear of the aggressive or unfriendly experimenter that leads to response suppression but rather negativism or resistance to his direction.

The depressing effect of an unfriendly experimenter has also been demonstrated by Weiss et al. (1959). Their subjects were college men, who were divided into two groups. One group was interviewed briefly by an experimenter who sneered at their inability to answer questions and made derogatory comments about their jobs and group affiliations. The other group was interviewed by a friendly, relaxed experimenter. Then both groups were placed in an operant verbal conditioning situation in which they were reinforced for using emotional words in telling stories to pictorial stimuli. The hostile interview significantly depressed the frequency of emotional words during conditioning in comparison to the friendly interview. As in Sapolsky's study, subjects reacted to the experimenter's hostility by decreasing their responsivity. There is considerable generality to this relationship, which holds across quite different operant verbal conditioning tasks and across sexes (Sapolsky's subjects being women and those of Weiss et al. being men).

Does the reinforced behavior generalize to another situation or to another task? Simkins (1960) attempted to answer this question, using the same hostile verbs that were used by Buss & Durkee (1958). The subjects, college men and women, were reinforced for using the hostile alternative. There were two experimental groups, and each had a control group matched for the number of hostile responses made during the free operant trials. One experimental group was reinforced by the experimenter's saying *Good* or *that's fine,* and the other was reinforced by receiving a point, with each point representing a penny to be collected at the end of the experiment. The two control groups received no reinforcement. After the conditioning trials, there was another series of trials without reinforcement. Before the conditioning began, all subjects took half of the Rosenzeig Picture-Frustration Study, and after conditioning they took the other half. The important Rosenzeig score was for Extrapunitiveness.

It was found that the control groups did not condition, but the two experimental groups learned rapidly. Both experimental groups made many hostile responses on the nonreinforced trials after conditioning, indicating that a high level of learning had occurred. The two experimental groups differed in the extent to which the hostile response generalized to the Rosenzeig Extrapunitive score. For the Good group there was no generalization, the Extrapunitive score being virtually the same before and after conditioning. For the group reinforced by points and pennies, there was significant generalization, the Extrapunitive score for the postconditioning half of the test being significantly higher than for the preconditioning half.

Generalization may depend on the task used to test for generalization. Weide (1959) reinforced college men for using malevolent words in sentences; the reinforcer was *Good,* and the generalization task was word associations. In comparison to a control group (not conditioned), there was significant generalization of malevolent words to the word association task. In this study *Good* led to generalization, but in Simkin's study it did not. The discrepancy may be due to the difference in generalization tasks: Picture-Frustration Study versus word association. Thus the dimension of generalization may be an important variable in determining whether generalization occurs.

Scrambled sentences. The Scrambled Sentences task was originated by Watson et al. (1955) in an attempt to demonstrate that neurotics are more hostile than normals. They had 60 scrambled sentences of the type

WINDOW THE WOUND OPEN

which can be unscrambled, after one word is dropped, to read Open The Wound or Open The Window. Note that one sentence is hostile and one is neutral. It was found that neurotics gave significantly more hostile solutions than normals.

The task has been adapted for use in operant conditioning, with the subject being reinforced for a neutral or a hostile solution. Scott (1958) studied the operant conditioning of acceptable aggressive and unacceptable aggressive sentences. He had student nurses rate sentences for social acceptability and used the extremes of the distribution. An example of each follows:

acceptable aggression: SWINDLER THE ATTACK INFORM
unacceptable aggression: THE MURDER UNDERSTAND CHILD

The subjects were college men, divided into three groups. One group was reinforced for constructing acceptable aggressive sentences, one group for unacceptable aggressive sentences, and a control group received no reinforcement.

Scott found that in all three groups there was significantly more acceptable aggression than unacceptable aggression. The group reinforced for acceptable aggression did condition, i.e., the curve of frequency of acceptable aggressive sentences was significantly steeper than that of the control group. There was no generalization to unacceptable aggressive statements. The group reinforced for unacceptable aggression did increase its frequency of such sentences, but the amount of learning (slope of the curve) was statistically insignificant. Evidently these college men were reluctant to unscramble sentences to form a sentence that conveys socially unacceptable aggression; not only was their initial operant rate low, but they resisted the experimenter's reinforcement of such responses.

Anderson (1958) also trained subjects to give the aggressive alternative in unscrambling sentences, but he did not distinguish between acceptable and unacceptable aggression. His subjects were college men and women, who were divided into high and low aggressiveness and punishment groups on the basis of their TAT stories. There were several TAT measures of aggression and punishment, but none of them was related to the conditioning of aggressive sentences on the Scrambled Sentences task, i.e., none of the differences in learning between high and low aggressive subjects, high and low punishment subjects (as measured by the TAT) was significant at the conventional (.05) level of significance for a two-tailed test.

Miscellaneous operant conditioning studies. Doehring (1958) attempted to condition the verbally aggressive responses of college men. The subjects read accounts of frustrating situations, each of which had an aggressive or a neutral reply. After a free operant period, half the subjects were reinforced for giving the aggressive reply, and the other half were not reinforced. The subjects were further divided into Shout and Whisper groups; one half were encouraged to shout their replies and the other half to whisper. Prior to the conditioning there was a pretest in which the subjects selected one of three replies to frustrating situations. In the posttest there was a similar task and similar instructions, differing from those given during conditioning in that during conditioning the subjects were instructed to give the reply they thought the experimenter wanted.

The dependent variable was performance on the posttest, with pretest performance controlled statistically. It was found that reinforcement of the aggressive alternative led to significantly more aggressive responses in the posttest than no reinforcement. The Shout and Whisper groups did not differ significantly.

Operant conditioning has also been shown to be effective in determining word associations. Zedek (1959) compiled a list of 50 neutral and 50 hostile words and presented them one at a time to college women. Each subject was instructed to give three associations to each word. After a free operant period, the experimenter reinforced hostile associations in one group and did not reinforce any responses in the other group. Hostile associations increased in the reinforced group but not in the control group.

Cushing (1957) instructed college men to say whether they liked or disliked a series of pictures. After an operant period one group was reinforced for dislike responses and one group for like responses. It was found that the "like" response could be conditioned, but the "dislike" response could not. There are two possible explanations of the failure to condition hostile responses. First, what was being conditioned was a dislike response rather than a specific hostile verb or hostile phrase, and it is possible that negative affective responses cannot be conditioned. Second, college men may be reluctant to increase their tendency to make dislike responses.

A study by Ekman & Friesen (1960) suggests that both explanations have merit. They attempted to condition dislike responses to pictures of peers and found that there was a negative correlation between learning and education. They were forced to discard all subjects with more than 12 years of schooling, which suggests that Cushing's failure to condition dislike responses may be attributed to his subjects being college students. Slightly less than half of the remaining subjects conditioned, suggesting that it may be difficult to condition dislike responses in any population.

Ekman & Friesen also attempted to demonstrate generalization of the dislike response to word associations but found no transfer; subjects who conditioned gave no more aggressive associations to words than those who did not condition. They did find generalization to a task similar to the conditioning task, that of assigning undesirable traits to photographs of peers, but this task was so similar to the learning task that it really does not demonstrate transfer. Note that the reinforcement in this study was one of the usual verbal reinforcers (Good). Simkins (1960) also found that there was no generalization when the reinforcer was verbal; he obtained transfer only when his subjects were reinforced with points and pennies. Thus the results with verbal reinforcers are clear; hostile verbalizations can be conditioned, but the tendency to make such hostile verbalizations is limited to the conditioning task or tasks very similar to it. The learning of a generalized tendency to make hostile verbal responses may require nonverbal reinforcers of the "reward" type, e.g., candy, cigarettes, money.

Galvanic Skin Response Studies

Several studies investigated galvanic skin responses (GSR) to hostile stimuli, GSR ostensibly being a measure of emotional reactivity. Ellsworth (1953) recorded GSRs of college women in a word association task. There were both hostile and neutral stimulus words, and the response measure was mean log conductance change from the resting state. There were greater GSR changes in response to hostile words than in response to neutral words, suggesting that hostile material evokes a greater emotional reaction than neutral material.

Another part of Ellsworth's study did not concern GSRs, but rather the learning of hostile material. Subjects were given syllogisms, scrambled sentences, a memory task, and a vocabulary test. An experimental group was then given a second series of tasks, this time the content being hostile; a control group was given a second series of neutral tasks similar in nature to those of the experimental group. The control group performed better on the second series of tasks than the experimental group; there was more learning of neutral material than of hostile material. This finding is in line with experiments on rote learning, which also found that hostile content tends to retard learning.

Diers (1955) measured both GSRs and random movements in response to spoken hostile sentences. The subjects (college men and women) listened to tape recordings of four hostile sentences, two in a woman's voice and two in a man's voice. Then they responded verbally to two of the sentences but inhibited responses to the other two.

The sex of the stimulus voice was found to have no effect on either the GSR measure or random movements. For the women, verbal responding produced a significantly greater change in GSR than inhibition of response, but there was no comparable effect for men. In the verbalization condition, the women showed significantly greater GSR changes than the men, despite an absence of sex differences in base conductance level. The effect of verbalization on random movements was in the opposite direction, men responding with significantly more random movements than women. Diers interpreted these results in terms of cultural conditioning. Women are taught to discharge aggressive tension verbally, and their tension, as measured by GSR, changed markedly when they verbalized. Men are taught that it is appropriate to discharge aggressive tension physically, and verbal discharge is therefore less satisfactory than in women. Thus the men's tension, as measured by GSR, changed significantly less than the women's tension under the condition of verbalization, but the men's random movements (physical discharge) were significantly greater.

Sines (1957) recorded GSR, respiration rate, and heart rate as responses to aggressive, passive-dependent, and heterosexual pictures. The subjects were male medical and psychiatric patients, who were divided into three groups on the basis of personality conflict: hostile-aggressive, passive-dependent, and heterosexual. The physiological measures were combined to yield an arousal score for each subject. The hostile group manifested the greatest physiological arousal to the hostile stimulus, and the other two groups showed greatest arousal to the stimuli dealing with their conflicts.

Two conclusions emerge from these three investigations. First, hostile stimuli elicit a greater physiological reaction than neutral stimuli, but the reaction is not necessarily any greater than that to other classes of "emotional stimuli." Second, the sex and personality of subjects are important determiners of GSR response to hostile stimuli.

Scaling of Hostile Words

Most experimenters working with hostile materials have controlled for meaningfulness, word frequency, or association value, and in several studies vividness has been controlled. One attempt was made to vary the intensity of the hostile words (Buss & Durkee, 1958), but only a crude differentiation was made. In the early stages of research in an area, most of the differences are qualitative. One mark of progress is quantification of the major independent variables so that they may be varied systematically throughout their range. What is needed is quantification of the intensity of hostile verbal materials, and the obvious method is psychological scaling. This section describes the scaling of hostile words along a dimension of intensity.

A list of 185 words was culled from various sources, with excessively pedantic and slang words omitted. They were arranged in alphabetical order and presented to 60 college men and 78 college women who were instructed to rate them for hostility from 1 (lowest intensity) to 9 (highest intensity). Means, medians, and standard deviations were computed for each sex separately, and scale values (method of successive intervals) were derived from the women's ratings. The women's medians correlated .90 with the scale

TABLE 7.1. MEDIAN SCALE VALUES AND THORNDIKE-LORGE FREQUENCIES* FOR HOSTILE WORDS

Word	Men	Women	Frequency Count	Word	Men	Women	Frequency Count
Competitive	1.8	2.0	8	Taunt	4.1	4.5	6
Contest	1.9	1.4	31	Critical	4.2	4.9	16
Plain-spoken	2.0	1.3	—	Quarrelsome	4.2	4.5	3
Frank	2.4	1.4	32	Reproachful	4.2	4.5	1
Controversy	2.4	4.7	12	Unfriendly	4.2	3.9	4
Debate	2.6	1.8	24	Troublesome	4.3	4.6	9
Abrupt	2.9	3.0	6	Nagging	4.4	4.1	5
Blunt	3.0	2.6	9	Irked	4.4	3.9	1
Disagreement	3.0	3.7	3	Interference	4.4	3.7	11
Depreciating	3.0	4.2	3	Impolite	4.4	3.9	16
Distaste	3.1	3.4	2	Grouchy	4.5	3.3	1
Dissent	3.1	3.3	4	Exasperated	4.5	4.7	5
Opposition	3.2	4.5	29	Grudge	4.5	4.6	10
Contrary	3.3	3.1	46	Argument	4.6	5.0	48
Curt	3.3	3.6	3	Accusation	4.6	5.1	9
Discontented	3.3	3.3	4	Disparaging	4.6	4.6	1
Displeasure	3.4	3.4	7	Wrangle	4.6	5.4	4
Outspoken	3.4	3.5	1	Scowling	4.6	4.3	10
Ill-humored	3.5	4.6	—	Suppressive	4.6	4.4	17
Peevish	3.5	3.3	2	Aggravation	4.7	4.8	1
Nuisance	3.6	3.7	10	Derisive	4.7	5.1	1
Teasing	3.6	2.5	14	Indignant	4.7	4.6	9
Adversary	3.6	4.0	7	Retort	4.7	4.7	15
Chiding	3.6	3.3	6	Repudiation	4.7	4.4	1
Reproof	3.7	3.9	4	Scuffle	4.7	5.1	2
Blame	3.7	3.6	A	Reprimand	4.8	4.2	2
Complaining	3.7	2.3	44	Scolding	4.8	4.8	19
Dissatisfied	3.7	3.1	3	Surly	4.8	5.1	3
Dislike	3.8	4.1	23	Contempt	4.9	5.8	18
Discord	3.8	5.0	6	Chastising	5.0	5.2	3
Annoyance	3.8	4.4	7	Dissaproval	5.0	3.5	5
Mischievous	3.8	2.9	6	Denunciation	5.0	5.2	2
Rivalry	3.9	4.6	5	Ill-will	5.0	4.9	—
Sullen	3.9	4.0	13	Rebuke	5.0	5.4	10
Touchy	3.9	3.7	1	Anger	5.1	5.7	A
Crabby	3.9	3.2		Browbeating	5.1	5.2	11
Bout	4.0	5.2	8	Conflict	5.1	5.3	30
Pest	4.0	3.8	6	Irritated	5.1	4.7	12
Bruise	4.1	4.0	17	Jeering	5.1	5.2	7
Dispute	4.1	4.5	40	Condemnation	5.2	5.6	4
Impatient	4.1	3.4	13	Hot-blooded	5.2	5.8	—
Petulant	4.1	3.7	2	Resentful	5.3	5.3	4
Spanking	4.1	4.7	9	Embittered	5.3	6.0	2

TABLE 7.1.   (*Continued*)

Word	Men	Women	Frequency Count	Word	Men	Women	Frequency Count
Fault-finding	5.3	5.0	—	Libel	6.5	7.0	2
Rudeness	5.4	5.0	1	Dictatorial	6.5	6.5	1
Destructive	5.4	7.3	9	Kicking	6.6	6.6	47
Bitterness	5.5	5.1	14	Lacerating	6.7	7.8	16
Maddened	5.5	6.0	4	Battle	6.7	8.0	AA
Persecuting	5.5	7.4	7	Malicious	6.7	8.0	6
Vengeful	5.5	7.5	1	Malice	6.8	7.8	10
Defiant	5.5	6.9	4	Brawl	6.8	7.0	5
Embittered	5.5	6.0	2	Enraged	6.9	7.7	6
Assaultive	5.6	7.7	22	Fight	6.9	7.5	AA
Curse	5.6	5.7	39	Assailant	7.0	7.9	6
Feud	5.6	6.2	6	Enemy	7.0	7.8	AA
Intimidating	5.6	4.5	1	Ferocious	7.1	7.7	4
Sneering	5.6	4.9	12	Revenge	7.2	7.2	29
Sarcastic	5.6	5.6	3	Furious	7.2	7.5	21
Temper	5.6	5.6	39	Hatred	7.4	8.5	20
Scorn	5.7	5.5	31	Brutal	7.4	8.6	—
Tormenting	5.7	6.5	18	Mauling	7.4	8.1	2
Combative	5.7	6.3	18	Terrorizing	7.6	7.9	1
Hurt	5.8	7.3	AA	Mangling	7.6	8.3	5
Menace	5.8	6.8	21	Attack	7.9	8.6	A
Abusive	5.9	7.3	1	Bomb	8.0	8.7	13
Insulting	6.0	5.9	21	Bloodthirsty	8.4	8.5	2
Wrath	6.1	7.5	21	War	8.4	8.8	AA
Spite	6.2	6.2	A	Annihilation	8.6	8.4	2
Thrashing	6.2	7.2	10	Mutilating	8.6	8.9	3
Loathing	6.4	7.6	7	Assassination	8.7	8.9	4
Cruel	6.4	7.1	46	Killing	8.7	8.9	AA
Slander	6.5	6.8	6	Torture	8.7	8.8	25
Rage	6.5	7.0	49	Murdering	8.8	8.9	A
Harm	6.5	6.5	A				

* A = 50 to 100/million.
  AA = 100 up to 1 million/million.

values derived from the method of successive intervals, and since medians are simple to compute and to comprehend, they were used as the scale values for both men and women.

The standard deviation and the range of ratings for each word are both measures of variability, and it was desirable to eliminate words with excessive variability. There was no uniform standard for eliminating words, the author deciding subjectively on the basis of both the range and the standard deviation. On this basis 39 words were discarded, leaving a list of 146 words scaled for intensity of hostility. They are presented in Table 7.1, with the words arranged in order of ascending intensity for male raters. Sex differences are clearly present, especially at the least intense and most intense ends of the dimension, with the women's scale values tending to be higher than the men's. While the sex differences are not large, it is advisable to keep the scale values separate because the particular words an investigator uses might be precisely those with a large discrepancy between men and women.

The standard deviation and range for each word are not presented. These values do not vary greatly from one word to the next, probably because the words with excessive variability in ratings were discarded. A difference of .1 between words is negligible; when the difference in scale values reaches .5, the words are somewhat different in intensity of hostility; differences of the order of 1.0 and larger represent clearly separate points of the intensity dimension.

There are several uses for words that have been scaled for intensity of hostility. They can be used to investigate stimulus generalization along a dimension of intensity of hostility, as will be described in the next section. They can be used in rote learning and operant conditioning studies, with the intensity of the hostile material being varied. They may also be separated into subareas: anger, hostility, physical aggression, verbal aggression, etc. Assuming the validity of this kind of separation, it would be possible to study the effect of different kinds of referents of hostile words, e.g., do physically aggressive words retard learning more than angry words?

Stimulus Generalization

Stimulus generalization is an important part of the individual's adjustive mechanisms. Mediated generalization is crucial because human interaction is primarily verbal, and this importance is reflected in the considerable research being done under the headings of stimulus predifferentiation, semantic conditioning, acquired equivalence of cues, and labeling. In previous research on generalization to verbal stimuli, the materials have been neutral. There has been no previous attempt to investigate stimulus generalization along a dimension of hostility, probably because of the lack of scaled stimuli. Adults tend to label the behavior of others, and in the labeling process the symbols (words) take on some of the emotional connotations of the behaviors they represent. Such labels are important in determining one's response to another's aggression. Most adults learn to grade aggression for intensity, and in learning to distinguish different intensities of aggression, language is of considerable help: one label is associated with a given intensity and another label with some other intensity. A word that has been linked with the aggressive event tends to connote the intensity of the event.

Since gradations in aggressive stimuli appear to be culturally important, the stimulus generalization paradigm would seem to be particularly appropriate for investigating aggressive stimuli. Assuming that the intensity of hostility is analogous to dimensions, such as loudness or brightness, a response may be conditioned to one part of the dimension, and the spread of the response to other parts of the stimulus dimension may be measured.

This is precisely what was done by Buss (1961).[1] Subjects were trained to make a response to either high or low hostile words. Then response frequencies were measured to words on other parts of the hostility dimension. Half the subjects generalized from high to low hostile words, and the other half generalized from low to high hostile words. The responses varied in intensity; one group of subjects was trained to shout, one group to read aloud, and one group to whisper. Significant differences were found in the slopes of the generalization gradients of these three groups. When the subjects generalized from high to low hostile words, the Shout gradient was steepest, the Aloud gradient next, and the Whisper gradient the flattest. When the subjects generalized from low to high hostile words, the Whisper gradient was steepest, Aloud next, and the Shout gradient was *inverse* (more shout responses to high hostile than to low hostile words). When generalization was from high to low hostile words, the gradients were significantly steeper than when generalization was from low to high hostile words.

Two explanatory principles can account for these results. The first is the stimulus intensity dynamism (Hull, 1951), which predicts a steeper gradient when generalization is from intense to weak stimuli than when generalization is from weak to intense stimuli. The second is a "matching principle": the tendency to match the intensity of the response to the intensity of the stimulus. High hostile words should elicit shout responses; low hostile words should elicit whisper responses. The matching principle explains why the Shout gradient was inverse when subjects generalized from low hostile stimuli. The tendency to shout high hostile stimuli was stronger than the tendency of the response to weaken as the stimuli were more distant from the (low hostile) training stimuli.

Evidence supporting the matching principle comes from a study by Geer (1960). He had subjects pull hard or soft on a hand brake in

[1] This research was supported by Research Grant M-2861 from the National Institute of Mental Health.

response to hostile words. On the first training trial, 24 of 30 subjects pulled hard to a high hostile word, while 21 of 30 different subjects pulled soft to a low hostile word. Thus there appears to be a pre-experimental tendency to grade the intensity of response to the intensity of the stimulus. Geer's generalization gradients provided further support for both the matching principle and direction of generalization (stimulus intensity dynamism).

This research on stimulus generalization with hostile stimuli suggests several avenues for further exploration. One possibility is the investigation of the generalization gradients of subjects known to differ in aggressiveness and hostility. Do more aggressive individuals tend to have flatter generalization gradients (characterize more stimuli as hostile) than less aggressive individuals? A further possibility is the study of generalization gradients in relation to anger level: Do angry subjects have flatter gradients than non-angry subjects?

Another line of investigation would seek to determine the generality of the matching principle. Does it hold for a variety of responses to the hostile stimuli or is it limited to just a few? Aside from hostile verbal stimuli, does the matching principle hold for other "emotional" stimuli? Does it hold for neutral stimuli that differ in intensity, for example, pitch, loudness?

REFERENCES

Anderson, D. E. Personality variables in verbal conditioning. Unpublished doctor's dissertation, University of Nebraska, 1958.

Binder, A., McConnell, D., & Sjoholm, Nancy A. Verbal conditioning as a function of experimenter characteristics. *J. abnorm. soc. Psychol.*, 1957, 55, 309–314.

Buss, A. H. & Durkee, Ann. Conditioning of hostile verbalizations in a situation resembling a clinical interview. *J. consult. Psychol.*, 1958, 22, 415–418.

Buss, A. H. Stimulus generalization and aggressive stimuli. *J. exp. Psychol.*, 1961, in press.

Cushing, M. C. Affective components of the response class as a factor in verbal conditioning. Unpublished doctor's dissertation, University of Nebraska, 1957.

Diers, W. C. A study of the effectiveness of verbalization in the homeostatic recovery from displacement induced by verbal-aggressive stimuli. Unpublished doctor's dissertation, University of Cincinnati, 1955.

Doehring, M. A test of a training procedure designed to increase the intensity of angry verbalization. Unpublished doctor's dissertation, University of Pittsburgh, 1958.

Ekman, P. & Friesen, W. V. The conditioning of hostile responses to photographs of peers. Paper read at Eastern Psychological Assn., 1960.

Ellsworth, R. B. The effects of hostility on related verbal problem-solving behavior. Unpublished doctor's dissertation, Pennsylvania State University, 1953.

Ferguson, D. & Buss, A. H.   Operant conditioning of hostile verbs in relation to experiments and subject characteristics. *J. consult. Psychol.*, 1960, **24**, 324–327.

Geer, J.   The effect of direction of generalization and amplitude of response on stimulus generalization with aggressive stimulus. Unpublished master's thesis, University of Pittsburgh, 1960.

Gofstein, A. G.   Hostile drive, conflict, and the recall of hostile material. Unpublished doctor's dissertation, Boston University, 1956.

Holzberg, J. D., Bursten, B., & Santiccioli, A.   The reporting of aggression as an indication of aggressive tension. *J. abnorm. soc. Psychol.*, 1955, **50**, 12–18.

Hull, C. L.   *Essentials of behavior.* New Haven: Yale University Press, 1951.

Mallet, J. J.   Verbal recall of hostile and neutral thematic contents by schizophrenic and normal subjects. Unpublished doctor's dissertation, Duke University, 1956.

Riggs, Margaret N.   Recall and organization of aggressive words under varied conditions of emphasis. *Percept. mot. Skills,* 1956, **6**, 273–284.

Robinson, B. W.   A study of hostility as reflected by the differential learning and retention of schizophrenic patients. Unpublished doctor's dissertation, Purdue University, 1954.

Sapolsky, A.   Effect of interpersonal relationships upon verbal conditioning. *J. abnorm. soc. Psychol.*, 1960, **60**, 241–246.

Scott, T. R.   Social reinforcement of aggressive sentences. Unpublished doctor's dissertation, University of Nebraska, 1958.

Simkins, L.   Generalization effects of hostile verb reinforcement as a function of stimulus similarity and type of reinforcer. Unpublished manuscript, 1960.

Sines, J. O.   Conflict-related stimuli as elicitors of selected physiological responses. *J. proj. Techn.*, 1957, **21**, 194–198.

Smith, J. G.   Influence of failure, expressed hostility, and stimulus characteristics on verbal learning and recognition. *J. Pers.*, 1954, **22**, 475–493.

Soffer, L.   Retroactive inhibition with aggressive and non-aggressive word lists in neurotic and normal subjects. Unpublished doctor's dissertation, University of Illinois, 1956.

Taffel, C.   Anxiety and the conditioning of behavior. *J. abnorm. soc. Psychol.*, 1955, **51**, 496–501.

Watson, R. E., Pritzker, L., & Madison, P.   Hostility in neurotics and normals. *J. abnorm. soc. Psychol.*, 1955, **50**, 36–40.

Weide, T. N.   Conditioning and generalization of the use of affect-relevant words. Unpublished doctor's dissertation, Stanford University, 1959.

Weiss, R. L., Krasner, L., & Ullmann, L. P.   Responsivity to verbal conditioning as a function of emotional atmosphere and pattern of reinforcement. Paper read at American Psychological Assn. meetings, 1959.

Williams, M.   Rate of learning as a function of ego-alien material. *J. Pers.*, 1951, **19**, 324–331.

Wolf, I.   Learning rate in relation to hostile drive strength and stimuli connoting hostility. Unpublished doctor's dissertation, Boston University, 1954.

Zedek, Meira E.   The conditioning of verbal behavior with negative cultural connotations. *J. Pers.*, 1959, **27**, 477–486.

PART TWO

8

Projective techniques

Projective techniques have been used for personality assessment for several decades and are now the most popular instruments for measuring enduring behavioral trends and psychopathology. The projective hypothesis that gives these instruments their name states that the subject imbues stimuli with meaning by projecting his own conflicts and needs into the ambiguous stimuli. These techniques are believed to measure fantasy responses, which relate to deeper personality trends of which the subject is unaware. A more recent approach is more behavioristic in its emphasis on response sampling and stimulus attributes rather than on dynamic mechanisms like repression and projection, e.g., Lesser (1958), Lubin (1960), and Solkoff (1960).

Regardless of viewpoint, the following developments seem to represent recent trends in research. There is much interest in the characteristics of the stimuli presented to the subject, for example, variations in the race of the characters portrayed in the TAT cards, variations in the color, shading, and amount of detail in the Rorschach ink blots. There is an increased emphasis on content in contrast to formal scoring. Normative data are being collected on subjects of varying age, occupation, degree of psychopathology, etc. The criterion issue has been accorded a more central role in the larger question of validity. No longer are projective techniques accepted as their own criteria, but investigators are attempting to discover just what these devices can predict.

127

This brief account of newer research trends and viewpoints may serve as background for a review of aggression in projective techniques. The subject's responses to the ambiguous stimuli usually contain elements of both aggression (people fighting, animals killing each other, many types of weapons) and hostility (threatening animals, disgusting objects, and various negative evaluations). Since the response to projective techniques contains both hostility and aggression, the two terms will be used interchangeably in describing *projective responses;* otherwise, they will be used in a fashion consistent with their definitions.

There are many studies of aggression in projective techniques, too many to review here. This chapter is limited to the major techniques, Rorschach and TAT. The studies to be reviewed deal with many issues, and it may help the exposition to state in advance the more salient ones:

1. The relationship between projective and behavioral aggression— direct or inverse.

2. The effectiveness of different scoring systems.

3. Projective aggression in different populations.

4. The ambiguity and scalability of the stimuli (this applies mainly to the TAT).

5. Aggression as a personality variable versus aggression in the laboratory.

RORSCHACH

Two kinds of scoring have been employed in Rorschach studies of aggression: scoring of hostile content and traditional scoring of formal elements (form level, movement, location, etc.). More investigators have used a hostile content scoring system, and these studies will be discussed first.

Content Scoring Systems

Scoring systems for hostile content have been used with a variety of subject populations, some systems predominantly with normals and others predominantly with deviants (psychiatric patients, prisoners, clients in psychotherapy).

Normals. The first scoring system for hostile content on the Rorschach was devised by Elizur (1949), and his scheme has been virtually the only one used with normal subjects. He distinguished two degrees of hostile content, and gave the more intense kind a score twice that of the milder one. Intensely hostile responses included reproach and hatred, expressions of stupidity and ugliness, killing and fighting, and aggressive objects like guns and arrows. Mildly hostile responses were not as direct: symbols like a war mask, aggressive objects like pliers or teeth, and injury to an animal or person. Rorschachs, interviews, questionnaires and self-ratings were collected on 30 college men.

The correlations between the Rorschach hostile content score and the other three measures were:

Questionnaire	.74
Interview	.60
Self-rating	.45

The first two correlations are especially high for this kind of research and suggest that Elizur's content scoring for hostility is closely related to external measures of aggression. Note that these external measures are all essentially self-report; the questionnaire and self-rating are self-report by definition, and the interview ratings were based on what the subject told the experimenter. Thus, rather than reveal deeper trends of which the subject is unaware, the Elizur scheme evidently taps aggressiveness that the subject can easily verbalize. Elizur's successful demonstration of his scoring system prompted other investigators to use it and to elaborate modifications of it.

Murstein (1956) expanded Elizur's two intensities into seven intensities of hostile content. His subjects were fraternity college men who rated themselves and each other on a dimension that ranged from friendliness to hostility. The pooled ratings from others determined whether a subject was friendly or hostile, and the extent of agreement between these pooled ratings and the self-rating determined whether a subject was "insightful" or "non-insightful." The two variables of hostility and insight generated four groups of subjects: hostile-insightful, hostile-non-insightful, friendly-insightful, and friendly-non-insightful. The hostile-insightful group scored significantly higher in hostile content than the other three groups, and there were no significant differences in these three remaining groups. Evidently intense hostility appears on the Rorschach only if the subject is aggressive (as noted by his peers) and knows it (insightful). If the subject is aggressive (peer ratings) but denies it (non-insightful), he manifests no more Rorschach hostility than subjects who are rated as friendly by peers. Again the Rorschach reveals only as much hostility as the subject can verbalize; subjects who are defensive (non-insightful) concerning aggression have low hostility scores on the Rorschach.

Vernallis (1955) related hostility on the Rorschach to teeth-grinding; he found that teeth-grinders had significantly higher Elizur hostility scores than students who did not grind their teeth. This may be regarded as evidence that the Elizur scale measures hostility only if hostility underlies teeth-grinding. Lit (1956) studied college students with excellent and with poor grades and compared them on a number of variables. The poor students had significantly higher Elizur hostile content scores than the superior students. Sanders & Cleveland (1953) found the Elizur scale useful in evaluating the effect of examiners' aggressiveness, and this study will be discussed in a later section. The last study with college students is that of Goodstein (1954), who failed to find a significant correlation between Elizur hostility scores and the hostility scale of the Iowa Picture Interpretation Test.

The Elizur has also been used with children and adolescents. Cummings (1954) compared the Elizur hostile content scores of children with their ratings on an index of nail biting and found a significant correlation of .34. Gorlow et al. (1952) used the Elizur scoring with delinquent and nondelinquent adolescents. The delinquents were more guarded, but, despite a smaller number of total responses, they gave significantly more hostile responses on the Rorschach.

With the exception of the Goodstein study, the Elizur system clearly distinguished between groups ostensibly differing in aggressiveness. In some instances the criterion groups might be questioned concerning relevance to aggression, but the total picture is one of a fair degree of construct validity for the scoring scheme. It would certainly appear to be useful in assessing hostility in normal populations.

Deviant populations. Three kinds of deviant populations have been used in the research to be reviewed in this section: prisoners, psychiatric patients, and those undergoing some form of therapy. Two kinds of criteria have been used: case records of assaultiveness and therapists' ratings of aggressiveness.

ASSAULTIVENESS. DeVos (1952) developed a hostile content scoring system that was subsequently used with assaultive prisoners. He distinguished eight varieties of Rorschach hostility: oral-aggressive responses, such as biting; depreciation or dehumanization of figures; direct aggression, such as fighting or arguments; indirect aggression, such as weapons; indirect aggression-anxiety, such as witch and blood; distorted figures, such as a torso without arms; responses indicating inner tension, such as volcano erupting; and sado-masochistic responses, such as a wolf that has been flattened by a car. DeVos had four judges score Rorschachs for hostile content and the mean intercorrelation was .77.

With slight modification the DeVos scoring was used by Kane (1955) in a study of assaultive and nonassaultive male prisoners. The assaultive group had attacked someone or threatened to do so; most had records of armed robbery, murder, and so forth. The non-assaultive prisoners were of comparable age, intelligence, and education but had neither threatened nor committed aggressive crimes. Kane assumed that fantasy would provide an outlet for hostility that would make it unnecessary to act out aggressive impulses (the familiar drainage hypothesis), and he predicted that the assaultives would show less Rorschach hostility than the nonassaultives. The results were in the opposite direction, the assaultive group scoring significantly higher on the modified DeVos hostile content scale than the nonassaultives. The Rorschach should be regarded as a sample of aggressive behavior rather than a channel for draining aggressive impulses.

As a complement to Kane's study of male prisoners, Sjostedt (1955) employed the DeVos scale with women prisoners. Her assaultives had attacked another person, and her nonassaultives had committed acquisitive crimes, such as illegally appropriating goods or money. The assaultives and acquisitives were matched for education, religion, and marital status, but the assaultives were on the average 12 years older and had spent 2 more years in prison than the acquisitives. The assaultives scored significantly higher than the acquisitives on the DeVos scale.

There have been several studies of physical attack on the part of psychiatric patients. Storment & Finney (1953) matched male psychiatric patients, who had exhibited violent activity, with nonviolent patients. They attempted to differentiate between the groups with a five-point scale that ranged from extremely passive responses to openly aggressive responses. The violent group scored significantly higher in hostile content than did the nonviolent group, and the biserial correlation was .71. In light of these very promising results Finney conducted a follow up study (1955) with a new sample from the same population of patients. He refined the scoring system and obtained an estimate of its inter-rater reliability. This new scoring system again significantly differentiated between violent and nonviolent patients, but this time with considerably less statistical reliability. Thus the refined system yielded a weaker relationship to aggression than did the original, crude hostile content scoring system. Finney's is one of the rare replication studies, and his results are typical; there is "shrinkage" from the first to the second study, some of the chance findings of the initial study tending to wash out on replication.

Wolf (1957) investigated anatomy responses and hostile content in assaultive and nonassaultive male psychiatric patients. Anatomy responses did not differentiate between the groups, but dividing the assaultive and nonassaultive patients into high and low hostile groups on the basis of hostile content yielded a significant Chi-square. Assaultiveness was associated with high hostile content scores and nonassaultiveness with low hostile content scores. The scoring system was modeled after that of Elizur.

Towbin (1959) found both positive and negative results when he compared the hostile content scores of assaultive and nonassaultive male psychiatric patients. The Rorschach was scored for three kinds of hostility: H_1—aggressive remarks directed at the Rorschach cards; H_2—aggressive objects like guns and knives; and H_3—aggressive figures like giants and witches, as well as aggressive actions like people dueling. The distributions of the three hostile content scores were dichotomized, and Chi-squares were computed. The only significant Chi-square was for the H_1 score; the phi-coefficient was .52. The scoring for H_1 was unique; hostile comments toward the cards is not usually included in hostile content systems. Yet this score was the only one that differentiated the assaultive from the nonassaultive group (the former scoring higher). The H_2 and H_3 scores included the content contained in most hostile content scoring systems, but these scores did not differentiate the groups.

Another unusual scoring scheme was developed by Sommer & Sommer (1958). They differentiated between explosive color responses (volcano, fire) and nonexplosive color responses; and between aggressive movement (kicking, fighting) and nonaggressive movement responses. The case histories of male psychiatric patients were rated for assaultiveness and for verbal aggression. When only color responses were examined, explosive-nonexplosive scoring significantly differentiated between assaultives and nonassaultives but was not related to verbal aggression. When assaultiveness and verbal aggression were combined into a single behavioral aggression score for each patient, the biserial correlation coefficient between this score and explosive color was .35. When aggressive movement was added, the biserial correlation rose to .55.

AGGRESSION IN THERAPY. The studies in this section employed ratings of therapists as the criterion of aggression. Walker (1951) had patients rated for frequency of direct verbal and physical aggression, withdrawal, reversal of roles, arguing, and tardiness. The Rorschach scoring system included four degrees of hostility, and the following examples are in descending order of intensity: fighting; animals shot, dead men; stupid men; mouse cut open; and old ladies gossiping, bugs with horns. Comparison of these scores with therapists' ratings of aggression yielded a phi-coefficient of .50.

Rader (1957) studied the Rorschach hostile content of male prisoners in group psychotherapy. Therapists rated members of their groups on a scale that ranged from submissive behavior through a neutral point of no aggression to assertive, bitter, verbal aggression. The Rorschachs were scored for: (a) hostility and mutilation responses and (b) indicators of a tendency to inhibit aggression— passivity, guilt, dependency, and inadequacy. The subjects were divided into two groups for the purpose of replication. Only the hostility mutilation score was found to be significantly related to the therapists' ratings, the correlations being .34 and .41 for the two samples. Rader noted that in group therapy there is reinforcement for verbal aggression, which would counteract inhibitions against expressing aggression. Verbal aggression is usually unpunished in therapy, which makes therapy behavior an excellent criterion of aggressiveness.

The last study to use therapists' ratings as the criterion concerns not psychotherapy but remedial reading. Smith & Coleman (1956) studied boys of 9 to 15 years who were in a remedial reading class. Teachers rated them for physical aggression, verbal aggression, and quarrelsomeness (the last probably being confounded with the first two). A hostile content scoring scheme similar to those of Elizur and Walker was developed, and it was predicted that the relationship between Rorschach hostility and behavioral aggression would be curvilinear. In order to test for curvilinearity, the hostile content scores were divided into quartiles, and the first and fourth quartiles were combined, as were the second and third quartiles. The following contingency coefficients were found between hostile content and behavioral aggression:

Rorschach hostile content versus

Physical aggression	.54
Verbal aggression	.41
Quarrelsomeness	.36

As predicted, the two middle groups in Rorschach hostile content were rated as more aggressive behaviorally than the highest and lowest groups in Rorschach hostility. This is the only study to discover a curvilinear relationship between Rorschach hostility and behavioral aggression. Perhaps the combination of a special population (schoolboys with reading difficulty) and the situation in which their behavior was observed (the classroom) accounts for this unusual finding.

Miscellaneous studies. There remain several studies that do not fall under the above headings. Wirt (1956), making a common clinical assumption that hostility covaries with degree of psychopathology, attempted to test this notion with schizophrenics, neurotics, and normals. He used Finney's scoring for hostile content and corrected for total number of responses. Neurotics scored significantly higher than schizophrenics, who scored significantly higher than normals. Thus the hypothesis was not confirmed; hostility does not covary with degrees of psychopathology. Finney's revised scoring system had four categories: derogatory remarks, possibly destructive responses, active destruction, and victim of destruction. Wirt grouped the first three into an "aggressor" category and kept the fourth as a "victim" category. Then he compared his three groups of subjects and found that normals tended to give the most aggressor responses and schizophrenics the most victim responses, with neurotics falling between in both categories. These significant differences were interpreted in terms of direction of punitiveness. The normals direct hostility outward, the schizophrenics inward, and the neurotics show no direction. This conclusion rests on the unverified assumption that aggressor and victim responses on the Rorschach are indicants of the direction of hostility.

A study by Gluck (1955) differs from all the others mentioned in that he used as a criterion the subjects' aggressive responses to frustration. The subjects were male psychiatric patients in an army hospital. Each subject was first given the Rorschach and then placed in a series of extremely frustrating situations and his aggressive behavior rated. A factor analysis of the various frustrating tasks yielded three factorially pure tasks, and the behavioral aggression score consisted of the average rating for these three tasks. The Rorschach was scored for overt aggression (two fellows in a duel) and covert aggression (spears, pistol, bat with torn wings). Behavioral aggression was correlated with overt, covert, and total Rorschach aggression, and in each instance the correlation was not significantly different from zero. Gluck noted that his subjects may have been inhibited from expressing aggression during the frustrating situations, which would serve to attenuate any relationship between Rorschach and behavioral aggression. A second possibility is that the frustrating tasks were not of the type to elicit aggression; it was noted in an earlier chapter that frustration often does not lead to aggression. The third possibility is that the Rorschach simply does not reflect transitory changes in aggression, such as those that Gluck attempted to induce in his subjects. The Rorschach may be a better measure of enduring aggressive trends than of temporary, experimentally induced behaviors.

The last study in this section is methodological; Sanders & Cleveland (1953) investigated the effect of examiner aggressiveness on Rorschach responses. The examiners were graduate students who administered Rorschachs to college men; each examiner also took the Rorschach. Each examinee filled out a questionnaire about his examiner that included five items about aggressiveness (critical, prying, disdainful, etc.). The questionnaires were used to rank the examiners for *overt* aggression, and the Elizur hostile content scores of the examiners' Rorschachs were used to rank them for *covert* aggression. When the examiner was overtly high aggressive, the examinees' hostility was significantly lower than when the examiner was overtly low aggressive; but high covert examiner aggression resulted in significantly more examinee hostility than low covert examiner aggression. Thus overt and covert examiner aggression work in opposite directions: overt aggression suppresses hostility, and covert aggression elicits it. This study points to a source of uncontrolled variance in Rorschach studies of hostility: the aggressiveness of the examiner. This variable is likely to be a source of error in any assessment technique that requires close interaction between examiner and examinee.

Formal Rorschach Scores

A number of studies have related formal Rorschach categories to aggression. Of all the Rorschach scores, the one whose traditional interpretation suggests a relationship to aggression is the white space response (*S*), which is believed to measure negativism. Two studies offer some support for this notion. Ingram (1954) divided college men into those who gave no S responses on the Rorschach and those who gave one or more. Both groups took part in a frustrating problem solving task and in a frustrating interview, and subjects were

rated for hostility and resistance. The high S group was rated significantly more hostile and resistive than the low S group in the interview situation and significantly more hostile in the problem solving
situation.

These results received partial corroboration from Bandura's study
(1954) of negativism in high school students. Students of both sexes
were rated by their teachers for negativism, and the partial correlation (a control for total number of Rorschach responses) between
white space responses and negativism was .34.

In both studies the relationship between S and negativism was
significant but weak. It is doubtful that a strong relationship could
be found because negativism is typically defined in a vague manner.
"Oppositional tendencies" may vary from the rebellion of an adolescent to the independence of a mature, thoughtful adult. Phillips &
Smith (1953) have pointed out the fallacy of lumping all kinds of
space responses under one heading because of the vast differences in
maturity levels of the responses so classified, a suggestion that receives support from the variety of personality variables associated
with the white space response in different studies (Murray, 1957).

Two hypnotism experiments have yielded negative results on the
relationship between aggression and S responses. Counts & Mensh
(1950) hypnotized college students of both sexes, giving the posthypnotic suggestion that they would be very angry with the Rorschach examiner but would not express their rage openly. Rorschachs were administered before hypnosis, immediately after hypnosis, and twice more after removal of the posthypnotic suggestion.
Half the subjects had no memory of the artificially induced anger,
and they manifested the most aggressive behavior during the administration of the immediate posthypnotic Rorschach. The Rorschachs were scored for the usual categories including S, but none
showed a significant change from one testing to the next.

Pattie (1954) hypnotized 14 college students and administered
the Rorschach twice. The first time, the subject was told that after
he came out of the trance he would take the test in a normal frame
of mind and then forget his responses. The second time, the posthypnotic suggestion was that the subject would feel "very hostile,
aggressive and angry" toward the examiner. All subjects reported
after the second testing that they had never taken the test before,
suggesting that the posthypnotic suggestion to forget responses
worked. None of the formal Rorschach scores, including S, differed
significantly from calm to hostile testing. However, a majority of
subjects showed more than a two-fold increase in hostile content,

and several others who did not show this increase vented their anger in card criticism on every card. Evidently the subjects were roused to anger, but it was reflected only in Rorschach content or in test behavior.

Several of the studies mentioned earlier under content scoring also used formal scoring, and they may be noted briefly. Lit (1956) found that out of 26 scores only S separated superior college students from poor achievers; but it was the superior students who had more S responses, whereas they had significantly *less* hostile content.

Storment & Finney (1953) found that only 1 out of 26 formal Rorschach scores (expected by chance alone) significantly differentiated between violent and nonviolent psychiatric patients. When Finney (1955) replicated the study, he found several of the formal scores were significant, but none of them had been significant in the original study. Thus no formal scores survived replication. Wolf (1957) found that anatomy responses did not differentiate between assaultive and nonassaultive patients. Finally, Sommer & Sommer (1958) could distinguish between assaultive and nonassaultive patients on the basis of color and movement only when content was added to these formal scores.

Comments on the Rorschach

Formal scoring on the Rorschach does not yield measures that are consistently related to aggression. On the other hand, hostile content on the Rorschach is related to a variety of aggressive behaviors in diverse populations. The relationship is a direct one; the more hostile content, the more aggressive the behavior. Thus hostile responses on the Rorschach are best regarded in terms of response sampling of a larger population of hostile responses, rather than in terms of drainage of a reservoir of hostility.

The hostile content scoring systems measure a personality variable of aggressiveness. The few studies of Rorschach hostility in relation to experimentally induced aggression suggest that there is no relationship. It is not clear why this is so. Perhaps the Rorschach can assess enduring behavioral trends but not transient ones. Perhaps the procedures for inducing aggression have been faulty. In any event, hostile content on the Rorschach is related only to long-time trends in aggression.

Hostile content scoring systems work in both normal and deviant populations. The scoring systems vary in complexity, but the simplest of them works as well as the most complex, and merely counting the number of hostile responses constitutes as good a scoring scheme as any devised. What is revealed by hostile content on the Rorschach is not any deep, latent hostility of which the subject is unaware but hostility that he and those around him clearly recognize.

The Rorschach is an unwieldy instrument for quick, efficient assessment of aggressive trends. Because it must be given in its entirety and requires almost an hour to administer, it is a poor measure for laboratory situations. Rorschach hostile content has been shown to separate the ends of the passive-aggressive dimension of personality, but it is incapable of finer discriminations. The Rorschach does not yield information that could not be obtained by other means, and perhaps preference should be given to instruments that focus directly on aggression—in contrast to the Rorschach with its ambitious attempt to assess personality globally.

THEMATIC APPERCEPTION TEST

In contrast to the Rorschach, the TAT is rarely scored in a formal fashion in everyday clinical use. Rather, the TAT is evaluated for thematic content, e.g., the hero, the dominant theme, the outcome of the story. There are almost as many scoring schemes as there are studies, which means that TAT investigations of aggression cannot be divided on the basis of the scoring system used.

A reasonable basis for dividing TAT studies of aggression is the context in which the TAT is used. Like the Rorschach, it has been used in clinical studies of aggression with both normal and deviant populations; unlike the Rorschach it has been used extensively in laboratory investigations of aggression. There are also several studies that do not seem to fall under any one heading and may best be labeled "miscellaneous." Finally, there have been modifications of the TAT for the purpose of more specific study of aggression or for the purpose of converting the TAT into a more objective instrument.

Clinical Studies

Several different populations have been used, and for expositional purposes they have been divided into deviant adults (prisoners and hospitalized patients), college students, and adolescents (normal and delinquent).

Deviant adults. As a captive population with obvious associations to aggression, prisoners have come in for their share of investigation. Stone (1956) divided army prisoners into three groups: (1) nonviolent crimes and no history of violence, (2) desertion with no history of violence, and (3) offenses of murder and intent to kill. Note that the first two groups are nonviolent and the third group is violent. The TAT categories of aggression were death, physical aggression, and verbal aggression, with weights of 3, 2, and 1, respectively. The violent group showed significantly more TAT aggression than the two nonviolent groups. It is noteworthy that this clear relationship between assaultiveness and TAT aggression occurred in a homogeneous population and with a simple scoring system.

Purcell (1956) also used army men as subjects, but they were patients in a psychiatric clinic. Two judges rated their case histories and placed them in one of three groups that varied in degree of antisocial aggressiveness. The TAT protocols were scored for: (1) aggression—fighting, criticizing, lying, cheating by the hero; (2) external punishment—assault, injury, deprivation directed against the hero; and (3) internal punishment—suicide, guilt, injury to a loved object by the hero. In contrast to the least antisocial group, the most antisocial group manifested the following significant differences on the TAT: higher aggression scores; more direct and undisguised aggression; less punishment anticipated; more themes of aggression as an excuse for aggression; fewer themes of punishment unrelated to aggression; and fewer themes of guilt or shame. Themes of guilt or shame constituted the best differentiator between the most and least antisocial groups, though the groups also differed in the strength and directness of TAT aggression.

Scodel & Lipetz (1957) used as subjects schizophrenics in a psychiatric hospital. One group had a history of assault or suicidal tendencies, and the other group had no history of acting out aggressively against either self or others. The TAT scoring for aggression was similar to Stone's, with assault receiving a heavier weight than verbal aggression. There was no significant difference between the groups in TAT aggression. This is not surprising because two kinds of behavior were lumped into a single group, assault and suicide. There is no compelling reason for including in the same group those who attack others and those who attempt to harm themselves, and this grouping negated the possibility of positive findings.

The studies just mentioned used case histories to derive a measure of behavioral aggression; the next group of studies all used ratings of hospital behavior. Pittluck (1950) had nurses evaluate the behavior of their psychiatric patients by means of a check list and ratings, the areas being: frequency of aggression, average rating of aggression, frequency of aggression accompanied by anger, and outbursts of rage. Unfortunately, these four measures are not independent, which makes it difficult to interpret the results of the many tests of significance that were computed. There were 10 scores for aggressive TAT themes, and these were compared with the four behavioral measures. Of the 40 Chi-squares only two were significant at the .05 level, a chance finding. The four behavioral measures were also compared with four measures of defenses against aggression on the TAT, and of the 16 comparisons, two were significant. Since there is no rationale for the way the defense scores were obtained, there is little meaning to these two significant comparisons. Finally, antisocial TAT themes were compared with the four behavioral measures, and one of the four was significant—outbursts on the ward. Thus the one unequivocal finding in Pittluck's study was the relationship between antisocial TAT aggression and outbursts of rage on the ward.

Bialick (1951) had nurses rate psychiatric patients for cooperativeness, dividing them into three groups—from most to least cooperative. The TAT stories were scored for verbal and physical aggression, destructiveness, and misfortune. There were no significant relationships between cooperativeness and TAT aggression, which is not surprising in light of the behavioral criterion. Uncooperativeness included faking symptoms, malingering, and demanding medication after hours, all of which would tend to annoy the nurses. The nurses' ratings of uncooperativeness were probably based as much on their own annoyance as on any aggressive behavior the patients might have displayed, and there is no reason to expect such ratings to be related to TAT aggression.

Another investigation that suffered from an inadequate criterion was Sturm's study (1956) of tuberculosis patients. Nurses rated them for conformity behavior on the ward, and the TAT protocols were scored for aggression and punishment. An aggression/punishment ratio failed to distinguish between conformers and nonconformers, but there was an interesting minor finding: middle class patients manifested more TAT aggression and lower class patients more punishment themes.

Summarizing the studies mentioned so far, several facts stand out. First, the TAT is a good measure of antisocial aggression but not of milder and more social forms of aggression. Second, using case histories as a source of criterion measures of aggressive behavior yields positive results, while ratings of hospital behavior yield negative results (except for outbursts of rage which approach antisocial aggression). Ratings by hospital personnel should be suspect because of their lack of training for the task, and ward behavior may be expected to reveal few instances of aggression, especially in these days of tranquilizers.

The last study in this section concerns a comparison between college normals and psychiatric patients (Haskin, 1958). Haskin distinguished between TAT themes of realistic aggression (constructive ways to overcome frustration, socially acceptable assaultiveness like self-defense against attack) and unrealistic aggression (self-destructive activities, rejection, unjustified assaultiveness, punitive orientation). Realistic aggression was inversely related to unrealistic aggression, and normals had significantly more realistic TAT aggression and less unrealistic aggression than patients. When unrealistic and realistic aggression on the TAT were added together, the normal group scored slightly but not significantly higher. Thus, while there was no difference in over-all aggression between normal and psychiatric groups, there were clear differences in the kind of aggression each manifests on the TAT. Realism of the aggression should perhaps be evaluated whenever normal subjects are being compared with psychiatric patients.

College students. There have been few clinical studies with college students, probably because of the difficulty of obtaining adequate criterion measures of aggressiveness. Lindzey & Tejessey (1956) were able to secure detailed information on young college men who were being assessed as part of a large scale investigation. A psychologist studied the interview and autobiographical data of the subjects and then rated them for aggression. A panel of experts made similar ratings, but theirs were contaminated by a knowledge of the subjects' TAT stories. There were 10 measures of TAT aggression, and one of them correlated significantly (.05 level) with the psychologist's ratings of behavioral aggression. This finding is not very different from what might be expected by chance alone. As an interesting sidelight, subjects' self-ratings of aggression were significantly related to 7 out of 10 TAT aggression scores, five of the correlations being above .50. Evidently the TAT, like the Rorschach, measures aggression that normal subjects are aware of and can verbalize.

Direction of aggression was noted in earlier chapters as a variable that might be important. Davids et al. (1955) conducted a study almost identical to that of Lindzey & Tejessey. This time the TAT protocols were scored for both amount and direction (in or out) of aggression. When only *amount* of TAT aggression was considered, there was no significant relationship between the TAT and either the psychologist's ratings or self-ratings. When *direction* of aggression was added, there were significant findings. "Anger out" on the TAT was associated with a high self-rating of aggression and "anger in" with a low self-rating. Inexplicably, no data were presented concerning the relationship between the psychologist's rating of amount and the TAT determination of anger in versus anger out, but for the psychologist alone, anger out was associated with a high rating of aggression and anger in with low aggression.

A point of confusion arises from these two very similar studies. Lindzey & Tejessey found that TAT aggression and self-ratings were significantly related, but Davids et al. did not. Davids et al. found a relationship between *direction* of TAT aggression and self-ratings of amount but not between amount of TAT and self-ratings. When two investigations as similar as these two fail to agree, there is reason to distrust the results of studies, especially with this number of subjects (20) and without any check on reliability of scoring the TAT or rating of behavioral aggression. In attempting to discover explanations for such discrepant data, perhaps the null hypothesis should not be forgotten.

Two studies of aggression in college students are unusual in that they attempt to relate TAT aggression to athletic activity. Husman (1955) had boxers, wrestlers, cross-country runners, and nonathletes take the TAT before and after the athletic season. The TAT protocols were scored for both amount and direction of aggression. The boxers had significantly less TAT aggression, less anger in, and more anger out than the other three groups. The amount of aggression increased from before to after the athletic season in the athletes but not in the nonathletes.

It might be argued that the low aggression of the boxers indicates that their aggressive urges were being drained off by aggressive athletic activity, assuming that boxing is more aggressive than wrestling or track. If this interpretation were correct, the boxer's TAT aggression would be lower at the end of the season than before the season, some having drained off. This expectation is opposed to the facts. The boxers increased in TAT aggression from before to after the season, like the other athletes. Thus the drainage notion does not hold. It might be more fruitful to regard the boxers as being aware of the intensely aggressive nature of boxing and defensive about their own aggressive tendencies. This would lead to a decrease in the amount of TAT aggression and to a greater turning inward of TAT aggression, both of which occurred in the boxers. It may be assumed that all the athletes were reinforced for aggressive and competitive activity during the season (praise from the coach, victory in competition), and the increased habit strength was reflected in their higher postseason TAT aggression scores.

Stone (1950) investigated TAT aggression in football players and matched controls, with somewhat different results. During the season the athletes and nonathletes did not differ in TAT aggression, but after the season the football players showed significantly less aggression on the TAT. This decrease is directly opposed to Husman's finding of an increase in boxers and track men. It is difficult to reconcile these conflicting results, but it may be concluded that: (1) of the various athletes studied, only boxers differ from nonathletes in TAT aggression and (2) the effect of competitive athletics is not clear. Note that in both studies the person who scored the TAT protocols knew when they had been administered, and there may have been unconscious bias in scoring for aggression. If the biases were to operate in different directions, the results would tend to be conflicting; this possibility cannot be ruled out.

Adolescents. In the study of adolescent aggression the same problems arises that plagues the study of college students: lack of criterion measures of aggression. The problem is not as serious with adolescents because they may also be observed in camp situations, but untrained observers are often used to obtain criterion measures of aggression.

Jensen (1957) had teachers select three groups of high school boys: Aggressive Bad—disruptive, unruly, defiant, destructive, surly; Aggressive Good—active, energetic, leading, tending to debate, competitive; and Passive—quiet, retiring, meek, timid, unassertive, withdrawn. All groups were administered the 10 TAT cards most likely to elicit themes of aggression and violence. The stories were scored for aggression, punishment, and defense, tabooed violence, and tabooed sex. It was found that the Aggressive Good group did not differ from the Passive group on any of the TAT variables, but both groups differed from the Aggressive Bad group. The Aggressive Bad group was highest in the proportion of aggressive stories having no punishment or defense theme, sex themes, tabooed sex themes, tabooed violence and tabooed language. The ordinary (non-taboo) measures of TAT aggression did not separate the aggressive from the passive boys nor the boys with acceptable behavior from the boys with unacceptable behavior. Evidently the best measure of unacceptable behavior is unacceptable themes on the TAT, whether or not they relate to aggression. Thus Jensen's findings are consistent with those of previous studies with other populations. Socially acceptable aggression cannot be distinguished from nonaggression by means of the TAT, but socially unacceptable aggression can be distinguished from nonaggression.

In Jensen's study it was the taboo themes that distinguished between his groups, the usual measure of TAT aggression failing to differentiate between groups. This result is corroborated by Heymann (1955), who had teachers rate their high school students for fighting, swearing, arguing, meanness, negativism, and creating a general disturbance. Ten TAT cards were administered in group fashion, five of the cards being the same as those used by Jensen. The protocols were scored for direct and indirect aggression, punishment, and defense but not for tabooed activities. TAT aggression was unrelated to classroom aggression. This finding, taken together with Jensen's negative findings with the usual TAT measures of aggression, suggests that the TAT is unrelated to the classroom aggressiveness of normal adolescent boys. Only themes of unacceptable behavior are indicants of unacceptable aggression in school.

Mussen & Naylor (1954) investigated TAT aggression in adolescents who had been semi-institutionalized for truancy, stealing, disorderly school behavior, etc. Cottage supervisors filled out a check list containing the following items: physical attack, bragging, threatening, teasing, impertinence, insulting, name calling, ridiculing, bullying, verbal castigation, malicious gossip, destructiveness, and temper tantrums. Ten TAT cards were administered individually, and the stories were scored for aggression and defense. TAT aggression was found to be significantly related to behavioral aggression, as measured by the check list. When TAT punishment was added, the differentiation was even sharper. The most aggressive boys behaviorally had the most TAT aggression and also the least number of punishment themes. Thus behavioral aggression was associated with high habit strength of aggression and little fear of punishment, and lack of behavioral aggression was associated with low habit strength of aggression and strong fear of punishment.

Miller (1953) used as subjects disturbed adolescents in a summer camp, who were given the TAT at the beginning of the camp session. Counselors rated them for physical aggression, and these ratings were compared with a number of TAT aggression variables. Unfortunately, the 12% level of confidence was accepted as significant, which makes the findings highly tentative. The behaviorally more aggressive boys scored significantly higher than the less aggressive boys on these TAT variables: attributing aggression to authority, direct aggression, and acceptance of aggression.

Both Miller and Mussen & Naylor used ratings of aggressiveness as the criterion measure in their studies with deviant adolescents. Gottfried (1958) simply used the categories *delinquent and nondelinquent* and attempted to discover differences in TAT aggression, using Jensen's scoring system. There were four TAT cards and six other pictures designed to elicit stories. For the TAT alone and the stories alone there were no significant differences between the delinquent and nondelinquent groups. When the entire 10 cards were pooled, it was found that the delinquents had significantly *less* thematic aggression. It is difficult to compare this study with the previous two investigations of deviant adolescents because in this study there is no way of knowing how aggressive either group was. One might assume that delinquents are more aggressive than nondelinquents, but there is probably a confounding of social behavior with aggressiveness. Since "delinquent" is a confused, amorphous category, it is perhaps not surprising that there are no clear-cut results when it is used as a criterion measure.

However, this group of studies on TAT aggression in adolescents raises the broader issue of the usefulness of TAT indices of aggression with this population. Jensen differentiated between his groups mainly on the basis of taboo material that rarely appears in TAT protocols, at least in those obtained individually. Miller's results are highly tentative because of his too easy rejection of the null hypothesis. Both Heymann and Gottfried found negative results, which leaves Mussen & Naylor as the only study with unequivocally positive findings. Though TAT is a useful indicant of aggressiveness in other populations, it may be of little use in assessing aggressiveness in adolescents.

Laboratory Studies

In the clinical studies, TAT aggression was related to aggressiveness, i.e., aggressive habit strength as a variable that endures over time. When the TAT is used in the laboratory, its purpose is to measure the short-term changes that are induced in the immediate situation. This requires the assumption that the TAT is sensitive to the transient changes in anger or aggression that occur under laboratory conditions.

Bellak (1944) used the TAT administration itself to induce anger. The subjects were paid college men who were administered 10 TAT cards. For the first five cards the administration was standard, but after the fifth card, the examiner was increasingly critical. The order of presentation was varied systematically, and the "card pull" for aggressive stories was controlled. The stories were analyzed simply by counting the number of aggressive words. Criticism by the experimenter led to significantly more TAT aggression than noncriticism.

Matarazzo (1954) replicated this study with hypertensive and normal men and women, the only change being in some of the TAT cards that had previously gone out of date. This time the number of aggressive words decreased (nonsignificantly) in response to criticism, and the only significant finding was that more normals (all of them women) refused to complete the experiment than hypertensives.

The discrepancy between these two studies points up two problems in this kind of research. First, it is difficult to replicate an experimental procedure in which the independent variable is the experimenter's behavior. One experimenter may incite his subjects to anger, and another may threaten his subjects into submission; it is important to sample the population of experimenters as well as of subjects. Second, differences in subject populations may be crucial. Matarazzo's subjects were clinic patients of both sexes, whereas Bellak's were paid, volunteer college men. The results of subsequent studies may be anticipated by noting that in the laboratory the TAT has worked better with college students than with other populations.

Lindzey & Kalnins (1958) re-analyzed the results of an earlier study in which college men were frustrated. Subjects were made to fail in such a way that they could blame only themselves. Four TAT cards were administered 2 months prior to the frustration and again immediately following frustration. A control group was given the cards at the same interval but without frustration. The stories were analyzed for aggression by the hero against himself, by the hero against others, by others against the hero, and by others against others. TAT aggression before frustration was subtracted from TAT aggression after frustration, each subject being in effect his own control. Also the control subjects' difference scores were subtracted from the experimental subjects' difference scores in order to cancel out the effect of repeated administration of the four TAT cards. It was found that two kinds of TAT aggression increased because of frustration: hero against other and other against hero. Since the category *hero against other* was the most important measure of aggression, these results are positive. Note that the frustration was severe and that the only outlet for anger was telling aggressive stories to TAT cards.

Feshbach (1955) insulted college students in groups, the study having been discussed in earlier chapters. He used four TAT cards, which were rated for aggression. The insulted group manifested significantly more TAT aggression than a control group. Interestingly, only one of the four TAT cards showed a significant difference when they were examined separately, the card that was least ambiguous with respect to aggression (a woman with her hands around the neck of another woman).

Gluck (1955) frustrated army psychiatric patients in a study that was described in the Rorschach section. Like his Rorschach results, his TAT findings were negative: the correlations between ratings of aggressive responses to frustration and TAT aggression approached zero.

In the foregoing studies there were attempts to anger subjects and determine the effect of such anger on TAT aggression. In the remaining studies in this section TAT aggression was related to laboratory aggression in the absence of anger. In a study mentioned earlier, Buss & Foliart (1958) had college students play the role of a person who is aggressively facing someone who has gossiped about him. A control group played the role of someone meeting an old acquaintance. Subjects were run individually by a college-age experimenter, who told all subjects that they had done well at the end of the role playing session. Four TAT cards were administered before and after role playing, and the stories were scored (blind) for violence. The control group showed a slight decrease TAT aggression from pre- to post-role playing, but the experimental group showed an increase that was significant only for male subjects. Thus reinforcement of vicarious aggression (role playing) tended to increase TAT aggression in the men.

The vicarious expression of aggression does not necessarily lead to an increase in TAT aggression; the kind of vicarious aggression, the reinforcement, and the kind of subject will all influence the outcome. Wilson (1958) used as subjects institutionalized adolescents who had committed various crimes. Since they had ostensibly aggressed against authority, they were given five TAT cards that tend to elicit themes of aggression against authority. Several weeks later they participated in a game in which they were required to express aggression, and the TAT cards were again administered. No relationship was found between the amount of aggression expressed during the game situation and aggression in the TAT, and there were no significant changes from before to after the aggressive game. The discrepancy between the results of this and the Buss & Foliart study might be attributed to: (1) a difference in subject populations, (2) a difference in settings—disciplinary versus voluntary; and (3) a difference in reinforcement—definite reinforcement for aggression in the Buss & Foliart study and no clear reinforcement in the Wilson study. One fact favoring the positive findings of the Buss & Foliart study is the consistency with data from other sources, e.g., Feshbach's finding (1958) that vicarious aggression increases aggressiveness and various doll play studies that have shown increases in doll play aggression in relation to reinforcement by the experimenter.

Goodrich (1953) related TAT aggression to the behavior of authoritarian and equalitarian college men in small discussion groups. Authoritarianism was measured by the California F scale, and the TAT stories were scored for aggression directed in, aggression directed out, and total aggression. The relationships were found to be curvilinear. For authoritarians the correlation between behavioral aggression and total TAT aggression was .56; between behavioral aggression and TAT aggression-in, .73; between behavioral aggression and aggression-out, not significantly different from zero. For the equalitarians there were no significant relationships between behavioral and TAT aggression. If it is assumed that the authoritarians are more extreme and less flexible in their group behavior, these results may be explained as follows. The less flexible authoritarians do not shift as much from one situation to the next; when faced with either TAT cards or with others in a group situation, their response is consistently aggressive or nonaggressive. Equalitarians manifest considerably more flexibility, and their behavior in one situation may have little to do with their behavior in the next situation. Thus they might or might not be consistent from group behavior to the TAT.

Miscellaneous Studies

The studies in this section are difficult to classify under the main headings of this section on the TAT. The first is an investigation of the dreams of college men and women, which were compared with their TAT stories (Osterberg, 1951). Both the dreams and the TAT were scored for aggression in the same way, scores being obtained for overt, covert, and total aggression. A number of ratios concerning aggression and various story characters were derived from both the

TAT protocols and the reports of dreams. A total of 48 correlations between TAT and dream aggression were computed, but only one was significant at the .05 level. Thus aggression in dreams does not relate to aggression on the TAT.

In the last two studies, which related Rorschach to TAT aggression, statistical issues cloud interpretation of the results. Carr (1956) compared the Rorschach and TAT protocols of male psychiatric patients, using Chi-squares as the measure of relationship and the 10% level of confidence. He did not state how many tests of significance were computed, but the number must have been large. There were several significant relationships between Rorschach formal scores and content on the one hand and TAT aggression on the other hand, but it is difficult to place much reliance on these findings because: (1) the 10% level of confidence is too lenient in rejecting the null hypothesis; (2) a large number of tests of significance were computed, and some of the results would be expected by chance alone; and (3) many of the measures were related, so that the separate tests of significance were not independent.

Fisher & Hinds (1951) conducted a large-scale investigation of aggression by means of eight different instruments administered to normals, paranoid schizophrenics, and schizophrenics who had attempted suicide. Among the eight instruments were the Rorschach and TAT. Out of a total of 51 tests of significance between the three groups, only eight measures were significant, and these manifested no consistent pattern. The various measures thus failed to discriminate among the three groups. Fisher & Hinds then divided the measures into those concerning "peripheral control" and those concerning "deep level control." They attempted to interpret a series of correlation coefficients by analyzing clusters, rather than by attempting factor analysis. Their interpretations rest on the assumption that the correlations differ significantly from zero. Of their 180 correlations, only 18 are significant at the .05 level, and since several of the variables were not independent, the number of reliably significant correlations is probably very small. Fisher & Hinds developed an elaborate scheme into which they fitted the correlational data. Unfortunately, since they did not distinguish between the 18 significant correlations and the others, there is no way of knowing how reliable are the patterns they describe, and their conclusions rest on precarious grounds. Since their theoretical presentation may have some intrinsic worth (aside from the questionable data), it is presented in a later chapter.

Modifications of the TAT

Stimuli resembling TAT pictures have been designed specifically for the elicitation of aggressive themes. The instructions to subjects are usually the same, and scoring procedures are similar, but with younger subjects the findings have been more positive than TAT studies with adolescents and children.

Kagan (1956) devised 13 pictures for use with middle-class school boys. Every picture contained at least one boy, and four of them depicted several boys in the absence of adults. Teachers rated the subjects for the tendency to start fights, and the ratings were used to divide the total group into five subgroups varying from very aggressive to very nonaggressive. The protocols were scored for fighting between boys, attacking an adult, destruction of property, stealing, and swearing. It was found that the more aggressive the group of boys, the more frequent were fantasy themes of fighting among boys. The other aggressive themes were not significantly related to behavioral aggression, either singly or together.

Since themes of fighting between boys occurred almost exclusively on the four cards with boy-boy interactions (in the absence of an adult figure), four cards were mainly responsible for the significant findings. The four cards were then rated for ambiguity, and it was found that the less ambiguous the card, the greater the number of subjects who produce fighting themes. Furthermore, the differences in thematic aggression between the most and least aggressive boys were much greater on the unambiguous cards than on the ambiguous cards. Even the least ambiguous card was not so well structured that all subjects told stories involving fighting, and in the most aggressive group only three quarters of the subjects gave fighting themes to the least ambiguous card. Of course, a maximally unambiguous card would be worthless because the stimulus would completely determine the response and all subjects would respond the same way. Kagan's pictorial stimuli appear to be of optimal ambiguity: they were structured enough to elicit many aggressive themes, yet discriminated between groups differing in behavioral aggressiveness.

Lesser (1957) used a similar series of 10 pictures that varied in the degree to which aggression is apparent. The subjects were schoolboys who rated each other for aggressiveness by means of the "Guess Who?" technique, e.g., "Here is someone who is always looking for a fight. Guess Who?" Teachers' ratings of aggressiveness correlated .76 with those of the children. The boys' mothers were interviewed to determine their attitudes and practices concerning the control of aggression, and they were divided into two groups: supporting aggression or discouraging aggression. For boys whose mothers encouraged aggression, the thematic versus behavioral aggression correlated .43; for boys whose mothers discouraged aggression, the correlation was —.41; both correlations were significant. The correlation of the entire sample was .07.

Thus the attitude and practices of the mother was a crucial determiner of the relationship between thematic and behavioral aggression. When aggression is encouraged, there is consistency from one situation to the other and a positive relationship between measures. When aggression is punished and discouraged, the less aggression that is manifested in behavior, the more that occurs thematically. For the latter group of boys, thematic responses appear to offer an outlet for their inhibited aggression, which is consistent with the drainage notion of aggressiveness. Lesser's data suggest that the drainage notion may hold for a certain class of subjects, namely those boys whose aggressiveness is inhibited by parental restrictions. Furthermore, the variable of parental control may account for some of the negative feelings with younger subjects. For Lesser's total sample there was no relationship between behavioral and thematic aggression, yet, when he divided his subjects on the basis of parental control of aggression, there were two significant relationships in opposite directions.

Both Kagan and Lesser found clear, positive results, and the basic difference between their investigations and previous ones that yielded contradictory findings is in the stimuli they used: pictures that were oriented toward a population of boys and that were designed to elicit aggressive themes.

The importance of the stimuli is emphasized by Lesser's scaling of his pictures (1958). He computed the percentage of aggressive themes given for each of his 10 stimuli and eliminated three pictures for which the percentages were higher than 80 or lower than 20. He then applied Guttman's scaling procedure and found a coefficient of reproducibility of .91 for the remaining seven pictures, which suggests that aggression is the single dominant variable in these stimuli. Auld, Eron & Laffal (1955) attempted to scale the TAT for aggression, but they found only three cards that elicited aggression with sufficient frequency (the percentages were 78, 22, and 21). For the remaining pictures, the occurrence of aggressive themes was too infrequent to permit scaling. The failure of TAT stimuli to be scaled for aggression is not surprising because it is an "omnibus" instrument, designed to yield information about a wide variety of behaviors.

Perhaps what is needed is an instrument that measures aggression specifically rather than an omnibus instrument.

The construction of a set of pictures specifically designed to assess aggression is no guarantee of positive results because stimulus variables, like ambiguity, and population variables are both important. For example, Burick (1952) devised a set of pictures for use with schizophrenic patients who were judged as overtly aggressive or non-aggressive. The two groups manifested no significant differences in thematic aggression.

Symonds & Jensen (1958) reported a follow-up study on adults who had been tested 13 years earlier (as adolescents) with a set of TAT-like pictures. In the earlier study many subjects had shown an inverse relationship between thematic aggression and behavioral aggression, and this finding has been widely cited as an example of the operation of the drainage principle. Interviews conducted 13 years later revealed that a number of these inhibited subjects (little behavioral aggression, much thematic aggression) did manifest aggressive tendencies subsequently, suggesting that the thematic aggression may have tapped latent aggressive trends. These later findings do not support the drainage notion, and a majority of studies have shown the relationship between thematic and behavioral aggression to be direct, not inverse.

Solkoff constructed a series of aggressive pictures that varied in intensity. The stories told in response to these pictures were scored for reaction time, total number of words, and inhibition. It was found that increasing the intensity of the hostile pictures resulted in significantly fewer words per story and more inhibition. Unfortunately, there was no scoring for hostile content, nor was there a comparison of the thematic material with a behavioral criterion of aggression.

Hurley (1955) used the original TAT pictures but substituted a multiple choice procedure for the usual method of having a subject tell a story. There were four alternatives, one each for Insecurity, Achievement, Hostility, and Blandness (defensiveness). This instrument has been used by several investigators at the State University of Iowa (e.g., Goodstein, 1954; Johnston, 1956), but none of them has related hostility to this Iowa Picture Interpretation Test.

Comments on the TAT

The use of the TAT in studying aggression has led to a confusing array of results, and in this section an attempt will be made to obtain order out of this chaos. The clinical studies yielded one clear-cut positive finding: TAT aggression is directly related to assaultiveness. This generalization holds for prisoners of both sexes and several kinds of patient populations. TAT aggression is not related to assertiveness, uncooperativeness, and other behaviors peripherally associated with aggression. In the clinical studies the most positive results were obtained when the subjects were from a deviant population and when the criterion of aggression was an unequivocal one like assault. Concerning college students, the results of clinical studies are equivocal, and weak positive results seem to emerge only when the direction of TAT aggression is taken into account. The population variable is also important in laboratory studies; the results with college students were clearly positive, and with various deviant populations the results were negative.

Several studies raised the issue of the relationship between TAT aggression and behavioral aggression—direct versus inverse. As with the Rorschach, there were one or two studies that yielded an inverse relationship between thematic and behavioral aggression, but the overwhelming majority of investigations with positive results found that there is a direct relationship between TAT and behavioral aggression. It seems likely that in adults, at least, there is consistency from thematic to behavioral aggression rather than an inverse relationship.

Unlike the Rorschach, the TAT is evidently sensitive to the kind of scoring system used to measure thematic aggression. It is true that simple scoring of aggressive themes did yield positive results, and even so crude a measure as counting the number of aggressive words (Bellak, 1944) proved to be sensitive enough to show changes in aggression. However, addition of a measure of anxiety clearly helped several studies to achieve more positive results, e.g., Mussen & Naylor (1954), achieved much sharper differentiation between groups differing in behavioral aggression when the variable of fear of punishment was added to the scoring for aggression on the TAT. A knowledge of anxiety over the consequences of aggression should help in making better predictions because, as was noted in the chapter on conflict, anxiety becomes attached to aggressive responses early in life. Therefore, a TAT measure of inhibition of aggression (anxiety, fear of punishment, guilt) should lead to a more precise prediction of behavioral aggression. and the data in part confirm this expectation. Other kinds of scoring were also found to be useful in different populations. The direction of aggression was shown to be important. especially in upper middle-class college stu-

154

THE PSYCHOLOGY OF AGGRESSION

dents. In comparing psychiatric patients with normals, the realism of the aggressive themes was an important variable. Finally, scoring for tabooed aggressive activities turned out to be the crucial variable in differentiating adolescent boys who engaged in antisocial aggression.

Research on the properties of the pictures that elicit the thematic material is a recent phenomenon, and several variables have proved to be important in the relationship between thematic and behavioral aggression. For adolescents, at least, it may be important to give them figures of their own age, perhaps so that identification occurs. Furthermore, the relationship between thematic and behavioral aggression is improved when the pictorial materials are scalable for aggression.

Finally, the more ambiguous the picture, the weaker is the tendency to respond with an aggressive story. The less ambiguous the picture, the more clearly is aggression depicted, which means that it is more intense than the neutral, ambiguous picture. Less ambiguous pictures elicit more aggressive responses and more intensely aggressive responses than more ambiguous pictures. Unambiguous pictures are the best stimuli for yielding indicants of behavioral aggression. This conclusion is strengthened by the results of a long-term study by Kagan (1959). He examined the TAT aggressive content of protocols obtained at three different times on the same children, with the total interval averaging approximately 5 years. Physical aggression was one of the few TAT contents to manifest stability on the two retests; stability was for the most part determined by a single card that unambiguously depicted a figure with a weapon.

CONCLUSIONS

The five issues that were raised at the beginning of the chapter have been discussed, and now it is appropriate to deal with the larger questions of the utility of such techniques as the Rorschach and TAT in the study of aggression. There are two major ways in which these instruments may be used: as measures of enduring aggressiveness and as measures of transient, laboratory-induced aggression.

Concerning aggression as a personality variable, the Rorschach and TAT can distinguish between extremely aggressive and extremely nonaggressive groups, but the evidence for finer discriminations is equivocal. Not only is there negative evidence concerning the relationship between projective and behavioral aggression, but a few studies have shown the relationship to be inverse rather than direct. It may be concluded that projective techniques should be used only as gross screening devices to separate groups differing greatly in aggressiveness.

Of course, such devices can be quite useful, and investigators of aggression are in no position to discard instruments that are capable of only gross screening. Contrary to the notion that projective techniques reveal underlying, deep aggressive trends, it is clear that they reveal only those aggressive trends that subjects, if given the opportunity, can verbalize. There seem to be two reasons for this. First, when a subject is administered a projective technique outside of a laboratory setting, he is usually aware that its purpose is personality assessment. Therefore, he inevitably responds with some guardedness, perhaps concealing what he is not ready to admit to others. Second, unambiguous stimuli do the best job of measuring aggression, and with such stimuli the subject must realize that his aggressiveness is being assessed. Thus the less ambiguous the stimuli (and these are the best stimuli for measuring aggression), the more the subject is aware of what area is being tapped and the closer will his projective responses match his self-reports.

It would seem that projective techniques have little to offer concerning measurement of aggression that could not be supplied by self-report techniques like inventories. This is especially true for normal subjects, who are capable of presenting an adequate and minimally defensive picture of themselves when asked in a proper fashion. This is less true of deviant populations, who tend to be either extremely defensive or who may be incapable of presenting a coherent self-picture. Therefore, the projective measurement of aggressiveness should be preferred when the subject is deviant.

Concerning aggression in the laboratory, the TAT and Rorschach offer different possibilities. The Rorschach is not only too long and inflexible but has yet to prove itself in the laboratory. The TAT is more flexible because it is possible to select just the few cards that tend to elicit aggressive trends; also, there is evidence that the TAT reflects laboratory changes in aggression. The positive evidence is restricted to college students, but since they constitute the major population used for the laboratory study of aggression, this restriction is not severe.

The best hope for future projective measurement of aggression would seem to lie in modifications of the TAT. Constructing pictures that focus on aggression and with less ambiguity than the standard series has been shown to lead to an improvement in measuring aggression. Since ambiguity has been shown to be more of a hindrance than a help, converting the TAT from free responding to multiple choice responding (as in the Iowa Picture Interpretation Test) would appear to be a promising innovation.

A final comment concerns exactly what it is that projective techniques measure. Some psychologists believe that projective techniques yield a measure of drive strength of aggression; this is incorrect. The intensity of aggression on projective techniques is determined jointly by habit strength of aggression and transient states of the organism. One of these transient states is anger, which represents aggressive drive if one is a drive theorist. The aggression score of a non-angry individual is determined only by habit strength (plus the inevitable error variance); the aggression score of an angry individual is determined by both habit strength and aggressive drive (anger). Thus an aggression score on a projective technique cannot be used as a measure of drive level because it is also determined by habit strength. Since most testing is done with non-angry subjects, projective techniques yield a measure of habit strength uncontaminated by drive.

REFERENCES

Auld, F., Eron, L. D., & Laffal, J. Application of Guttman's scaling method to the TAT. *Educ. Psychol. Meas.*, 1955, 15, 422–435.

Bandura, A. The Rorschach white space response and "oppositional" behavior. *J. consult. Psychol.*, 1954, 18, 17–21.

Bellak, L. The concept of projection. *Psychiatry*, 1944, 7, 353–370.

Bialick, I. The relationship between reactions to authority figures on the TAT and overt behavior in an authority situation by hospital patients. Unpublished doctor's dissertation, University of Pittsburgh, 1951.

Burik, T. E. An investigation of perceptual and interpretive processes of a group of overtly aggressive as contrasted with a group of overtly nonaggressive schizophrenic patients. Unpublished doctor's dissertation, Fordham University, 1952.

Buss, A. H. & Foliart, R. Role-playing aggression and the catharsis hypothesis. Unpublished research, 1958.

Carr, A. C. The relation of certain Rorschach variables to expression of affect in the TAT and SCT. *J. proj. Tech.*, 1956, 20, 137–142.

Counts, R. M. & Mensh, I. N. Personality characteristics in hypnotically induced hostility. *J. clin. Psychol.*, 1950, 6, 325–330.

Cummings, C. The role of various psychological variables in children's nail biting behavior. Unpublished doctor's dissertation, University of Pennsylvania, 1954.

Davids, A., Henry, A. F., McArthur, C. C., & McNamara, L. F. Projection, self-evaluation, and clinical evaluation of aggression. *J. consult. Psychol.*, 1955, **19**, 437–440.

DeVos, G. A. A quantitative approach to affective symbolism in Rorschach responses. *J. proj. Tech.*, 1952, **16**, 133–150.

Elizur, A. Content analysis of the Rorschach with regard to anxiety and hostility. *J. proj. Tech.*, 1949, **13**, 247–284.

Feshbach, S. The drive-reducing function of fantasy behavior. *J. abnorm. soc. Psychol.*, 1955, **50**, 3–11.

Feshbach, S. The stimulating versus cathartic effects of vicarious aggressive activity. Paper read at Eastern Psychological Assn. meetings, 1958.

Finney, B. C. Rorschach correlates of assaultive behavior. *J. proj. Tech.*, 1955, **19**, 6–16.

Fisher, S. & Hinds, Edith. The organization of hostility controls in various personality structures. *Genet. Psychol. Monogr.*, 1951, **44**, 3–68.

Gluck, M. R. The relationship between hostility in the TAT and behavioral hostility. *J. proj. Tech.*, 1955, **19**, 21–26.

Gluck, M. R. Rorschach content and hostile behavior. *J. consult. Psychol.*, 1955, **19**, 475–478.

Goodrich, D. C. Some manifestations of aggression in authoritarian and equalitarian discussion groups. Unpublished doctor's dissertation, University of Rochester, 1953.

Goodstein, L. Interrelationships among several measures of anxiety and hostility. *J. consult. Psychol.*, 1954, **18**, 35–39.

Gorlow, L., Zimet, P., & Fine, R. The validity of anxiety and hostility Rorschach content scores among adolescents. *J. consult. Psychol.* 1952, **16**, 73–75.

Haskin, P. R. A study of the relationship between realistic and unrealistic aggression, reliance on categorical attitudes, and constructiveness of adjustment. Unpublished doctor's dissertation, Western Reserve University, 1958.

Heymann, G. M. Some relationships among hostility, fantasy aggression, and aggressive behavior. Unpublished doctor's dissertation, Michigan State University, 1955.

Hurley, J. R. The Iowa Picture Interpretation Test: a multiple choice version of the TAT. *J. consult. Psychol.*, 1955, **19**, 372–376.

Husman, B. F. Aggression in boxers and wrestlers as measured by projective techniques. *Res. Quart. Amer. Ass. Hlth. Phys. Educ.*, 1955, **26**, 421–425.

Ingram, Winifred. Prediction of aggression from the Rorschach. *J. consult. Psychol.*, 1954, **18**, 23–28.

Jensen, A. R. Aggression in fantasy and overt behavior. *Psychol. Monogr.*, 1957, **71**, Whole No. 445.

Johnston, R. A. A methdological analysis of several revised forms of the Iowa Picture Interpretation Test. *J. Pers.*, 1956, **25**, 283–289.

Kagan, J. The stability of TAT fantasy and stimulus ambiguity. *J. consult. Psychol.*, 1959, **23**, 266–271.

Kagan, J. The measurement of overt aggression from fantasy. *J. abnorm. soc. Psychol.*, 1956, **52**, 390–393.

Kane, P. Availability of hostile fantasy related to overt behavior. Unpublished doctor's dissertation, University of Chicago, 1955.

Lesser, G. S. Application of Guttman's scaling method to aggressive fantasy in children. *Educ. psychol. Measmt.*, 1958, **18**, 543–551.

Lesser, G. S.   The relationship between overt and fantasy aggression as a function of maternal response to aggression.   *J. abnorm. soc. Psychol.*, 1957, 55, 218–221.

Lindzey, G. & Kalnins, D.   Thematic Apperception Test: some evidence bearing on the "hero assumption."   *J. abnorm soc. Psychol.*, 1958, 57, 76–83.

Lindzey, G. & Tejessey, Charlotte.   Thematic Apperception Test: indices of aggression in relation to overt and covert behavior.   *Amer. J. Orthopsychiat.*, 1956, 26, 567–576.

Lit, J.   Formal and content factors of projective tests in relation to academic achievement.   Unpublished doctor's dissertation, Temple University, 1956.

Lubin, B.   Some effects of set and stimulus properties on TAT stories.   *J. proj. Tech.*, 1960, 24, 11–16.

Matarazzo, J. D.   An experimental study of aggression in the hypertensive patient.   *J. Pers.* 1954, 22, 423–447.

Miller, L. C.   Relationships between fantasy aggression and behavioral aggression.   Unpublished doctor's dissertation, Harvard University, 1953.

Murray, D. C.   White space on the Rorschach: interpretation and validity.   *J. proj. Tech.*, 1957, 27, 47–53.

Murstein, B. I.   The projection of hostility on the Rorschach and as a result of ego-threat.   *J. proj. Tech.*, 1956, 20, 418–438.

Mussen, P. H. & Naylor, H. K.   The relationships between overt and fantasy aggression.   *J. abnorm. soc. Psychol.*, 1954, 49, 235–240.

Osterberg, Mary N.   A comparison of aggression in dreams and TAT stories.   Unpublished master's thesis, Western Reserve University, 1951.

Pattie, F. A.   The effect of hypnotically induced hostility on Rorschach responses.   *J. clin. Psychol.*, 1954, 10, 161–164.

Phillips, L. & Smith, J. G.   *Rorschach interpretation: advanced technique.*   New York: Grune & Stratton, 1953.

Pittluck, P.   The relation between aggressive fantasy and overt behavior.   Unpublished doctor's dissertation, Yale University, 1950.

Purcell, K.   The TAT and antisocial behavior.   *J. consult. Psychol.*, 1956, 20, 448–456.

Radar, G. E.   The prediction of overt verbal behavior from Rorschach content.   *J. proj. Tech.*, 1957, 21, 294–306.

Sanders, R. & Cleveland, S. E.   The relationship between certain examiner personality variables and subject's Rorschach scores.   *J. proj. Tech.*, 1953, 17, 34–50.

Scodel, A. & Lipetz, M. E.   TAT hostility and psychopathology.   *J. proj. Tech.*, 1957, 21, 161–165.

Sjostedt, Elsie M.   A study of the personality variables related to assaultive and acquisitive crimes.   Unpublished doctor's dissertation, Purdue University, 1955.

Smith, J. R. & Coleman, J. C.   The relationship between manifestations of hostility in projective tests and overt behavior.   *J. proj. Tech.*, 1956, 20, 326–334.

Solkoff, N.   Effects of a variation in instructions and pictorial stimuli on response to TAT like cards.   *J. proj. Tech.*, 1959, 23, 76–82.

Sommer, R. & Sommer, Dorothy T.   Assaultiveness and two types of Rorschach color responses.   *J. consult. Psychol.*, 1958, 22, 57–62.

Stone, A. A. The effect of sanctioned overt aggression on total instigation to aggressive responses. Unpublished honors thesis, Harvard University, 1950.

Stone, H. The TAT aggressive content scale. *J. proj. Tech.*, 1956, **20**, 445–452.

Storment, C. T. & Finney, B. C. Projection and behavior: a Rorschach study of assaultive mental hospital patients. *J. proj. Tech.*, 1953, **17**, 349–360.

Sturm, R. J. The relationship between aggressive fantasy and non-conformative behavior. Unpublished doctor's dissertation, University of Texas, 1956.

Symonds, P. M. & Jensen, A. R. The predictive significance of fantasy. *Amer. J. Orthopsychiat.*, 1958, **28**, 73–84.

Towbin, A. P. Hostility in Rorschach content and behavior. *J. abnorm. soc. Psychol.*, 1959, **58**, 312–316.

Vernallis, F. F. Teeth grinding: some relationships to anxiety, hostility, and hyperactivity. *J. clin. Psychol.*, 1955, **11**, 389–391.

Walker, R. G. A comparison of clinical manifestations of hostility with Rorschach and MAPS test performances. *J. proj. Tech.*, 1951, **15**, 444–460.

Wilson, Helen E. Overt and fantasied hostility as a function of channels of expression. Unpublished doctor's dissertation, University of Utah, 1958.

Wirt, R. D. Ideational expression of hostile impulses. *J. consult. Psychol.*, 1956, **20**, 185–189.

Wolf, I. Hostile acting out and Rorschach test content. *J. proj. Tech.*, 1957, **21**, 414–419.

9

Inventories

The inventories to be discussed in this chapter attempt to assess aggression as a personality variable, in contrast to the questionnaires mentioned in Chapter 3, which attempt to assess transient attitudes in the laboratory. Inventories of aggressiveness differ in several ways from projective techniques, and a few of these differences should be mentioned before discussing the inventories themselves.

Projective techniques present ambiguous stimuli and attempt to conceal from the subject the purpose of the instrument. Because the subject's response is relatively unrestricted, it is difficult to score. The emphasis is on dynamics and defenses, and usually qualitative description is all that is attempted. A trained examiner is needed to administer, score, and interpret projective techniques. Inventories, on the other hand, present relatively unambiguous stimuli in the form of questions, and there is little attempt to conceal the content of the questions. The subject's response is severely restricted (yes-or-no, more-or-less), and scoring is merely a matter of counting. The emphasis is on quantitative assessment and on test development procedures: collection of norms, factor analyses, and item analyses. Little attention is paid to dynamics or defenses, and inventories can be administered and scored by a clerk.

The background of projective techniques is psychoanalytic or neo-psychoanalytic theories, which have emphasized the importance of aggression as a personality variable; this emphasis is reflected in the large number of projective studies of aggression. The psychometric orientation that underlies the use of inventories has directed little attention to aggression, and only within the last few years has there been any attempt to assess aggressiveness by means of questionnaires.

In attempting to assess aggression by means of an inventory, one source of items is inventories that already exist. Several investigators have attempted to construct aggression inventories from Minnesota Multiphasic Personality Inventory (MMPI) items. Such inventories are reviewed in the first section of the chapter. Others have started from scratch and constructed their own inventories, and their efforts are reviewed in the second section. The last section of the chapter deals with the development of an aggression inventory by the author and Ann Durkee.

INVENTORIES DERIVED FROM THE MMPI

One of the earliest aggression inventories derived from the MMPI was devised by Moldawsky (1953), who submitted 100 MMPI items to psychologists. These judges were able to agree on 45 items, and these 45 comprise the aggression inventory. Dinwiddie (1954) related this inventory to self-ratings and psychotherapists' ratings of male psychiatric clinic patients. Both sets of ratings took the form of answers to three questions: (1) Compared with others, how hostile is he? Does he bear little hostility or a high degree of ill will, resentment, bitterness, and hate?; (2) How does he tend to perceive the world? Does he perceive it as predominantly hostile, threatening or depriving, or as friendly, nonthreatening and nondepriving?; (3) Does he tend to feel hostile, resentful or rebellious toward adults in authority? Or, is he more inclined to feel compliant and accepting? The statements were reworded for self-ratings and the ratings ranged from one to six. These ratings were correlated with the Iowa Hostility Inventory, with the following results:

Statement	Therapist's Ratings	Self-ratings
1. How hostile	.59	.67
2. Perception of the world	.50	.54
3. Hostile toward authority	.20	.37

All but the .20 correlation are significantly different from zero. The significant correlations between the inventory and self-ratings are not unexpected because of the similarity between self-report (inventory) and self-ratings. The significant relationships between therapists' ratings and the inventory suggest that the inventory has moderate validity. The inventory appears to tap hostility, a generalized negative attitude toward the world.

162 THE PSYCHOLOGY OF AGGRESSION

Therapists's evaluations of their clients would seem to be an excellent criterion measure of aggression and hostility because during the prolonged course of psychotherapy, the therapist has ample opportunity to see through the client's defenses and evasions. On the other hand, much of the therapist's information comes directly from the verbalizations of the client, and there may be a built-in relationship between the therapist's evaluation and the client's self-report. It is necessary to correct for the inherent bias connected with information obtained directly from the subject.

Buss et al. (1956) interviewed psychiatric inpatients, attempting to allow for the patient's bias in describing himself. This attempt was facilitated by their being able to observe the patient's behavior during a half-hour interview. Seven different kinds of behavior were rated:

1. *Resentment*—a feeling of anger over real or fancied mistreatment, verbalized in terms of annoyance, whining, complaining, and demanding.

2. *Suspicion*—an attitude of distrust in which hostility or aggressiveness is projected onto others; included are beliefs of being persecuted and punished.

3. *Verbal*—style of verbalization rather than content; included are yelling, cursing, screaming, arguing, shouting, and being caustic, ironic, and teasing.

4. *Assault*—acts of violence against people or objects; included are fighting and striking others, defending against attack, and breaking or destroying objects.

5. *Indirect*—aggression expressed in a roundabout or passive fashion; included are negativism, recalcitrance, spiteful silence, slamming doors, and such acts as smashing the hated person's car.

6. *Strength of aggressive urges*—the intensity of the urge to aggress, whether or not it was expressed behaviorally.

7. *Over-all rating*—a global assessment of aggression-hostility.

These seven varieties may be grouped into several categories. Resentment and Suspicion clearly fall under the heading of hostility, which has been defined in terms of negative labels and conditioned anger. Verbal, Indirect, and Assault all refer to attacking behaviors of varying styles and directness. Strength of Aggressive Urges does not refer to behavior but rather to something akin to habit strength in the absence of any inhibitions against expressing aggression. The last rating concerns a global evaluation that more or less contained all the previous ratings.

There were four judges, and inter-rater agreement ranged from an average correlation of .77 for Resentment to .95 for Assault, with the exception of Strength of Aggressive Urges, for which the correlation was .57. The lower agreement for Strength of Aggressive Urges may be ascribed to the vagueness of the required rating, which involved inference from behavior rather than behavior itself.

The correlations between the inventory and the pooled ratings are presented in Table 9.1. There are clear-cut sex differences. Only

TABLE 9.1. CORRELATIONS BETWEEN THE IOWA HOSTILITY INVENTORY AND RATINGS OF AGGRESSION AND HOSTILITY

	Men	Women
Resentment	.30	.51
Suspicion	.24	.56
Verbal	.26	.46
Assault	.36	.41
Indirect	.24	.29
Strength of urges	.37	.32
Overall	.39	.54

$p = .05$ when $r = .37$.

two out of seven correlations are significant for men, while five are significant for women. For men, only Strength of Urges and the Over-all Rating were significantly related to the inventory scores. For women, only the two most covert aspects failed to correlate significantly with the inventory scores: Strength of Urges and Indirect. The highest correlations for women were between the inventory and the two hostility categories.

Thus the Iowa Hostility Inventory is significantly related to an over-all measure of hostility-aggression in psychiatric patients, but the relationship is stronger for women than for men. The inventory is significantly related to specific, overt kinds of hostility and aggression in women. For the women only the correlations for the two hostility categories (Resentment and Suspicion) were of the same order—in the fifties—as the comparable correlations for men in Dinwiddie's study.

The Iowa Hostility Inventory has been found to be related to therapist's ratings and interviewer's ratings of psychiatric patients' hostility. Charen (1955) attempted to relate the inventory to nurses' ratings of male tuberculosis patients. The ratings concerned hostility: patient perceives the world as hostile, threatening, depriving; tends to be resentful of authority; inclined to feel unwanted and rejected by others. Two sets of nurses rated the patients, and the correlations with the inventory were not significantly different from zero. These negative findings lead to two possible conclusions. First, nurses' ratings may be a poor criterion of hostility; second, the inventory is not related to hostility in male, hospitalized patients, which is consistent with the findings of Buss et al. (1956).

A study by Smith (1954) offers some evidence of construct validity. He used the Iowa Hostility Inventory to select high and low aggressive groups of college students, who learned hostile and neutral word lists by the paired associates method. The high aggressive group learned neutral words faster than hostile words, but there was no similar difference for the low aggressive group. This is not strong evidence, but it does suggest that the inventory is relevant to hostility, since it leads to positive results concerning the learning of hostile material. The evidence from these studies leads to the conclusion that the Iowa Hostility Inventory is an adequate measure of hostile attitudes, but its value in assessing aggressiveness has yet to be demonstrated.

Another MMPI-derived hostility inventory was devised by Cook & Medley (1954) in the course of developing an inventory of teacher attitudes. From 250 items relating to teacher attitudes, 77 were selected as reflecting hostility. These were judged for hostility by five clinical psychologists, who agreed on 50 of the items; these 50 comprise the hostility inventory.

McGee (1954) related the Cook-Medley inventory to two tasks, using college students as subjects. The first task involved associations to 10 hostile words. Judges rated responses as hostile or non-hostile, and response time was recorded. Neither measure correlated significantly with inventory scores. The second task involved the subject's judging Szondi pictures as dangerous, tricky, deceitful, or none of these. This "danger" score was found to correlate .44 with inventory scores, suggesting that the inventory is related to perception of others as threatening. This is in accord with the statement by Cook & Medley that their hostility scale "reveals a type of individual characterized by dislike for and distrust of others." (p. 418)

Merrill & Heathers (1956) report a significant correlation of .33 between the Cook & Medley scale and the Aggression scale of the Edwards Personal Preference schedule. Snoke (1955) used the inventory to select high and low hostile college men, and then observed their behavior in a small group situation. There were two degrees of clarity in the situation, and it was found that high hostile men perceived the ambiguous situation as less ambiguous than low hostile men. There were no significant differences between high and low hostile men in either willingness to participate in discussion or in their evaluation of whether the sessions were worthwhile. Among the high hostile men, those who agreed to attend the sessions and then failed to appear had significantly higher inventory scores than those who attended. Thus the study offers weak evidence that the Cook & Medley inventory is meaningfully related to laboratory activities that ostensibly tap hostility. The positive findings are in part negated by the failure to find a significant difference between high and low hostile men in their evaluation of the sessions. It appears that the Cook & Medley inventory has less to recommend it in terms of positive findings than the Iowa Hostility Inventory.

A third MMPI-derived hostility scale was constructed by Siegel (1956). He began by selecting 110 MMPI items and adding four of his own. These were trimmed to 50 by four judges, the basis of selection being 80% agreement. The 50-item scale was administered to male college students and applicants to a mental hygiene clinic. In addition, the Rorschach and the California F scale were given.

The rank-order correlations between the hostility inventory and Elizur hostile content on the Rorschach approached zero for both groups of subjects. The F scale was used to divide each sample into high, middle, and low authoritarians. In both the college and clinic samples, high authoritarians scored significantly higher on the hostility inventory than low authoritarians; assuming authoritarians are hostile, this finding is evidence for construct validity of Siegel's hostility scale. On the other hand, it should be noted that both the F scale and the inventory are paper-and-pencil self-report measures, and both are susceptible to the same kinds of response sets. Furthermore, some of the item contents overlap. The relationship between authoritarianism and Siegel's hostility inventory would be more meaningful if the measuring instruments were clearly independent.

The three previous inventories were all derived rationally; one or more judges selected items from the MMPI believed to tap hostility or aggressiveness. Schultz (1954) used a strictly empirical approach, selecting only those items that correlated with a criterion. He used five different criteria, all based on therapist ratings of male psychiatric clinic patients: (1) adequacy of methods of dealing with hostility, (2) frequency of overt aggression, (3) direction of aggression, (4) duration of aggressive impulses prior to expression, and (5) frequency of covert aggression.

The ratings for each criterion were divided into quartiles, and the upper and lower quartiles were used to select items. Since there are 550 MMPI items and five criteria, 2750 statistics were computed. Using the .10 level of confidence, 574 items were significantly related to the five criteria (there being item overlap among the five sets). Thus, approximately one fifth of the total possible combinations proved to be significant at the .10 level, with slightly less than half of these being expected to attain the .10 level by chance alone (275 out of 2750). Therapists' ratings and MMPIs were collected on a new sample, and of the 574 items, 55 held up on replication.

Schultz discovered that several of the therapist's rating categories were related. Adequacy of dealing with hostility and duration of aggressive impulses correlated .63; therefore, the latter category was dropped and its items added to adequacy of dealing with hostility. Similarly, a correlation of .66 between frequency of overt aggression and direction of aggression led to the latter's being dropped and its items added to frequency of overt aggression. The final inventory consisted of three categories, with a total of 55 items related to them.

These 55 items were derived from 2750 total possible combinations. Even with the "shrinkage" that is inevitable in cross-validation, Schultz was assured of retaining a fair number of items by chance alone. Further shrinkage with a new sample seems highly probable, and examination of the content of some of the items strengthens this argument. Significantly related to adequacy of dealing with hostility in both samples were:

My daily life is full of things that keep me interested.

I used to keep a diary.

If I were a reporter, I would very much like to report sporting news.

I very much like horseback riding.

The other two categories contain similar items that have no connection with aggression or hostility. All three categories also include items whose content deals with hostility and aggression, but there are many "fillers" of the type listed above, and surely these would disappear with further replication. When the initial pool of items is sufficiently large, a fair number of significant items is guaranteed by chance alone. When there is no rationale for selection of items, it is necessary to be more conservative in setting confidence limits, e.g., the .01 level rather than the .10 level of confidence.

OTHER INVENTORIES

Fisher (1956) used the same empirical approach as Schultz but carried the process through to a second replication. He started with a pool of 667 items (newly constructed or borrowed) and administered them to 20 male psychiatric patients, 10 assaultives and 10 nonassaultives. The assaultives had struck or kicked someone at least twice in 6 months with minimal provocation, and the nonassaultives had no record of any such aggression. Of the original 667 items, 221 were found to discriminate between the two groups. These were tried on new groups of assaultive and nonassaultive patients, and the number of discriminating items dropped to 13. The point biserial correlation between assaultive-nonassaultive groups and scores on these 13 items was .54.

The 13-item scale was then given to a third sample, which contained patients from various psychiatric hospitals. The correlation dropped to .33. This is the kind of shrinkage that was predicted for Schultz's inventory had he used a third sample, and it makes clear the dangers of the empirical approach in the absence of a guiding rationale. A single replication may be insufficient when the original pool of items is very large.

Inventories typically involve self-report, with the content of the items being undisguised. Bass (1956) developed a hostility scale based on agree-disagree responses to proverbs. The proverbs represented Murray's list of needs, and an initial pool of 300 was administered to approximately 2000 subjects. A factor analysis yielded four factors, one of them labeled Hostility and consisting of the needs Aggression, Autonomy, and Rejection (loadings of .76, .65, and .64, respectively). Next, the 300 items were item-analyzed, using the method of upper and lower 25% of the groups; this yielded 30 items for the hostility scale.

Bass then collected norms for different groups, e.g., salesmen, nurses, marines (1957). The following significant differences were found for the hostility scale:

1. Salesmen score higher than nonsalesmen.
2. Prisoners score higher than nonprisoners.
3. High school students score higher than college students.
4. Southerners score higher than non-Southerners.

In addition, the scale correlated .29 with the Cook & Medley hostility scale. This low correlation suggests that though the scales have the same name, they are measuring different behaviors. Bass' careful construction of the hostility scale and collection of norms for a variety of groups contrasts with several of the inventories mentioned previously.

One of the 15 scales on the Edwards Personal Preference Inventory (EPPS) is labeled Aggression (Edwards, 1954). This scale includes the following:

To attack contrary points of view.
To tell others what one thinks of them.
To criticize others publicly.
To make fun of others.
To tell others off when disagreeing with them.
To get revenge for insults.
To become angry.
To blame others when things go wrong.
To read newspaper accounts of violence.

The EPPS is a forced-choice inventory, the first self-report instrument to control for social desirability. Items were matched for social desirability in order to preclude choosing an alternative simply because it would appear better in the eyes of others. The EPPS has been administered to numerous groups within the population, and norms for the various groups are available (Klett, 1957). Edwards (1954) reported that men score significantly higher on aggression than women. So far the aggression scale has not been related to aggressive behavior, either in field studies or in the laboratory, and it will be interesting to see how it holds up against such criteria.

Zaks & Walters (1959) have devised the most recent aggression scale. As part of a larger inventory, 33 items were administered to assaultive criminals and noncriminal controls, all men. Twelve items discriminated between the two groups, and these constitute the aggression scale; four of the items refer to difficulties with the law or rationalizations for crime. The 12-item scale was then administered to several other populations. It was found that institutionalized juvenile offenders score significantly higher than high school controls and that drug addicts score significantly higher than controls. It would be interesting to discover whether the discrimination between these two institutionalized groups and their controls was due mainly to the four items dealing with the law, but no item analysis data are reported.

In a second study (Walters & Zaks, 1959), aggression scores were found to be higher for a group just frustrated than for a group taking the scale in the usual way. The scale was also related to the peer ratings of young adult members of a community center. Those rated in the upper third of aggressiveness scored significantly higher on the scale than those rated in the lower third.

Thus the aggression scale discriminated between the extremes of aggression in normal and criminal populations, and it reflects the effect of frustration. These findings suggest that this brief scale has considerable promise. One limitation of the results is the reliance on *t* tests, to the exclusion of correlation coefficients. Examination of the means and standard deviations reveals considerable overlap in the various distributions reported in the two studies. When the number of subjects is large (as it was in these studies), small differences in means yield significant *t* values. It would be interesting to see correlations between this potentially valuable scale and other measures of aggressiveness.

THE BUSS-DURKEE INVENTORY[1]

With the exception of Schultz's scale, all the aggression-hostility inventories reviewed previously have been omnibus instruments. They tap a variety of hostile attitudes and aggressive behaviors and combine all of these into a single score. The unstated assumption made in using a single summary score is that hostile-aggressive behaviors do not need to be divided into subclasses. Thus a suspicious, nonassaultive person might receive the same score as a nonsuspicious, assaultive person.

In constructing the Buss-Durkee inventory the alternate assumption was made: it is necessary and useful to divide hostile-aggressive behavior into subclasses. Initially the subclasses used in the Buss, Durkee & Baer study (1956) were used, but these were elaborated further into the following:

1. *Assault*—physical violence against others. This includes getting into fights with others but not destroying objects.
2. *Indirect aggression*—both roundabout and undirected aggression. Roundabout behavior like malicious gossip or practical jokes is indirect in the sense that the hated person is not attacked directly but by devious means. Undirected aggression, such as temper tantrums and slamming doors, consists of a discharge of negative affect against no one in particular.
3. *Irritability*—a readiness to explode at the slightest provocation. This includes quick temper, grouchiness, exasperation, and rudeness.
4. *Negativism*—oppositional behavior, usually directed against au-

[1] Much of the material in this section is taken from Buss & Durkee, 1957.

thority. This involves a refusal to cooperate that may vary from passive noncompliance to open rebellion against rules or conventions.

5. *Resentment*—jealousy and hatred of others. This refers to a feeling of anger at the world over real or fancied mistreatment.

6. *Suspicion*—projection of hostility onto others. This varies from merely being distrustful and wary of people to beliefs that others are being derogatory or are planning harm.

7. *Verbal aggression*—negative affect expressed in both the style and content of speech. Style includes arguing, shouting, and screaming; content includes threats, curses, and being overcritical.

This classification includes two kinds of hostility (resentment and suspicion) and five kinds of aggression (assault, indirect, irritability, negativism, and verbal). A Guilt category was added because of interest in observing the relationship of the inhibiting influence of guilt to the expression of behaviors that are often inhibited. Guilt was defined in terms of feelings of being bad, having done wrong, and suffering pangs of conscience.

Item-Writing Techniques

A pool of items was written and supplemented with items borrowed from previous inventories. Items should be worded so as to minimize defensiveness in responding. It has been established that social desirability accounts for much of the variance of a normal's responses to inventories. In attempting to facilitate respondents' admitting socially undesirable behavior, three item-writing techniques were employed:

First, assume that the socially undesirable state already exists and ask how it is expressed; "When I really lose my temper I am capable of slapping someone," "When I get mad, I say nasty things." In these items the loss of temper is assumed and the subject is asked only whether he expresses it. This procedure emphasizes a report of behavior and tends to minimize the value judgments associated with hostility.

Second, provide justification for the occurrence of aggression; "Whoever insults me or my family is asking for a fight," "People who continually pester you are asking for a punch in the nose," "Like most sensitive people, I am easily annoyed by the bad manners of others." When the item provides a rationale for aggression, the subject's defensive and guilt reactions are reduced, and he does not necessarily answer in the direction of social desirability.

Third, use idioms; "If somebody hits me first, I let him have it," "When I am mad at someone, I will give him the silent treatment." Idioms have a high frequency of usage in everyday life, and these phrases are typically used by subjects to describe their own behavior and feelings to others. Therefore, when such phrases apply, they should be readily accepted and admitted.

Item Analysis

The first version of the inventory consisted of 105 items, with items from each scale randomly scattered throughout the inventory. It was administered in group fashion to 85 male and 74 female college students. In an attempt to reduce defensiveness, all protocols were anonymous. The various scales were scored, and separate item analyses were performed for men and women (see Buss & Durkee, 1957, for details of the item analysis).

Item analysis yielded 75 items, 66 for hostility and 9 for guilt. The items comprising the final form of the inventory are listed in

TABLE 9.2. ITEMS COMPRISING THE INVENTORY

Assault

  1. Once in a while I cannot control my urge to harm others.
 2F. I can think of no good reason for ever hitting anyone.
  3. If somebody hits me first, I let him have it.
  4. Whoever insults me or my family is asking for a fight.
  5. People who continually pester you are asking for a punch in the nose.
 6F. I seldom strike back, even if someone hits me first.
  7. When I really lose my temper, I am capable of slapping someone.
  8. I get into fights about as often as the next person.
  9. If I have to resort to physical violence to defend my rights, I will.
  10. I have known people who pushed me so far that we came to blows.

Indirect

  1. I sometimes spread gossip about people I don't like.
 2F. I never get mad enough to throw things.
  3. When I am mad, I sometimes slam doors.
 4F. I never play practical jokes.
  5. When I am angry, I sometimes sulk.
  6. I sometimes pout when I don't get my own way.
 7F. Since the age of ten, I have never had a temper tantrum.
  8. I can remember being so angry that I picked up the nearest thing and broke it.
  9. I sometimes show my anger by banging on the table.

TABLE 9.2. (*Continued*)

Irritability

   1. I lose my temper easily but get over it quickly.
2F. I am always patient with others.
   3. I am irritated a great deal more than people are aware of.
   4. It makes my blood boil to have somebody make fun of me.
5F. If someone doesn't treat me right, I don't let it annoy me.
   6. Sometimes people bother me just by being around.
   7. I often feel like a powder keg ready to explode.
   8. I sometimes carry a chip on my shoulder.
   9. I can't help being a little rude to people I don't like.
10F. I don't let a lot of unimportant things irritate me.
  11. Lately, I have been kind of grouchy.

Negativism

1. Unless somebody asks me in a nice way, I won't do what they want.
2. When someone makes a rule I don't like, I am tempted to break it.
3. When someone is bossy, I do the opposite of what he asks.
4. When people are bossy, I take my time just to show them.
5. Occasionally when I am mad at someone I will give him the "silent treatment."

Resentment

1. I don't seem to get what's coming to me.
2. Other people always seem to get the breaks.
3. When I look back on what's happened to me, I can't help feeling mildly resentful.
4. Almost every week I see someone I dislike.
5. Although I don't show it, I am sometimes eaten up with jealousy.
6F. I don't know any people that I downright hate.
7. If I let people see the way I feel, I'd be considered a hard person to get along with.
8. At times I feel I get a raw deal out of life.

Suspicion

1. I know that people tend to talk about me behind my back.
2. I tend to be on my guard with people who are somewhat more friendly than I expected.
3. There are a number of people who seem to dislike me very much.
4. There are a number of people who seem to be jealous of me.
5. I sometimes have the feeling that others are laughing at me.
6. My motto is "Never trust strangers."
7. I commonly wonder what hidden reason another person may have for doing something nice for me.

TABLE 9.2. (*Continued*)

8. I used to think that most people told the truth but now I know otherwise.
9F. I have no enemies who really wish to harm me.
10F. I seldom feel that people are trying to anger or insult me.

Verbal

1. When I disapprove of my friends' behavior, I let them know it.
2. I often find myself disagreeing with people.
3. I can't help getting into arguments when people disagree with me.
4. I demand that people respect my rights.
5F. Even when my anger is aroused, I don't use "strong language."
6. If somebody annoys me, I am apt to tell him what I think of him.
7. When people yell at me, I yell back.
8. When I get mad, I say nasty things.
9F. I could not put someone in his place, even if he needed it.
10. I often make threats I don't really mean to carry out.
11. When arguing, I tend to raise my voice.
12F. I generally cover up my poor opinion of others.
13F. I would rather concede a point than get into an argument about it.

Guilt

1. The few times I have cheated, I have suffered unbearable feelings of remorse.
2. I sometimes have bad thoughts which make me feel ashamed of myself.
3. People who shirk on the job must feel very guilty.
4. It depresses me that I did not do more for my parents.
5. I am concerned about being forgiven for my sins.
6. I do many things that make me feel remorseful afterwards.
7. Failure gives me a feeling of remorse.
8. When I do wrong, my conscience punishes me severely.
9. I often feel that I have not lived the right kind of life.

Table 9.2. Each item is grouped with the other items in its scale, and the False items are marked "F."

Factor Analyses

The final form of the inventory was administered in group fashion to 85 college men and 88 college women. The eight scales were scored, and product-moment correlations were computed among them for men and women separately. The correlation matrices are presented elsewhere (Buss & Durkee, 1957). None of the women's correlations was above .50 and only two of the men's were above .50, indicating that the various scales are tapping at least partially independent classes of behavior. Thurstone's centroid method was used to extract two factors from each correlation matrix. The axes for men and women were rotated to the same oblique, simple structure so that the factor loadings of the two sexes would be comparable. These loadings are presented in Table 9.3, with loadings .40 or above marked with an asterisk.

TABLE 9.3. ROTATED FACTOR LOADINGS FOR MEN AND WOMEN

Variable	Men		Women	
	I	II	I	II
Assault	.17	.54*	.19	.61*
Indirect	.19	.40*	.00	.48*
Irritability	.11	.57*	.14	.47*
Negativism	.23	.22	−.03	.48*
Resentment	.59*	.12	.57*	.04
Suspicion	.66*	−.02	.54*	.02
Verbal	.05	.63*	.04	.49*
Guilt	.29	.03	.50*	.28

There is no universally accepted criterion for the size of factor loadings, and it is necessary to choose some arbitrary cut-off point. Accordingly, only factor loadings of .40 and over are considered meaningful. On this basis the first factor is defined by Resentment and Suspicion for men, and by Resentment, Suspicion, and Guilt for women. The second factor is defined by Assault, Indirect, Irritability, and Verbal for both sexes, with the addition of Negativism for women. Both Guilt and Negativism had positive loadings on their respective factors for the men and the sex differences just noted are slight. The men's and women's factor loadings are generally similar, differences being small and random. Since the same axes were used for men and women, this similarity of factor loadings suggests that the factor structure is stable.

The two factors extracted from the correlation matrix roughly parallel hostility and aggression. Negativism, which is part of the first factor for women does not fit in with this scheme. However, Resentment and Suspicion clearly fall under the heading of hostility, having to do with the attitude that involves negative labels, e.g., "People are no damn good." Assault, Indirect, and Verbal all fall under the heading of aggression, having to do with a variety of attacking responses: direct and indirect, physical and verbal. Irritability comes closest to anger: loss of temper, "blood boiling," impatience, "powder keg," etc. But irritability is an enduring disposition to become angry, and, therefore, it is not surprising to find that Irritability loads up on the Aggression factor. Thus the factor analysis reveals that the inventory assesses behaviors that fall under the headings used throughout the book: aggression, anger, and hostility. The factorial evidence strengthens the case for this analysis of aggression and hostility, though the Guilt and Negativism loadings for women do not fit too well.

Stability

A group of 29 college men and women were retested in group fashion after a 5-week interval. The product-moment correlations for the two testings were:

1. Assault	.78
2. Indirect	.72
3. Irritability	.65
4. Negativism	.46
5. Resentment	.61
6. Suspicion	.67
7. Verbal	.72
8. Guilt	.64
Sum 1–7	.82

These correlations indicate moderate stability for most of the scales and poor stability for Negativism. The Negativism scale contains only five items, which probably reduced the correlation to a considerable extent. The opposite effect is seen in the test-retest correlation of .82 for the summary score, which included 66 items. Thus the item analyses, which reduced the number of items of each scale, tended to work against stability. In order to add items and thereby increase reliability of the scales, it would be necessary to adopt less stringent criteria for item analysis. It was felt that allowing some unreliability was the lesser of the two evils.

Norms

The collection of norms for a new instrument is a long-range endeavor, and in the present instance the process has just begun. Several sets of norms are available on college students and psychiatric patients. The first set of norms for college students was collected at Indiana University on 85 men and 88 women, and the data are presented in Table 9.4. Inspection of this table reveals that the only appreciable sex difference was for Assault, and the higher score for men is not surprising in light of cultural training regarding physical aggression.

TABLE 9.4. MEANS AND STANDARD DEVIATIONS FOR INDIANA SAMPLE

	Men		No. of	Women	
	Mean	SD	Items	Mean	SD
1. Assault	5.1	2.5	10	3.3	2.3
2. Indirect	4.5	2.2	9	5.2	2.0
3. Irritability	5.9	2.7	11	6.1	2.8
4. Negativism	2.2	1.3	5	2.3	1.2
5. Resentment	2.3	1.9	8	1.8	1.6
6. Suspicion	3.4	2.1	10	2.3	1.8
7. Verbal	7.6	2.7	13	6.8	2.6
8. Guilt	5.3	1.9	9	4.4	2.3
Sum 1–7	30.9	10.2	66	27.7	8.8

TABLE 9.5. NORMS FOR UNIVERSITY OF PITTSBURGH STUDENTS

	Men		Women	
	Mean	SD	Mean	SD
1. Assault	4.6	2.6	2.9	2.0
2. Indirect	4.2	2.1	4.6	2.1
3. Irritability	3.9	2.5	4.5	2.2
4. Negativism	1.8	1.1	1.9	.9
5. Resentment	1.2	1.7	1.3	1.4
6. Suspicion	1.7	1.7	1.8	1.4
7. Verbal	7.2	2.6	6.0	2.3
8. Guilt	3.2	2.1	4.1	1.9
Sum 1–7	24.6	*	22.9	*

* These SDs were not available.

A second set of norms was collected at the University of Pittsburgh on 50 men and 85 women, and they are presented in Table 9.5. The Pittsburgh sample has lower scores than the Indiana sample on every scale. The samples are, of course, from different regions, but the data were undoubtedly affected by another variable—anonymity. The Pittsburgh inventories were signed, and the Indiana inventories were anonymous. Thus regional differences and anonymity were confounded.

Data reported by Dr. James Flynn[2] with Washington State College students suggest that the anonymity variable is of greater significance than regional differences. He administered the inventory to two groups, one anonymous and one signed, and the results are presented in Table 9.6. The scores for the anonymous inventories are

TABLE 9.6. WASHINGTON STATE COLLEGE SAMPLE

	Anonymous				Signed			
	Men (N = 73)		Women (N = 104)		Men (N = 70)		Women (N = 58)	
	Mean	SD	Mean	SD	Mean	SD	Mean	SD
1. Assault	5.2	2.5	3.1	1.9	4.9	2.7	2.9	1.9
2. Indirect	4.8	2.4	5.0	2.0	4.4	2.1	4.9	2.0
3. Irritability	5.5	2.4	5.4	2.5	5.1	2.6	4.6	2.0
4. Negativism	2.3	1.4	2.1	1.3	1.9	1.2	1.9	1.2
5. Resentment	2.1	1.9	1.7	1.7	1.9	1.7	1.3	1.4
6. Suspicion	2.7	1.9	2.1	2.1	2.6	1.7	1.8	1.4
7. Verbal	7.3	2.8	5.8	2.6	7.4	1.9	5.5	2.7
8. Guilt	4.6	2.1	4.6	2.2	3.8	2.7	3.3	2.4
Sum 1–7	35.1	10.2	29.7	10.7	33.4	9.4	27.3	9.2

consistently higher than those of the signed inventories, with few exceptions. The differences are small but consistent. Since in most instances the respondents sign their names, it seems best to use the signed norms rather than the anonymous norms.

The last set of norms comes from Dr. Charles Spielberger,[3] who collected data on 29 men and 31 women, students at Duke University. He reports Verbal scale scores of 7.87 and 6.42 and Sum Hostility scores of 31.26 and 25.00, for men and women, respectively. These scores for signed inventories are similar to the scores of the Indiana sample for anonymous inventories.

Two conclusions emerge from the four sets of college norms: (a) there are no consistent regional differences and (b) the scores are slightly higher when the inventory is taken anonymously than when it is signed.

The inventory has also been tried out with psychiatric patients, the

[2] Personal communication.
[3] Personal communication.

first sample consisting of 53 men and 114 women from Carter Me-
morial Hospital, Indianapolis. The data are presented in Table 9.7.

The scores for the signed patients's inventories differ from those
of the various samples of college students reported above, but the
signed patient's scores are more similar to the signed college scores
than to the anonymous ones. Comparison of patients' with students'
scores reveals: (1) the students generally score lower on Resentment
and Suspicion, suggesting a lower intensity of hostility and (2) the
students generally score higher on Verbal. If these self-reports are
taken at face value, the psychiatric patients are more hostile but
verbally less aggressive. This pattern is consistent with clinical de-
scriptions of many patients as being unable to express openly the
deep resentment they harbor.

TABLE 9.7.   NORMS FOR CARTER HOSPITAL PSYCHIATRIC PATIENTS

| | Men | | Women | |
	Mean	SD	Mean	SD
1. Assault	3.3	2.2	2.5	2.2
2. Indirect Hostility	3.6	2.0	3.9	2.0
3. Irritability	5.0	2.8	5.7	2.8
4. Negativism	1.6	1.4	1.6	1.0
5. Resentment	2.9	2.0	2.6	1.7
6. Suspicion	3.3	2.2	3.3	2.5
7. Verbal	5.3	2.7	4.7	2.7
8. Guilt	5.6	2.0	5.5	2.2
Sum 1–7	24.9	12.8	23.8	11.4

Dr. James Flynn also administered the inventory to psychiatric
patients from Eastern State Hospital, Medical Lake, Washington,
with approximately half signing it and half remaining anonymous.
The data are presented in Table 9.8. The anonymous patients
scored higher on every scale, corroborating the similar finding with
college students. The signed inventory scores agree reasonably well
with the scores for the Carter Hospital sample (also signed). Most
of the differences are small, and the few larger differences follow no
systematic pattern. The anonymous Eastern State Hospital scores
are, of course, higher than the signed Carter Hospital scores.

Concerning the norms for both college and psychiatric patient
populations, some of the differences may be attributed to anonymity,
but even when anonymity is not a variable, there are differences
among samples. The differences between patients and college stu-

TABLE 9.8. Norms for Eastern State Hospital Patients

| | Anonymous | | | | Signed | | | |
| | Men (N = 49) | | Women (N = 77) | | Men (N = 52) | | Women (N = 73) | |
	Mean	SD	Mean	SD	Mean	SD	Mean	SD
1. Assault	4.8	2.8	3.0	2.3	4.1	2.3	2.9	2.1
2. Indirect	3.7	2.5	3.7	2.2	3.4	2.4	3.1	2.1
3. Irritability	5.0	2.6	4.9	2.8	4.0	3.0	4.2	2.4
4. Negativism	2.1	1.4	2.1	1.4	1.8	1.4	1.6	1.4
5. Resentment	3.1	2.0	3.0	2.0	2.2	1.9	2.2	1.8
6. Suspicion	4.6	2.6	4.4	2.9	3.1	2.3	3.0	2.5
7. Verbal	6.4	3.1	5.5	2.8	5.7	3.0	4.9	2.7
8. Guilt	5.4	2.3	5.4	2.3	4.7	2.7	4.6	2.3
Sum 1–7	35.0	13.2	31.9	12.7	28.9	13.2	26.4	10.6

dents follow a pattern that makes sense in terms of a clinical approach to aggression and hostility in disturbed individuals; but within the college and patient populations differences from one sample to the next appear to be random. These random variations may be attributed to unreliability of the scales. Fortunately, for most of the individual scales the differences from one sample to the next are less than 1.0.

Social Desirability

Responses to inventory items are determined in part by the respondent's desire to place himself in a favorable light. This tendency assumes great importance in a hostility inventory, which deals with behaviors that are generally regarded as socially unacceptable. Edwards (1953) had college students assign each of 140 personality trait items to one of nine intervals of social desirability. Scale values for social desirability were obtained by the method of successive intervals. Then the 140 items were administered to different college students, with standard inventory instructions. The correlation between social desirability and probability of endorsing the items was .87. Subsequent studies with other inventories have confirmed the fact that social desirability is an important uncontrolled variable in many present-day inventories.

In constructing the present inventory, an attempt was made to minimize the variable of social desirability. In order to test the success of this attempt, the 66 hostility items of the final inventory were scaled for social desirability, using the method of successive intervals. The judges were 85 male and 35 female college students. The men's and women's judgments were quite similar, and they were pooled. Next, the inventories of 62 men and 58 women (who had previously taken the inventory and were different from the judges) were used to determine the probability of endorsement for each of the 66 hostility items. The product-moment r's were .27 for the men and .30 for the women. Both correlations are considerably lower than the .87 reported by Edwards. The diminished effect of social desirability on responding to the Buss-Durkee inventory may be attributed to the techniques employed in item construction: (a) assuming that anger was present and inquiring only what kind of attack ensued; (b) providing justification for admitting aggressive acts; and (c) including cliches and idioms that would find ready acceptance. These techniques are in marked contrast to both Edwards' list of unelaborated personality trait names and virtually all inventories, the construction of which includes no attempt to manipulate the wording of items.

The importance of item-writing techniques was further demonstrated by Buss (1959) who systematically varied styles and observed their effect on social desirability and frequency of endorsement. It was found that with item content controlled, item style was responsible for variations in frequency of endorsement that ranged from 26 to 48%. In addition, there were significant effects of style on social desirability.

SUMMARY AND CONCLUSIONS

In contrast to projective techniques, inventories have received little use in the study of aggression, and they have yet to be established as adequate measures of aggressiveness. It is not so much a matter of negative findings as of a paucity of research, and it may well be that inventories will prove to be efficient measures of aggressiveness in a variety of populations.

For the most part, aggression inventories tap a variety of aggressive behaviors and yield a single omnibus score. The items are usually selected from a larger pool of items by judges, and often there is no underlying rationale of item analysis. These comments apply to the majority of inventories, the exceptions being the Iowa Hostility Inventory and the Zaks-Walters Aggression Scale, which have been related to clinical and laboratory measures of aggression.

However, the inventory that appears to show the most promise is the Buss-Durkee Inventory. Whatever the bias involved in this assertion, there are facts to sustain it. The items were selected on the basis of a rationale, which consisted of a classification of the varieties of aggressive behavior. In constructing items, several different item-writing techniques were used in an attempt to minimize artifacts in the subjects' responding. The inventory was developed along standard test construction lines, with the use of item analysis, factor analysis, and the collection of norms. The factor analysis yielded two factors that are consistent with the frequently used division between aggressiveness and hostility. Responses to the inventory were found to be relatively free from the influence of the social desirability variable.

The inventory is being used as part of a large-scale study of aggression and hostility in psychiatric patients; a full report of this study will be published in the near future. Tentative findings indicate that the inventory shows a weak relationship with clinical ratings of aggression and a strong relationship with performance on the scrambled sentences task, operant level of hostile responding, and the Iowa Picture Interpretation Test. A preliminary factor analysis of the patients' inventories fails to yield factors of aggressiveness and hostility. However, factor analysis of three sets of clinical ratings yield factors of aggressiveness and hostility that are virtually identical to those found in college students' inventories.

REFERENCES

Bass, B. M. Development of a structured disguised personality inventory. *J. appl. Psychol.*, 1956, **40**, 393–397.

Bass, B. M. Validity studies of a Proverbs Personality Test. *J. appl. Psychol.*, 1957, **41**, 158–160.

Buss, A. H. The effect of item style on social desirability and frequency of endorsement. *J. consult. Psychol.*, 1959, **23**, 510–513.

Buss, A. H. & Durkee, Ann. An inventory for assessing different kinds of hostility. *J. consult. Psychol.*, 1957, **21**, 343–348.

Buss, A. H., Durkee, Ann, & Baer, M. The measurement of hostility in clinical situations. *J. abnorm. soc. Psychol.*, 1956, **52**, 84–86.

Cook, W. W. & Medley, D. M. Proposed hostility and pharisaic-virtue scales for the MMPI. *J. appl. Psychol.*, 1954, **38**, 414–418.

Charen, S. The awareness of hostile feelings in patients by their nurses. *J. consult. Psychol.*, 1955, **19**, 290.

Dinwiddie, F. W. An application of the principle of response generalization to the prediction of aggressive responses. Unpublished doctor's dissertation, Catholic University of America, 1954.

Edwards, A. E. *Manual for the Edwards Personal Preference Schedule.* New York: Psychological Corp., 1954.

Edwards, A. L. The relationship between the judged desirability of a trait and the probability that the trait will be endorsed. *J. appl. Psychol.,* 1953, **37,** 90–93.

Fisher, M. G. The prediction of assaultiveness in hospitalized mental patients. Unpublished doctor's dissertation, Pennsylvania State University, 1956.

Klett, C. J. Performance of high school students on the Edwards Personal Preference Schedule. *J. consult. Psychol.,* 1957, **21,** 68–72.

McGee, Shanna. Measurement of hostility: a pilot study. *J. clin. Psychol.,* 1954, **10,** 280–282.

Merrill, R. M. & Heathers, Louise B. The relation of the MMPI to the Edwards Personal Preference Schedule. *J. consult. Psychol.,* 1956, **20,** 310–314.

Moldawsky, Patricia. A study of personality variables in patients with skin disorders. Unpublished doctor's dissertation, State University, Iowa, 1953.

Schultz, S. D. A differentiation of several forms of hostility by scales empirically constructed from significant items on the Minnesota Multiphasic Personality Inventory. Unpublished doctor's dissertation, Pennsylvania State College, 1954.

Siegel, S. M. The relationship of hostility to authoritarianism. *J. abnorm. soc. Psychol.,* 1956, **52,** 368–373.

Smith, J. G. Influence of failure, expressed hostility, and stimulus characteristics on verbal learning and recognition. *J. Pers.,* 1954, **22,** 475–493.

Snoke, M. L. A study in the behavior of men students of high and low measured hostility under two conditions of goal clarity. Unpublished doctor's dissertation, University of Minnesota, 1955.

Walters, R. H. & Zaks, M. S. Validation studies of an aggression scale. *J. Psychol.,* 1959, **47,** 209–218.

Zaks, M. S. & Walters, R. H. First steps in the construction of a scale for the measurement of aggression. *J. Psychol.,* 1959, **47,** 199–208.

10

Personality theories of aggression

The theories of aggression included in this chapter are for the most part psychoanalytic or neo-psychoanalytic, and in general they emphasize broader aspects of aggression than behavioral approaches. Freud's approach and its offshoots assume the presence of unconscious processes, systems of inner tension, bodily oriented concepts (oral, anal, phallic), inner and outer life, superficial and deep level controls, and so on. The observations from which these theories arose and which are used to support them have been made in clinical situations, and there have been only rare attempts to subject the theories to rigorous test. Laboratory study is rejected as being too atomistic and artificial; only in the clinic can the whole person be seen. Because of the clinical derivation of the theories, they are oriented toward psychopathology. Most of the theories emphasize the critical period of early childhood in the development of enduring aggressive trends.

The theories deal with aggressiveness and hostility as global variables, and because of the sweeping nature of the statements, there are no precise predictions that can be tested under controlled conditions. Acceptance of them is based not on how well they predict or the tenability of their assumptions but on how well they account for what is known about the developmental or psychopathological aspects of aggression. Acceptance is not a matter of evaluating evidence but a strategic judgment of the best bet for explaining quasi-empirical facts. Which theory is accepted is determined by one's training and general orientation to psychology, and the ultimate test of these theories will be their survival over time, rather than their survival of a series of experimental tests. In light of these considera-

183

tions there will be no critique of the personality theories of aggression, only an account of the major ones plus the author's ideas concerning aggressiveness.

Freud

Any account of personality theories of aggression must begin with Freud. Since his ideas about aggression underwent considerable change during his long creative period, it seems best to treat his views historically. They may be divided into three phases. In his earliest writings Freud was preoccupied with libido (sexual energy) and psychosexual development, as he attempted to establish the notion that sexuality (defined broadly) underlay all neurotic conflicts. The emphasis on libido had the effect of relegating aggression to a minor role, aggressive impulses becoming manifest only in relation to the stages of psychosexual development. In the late oral stage the child acquires teeth, and his tendency to bite objects (including the mother's breast) is an expression of oral-sadistic impulses. The peak of aggression is reached during the anal stage, when sadistic urges to hurt and dominate others are notable for their frequency and intensity. Finally, in the Oedipal stage, rivalry with the same-sex parent for the love of the opposite-sex parent leads to death wishes toward the hated rival. In this scheme sadism appears first in the sequence, and only later is masochism seen (as the inversion of outwardly directed aggressive impulses).

In the next phase of Freud's theorizing he explored more fully the question of "ego instincts," and nonlibidinal urges played an increasingly important role in his formulations. He was no longer as concerned with the source of instincts as with their aims, e.g., the prototype of an ego instinct would be hatred (which has an aim) rather than hunger (which has a source but no particular aim). The general aim of ego instincts was self-preservation, and the major constituent of such instincts was aggression. Aggressive trends were thus transferred from aspects of libido to part of the ego instincts, and Freud believed that aggressive urges could occur in the absence of sexual conflict:

> The ego hates, abhors and pursues with intent to destroy all objects which are for it a source of painful feelings, without taking into account whether they mean to it frustration of sexual satisfaction or gratification of the needs of self-preservation. Indeed, it may be asserted that the true prototypes of the hate relation are derived not from sexual life, but from the struggle of the ego for self-preservation and self-maintenance. (1925, vol. 4, p. 81)

This revision of earlier views emphasized the reactive nature of aggressive urges. Their source was not biological, as were sexual urges, but in the self-preservative tendency of the ego to strike back at whatever threatens it or denies it satisfaction. This reactive view was adopted two decades later by the Yale group, who expressed it in more behavioral terms as the frustration-aggression hypothesis (Dollard et al., 1939).

The destructiveness of World War I evidently had a profound effect on Freud's theorizing, and subsequently he gave aggressiveness an even more important role in his theorizing. Freud's final theory of aggression is more balanced in terms of the polarities that characterize psychoanalytic theories; life-death, expression-suppression, tension-increase versus tension-decrease. The novelty in the revision was the postulation of a death instinct,[1] which represents the organism's wish to return to the state of nothingness whence it emerged. This notion is consistent with the "conservative" nature of all instincts, which orient the organism toward conservation of energy, i.e., a return to a tensionless state. The death instinct is opposed by the life instinct, which consists of both libido and self-preservative tendencies. Both life and death instincts have the aim of reducing tension, the life instinct seeking release mainly from sexual tension and the death instinct seeking release from the tension of simply living. Since all life is a tension state that ends with death, the death instinct predominates ultimately. The organism's wish to return to the passive, tensionless state of death is opposed by the life instinct, whose aim is to maintain life and allow the release of only sexual tension, not all tension.

If the organism did not prevent death instinct from fulfilling its aim, death would soon ensue; and the deaths that ostensibly occur when infants are not fondled are cited by Freudians who adopt this view. Most individuals do not allow this primal self-destructiveness to manifest itself in behavior; self-destructiveness is opposed by the life instinct, which succeeds, at least in part, in turning destructive urges from the self to external objects. The life history of every individual may be construed as a struggle between the life and death instincts, ending only when the life instinct is no longer capable of opposing the death instinct. The stronger the death instinct in a person, the more necessary is it for him to direct aggression outward against objects and people. Whatever aggression is not vented against external objects will be turned back on the self. In this

[1] In the literature "death instinct" has been used both as a singular and as a plural phrase (death instincts); the singular will be used throughout the chapter.

scheme there is a primal masochism (self-destructiveness) that must be directed outward and turned into sadism; to the extent that it is not expressed in sadism, this aggressiveness is turned back on the self in the form of secondary masochism. This is clearly an inversion of the earlier formulation, in which sadism antedated masochism.

In this final formulation, the parallel between sexual instinct and destructive instinct is exact. Sexual instinct derives from life instinct, which also includes self-preservation. In the developmental scheme of sexual instinct, primary narcissism (self-love) is followed by object libido, i.e., love is diverted from the self to external objects. This may be followed in turn by secondary narcissism, a return to self-love, when sexual impulses cannot be completely discharged onto external objects.

Destructive instinct derives from death instinct. In the developmental scheme of destructive instinct, primary masochism is followed by sadism; aggressiveness is diverted from the self to external objects. This may be followed by a return to (secondary) masochism when destructive impulses cannot fully be discharged against external objects. Thus narcissism and masochism follow parallel paths during the developmental sequence.

Freud realized that there is no direct evidence for the existence of a death instinct, but he reasoned that the absence of its manifestations was due to its being a "silent instinct." Its actions are ostensibly concealed by those of the more obvious and flamboyant life instinct, which blocks and fuses with the death instinct in order to prevent it from fulfilling its aim. The most direct fusion of life and death instincts leads to masochism, the pleasurable experiencing of pain. Freud was not concerned with behavioral proof of the death instinct because he believed that the existence of any instinct was a matter best reserved for chemists to decide. He predicted that eventually instinct would be placed on a firm foundation of physiology, a belief that is consistent with his biological approach when discussing the fundamentals of behavior.

Reactions of Freudians

Freud's theory of the death instinct split psychoanalysts into three camps. One group accepted it fully; one group rejected the death instinct with its metaphysical connotations but accepted aggression as an instinct of equal importance with libido; and the third group rejected the entire revision, retaining Freud's earlier version of aggression as reactive and noninstinctual.

Complete acceptance. Even among those who fully accept death instinct there is room for a difference of opinion, and this group may be divided into the extremists and the moderates on the basis of whether they are willing to consider any modifications. The views of Nunberg (1955) may be taken as an example of the extremists. He follows Freud in regarding the death instinct as silent and not striving for objects but is more active than Freud in seeking evidence for it. He regards an infant's gnawing at its fingers or toes as evidence of primal masochism, the earliest manifestation of the death instinct. He distinguishes between this primal masochism and "actual" masochism, in which the death instinct fuses with narcissistic libido to acquire an erotic tinge. Nunberg also proceeds further than Freud in attempting to specify the "organs" of aggression; he notes that, just as the genital is the instrument of sexuality, the striped muscles of the extremities and trunk constitute the instrument of aggression.

Nunberg's view of psychosexual development deviates from that of other Freudians mainly in the way he sees the oral period. He assumes that from the earliest period the destructive instinct attempts to protect the ego from *all* external stimuli. When tension in the erotogenic zones of the mouth disturbs the infant's rest, this tension is projected to the mother's breast, which must be destroyed. The early oral period is marked not only by primal masochism (gnawing on his own fingers and toes) but also by cannibalistic tendencies to incorporate the mother, or at least her breast. In the anal-sadistic period the child acts out wishes to take possession of and destroy objects, using as a means of aggression the muscles of the extremities and trunk. The phallic period is also marked by destructiveness, but now inflicting pain is associated with pleasurable genital sensations, as hatred of objects appears for the first time.

Waelder also accepts death instincts (1956) but has more moderate views. He distinguishes between reactive and essential destructiveness, the former arising from three sources. First, there are threats to ambition or self-preservation and frustration of libidinal impulses; second, there are aggressive by-products of the ego's attempts to control its own body and to master the external world; and third, aggression may be a part of libidinal drive, as in incorporation and penetration fantasies. Aggression from these three sources is reactive, and there is no need to postulate a death instinct.

Essential destructiveness, on the other hand, requires postulation of a death instinct because the aggression is too deeply rooted in the individual to be ascribed to any other source. Consider psychotic acts of murder and suicide, and acts of revenge that occur 10 or 20 years after their instigation; Waelder argues that such acts cannot be accounted for by a transient, reactive aggressiveness but must be attributed to an inborn drive to destroy.

Partial acceptance. Most psychoanalysts reject the metaphysical notion of death instinct but accept aggression as an instinct. Loewenstein (1940), one of the leading proponents of this view, distinguishes three aspects of the theory of death instinct:

1. A primary self-destructive instinct
2. The turning outward and projection of self-destructive instinct, which leads to aggression
3. Destructiveness as an independent instinct, opposed to the united sexual and life instincts.

He rejects the first two assumptions but accepts the third, and in collaboration with others (Hartmann, Kris & Loewenstein, 1949) has formulated a theory of aggression as an independent instinct, as follows.

Libido and aggression may be compared as to source, nature of discharge, and aims. Certain organ zones are the source of both stimulation and gratification of libido, but aggression is not zone-specific as to source or gratification, and the zones involved in discharge involve widespread musculature. Aggressive discharge is less structured than libidinal discharge, but there are elements of fore-pleasure and satisfaction in aggressive behavior as well as in sexual behavior. While the aims of sexuality are diversified, the aims of aggression are rigid and narrow; but the plasticity of aggression may be seen in the variety of *means* that can lead to satisfaction.

Hartmann et al. reject the formulation that internalized aggression leads to self-destruction because internalized aggression, once it has been neutralized by the ego, constitutes part of the motive power of both the ego and superego. Internalized aggression is necessary for the normal development of the superego, and only in rare instances of psychopathology is the superego self-destructive.

The impact of aggression may be modified by four processes: (1) the destructive urge may be displaced from the original "object" to "objects" that do not retaliate or are not prized by society; (2) the aims of aggression may be restricted by a scaling down of the intensity of the act, e.g., intent to injure becomes intent to humiliate; (3) aggression may be sublimated and directed into socially acceptable channels, such as fighting disease or crime; and (4) there may be a fusion of aggression with libido, e.g., mastery of man over woman in the sexual act.

Although these various means of modifying aggressive urges are at the disposal of the ego, it cannot prevent conflicts over aggression. Hartmann et al. outline four kinds of conflict. The first may be labeled instinctual conflict: aggressive drive versus the libido when both are directed toward the same object. The dual impulse to love and destroy the same person must lead to severe conflict and turmoil. Most affectional relationships are marked by ambivalence, but individual members of society fail to understand the dual nature of their feelings toward another. It is considered reprehensible to harbor ill will toward loved ones. Often aggressive urges are repressed, to the accompaniment of considerable anxiety and guilt.

The second kind of conflict is between instinct and reality. The aggressive act would be met with retribution, endangering the aggressor. No one can escape punishment for his aggressive acts, at least not during childhood, and the awareness of punishment for aggression sets up an approach-avoidance conflict.

The third type of conflict is similar to the first type, but it involves only the ego. The ego may identify with the "object" of destructive urges; the child identifies with the parent against whose domination he is rebelling. Since the ego has an investment in the victim, any attack against the victim is similar to an attack against the self.

The fourth type of conflict involves the superego. When the lessons of civilization ("Thou shalt not . . . .") have been well learned, the inhibitions against aggression are strong. After parental disapproval of aggression has been introjected, there is self-disapproval whenever aggression occurs. The discharge of aggressive drive is held back by the superego, which severely punishes the ego for transgressions. If the conflict becomes severe, thought may be equated with action, and the superego punishes the ego merely for the impulses to aggress.

The outcomes of these conflicts depend on the strength and maturity of the ego and superego. An immature ego has weak identifications and is insufficiently aware of reality; consequently there will be little inhibition of aggressive urges. An undeveloped superego has not introjected the values of society, and it fails to inhibit aggressive acting out. On the other hand, the ego may overestimate the danger of possible punishment and place excessive inhibitions on aggressive acts. Similarly, the superego may be too demanding, refusing to allow even the mildest forms of aggression. Finally, in the mature individual there is a balance between instinctual demands for aggression and ego inhibitions against aggression, permitting the expression of modulated aggression along lines that do not endanger the ego and are acceptable to society. When there is a clear danger signal, the normal individual can aggress; but if danger situations become sexualized, the result is likely to be masochism, i.e., danger and pain become a source of sexual stimulation.

In the face of danger, aggressive energy has only two courses, discharge or internalization. *Internalized aggression* may follow three paths: (1) it may be neutralized by the ego in ways outlined above, with the individual's integrity remaining intact; (2) it may be used by the superego to attack the ego via guilt feelings; and (3) it may become a source of self-destructive impulses. This last path reveals a crucial difference between the doctrine of aggressive instinct and the doctrine of death instinct. The death instinct doctrine states that there is a primal masochism that must somehow be turned outward against others; the aggressive instinct doctrine states that there is a primal aggressiveness against others that may be turned inward under certain circumstances.

Building on the formulation of Hartmann et al., Beres (1952) described the varieties of maladaptive behavior that result from faulty fusion of aggression and libido. Oral drive merging with aggression may lead to insatiable demands for food and its psychic equivalent, nurturance, e.g., continued demands for attention and affection (aggressive helplessness). Combined aggressive and anal drive may lead to clutching, possessive love, in which the person must dominate and ensnare the partner; or it may lead to sadism, which is seen early in childhood in tormenting animals and later in the infliction of pain. In combination with phallic drive, aggressive drive may give rise to exhibitionism and competitiveness.

Rejection. Most European psychoanalysts accept the doctrine of death instinct; most American psychoanalysts reject death instinct but accept the notion of aggressive instinct. Some psychoanalysts reject both notions; they adhere to Freud's previous view of aggression as a reaction to frustration. The writings of Saul serve to illustrate the last position.

Saul (1956) notes that there is no evidence that hostility is inherited and immutable, and he emphasizes the importance of events during the early formative years in the genesis of hostility:

Hostility is a disease of development and has its chief sources within the personality. The distortions which cause it may be in the id (excessive demands, dependence, envy and the like), in the superego (either through hostile imagos which stimulate hostility or through deficiencies and disorders of standards and ideals), or finally in the ego (the highest faculties), insofar as an individual's whole way of thinking and outlook are warped by the persisting emotional effects of unwholesome childhood influences. (1956, p. 61)

Non-Freudian Psychoanalytic Views

Within the psychoanalytic movement there were a number of deviations from Freudian doctrine, the earliest and most important being those of Adler and Jung. During the last few decades there have been numerous modifications of psychoanalytic theory, but of the latter-day deviationists only Horney has written extensively on aggression. Psychoanalytic views are, of course, not limited to psychoanalysts, and there have been systematic contributions from psychologists. The major statement on aggression by a psychoanalytically oriented psychologist is that of Munroe, and her views will be discussed after those of Adler, Jung, and Horney.

Adler. Many of Adler's previously untranslated writings were translated by Ansbacher & Ansbacher (1956), and the following account leans heavily on their volume. Adler's early views on aggression date back to 1908, but his approach is similar to that of many present-day psychoanalysts. He saw aggression as a drive (instinct) toward fighting for satisfaction of all needs, a drive not restricted to a single organ or organ system. Aggressive drive dominates all aspects of motor behavior: in pure form aggression is seen in fighting and cruelty; in modified form in sports and war; and when directed against the self, in masochism and exaggerated submissiveness.

Aggressive drive may be directed into a number of channels or modes of expression. If it is expressed in fantasy by an artist or poet, the creation will show cruelty or destructiveness. If it is expressed in terms of an individual's occupation, it may show up in such diverse roles as criminal, revolutionary, or police officer. Or it may undergo cultural transformation and emerge as converse behavior (reaction formation), as in charitableness, sympathy, and altruism.

In normals, aggression is seen predominantly in modified and modulated forms, but in neurotics and psychotics it is more intense and naked. It can be seen directly in temper tantrums, hysteria, epilepsy, and paranoia—all directed against others. Directed against the self, it emerges as hypochondria, hysterical pain, accident neurosis, ideas of reference and persecution, or self-mutilation and suicide. In this early formulation, anxiety was seen as a phase of aggression inverted against the self, occurring only when aggression is suppressed. The inverted aggression (anxiety) may be expressed in the motor system as tremors and in other body systems as blushing, palpitations, sweating, and vomiting.

Freud knew about these 1908 views of Adler, and in a paper written in 1909 he stated his reaction:

Alfred Adler, in a suggestive paper, has recently developed the view that anxiety arises from the suppression of what he calls the "aggressive instinct," and by a very sweeping synthetic process he ascribes to that instinct the chief part in human events, "in real life and in the neuroses" . . . . I cannot bring myself to assume the existence of a special aggressive instinct alongside of the familiar instincts of self-preservation and of sex, and on an equal footing with them. It appears to me that Adler has mistakenly hypostatized into a special instinct what is in reality a universal and indispensable attribute of all instincts and impulses—their "impulsive" and dynamic character, what might be described as their capacity for initiating motion. Nothing would remain of the other instincts but their relation to an aim, for their relation to the means of reaching that aim would have been taken over from them by the "aggressive instinct." In spite of all the uncertainty and obscurity of our theory of instincts I should prefer for the present to adhere to the usual view, which leaves each instinct its own power of becoming aggressive. (1925, vol. 3, pp. 281–282)

Many years later Freud was forced to recant his strict opposition to aggression as an instinct, but he never agreed with Adler. When Freud elevated aggression to an equal position with libido, it was in the form of death instinct that could be turned outward toward external objects. He refused to the end to acquiesce to Adler's views on aggression, despite their partial similarity to his own. History has many strange quirks. While most Freudians have rejected Freud's doctrine of death instinct, they have accepted the notion of aggression as an instinct; but it is clear from both Adler's 1908 paper and Freud's reply, that the idea of an instinct of aggression and the ways in which it is manifested are Adlerian.

Adler tended to play down the role of aggression in his later formulations. Aggression was no longer considered a drive (instinct), but a partly conscious, partly irrational reactive tendency toward overcoming obstacles and everyday life tasks. It was seen as subordinate to a general striving for superiority and power, aggression being a pathological form of the more general tendency to "overcome."

Thus the paths of Adler and Freud crossed, going in opposite directions. Adler's formulation of aggression as a basic (biological) instinct yielded to a later view of aggression as reactive and non-instinctual and of relatively minor importance. Freud started out by assigning aggression to a minor role; then promoted it to a major ego instinct; and finally gave it equal status with libido as an instinct (death instinct). It changed from a reactive tendency to a basic, biological tendency of the individual.

Jung. Jung did not spell out his views on aggression in detail, and they may be stated briefly. He grouped life and death instincts into a single drive, libido. This single, all-encompassing drive becomes differentiated in its manifestations into polar opposites, e.g., life-death, love-hate. Since libido is dynamic, when one aspect does not operate, its opposite must function: when it cannot create, it must destroy. When an undifferentiated function sinks to a lower level in the unconscious, it necessarily becomes destructive.

Note the contrast to Freud's doctrine of death instinct. Freud opposed death instinct with life instinct, and the various personality processes reflected the fusion and conflicts between these polar opposites. Jung started out with a single instinct, out of which emerged the polar opposites of life and death instincts.

Horney. Horney (1939, 1945) was explicit in rejecting both death and aggressive instincts. She attributed aggressiveness and hostility to the individual's response to "basic anxiety." Basic anxiety supplies the core motivation for all tendencies; briefly it is " . . . the feeling a child has of being isolated and helpless in a potentially hostile world." (1945, p. 41) The response to this feeling may crystallize into one of three patterns: moving toward, moving against, and moving away from people. In the normal person all three approaches are possible, and the individual is capable of shifting his approach as conditions demand it. The neurotic, however, is stuck in one or the other of these three molds and is incapable of shifting.

The individual who moves against people is an aggressive personality. He takes for granted the hostile nature of the world and reacts by fighting; people cannot be trusted, and in the jungle of life one must strike first. Beyond fighting for his own protection, he is also strongly motivated toward revenge, which is closely related to sadism. As might be expected, Horney rejects sexuality as the basis for sadism. She traces the roots of sadism to hopelessness and futility. The miserable person, unhappy with his own lot and jealous of others' happiness, seeks to impart suffering to others. His own self-loathing must be projected onto others, and by hating them, he has less need to hate himself: "The degrading of others not only allays his intolerable self-contempt but by the same token gives himself a feeling of superiority." (1945, p. 206) His torture of others not only projects his self-hatred but also lifts him from self-negating futility by allowing him to step on those he humiliates. The sadistic individual thus lives aggressively and destructively, but he achieves meaning for his life only vicariously, i.e., through the suffering he causes.

Horney makes hostility an all-pervasive tendency rooted in rejection. The child wishes only to be cared for and loved, hopes only that the world will be kind. Since the world is not a comfortable, warm place and because some rejection and hostility are inevitable, there must be at least some hatred in everyone. What is not made clear is the basis for some individuals tending to move against others, while others tend to move away. In the face of rejection and hostility, moving against people is no more probable than moving away from them, and Horney's failure to state the conditions for the development of one or the other tendency is a weakness in her theorizing.

Munroe. Munroe's views may be described as eclectic psychoanalytic. While she is predominantly Freudian, her position reflects other psychoanalytic views, and, in part, those of modern psychology. She notes that several different kinds of behavior are lumped under the heading of aggression and attempts to distinguish between them. Some aspects of aggression, she argues, stem from the ordinary activities of the individual as he makes his way in the world. While they might be interpreted as aggression, they are more likely " . . . essentially neutral behavior, or a by-product of the effort to establish an effective idea of the self." (1955, p. 635)

Another aspect of aggression is the emotional response to danger or frustration, namely rage. Unlike sex or hunger, rage is a response to an external stimulus, rather than a tension arising from within the organism. Yet the antecedents of rage are so universal in early childhood, and the rage response is so much more than an appropriate reaction to stimuli that it has the same drive qualities as sex and hunger. Thus Munroe comes close to an instinctual view of aggression, without becoming involved in the theoretical complexities of instinct doctrine.

Fisher & Hinds. Psychoanalytic theory makes extensive use of the hydraulic analogy, with implications of deep level tensions exerting pressure on surface structures. The analogy is spelled out in some detail by Fisher & Hinds (1951), who compare normal with patho-logical control over aggressive impulses. They distinguish between deep level hostility, which is entirely unconscious, and peripheral hostility, which is under more conscious control. In the normal per-sonality, surface and deep level controls over aggression function as follows. Surface controls operate primarily to discharge anger out-ward and secondarily to turn anger inward; the number of outward channels should exceed the number of inward channels. Outward channels function cooperatively, so that when one channel is directing hostility outward, the others are also operating. On the other hand, the relationship between outward-directing and inward-directing channels is reciprocal: the more hostility directed outward, the less directed inward.

Normal deep level control involves a distinction between hostile urges associated with guilt and hostile urges associated with assertive-ness (which do not arouse anxiety). The adjusted person does not confuse these two kinds of aggressive urges. Deep level assertive urges are allowed expression, but anxiety-laden aggression is in-hibited. The inhibition of disturbing hostile urges is not complete because there is at least minimal drainage in order to prevent the build-up of too much tension due to unexpected deep level urges. When such urges do accumulate, there is an increase of peripheral hostility directed outward and a decrease of peripheral self-blame, both of which allow sufficient drainage of deep level impulses (like water spilling over a dam).

Maladjustment tends to disrupt the functioning of this complex system of controls. Mild maladjustment affects only peripheral con-trols, leaving deep level controls unaffected; deep level controls must be left free to operate in an organized fashion, and, fortunately, they show the greatest resistance to disturbance. As the personality dis-turbance becomes more severe, deep level controls become more disorganized. In the extreme of maladjustment, psychosis, the major effect is on deep level controls, surface controls remaining virtually unaffected. The psychotic cannot distinguish between realistic ag-gressive urges and those laden with guilt or anxiety. All aggressive urges are inhibited, and too many are directed inward by peripheral controls. The subsequent tension serves to increase confusion and disorganization, creating a spiral of ever-increasing turmoil. Surface controls cannot channel enough of the deep level hostile impulses, and in persons with suicidal tendencies the resulting tension may spark an attempt at self-destruction.

Aggression as an Instinct

Aggressive instinct is, in the main, an accepted notion in psychoanalysis. The various arguments for an instinct of aggression, self-destruction, or destruction may be summarized briefly. Aggression is pervasive and universal, and much aggression cannot be explained on a reactive basis; psychotic acts of murder, suicide, or long-awaited revenge. The phenomena of sadism and masochism indicate the presence of an innate pleasure in inflecting pain on others or the self. There is an unlearned physiological pattern for rage, the predecessor of attack. Finally, aggression occurs so early in development that it must be innate.

In evaluating these arguments it may help to mention some recent views on instinct. The major basis for assuming an instinct appears to be the presence of unlearned behavior, but it is difficult to establish whether a given behavior is unlearned, especially in humans. Because of this difficulty, the learned-unlearned dichotomy has been discarded, just as the earlier heredity-environment dichotomy was discarded. Instinct may be a useful notion for summarizing a complex behavioral sequence, but it cannot be used as a motivational construct without circularity (Allee et al., 1953). Particularly relevant to the study of aggression is the point made by Beach:

. . . the degree of assurance with which instincts are attributed to a given species is inversely related to the extent to which that species has been studied, particularly from the developmental view. Before the development of complex behavior in human infants had been carefully analyzed, it was as we have seen, a common practice to describe many human instincts. Longitudinal studies of behavior have reduced the "unlearned" components to three or four simple responses not much more complex than reflexes. (1955, p. 405)

Although there have been developmental studies of aggression, there is as yet little of the detailed analysis needed to establish the presence of unlearned aggression. Furthermore, on the basis of what is known, aggressive responses appear to be learned. One distinction that does stand up is that between internal and external sources of stimuli. Thus hunger may be regarded as a condition involving chemical changes over time and leading to food-searching behavior; aggression, on the other hand, has no internal stimulus but requires an external stimulus to initiate it.

Aggression is unquestionably a pervasive and universal response, but so is walking. No one regards walking as an instinct, despite its pervasiveness; a behavior's being widespread is not a sufficient reason for labeling it instinctual.

Psychotic murder and suicide were suggested by Waelder (1956) as being so far beyond reactive aggression as to necessitate postulation of an essential destructiveness, the death instinct. Apparently Waelder is impressed with the senselessness of such acts, but behavior cannot be ascribed to an instinctual source merely because it is bizarre and pathological. Unfortunately, there appears to be an implicit equating of rational with learned and of irrational with unlearned or instinctual; while this assumption is never stated clearly in psychoanalytic literature, it would seem to underlie much of the theoretical reasoning about sexual and aggressive instincts.

Sadism and masochism are also offered as indications of the presence of aggressive instinct or death instinct. Again the notion of bizarre or irrational being equal to instinctual appears to underlie this conclusion. It may be countered with the notion of the extreme conditionability of the human organism. Humans can be conditioned to bear intense pain in the expectation of future pleasure, and pride in enduring discomfort plays at least a minor part in identification with the masculine role. Virtually any stimulus can become a reinforcer with appropriate conditioning, including the stimuli of others' pain (sadism) and one's own pain (masochism).

There is an unlearned psysiological rage pattern, though, as was noted in an earlier chapter, it overlaps the pattern for anxiety. Rage is often not followed by aggression, and aggression often occurs in the absence of rage, not only in humans but also in rats (Scott, 1958). Furthermore, in humans there is no external stimulus that is guaranteed to evoke rage; rather, the rage reaction is one that becomes conditioned to a number of antecedent events, and there is much variability among individuals in the stimuli that evoke rage. Thus the presence of an unlearned physiological pattern of rage is not a sufficient reason for postulating an aggressive instinct.

Finally, the appearance of aggression very early in the developmental sequence has been used as an argument for regarding aggression as an instinct. But attacking behavior occurs no earlier than talking or walking; like them, it requires some maturation, and, like them, aggressive responses must be learned. Beach's point about the relationship between lack of knowledge and the postulation of instincts is particularly appropriate here: there has been little investigation of the early patterning of aggression, and those who espouse the notion of an aggressive instinct appear to be least concerned with early development. From what is known of early childhood, it appears that efficient attacking responses, like efficient locomotor responses, are learned slowly.

In brief, none of the arguments for the presence of an instinct of aggression seems to stand up under analysis. There is a paucity of evidence for the notion; for the present it seems best to reject the idea of an instinct of aggression and to focus on the study of attacking responses as they develop in young children.

A Behavioral Approach to Aggressiveness

Aggressiveness is a personality variable, a class of responses that is both enduring and pervasive. In this behavioral approach to aggressiveness a crucial role is played by *habit*: aggressiveness is the habit of attacking. For the present, aggressiveness is treated as an entity in order to simplify the exposition, but it is really a habit system with component habits (physical aggression, verbal aggression, etc.) that will be discussed separately in the last part of this section.

Though psychoanalytic and neo-psychoanalytic theories have dealt with developmental and pathological aspects of aggression, the behavioral approach outlined here will not deal with these aspects. They will be discussed in later chapters. Since it is not possible to distinguish between anger and fear in the infant's diffuse emotional reaction to noxious stimuli, and little is known of the stimuli that elicit anger and aggression in early childhood, it seems fruitless to speculate about innate aggressive responses and about intense feelings of hatred in infants.

Determinants of aggressive habit strength. The strength of aggressive responses is determined by four variables: antecedents of aggression, reinforcement history, social facilitation, and temperament.

ANTECEDENTS OF AGGRESSION. The antecedents of anger and aggression (attack, frustration, and annoyers) have been described in detail; the frequency and intensity of these antecedents constitute one determiner of aggressiveness. The individual who has been the recipient of many anger stimuli is more likely to be chronically aggressive than the one who has been the recipient of few anger stimuli.

REINFORCEMENT HISTORY. Like any other response, aggression owes its habit strength to the consequences that follow it. Frequent, strong reinforcement of attacking responses leads to a strong attacking habit; infrequent, weak reinforcement leads to a weak attacking habit. The reinforcement may be internal, as in a sharp drop in anger level; or it may be external, as in the elimination of a noxious stimulus or the attainment of a reward. If rewards follow aggression often and early in the individual's development, the habit may be extremely resistant to extinction. The tendency to attack may become so strong that it pervades virtually all areas of adjustment, making it impossible for the individual to distinguish between situations calling for aggression and those calling for more peaceful responses. In war men are strongly reinforced for killing other men; in the aftermath of war some men cannot adjust to the peace because killing has become too strong a habit. They have difficulty in extinguishing their tendency to attack and substituting other instrumental responses that lead to rewards in a peaceful society. A less extreme example is the individual who fights his way out of poverty by knocking down anyone who blocks his path to success. Such a person typically continues his aggressive ways after he has attained success, despite changed conditions that no longer call for aggression. The aggressive habit is too strong and too pervasive to fade away.

Fortunately, aggression is not always reinforced. Often the attack does not succeed in attaining the reinforcer; often the drop in anger level is not sufficient to be a strong reinforcer of the preceding aggression. Some children are too weak to win a contest of strength, and, failing to achieve the reward of winning, they soon learn to be nonaggressive (at least physically nonaggressive). Others tend to aggress when an attack is inappropriate in terms of attaining the goal; they coerce when quiet pleading or patience would be more appropriate. Inappropriate aggression is not reinforced, and when the reward does not follow such aggression, there may well be generalization to all aggression, leading to weak aggressive habit strength.

Habit strength of aggression is also weakened by punishment, whether the mechanism is direct weakening of the habit or the strengthening of incompatible habits. Punishment may lead to anxiety or guilt, and the following are speculations concerning the development of these two reactions. Direct verbal and physical punishment constitute strong, focused attacks on the individual who has aggressed. Assuming these noxious stimuli originate with powerful figures, the aggressor becomes anxious, i.e., aggressive responses become a signal for the visceral reaction of anxiety. The anxiety response occurs only in the presence of the punishing agents. However, if the punishment occurs in enough different situations and if it is sufficiently severe, it may generalize to all situations. Now the individual does not discriminate between presence and absence of punishing agents; anxiety is associated with all aggression. The aggressive habit becomes weak, and the individual is chronically nonaggressive.

Indirect punishment, such as shaming and threatened loss of love, would seem to lead to guilt, a more complex and socialized reaction than anxiety. The guilt reaction is associated with a conceptualization of one's behavior and the learning of rules of conduct, whereby certain classes of behavior must be inhibited. Developing children are required to learn a complex set of rules governing the expression of aggression. For example, boys learn that though they may assault other boys, they should not attack girls physically; only such forms of aggression as teasing and mocking are permissible when the target is a girl. Beyond the preschool years when a boy strikes a girl, he is likely to be shamed for breaking the rule; he may also be punished more directly by either the girl or an adult. The shaming is ultimately more effective than the anxiety caused by direct punishment, and the tendency to hit girls is inhibited not so much by anxiety as by guilt. Rules of conduct are probably better inhibitors of aggression than direct punishment that leads to anxiety, but such rules depend for their effectiveness on at least a modicum of maturity on the part of the individual and consistent pressure on the part of those figures who are important in shaping his behavior.

SOCIAL FACILITATION. Group tendencies and attitudes toward aggression are an important determinant of its habit strength, whether the group is the family, the community, the social class, or the entire culture. Anthropologists have demonstrated the wide range of differences in aggressiveness to be found in different cultures and also the link between aggressiveness and child training practices. Much of the learning that occurs in childhood is of the imitative variety, the child mimicking his peers and older members of the group. When aggression predominates in the group, there is ample opportunity for the child to acquire a strong aggressive habit merely by following in the footsteps of other group members. When aggression is relatively absent in the group, the models of behavior that the child imitates are marked by nonaggressiveness, and the tendency to attack remains weak.

When aggression predominates in the group, there is inevitably considerable intra-group friction, and any single member must frequently be subjected to attacks from other members of the group. There are more frequent and probably more intense anger stimuli and more frequent and intense aggression. Since aggression is one of the most potent antecedents of aggression, attack leading to counterattack, a group marked by aggression inevitably produces members with a strong tendency to aggress. Furthermore, since aggression must be valued or at least condoned in such a group, aggression receives powerful reinforcement.

Thus the group can facilitate the development of aggressive personalities by providing aggressive models for children to imitate, by supplying provocation to aggression, and by supplying social reinforcement for aggression once it has occurred.

TEMPERAMENT. Temperament refers to characteristics of behavior that appear early in life and remain relatively unchanged. It is not clear whether these characteristics are more innate than learned or more learned than innate, and, as was noted earlier, attempting to establish innateness is probably a fruitless quest. Temperament variables affect all behavior, not just aggression, and temperament is part of the "style" or typical *mode* of responding of an individual. Style may be contrasted with content of behavior. Content refers to a particular response class, such as aggressive behavior and sexual behavior. Style refers to *how* the response is made, e.g., quickly, with much intensity, and so on.

The temperament variables that influence the development of aggressiveness are impulsiveness, intensity of reaction, activity level, and independence. While these variables are undoubtedly related, each of them may act independently in the development of aggressiveness. There has been little research on temperament variables outside of questionnaire studies. Guilford (1959) reports several factors that emerged from factor analyses of questionnaires, and some of his factors are similar to the four variables listed here, though the names he gives them are different.

Impulsiveness. All infants are impulsive, being unable to inhibit responses. As children mature they are expected to delay, to think before acting, and the ability to delay a response is one sign of maturity. Individuals differ considerably in their ability to delay, to tolerate frustration. Those who cannot wait are more likely to be aggressive than those who can tolerate the tension of having to delay. When an anger stimulus occurs, the impulsive person tends to become angry and respond with aggression immediately. There is insufficient time to develop inhibition of the attacking response, to allow for the learning of responses incompatible with aggression. Once the aggression occurs, its habit strength depends upon the consequences (positive or negative), but the impulsive person tends to make more frequent aggressive responses because of the lack of inhibition. The overdeliberate person should, other things being equal, be at the other extreme, low aggressiveness. His latency of aggression is sufficiently long for responses incompatible with aggression to be well learned. He tends to delay responding to an anger stimulus, and sometimes the delay is so long that an aggressive response is unnecessary. Thus extreme deliberation before responding may tend to prevent the occurrence of an aggressive response when the individual is presented with an anger stimulus.

Activity level. Activity level refers to the amount of energy expended in everyday activities, and it is determined in part by hormones. Individuals may be ranged on a continuum from sluggishness to hypomania, and their place on this continuum is one determinant of aggressiveness. High activity means involvement in a greater variety of situations and often leads to social intrusiveness. In his busy activity the energetic person inevitably involves himself in more interactions with others, especially competitive, conflicting interactions. By serving as an irritant to others in his everyday interactions, the active person produces anger in others, which is fed back to him. Thus the more active person is likely to be presented with more anger stimuli than the less active person. Since the frequency of anger stimuli is one determinant of aggressiveness, the greater the activity level, the higher the probability of a strong aggressive habit.

Intensity of reaction. Some individuals tend to react with intensity to situations that elicit milder responses from most people. While there are only uncontrolled observations of small children and clinic cases to substantiate this statement, there are well-established differences among individuals in physiological reactivity (Lacey, 1950). There are similar differences in behavioral reactivity, e.g., explosive laughter, excessive weeping, and a generally "labile affect."

Of particular relevance is the tendency of some people to have an intense rage reaction in response to stimuli that elicit only mild anger from most others. The greater the intensity of rage, the higher the probability and the greater the intensity of aggression. Since frequency and intensity of aggressive response are indicants of habit strength, the highly reactive individual should be more aggressive than less reactive individuals.

Independence. Independence refers to a tendency toward self-sufficiency and resistance of group pressures. It may be seen in the child who refuses to sit on an adult's lap, who will not sit still and accept adult affection; in contrast, a more dependent child thrives on being held and kissed and later is more susceptible to group pressures. For the independent individual there are more irritants in his everyday interactions because of strong pressures for conformity and submission to the demands of others. Thus in his interactions with others, the independent individual chafes and becomes angry; on the stimulus side there are more frequent anger stimuli than there are for more dependent people.

On the response side the tendency to rebel is an important component in independence, and rebelliousness is part of aggressiveness. The need to assert one's own individuality not only produces more irritants for oneself and for others, but by the very content of the rebellious response the individual is engaging in aggression. Thus the independent person, almost by definition, has a stronger aggressive habit than the dependent, conforming person.

Varieties of aggression. In the foregoing account, aggressive habit strength was treated as a global variable for simplicity of exposition. However, a personality approach to aggression must distinguish between the subclasses of aggression because many individuals have characteristic modes of attacking and do not utilize all the different responses that fall under the heading of aggression. Aggression may be divided into three dichotomies: physical-verbal, active-passive, and direct-indirect. Most people engage in all types of aggression at one time or another, shifting as the stimulus situation demands, but there are extreme individuals who rigidly adhere to one or the other part of these dichotomies; their style of aggression is sufficiently enduring and characteristic to fall under the heading of a personality variable.

There are extremes of the physical-verbal dichotomy. The individual (almost exclusively male) who is quiet and verbally unaggressive, but assaultive and perhaps murderous, is a rare type, but he exists. Complementing him is the more frequent individual who criticizes, nags, and perhaps threatens or curses but who does not attack physically. Both types are at the active end of the active-passive dichotomy; the passive end is represented by those who resist passively and do not initiate aggression. All the preceding personality types aggress directly, occupying one part of the direct-indirect dichotomy. At the indirect end are those who typically are sly and circumspect in their attacking behavior; their aggression is mediated by events and people, and its indirectness makes it more difficult to detect and retaliate against.

Although these various modes of aggression may be characteristic of an individual, it would be a mistake to suppose that these styles characterize only aggressive behavior. The person who attacks physically but not verbally is undoubtedly predominantly physical in all areas of behavior; the person who engages only in passive aggression is undoubtedly passive in virtually all of his interactions with others. The person who rigidly adheres to one mode of aggression also rigidly adheres to this style in other areas of behavior. Style develops partly through imitation and partly through selective reinforcement. Since style transcends aggression, it is not necessary in the present context to attempt a more detailed discussion of its development.

Hostility. Evidence was presented in Chapter 9 that aggressiveness and hostility are different. Factor analysis of college students' self-reports and of evaluations of psychiatric patients by psychologists, psychiatrists, and relatives all yielded an aggression factor and a hostility factor. The hostility factor was defined by resentment and suspicion. An individual may mull over past ill treatment and be suspicious of the motives of others without engaging in aggressive behavior, or he may attack others without being hostile. Thus while hostility and aggressiveness may coincide, the hostile person is not necessarily aggressive and the aggressive person is not necessarily hostile.

Since hostility can be kept relatively unobtrusive, the variables that might inhibit it (negative reinforcement, cultural taboos, etc.) do not affect it. Hatred may increase in the hostile person, without others being aware of it, and aggression need not accompany it. Usually, however, increases in hostility tend to be accompanied by verbalizations of the hatred and by at least indirect attacks against the hated person. Hostility is focused against one or more hated persons, and in this respect it is different from aggressiveness. The habit of aggressing is more generalized; individuals do not attack only one or two people, but many people; anger is a diffuse emotional response. Hostility, on the other hand, is specifically directed to a particular person or group. Its directive character is facilitated by the verbal mediation that is one of its major components; words sharpen the discrimination, allowing the hatred to be focused rather than generalized. There are some individuals who tend to hate everyone, but such misanthropes are rare, especially outside of mental hospitals.

Since hostility is a conditioned anger response, its development depends upon the individual's being angered. The more anger stimuli that impinge on an individual, the more likely he is to be hostile. If there is an excess of the antecedents of anger (attacks, frustrations, annoyances), there is likely to be an excess of hostility.

Of the various antecedents, attack is the most likely to lead to hostility because it is the most focused antecedent. Both frustrations and annoyances are generalized events that are not selective in their targets, whereas attack is usually directed toward a specific target. The victim of attack has been singled out, and his observing-labeling responses, together with his anger reaction, are the basis for his subsequent hostility. If he can fight back, his anger level may drop quickly enough for there to be little conditioned anger or hostility. When the attack consists of rejection, there is little opportunity to fight back. When one is cast out of a group, it is difficult to retaliate by attacking. The rejected person has been branded as aversive and has been isolated; the rejecting individual does not remain in his victim's presence, and the latter in his isolation finds it extremely difficult to attack. Rather, he mulls over the rejection, making the verbal responses (explicit or implicit) that serve as a basis for later hostility.

Since verbal mediation is an important part of hostility, those who tend to make more implicit verbal responses would be more likely to become hostile; for example, "ideational characters," who tend to spin fantasies, who tend to think rather than act, who have a rich imagination. Excessive ideation, when it reaches pathological dimensions, is seen in obsessives, who ruminate and ponder but never get around to acting; it is also seen in paranoids. These individuals are most likely to make the implicit responses that constitute hostility.

NOTES

In the discussion of psychoanalytic reactions to Freud's death instinct doctrine, only a few representative works were cited. Other writings that contributed to the discussion are Bibring, 1941; Fairbairn, 1940; Anna Freud, 1949; Hitchmann, 1948; Loewenstein, 1940; and Szasz, 1952. The writings of three important psychoanalysts or neo-psychoanalysts were omitted because aggressiveness is peripheral to their main themes and therefore receives little attention: Fromm, Schilder, and Sullivan.

The nonpsychoanalytic approach of Kelly (1955) was omitted. His definitions of aggression and hostility belong in the context of a theory of personal constructs, and they depart radically from commonly accepted definitions. His views on aggression cannot be presented fairly out of the context of his two-volume work (1955).

REFERENCES

Allee, W. C., Nissen, H. W., & Nimkoff, M. F. A re-examination of the concept of instinct. *Psychol. Rev.*, 1953, **60**, 287–297.

Ansbacher, H. L. & Ansbacher, Rowena R. *The individual psychology of Alfred Adler.* New York: Basic Books, 1956.

Beach, F. A. The descent of instinct. *Psychol. Rev.*, 1955, **62**, 401–410.

Beres, D. Clinical notes on aggression in children. *Psychoanal. Stud. Child.*, 1952, **7**, 241–263.

Bibring, E. The development and problems of the theory of the instincts. *Int. J. Psychoanal.*, 1941, **22**, 102–131.

Dollard, J., Doob, L. W., Miller, N. E., Mowrer, O. H., & Sears, R. R. *Frustration and aggression.* New Haven: Yale University Press, 1939.

Dollard, J. & Miller, N. E. *Personality and psychotherapy.* New York: McGraw-Hill, 1950.

Fairbairn, W. R. D. Is aggression an irreducible factor? *Brit. J. Med. Psychol.*, 1940, **18**, 163–170.

Fisher, S. & Hinds, Edith. The organization of hostility controls in various personality structures. *Genet. Psychol. Monogr.*, 1951, **44**, 3–68.

Freud, Anna. Notes on aggression. *Bull. Menninger Clin.*, 1949, **13**, 143–151.

Freud, S. *Collected papers.* London: Hogarth Press, 1925.

Freud, S. *Beyond the pleasure principle.* New York: Boni & Liveright, 1927.

Guilford, J. P. *Personality.* New York: McGraw-Hill, 1959.

Hartmann, H., Kris, E., & Loewenstein, R. Notes on the theory of aggression. In *Psychoanal. Study Child.* 1949, **3**, 9–36.

Hitschman, E. The history of the aggressive impulse. *Yearbook of psychoanalysis*, 1948, **4**, 70–74.

Horney, Karen. *New ways in psychoanalysis.* New York: Norton, 1939.

Horney, Karen. *Our inner conflicts.* New York: Norton, 1945.

Kelly, G. A. *The psychology of personal constructs.* New York: Norton, 1955.

Lacey, J. I. Individual differences in somatic response patterns. *J. comp. physiol. Psychol.*, 1950, **43**, 338–350.

Loewenstein, R. The vital or somatic instincts. *Int. J. Psychoanal.*, 1940, **21**, 377–400.

Munroe, Ruth L. *Schools of psychoanalytic thought.* New York: Dryden, 1955.

Nunberg, H. *Principles of psychoanalysis.* New York: International University Press, 1955.

Saul, L. J. *The hostile mind.* New York: Random House, 1956.

Scott, J. P. *Aggression.* Chicago: University of Chicago Press, 1958.

Szasz, T. S. On the psychoanalytic theory of instincts. *Psychoanalyt. Quart.*, 1952, **21**, 25–48.

Waelder, R. Critical discussion of the concept of an instinct of destruction. *Bull. Phila. Ass. Psychoanal.*, 1956, **6**, 97–109.

11

Psychopathology

Both hostility and aggression play an important role in the development of psychopathology. Resentment, envy, and jealousy tend to keep the individual isolated from others, preventing hostility from diminishing (Newcomb, 1947) and preventing him from achieving the affectional relationships necessary for adjustment. Society specifies the targets, the amount, and the modes of aggression; those who do not conform are maladjusted. The person who cannot modulate his aggressive tendencies not only drives others away and is punished for his aggression but also usually fails to achieve his goal because society generally rewards only those who adopt prevailing response modes. The person who fails to manifest sufficient aggression is also maladjusted. He lacks the minimal assertiveness necessary to succeed in competition with others and is assailed by doubts and fears in situations calling for aggressive behavior.

This chapter is a survey of the role of hostility and aggression in psychopathology; the treatment is brief because a full discussion would occupy a volume of its own. No attempt is made to deal with criminal personalities, and aggression in childhood psychopathology will be discussed in Chapter 14. The plan of the chapter is to discuss classifications of aggression in psychopathology; neurosis, psychosis, and, finally, prognosis.

Classifications

Thorne (1953) specified three types of aggressive reactions. The first is a simple anger reaction, a direct response to thwarting that is analogous to the fear response to danger; it is acute and tends to subside when the irritation is removed. The second is the psychoneurotic reaction, which is more intense, enduring, and related to unconscious motivation. The third represents the most extreme psychopathology, the paranoid reaction; hostility is projected to others, enabling the patient to justify his own hatred.

Saul's classification (1956) is more comprehensive; he divided hostility and aggressiveness into three types: normal (social), private, and asocial. Private hostility includes three kinds of deviant personalities: neurotic character, classical neurotic, and psychosomatic patient. The neurotic character may provoke punishment from others in order to assuage his own guilt, but he does not devleop neurotic symptoms. His problems arise from his typical response modes, indirect and underhanded aggression, which are a source of great discomfort to those around him. Nacht (1948) has pointed out that neurotic characters are sadistic but without insight into their behavior; when they do achieve partial insight, they may be as ruthless and pitiless in condemning themselves as they are in attacking others. Examples may be found in martinets who insist on conformity to the letter of the law and strict mothers who use child training as an excuse to punish their children.

The classical neurotic also represses hostility, but the repression leads to neurotic symptoms that vary from simple anxiety (fear of loss of control) to obsessive thoughts of killing. The psychosomatic patient also represses hostility but at the cost of somatic discomfort.

Saul's asocial hostility includes criminals, "criminoids," and neurotic criminals, but, as noted above, a discussion of these types is beyond the scope of this book.

Hostility and aggression are important in the interaction between client and therapist, and psychoanalysts have emphasized the crucial role of "negative transference." The various kinds of negative transferences have been classified by Romano (1959), whose scheme is presented in Table 11.1. The orally hostile patient craves love but fears rejection and abandonment; he also fears that he will "devour" the therapist if the latter continually furnishes love and attention. The passive, anally hostile patient is adept at withholding information, his silence representing negativism and a desire not to "give." The active, anally hostile patient may deluge the therapist with associations ("feces") that block therapeutic progress. Active or passive, the patient with anal rage seeks to manipulate, attack, and destroy the therapist. Phallic hostility leads to competition with the therapist, the patient attacking the therapist as a rival.

Alexander & Pope (1956) have also classified aggression and hostility in psychotherapy, their approach being less psychoanalytic. Their list leads to the following types. First, the patient with little tolerance for frustration or criticism is easily angered by the therapist's questions or interpretations.   Partly as a reaction to inferiority, he interprets the therapist's actions as hostile and rejecting; his reaction is to have a "chip on the shoulder."

Second, the patient who must prove to himself that others are cruel becomes pseudo-aggressive in an attempt to elicit anger and aggression from the therapist.   When the therapist obliges with a verbal attack, the patient has proved his case.

TABLE 11.1. Types of Transference Hostility[*]

	Oral	Anal	Phallic
Aim	Fusion with object.	Mastery of object by deprivation and/or annihilation.	Possession of object and establishment of superiority.
Warded off wish	"I wish to eat you."	"I won't give to you." "I defecate on you."	"I shall castrate you." "I am bigger (penis) than you."
Fantasies	Eating, biting, sucking.	Soiling, wetting	Penetration, rape.
Fears	Loss of identity, abandonment.	Counterhostility and punishment.	Counterhostility (castration).
	—	Fear of destruction of the object	—

[*] Romano, 1959, p. 12.

Third, the deviously aggressive patient attempts to manipulate the therapist by making excessive demands on his time, telephoning between sessions, stubbornly adhering to ideas, and even falling asleep during the therapy session.

Fourth, the patient who is too inhibited to attack the therapist often becomes tense and anxious.   He complains that the room is too hot or too cold and that he is becoming confused—signs of anxiety over loss of control.   His aggressive tendencies may appear in the form of fantasies about the therapist's injury or death.   A number of neurotic defense mechanisms may occur, which will be discussed in the next section.

Neurosis

Bergler (1946) has made the most comprehensive attempt to distinguish between normal and neurotic aggression, as follows.   Normal aggression is used only in self-defense against a real enemy;

there is no guilt, and the amount of aggression corresponds roughly to the provocation; aggression is always used to harm an enemy; the normal person is not easily provoked and has the ability to wait until the enemy is vulnerable before attacking; he regards aggression as a necessary but disagreeable task, and he anticipates success. The neurotic uses aggression indiscriminately, and slight provocation may elicit massive aggression; there is much guilt, and retaliation leads to masochistic satisfaction; he is easily provoked and cannot wait to attack; aggression is regarded as a sadomasochistic game, with defeat anticipated.

These distinctions by Bergler are overdrawn. Normal aggression is rarely so mature and adjusted, nor is neurotic aggression usually so explosive and masochistic. Neurotic aggression is like any other neurotic behavior. It is expressed tentatively, with ambivalence and guilt, with inadequate appreciation of the realities of the situation, and with fear concerning the outcome.

It might be inferred from Bergler's account that the neurotic is more aggressive than the normal. Whether or not the inference is correct, it is doubtful that the neurotic is more aggressive than the normal. The neurotic is assailed by fears and doubts, by inhibitions that have generalized far beyond the punishment situations. Since the neurotic is ambivalent and fearful, he is less likely to *aggress* than the normal. On the other hand, since the neurotic often feels rejected and is often frustrated (by his own inadequacy as much as by the environment), he is likely to be more *hostile* than the normal.

Watson et al. (1955) compared neurotics and normals on the Scrambled Sentences task and found that neurotics constructed significantly more hostile sentences than the normal. Wahler (1959) also used the Scrambled Sentences task, but he had both human and nonhuman content. Neurotics gave significantly more hostile solutions than normals only when the content was human. Wirt (1956) compared neurotics, psychotics, and normals on the Rorschach and found that neurotics had significantly more hostile content than normals and psychotics. These studies tend to corroborate the hypothesis noted above: neurotics are more hostile than normals.

What marks the neurotic is his utilization of one or more defense mechanisms. He is relatively incapable of making necessary discriminations and tends to overgeneralize inhibitions (Dollard & Miller, 1950). In situations calling for aggression he is thrown into an approach-avoidance conflict, which he attempts to cope with in one of the following ways.

One defense is simple inhibition, the generalized avoidance of aggression. The individual remains passive and inert in the face of anger stimuli or environmental demands for aggression. Such behavior is typical of the anxiety neurotic, who cannot verbalize what it is he fears. The fear is of losing control, aggressing, and then being punished.

Generalized anxiety may be limited to a few circumscribed situations, as in phobias. It has been speculated that the fear of open spaces is based on anxiety lest control be lost, and the agoraphobic indulge in the very sexual or aggressive impulses he has been attempting to repress (Fenichel, 1945). A neurotic may develop an intense fear of guns because of the possibility of surrendering to his strongly inhibited tendency to shoot someone. The anxiety that is initially associated with aggression subsequently becomes linked to *stimuli* associated with aggression (guns). The neurotic may then contain his anxiety by avoiding such stimuli; or the anxiety may become conditioned to such a variety of stimuli that he is unable to avoid stimuli that have connotations of aggression.

The conflict between attacking and avoiding behavior may be manifested directly in motor behavior. A tic shown by a disturbed, hospitalized boy illustrates such a conflict. This boy had a strong tendency both to control and to abandon himself to the impulse. He showed both sides of the conflict by pushing his hands back and forth in front of him whenever he became excited. The forward push represented his tendency to attack by shoving someone, and the pull back represented his tendency to withdraw.

In adults, ideational symptoms of the conflict are more common than motor symptoms. The neurotic who uses obsessiveness as a defense tends to think excessively before acting but does not act. He mulls over the pros and cons of attacking or, in some instances, the particular mode of aggression to be used, but, rather than helping him to attack, these implicit responses tend to prevent him from acting. So long as he can debate with himself, he is protected from the anxiety that would ensue from making the aggressive response itself. Unfortunately, the tendency to attack may become so strong that the neurotic cannot help but think about aggressing. He then becomes preoccupied with obsessive thoughts of killing others, or, one step removed, with obsessive fantasies of accidental injury or death to others. The presence of such obsessions means that the neurotic is losing control and is having difficulty in stemming his aggressive tendencies.

An extreme defense against aggression is reaction formation, which consists of attempts by the neurotic to prove to himself and others that he is not aggressive by going to the opposite extreme of peaceful, loving helpfulness. He feels compelled to deny even the mildest tendency to aggress, even the slightest hint of anger. This is accomplished by proclaiming his solicitude and desire to help others, and the stronger the original tendency to aggress, the more extreme must be its denial by doing the opposite. It is the rigid overstating of his case that distinguishes the neurotic with reaction formation from the genuine "good Samaritan." The latter can show a bit of temper or aggressiveness, and he can aggress if it is necessary. The neurotic is inflexible concerning aggression and rage; in fact, he may be aggressively helpful, forcing his solicitude and help on those who may not want them. The neurotic is impelled to "help," not by others' need but by his own need to deny aggression.

Another defense is sublimation, which refers to the channeling of immature response tendencies into socially acceptable and useful modes. A strong tendency toward destruction may be converted into useful acts, such as demolishing slum housing in order to clear the way for new housing, fighting disease, or fighting crime. The satisfaction derives from the useful service and not from the aggressive act itself. The surgeon who finds it necessary to amputate a limb derives satisfaction from the knowledge that he is saving a life, not from the act of removing the limb. Were the surgeon to enjoy cutting off a limb, it would be an instance of *partial* sublimation.

The mechanism of projection consists of attributing one's own feelings or impulses to others: "I do not hate them; they hate me." Since aggression tends to be commonplace, there is a grain of truth in the assertion that others are hostile or aggressive. Usually the individual who projects is more hostile than aggressive. If he could express his aggression, there would be little need for attributing aggressiveness and hatred to others. His failure to aggress is accompanied by intense hatred of those around him; he sees himself surrounded by enemies in a cold, threatening world. The mechanism of projection enables him to preserve the nonhostile façade and to forestall guilt because it is not he who hates but "those others." He need not fear his own conscience, for he has disowned hostility and aggression, but he must fear the actions of others, who are filled with hostility and aggressiveness. He trades a sense of guilt for a feeling of anxiety.

Psychosis

Psychotics manifest greater variability in aggressiveness and hostility than neurotics. Psychotics tend to withdraw from the frightening reality of everyday life, and, for the most part, they are too pre-occupied with their own distorted world to become involved in even the minimal interpersonal relationship involved in attacking someone. This does not mean that tendencies toward aggression are absent, for occasionally a psychotic who has been quiescent for years may erupt into manic violence.

Some psychoanalysts are sufficiently impressed with the role of aggression in psychosis to suggest that it is of paramount importance. Bak (1954) believes that psychosis is the result of a conflict between the ego and aggression, in contrast to neurosis, which is a conflict between the ego and sexuality. When the ego cannot neutralize aggressive "drive," the individual has started down the road to psychosis; the more the clinical picture approximates psychosis, the more dominant is the conflict between the ego and aggression. The different clinical pictures in psychosis are in part determined by the defense the ego tries instead of attempting to neutralize aggression. Thus there is turning against the self in depression, projection in paranoia, and the complete failure of defense in catatonic excitement (liberation of tremendous quantities of aggression).

Although Bak's formulation is too sweeping to be correct (aggression is not always crucial in psychosis), his insistence on the importance of aggression in psychosis seems well taken. Some psychotics are petrified of close contact with others because of the dual fear of killing and being killed. As noted earlier, there is a wide range of symptomatology among psychotics, and it seems best to avoid the pitfalls of nosology, especially those associated with schizophrenia. Schizophrenics vary not only in their symptom pictures but also in the amount and form of aggression, and it would be fruitless to discuss aggression in relation to this heterogeneous group of patients. Therefore, the following account is limited to the two psychotic groups that manifest at least a modicum of homogeneity with respect to aggression and hostility: manic-depressives and paranoids.

Manic-Depressives. It is generally acknowledged that most depressives do not have manic phases, and a true manic-depressive is rarely seen. This section deals principally with depression, but the role of aggression in mania will be noted briefly.

Although euphoria and over-activity are the most salient features of the manic's behavior, the most dangerous feature is his aggressiveness. During manic episodes bystanders may be in real peril; this is especially true of the patient's immediate family—his most likely victims. The manic has a weak conscience and little ability to inhibit intense physical aggression (Othman & Friedman, 1943). He appears to regress back to the earliest stages of childhood during which there is no capacity for delay or restraint.

Depression represents the opposite of mania: instead of attacking others, the depressive attacks himself. Any tendency to attack others is rigidly suppressed; nor can any feelings of hostility toward others be admitted because they would arouse intense feelings of guilt. The essence of psychotic depression is guilt, and the psychotic's guilt concerns both real and fantasied behavior. The depressive suffers from a sense of worthlessness and inferiority; he believes that he should not be allowed to live.

While the profound guilt precludes any direct aggression against others, the depressive still hates and aggresses—the target being himself. Even though the self-aggression is usually verbal (tongue lashings and self-depreciation), there may also be attempts at self-mutilation or suicide.

There are two kinds of speculation concerning the development of depression. The first is psychoanalytic (Freud, 1925; Nacht, 1948). It assumes that both a hated and a loved object are represented within the individual. The depressive is ambivalent toward the internalized object, and there is an aggressive explosion against this loved-hated object. The good part is the ego, and the bad part the superego; the depressive's attempt at suicide represents an attempt of the ego to kill the bad part of himself, the superego.

The second kind of speculation is behavioral. The depressive is both hostile and verbally aggressive toward himself, but there is essentially no self-anger. In tracing the development of these features, it is important to distinguish between self-hate and anger. The child learns to hate himself by imitating his parents, the crucial figures in his life with respect to love and discipline. All children receive a combination of praise and punishment from their parents, but for the depressive this combination is weighted heavily with punishment. It is not just any punishment, but punishment that consists largely of negative labeling, shaming, and rejection; the parent responds toward the child with negative verbal labels and with the clear implication that the child is unworthy. Because the parent is usually not only the child's major source of affection but also the major source of value judgments, the child learns that he is inferior and bad. To the extent that he identifies with his parents, he accepts their value judgments and comes to make the same negative verbal responses toward himself that his parents did. He learns that when blame is to be apportioned, it should be attributed to himself and not to others; he may go so far as to accept other's blame as his own (the mechanism of introjection).

While the parent is not only rejecting but also loving, rejection is so dominant that the child cannot depend on himself for self-esteem. As a child, and later as an adult, he needs continual reassurance (by way of attention and affection) that he is wanted, that he is worthy. He never learns to cope with rejection because not only does he lack the self-esteem to counteract the implied hostility but also he has learned to make negative responses toward himself. The strongest implicit verbal response in his hierarchy is self-condemnation, but so long as there is a crucial figure around to reassure him that he is esteemed, he can remain at least ambivalent about his worth. When such external esteem is withdrawn, it is a double blow. In addition to constituting a fresh rejection, the withdrawal removes the sole opposition to his negative self-labels. His self-hatred is no longer opposed by the affection and esteem of a valued parent-figure, and the result is depression.

The development of low self-esteem requires that parental punishment consist mainly of rejection and negative labeling. If the parent becomes angry or uses physical punishment, the outcome is not low self-esteem. Rather, the child becomes angry and attempts to retaliate against the parent. If he cannot aggress against the parents because they are too punitive, he will turn to weaker targets, such as younger siblings and peers. He will "identify with the aggressor," adopting his parent's response mode (aggression) but not the parent's attitude toward him. In face of parental anger and physical punishment, the child is likely to learn rebellion.

Thus the type of parental punishment is probably a crucial variable in the development of depression and rebellion. In the development of depression, the parent punishes mainly by rejection and negative labeling, actions that arouse anxiety in the child rather than anger. If the child happened to attack his parents, it would become another occasion for rejection and for parental negative evaluation. The child learns by imitation to aggress verbally against himself; aggression directed toward others is punished and, therefore, never acquires much habit strength. In the development of rebellion, the parent punishes mainly by physical aggression and with considerable anger. Such punishment is a stimulus for counteraggression on the part of the child, and the child learns by imitation to be angry.

For simplicity, the types of parental discipline have been overemphasized as determiners of later hostility and aggression. The child's development is complicated by a number of other determinants (e.g., temperament variables, ordinal position in the family, extra-home training), which cannot be discussed here. The major assumption in this behavioral approach is that the individual can learn self-hatred and verbal self-aggression just as he learns any other response.

The hypothesis that rejection leads to self-aggression receives support from a study by Moulton (1958). Hospitalized psychotic men were divided into those directing aggression toward themselves (self-blame, attempted suicide, etc.) and those directing aggression toward others (threats, verbal aggression, attempted assault, etc.); the two groups will be called the "Ins" and the "Outs." Their mothers were interviewed concerning child rearing techniques and attitudes. It was found that mothers of the "Ins" tended to use psychological punishment, such as rejection, for the child's misbehavior, while mothers of the "Outs" tended to use more physical punishment. Mothers of the "Ins" emphasized self-control on their own part in dealing with the child, whereas mothers of the "Outs" saw no reason to restrain their own anger and tended to express it toward the child. Thus the type of maternal discipline did affect the direction of aggression that was seen subsequently in the adult psychiatric patients.

Paranoia. The term *paranoia* as used here refers to behavior involving projection—attribution of one's own (negative) traits and impulses to others. In this context it cuts across the diagnostic boundaries of paranoia, paranoid schizophrenia, and paranoid character. Paranoids share one common feature, delusions, but since all delusions are not persecutory or aggressive, the exposition is limited to those paranoids whose hostility spills over into their delusional symptoms.

It is important to distinguish between hostility and aggression in discussing the paranoid. The paranoid starts out with a fund of hostility that, ostensibly, is based on a long history of rejections, frustrations, punishments, annoyances, and so forth. Society does not tolerate such hatred, and the paranoid accepts the verdict of society. He therefore defends against recognizing his own hostility by denying and projecting it. He denies that he is the hostile one, stating that he is merely an innocent victim of others' cruelty; he believes that those around him hate him and are working against him. If he dislikes them or attacks them, these are countermeasures used in self-defense.

While most paranoids are hostile, they are relatively nonaggressive because of fear of others. Aggression implies at least a minimal interpersonal relationship, and the paranoid is frightened of interpersonal relationships. If the paranoid had been able to ventilate some of his anger, he would not have become so suspicious and distrustful of others.   Although he hates others, he is no more aggressive than the depressive, who hates himself.

This hypothesis receives support from a study by Caine (1960), who compared the performance of depressive and paranoid women on the Scrambled Sentences task and the MMPI. There were three kinds of scrambled sentences:

Aggressive	Hit You I'll Take
Hostile	They'd Me Cheat Find
Self-Critical/Guilt	Courage No Books I've.

The alternative solutions are aggressive-neutral, hostile-neutral, and guilt-neutral, respectively. It was found that the depressives and paranoids did not differ significantly in aggressive solutions; but the paranoids gave significantly more hostile solutions than the depressives, and the depressives gave significantly more guilt solutions than the paranoids.

The MMPI was divided into aggression, hostility, and guilt scales, and the results were the same: no differences on aggression, paranoids more hostile, and depressives more guilty.   Note that both aggression and hostility were directed toward others and that guilt represented hostility directed toward the self.   Thus both self-reports (MMPI) and hostile materials yield findings consistent with this formulation: there is essentially no difference between these two kinds of patients in aggressiveness, but there is in hostility—depressives hate themselves and paranoids hate others.

Prognosis

This section deals with the relationship between direction of aggression and prognosis. The importance of direction of aggression stems from its association with the developmental sequence. The young child often employs attack against others in order to achieve a goal or in response to frustration, rejection, or attack. As he grows older, he is taught to inhibit his aggression in most situations and to modify its intensity when aggression is appropriate. His identification with parents and other significant adult figures leads him to adopt their attitudes and responses toward himself. He learns to direct verbal aggression and hostile attitudes toward himself after wrongdoing, just as his parents do. These self-aggressive responses are part of the development of conscience, which becomes a more potent determiner of behavior as the child progresses toward maturity. Thus aggression directed toward others occurs earlier in the developmental sequence than aggression directed toward the self, and self-directed aggression is a sign of greater maturity than other-directed aggression.

These considerations and the assumption that a higher maturity level indicates a better prognosis led Albee (1950) to suggest that outwardly directed aggression would be more prevalent in schizophrenics than in nonschizophrenics and that it would lead to a poorer prognosis than inwardly directed aggression. On the basis of accident and injury reports, he classified psychiatric inpatients as either extrapunitive or intropunitive. Diagnosis was dichotomized as schizophrenic-nonschizophrenic, and outcome of hospital stay was split into improved-unimproved.

Since the prognosis findings might be confounded with the generally unfavorable prognosis for schizophrenia, Albee examined the relationship between direction of aggression and prognosis for schizophrenics only. The findings were the same; outwardly directed aggression is associated with a poor prognosis.

Smith (1951) followed up Albee's study, again using accident and injury reports, and she corroborated Albee's finding of an association between direction of aggression and prognosis. In addition, outwardly directed aggression tended to be associated with symptoms of extreme psychopathology: withdrawal, silliness, and delusions of persecution.

In a similar study by Feldman et al. (1954), the criteria for improvement and unimprovement were more stringent, being based on status one year after discharge. Direction of aggression was determined by examination of case reports in hospital files. A nine-point scale that ranged from homicidal attack to suicide attempt was used. Thus both the prognosis and direction of aggression variables were measured differently from the first two studies. The biserial r between direction of aggression and prognosis was .67.

It was found that a number of variables significantly correlated with direction of aggression: affective expression, orientation, diagnosis, onset of illness, duration of illness, kind of treatment, and marital status. When the effects of these variables were partialled out statistically, the biserial r between direction of aggression and prognosis dropped from .67 to .23. This finding suggests that, while direction of aggression is related to maturity level, it is only one of several variables that bear such a relationship. Furthermore, the expression of aggression against others is more likely to arouse the anger of hospital personnel than self-aggression, which might affect the kind of treatment received by the patient. It is clear that outwardly directed aggression is associated with a poor prognosis, but this relationship may be mediated by the action of other variables (kind of treatment, general maturity level, etc.).

Direction of aggression has also been found to be important in the outcome of electroshock therapy. Carpenter (1957) used MMPI scales and clinical ratings of improvement as criteria of the outcome of therapy. Scores on a number of tests were used to determine whether a patient was intropunitive or extrapunitive. It was found that intropunitiveness was associated with improvement and extrapunitiveness with an unfavorable outcome after electroshock therapy. These results are in agreement with the clinical notion that depressives are considerably better risks for electroshock therapy than paranoids, depression representing inwardly directed aggression and paranoia representing outwardly directed aggression.

REFERENCES

Albee, G. W. Patterns of aggression in psychopathology. *J. consult. Psychol.,* 1950, **14,** 465–468.

Alexander, R. P. & Pope, H. L., Jr. The negative transference: some comments on its manifestations, development and management. *Amer. J. Psychother.,* 1956, **10,** 5–17.

Bak, R. C. The schizophrenic defense against aggression. *Int. J. Psycho-Anal.,* 1954, **35,** 129–133.

Bergler, E. Differential diagnosis between "normal" and "neurotic" aggression. *Quart. rev. psychiat. Neurol.,* 1946, **1,** 1–5.

Caine, T. M. The expression of hostility and guilt in melancholic and paranoid women. *J. consult. Psychol.,* 1960, **24,** 18–22.

Carpenter, L. G. Relation of aggression in the personality to outcome with electro-convulsive shock therapy. *J. gen. Psychol.,* 1957, **57,** 3–22.

Dollard, J. & Miller, N. E. *Personality and psychotherapy.* New York: McGraw-Hill, 1950.

Feldman, Dorothy A., Pascal, G. R., & Swensen, C. H. Direction of aggression as a prognostic variable in mental illness. *J. consult. Psychol.,* 1954, **18,** 167–170.

Fenichel, O. *The psychoanalytic theory of neurosis.* New York: Norton, 1945.

Freud, S. Mourning and melancholia. In *Collected papers.* London: Hogarth, 1925.

Moulton, R. W. Antecedents of aggressive expression in psychosis. Unpublished doctor's dissertation, University of Michigan, 1958.

Nacht, S. Clinical manifestations of aggression and their role in psychoanalytic treatment. *Int. J. Psychoanal.,* 1948, **29,** 201–223.

Newcomb, T. M. Autistic hostility and social reality. *Hum. Rel.,* 1947, **21,** 69–86.

Othman, Jane E., & Friedman, S. The role of hostility in affective psychosis. *J. nerv. ment. Dis.,* 1943, **97,** 170–196.

Romano, R. L.   Forms of hostility in the transference. *Psychoanal. psycho-analyt. Rev.,* 1959, **46,** 3–19.

Saul, L. J.   *The hostile mind.* New York: Random House, 1956.

Smith, Dorothea M.   An analysis of aggression among patients in a mental hospital.   Unpublished doctor's dissertation, University of Pittsburgh, 1951.

Thorne, F. C.   The frustration-anger-hostility states: a new diagnostic classification.   *J. clin. Psychol.,* 1953, **9,** 334–339.

Wahler, H. J.   Hostility and aversion for expressing hostility in neurotics and controls.   *J. abnorm. soc. Psychol.,* 1959, **59,** 193–198.

Watson, R. E., Pritzker, L., & Madison, P.   Hostility in neurotics and normals. *J. abnorm. soc. Psychol.,* 1955, **50,** 36–40.

Wirt, R. D.   Ideational expression of hostile impulses.   *J. consult. Psychol.,* 1956, **20,** 185–189.

12

Psychosomatics

A psychosomatic disorder may be defined as a vegetative dysfunction or tissue change whose most important etiological variable is psychological conflict. Hostility and anger are undoubtedly present in most patients with psychosomatic ills, probably because of the prevalence of resentment not only among those with conflicts but also in the population as a whole. Thus patients with ulcerative colitis, peptic ulcer, migraine headache, and other ailments, have been reported to have conflicts concerning resentment toward others and concerning the expression of their aggressive tendencies. However, there are only two psychosomatic disorders that have been consistently related to conflict over hostility and aggression, and these will be discussed in this chapter: essential hypertension and neurodermatitis.

ESSENTIAL HYPERTENSION

In hypertension blood pressure is chronically elevated. High blood pressure often results from kidney dysfunction, and there are other kinds of physiological malfunction and disease that culminate in a chronically elevated blood pressure. When there is no apparent organic basis for the high blood pressure, it is called essential hypertension.

Hambling (1952) distinguishes three stages in the development of essential hypertension. The first, *diastolic reaction,* occurs in *pre-hypertensives,* who react to psychological stress or to the pain of the cold pressor test (immersion of a hand or a foot in ice water for one minute) with a diastolic blood pressure of more than 95.[1] The sec-

[1] The numbers associated with blood pressure readings will be given without adding "millimeters of mercury."

221

ond stage is called *benign hypertension:* diastolic blood pressure is as mobile as in the first stage but is now permanently raised during resting to 95 or above. Related to the chronically elevated pressure is a thickening of the arterioles, which still retain some elasticity. In the third stage, *malignant hypertension,* diastolic pressure is permanently above 130, probably because of a renal pressor substance. Under the severe stress of the abnormally high blood pressure, there is malfunctioning of the kidneys, retinae of the eyes, etc.

Etiology of Essential Hypertension

The dynamics of essential hypertension have been described (Alexander, 1939, 1950; Hamilton, 1942), and the importance of suppressed rage has been accepted with only minor dissent. When an individual becomes angry, his blood pressure rises. Since anger is a temporary reaction, the elevation in blood pressure is temporary. Some individuals inhibit the expression of anger, and their rage subsides slowly. They are chronically hostile and resentful, and their blood pressure is chronically high.

This account is weakest in bridging the gap between temporary rises in blood pressure and chronic blood pressure elevation. It is an oversimplification to state that chronic resentment leads to chronic high blood pressure, and the problem remains of accounting for the change from the stage of diastolic reaction to the stage of benign hypertension. The following formulation attempts to do just this.

The potential hypertensive has an excessively mobile blood pressure, as shown by his response to the cold pressor test. Like anyone else, he reacts to an anger stimulus with an elevation in blood pressure, but the blood pressure rise is considerably higher than average. Because the deviation from resting blood pressure is greater, more time is required to return to resting level than the average person. Because he is fearful of the consequences of anger (either punishment or his own guilt), the prehypertensive suppresses expressions of rage. Unlike the neurotic, he has no systematic defense against anger stimuli or his own tendency to aggress. He cannot retreat into rituals as does the compulsive, nor can he avoid specific anger stimuli as does the phobic. Instead, the prehypertensive works himself up to the final stages of physiological preparation for attack before he suppresses action. His readiness to aggress is at a peak, and in the absence of an attacking response or a temper tantrum, his tension state remains at a high level for some time. Thus his blood pressure remains high not only because it deviates so far from resting state but also because the tension state is not alleviated by an explosive behavioral reaction. This is the first stage—diastolic reaction.

Since the prehypertensive tends to suppress aggression, it follows that he is more sensitive than the average person to the presence of anger stimuli. The person who fears the consequences of venting rage tends to perceive anger stimuli in the neutral stimuli that impinge on him. The prehypertensive should, therefore, become angry more often than the average person, which means that his blood pressure should rise more often. With the passage of time, the cycle proceeds toward more frequent elevations in blood pressure and longer periods during which it is high. This period continues for years, with the interval between successive elevations of blood pressure becoming smaller and smaller. It becomes more and more difficult to distinguish resting blood pressure from temporary rises. The excessive and prolonged increases in blood pressure activate minor changes in the arterioles, which tend to thicken in response to the additional stress placed upon them. This thickening constricts the arteriolar bed, thus elevating resting blood pressure.

Eventually the interval between successive blood pressure elevations becomes so small that blood pressure does not have time to return to resting level before another anger stimulus initiates the next rise in blood pressure. Blood pressure is still excessively mobile, but resting level is now higher. The peaks and the valleys are the same as before, but resting diastolic level is above 95—the stage of benign hypertension. Once this second stage has been reached, the cycle proceeds inexorably to the third stage (malignant hypertension) by means of bodily reactions to the abnormally high blood pressure: more thickening of the arterioles and the arteries, interference with kidney filtration, and so on.

This account of the etiology of essential hypertension makes three assumptions. First, the potential hypertensive has a labile blood pressure. This has been reported in Harris et al. (1952), and it evidently carries through to the second stage—hypertensives are hyperreactive on the cold pressor test (Thacker, 1940). Second, potential hypertensives are more susceptible to anger, being resentful, jealous, and oversensitive to slights. They are triggered into anger more quickly than the average person. Third, they cannot cope with rage, failing to express aggression against those they blame. They are too insecure and frightened of retaliation, too guilt-stricken to launch an attack against those who anger them. Helpless to stem their recurrent rages or to alleviate tension by exploding into aggression, they remain tense and uncomfortable.

These last two assumptions have not been tested in an experiment or series of experiments. There is, however, a body of evidence that indicates their essential correctness, and this evidence will be reviewed after a brief discussion of the specificity issue.

The Problem of Specificity

An elevation in blood pressure is only one of the changes that occur in rage. There are also changes in such factors as heart rate, skin temperature, and stroke volume of the heart (Ax, 1953; Schachter, 1957). Why should suppressed rage lead to essential hypertension rather than neurodermatitis, which is also related to unexpressed anger? The answer may lie more in the realm of physiology than of psychology. It may be assumed that some individuals are more susceptible to cardiovascular disability, while others are more susceptible to skin disorders. It is not known whether such tendencies are hereditary, but the genetic component must exercise some influence. Special sensitivity has been amply demonstrated in allergic reactions, the organism being oversensitive to very small quantities of dust, pollen, seeds, proteins, etc. There has been no similar demonstration for cardiovascular disorders, although it is known that potential hypertensives overreact to the pain of the cold pressor test. It may be guessed that potential hypertensives have a lower threshold for stimuli that initiate a large blood pressure response, an oversensitivity similar to that seen in allergies.

There is also evidence for the notion of specificity in the work of Lacey (1950) and Schnore (1959), whose subjects displayed wide individual differences in physiological response. One individual might respond with a large jump in blood pressure and only a small rise in skin temperature; another might respond to the same stimulus with a slight blood pressure elevation but a maximal rise in skin temperature. Within a single individual the pattern tends to be consistent over time and across different stimuli. These works provide a physiological rationale for individual differences in symptom formation when the conflict concerns expression of aggression; one person might show a cardiovascular overreaction and another a skin overreaction.

Lacey's work on individual differences does not negate distinct patterns for anger and fear across individuals. It was shown in Chapter 6 that anger tends to increase blood pressure; in one subject the increase might be small and in another subject it might be large, but both subjects would show an increase. Thus the *direction* of blood pressure change in anger is always up, regardless of individual differences in *extent* of change. How much of an increase is determined by a number of psychological and physiological variables, which in proper combination may lead to essential hypertension.

Laboratory Studies of Essential Hypertension

Investigation of the dynamics of essential hypertension may take two forms. The first (laboratory) consists of angering the subject or bringing up topics about which he is resentful and then measuring his cardiovascular reactions. The second consists of the clinical study of personality characteristics in essential hypertensives. This section reviews laboratory studies.

Schachter (1957) divided subjects into three groups: hypertensives, 140/90 or over; potential hypertensives, initially 140/90 or over but dropping to below 135/85 after 30 minutes of rest; and normals, below 140/90 at all times (average blood pressure of 123/80). His anger situation, described in detail in Chapter 6, involved an assistant's verbally abusing and jostling the subjects. Only systolic blood pressure yielded significant differences in anger; hypertensives increased the most, followed by potential hypertensives and then normals. Diastolic pressure rose in all three groups, and the differences between groups were not significant. There was also a fear stimulus, and there were significant differences between groups in diastolic pressure; normals increased less than the other two groups. These findings offer only partial support for the dynamic formulation of hypertension mentioned earlier. The differential rise of systolic pressure in anger is supporting; the failure of diastolic pressure to rise differentially and the significant diastolic changes in fear suggest that the formulation needs amending. Evidently fear is as much a trigger for large jumps in blood pressure as is anger.

Neiberg (1957) compared hypertensives and patients with middle ear infection in an anger-arousing situation. The Wisconsin Card Sorting Test was administered, and subjects were failed randomly throughout the test, with the experimenter making nasty, derogatory comments about the subjects' performance. Mean blood pressure (a combined measure of both systolic and diastolic pressures) increased approximately the same for both groups, the hypertensives' resting and final levels being higher than those of the controls. The discrepancy between these findings and Schachter's may be due to either the difference in measures or the difference in anger-arousing situations.

Two other studies used anger arousal in the laboratory with hypertensive patients, but in neither instance was blood pressure the dependent variable. Matarazzo (1954) badgered hypertensives and controls during a TAT administration but found no differences in TAT aggression. Harris et al. (1953) had potential hypertensive women and controls role play in a situation that induced anger, and their behavior was rated by judges. The potential hypertensives were judged as being more irritable, more resentful, and less controlled in their emotional responses. In both these studies the dependent variable was personality characteristics; and in the four studies mentioned so far, anger was aroused in the laboratory. In the following investigations, hypertensives were stressed in clinical situations, and the dependent variable was blood pressure change.

Schneider & Zangari (1951) interviewed a normotensive anxiety hysteric and a hypertensive patient, in both instances bringing up affect-laden material during the interviews. The anxiety hysteric manifested no systematic fluctuation in blood pressure. When the hypertensive patient became anxious and resentful, both diastolic and systolic blood pressure rose steeply, returning to the resting state only after strong reassurance.

Wolf & Wolff (1951) interviewed a large number of hypertensives and controls. After a period during which the subject was placid, there was an abrupt switch to a discussion of significant and disturbing interpersonal problems. The subjects were divided into two groups on the basis of their reported reactions to this stress. One group reported being menaced and trapped, feeling not only anxious but resentful. Their blood pressure rose sharply: hypertensives' blood pressure increased from a mean of 165/103 to 189/117 and controls' from 119/76 to 131/81. The second group reported feeling defeated and overwhelmed, experiencing no resentment but only terror and despair. The blood pressure of both hypertensives and controls in this group *fell* below what it had been during the placid state. Note that both groups were anxious, but while the first group was also angry, the second group was not. Thus with anxiety held more or less constant, resentment elevated blood pressure and despair or depression lowered it. This is the strongest evidence available for the role of suppressed anger in the etiology of essential hypertension.

Moses et al. (1956) recorded the blood pressure of essential hypertensives undergoing psychoanalysis, attempting to relate blood pressure changes to the anxiety and anger that occurred during therapy. They found that rage and resentment predominated when blood pressure was in the 160/100—200/130 range, but anxiety predominated in the 140/90—160/100 range. During the course of therapy it was found that excessive rage reactions diminished, with a concomitant drop in blood pressure. Blood pressure never descended below borderline hypertensive levels, but it was accompanied by persistent anxiety. The investigators concluded that anxiety raises blood pressure to hypertensive levels, but rage elevates it beyond these levels.

These various laboratory studies raise two issues that are difficult for any dynamic formulation of hypertension to handle. First, there is evidence that in anger the blood pressure increase of normals is often no less than that of hypertensives. There are reasons, however, for believing that hypertensives have a more labile blood pressure than normals. It has been demonstrated on a large number of subjects that the blood pressure reaction of hypertensives to the cold pressor test is considerably more intense than that of normals (Thacker, 1940). Those with a normal resting blood pressure but an overlabile reaction to the cold pressor test have been shown to be especially susceptible to hypertension in later years.

The absence of a differential rise in blood pressure between hypertensives and normals may be due to artifacts. Because of sampling errors, a particular group of normal subjects might be more susceptible to anger than a given group of hypertensives; in this event, the lability of the hypertensives' blood pressure would be canceled out by the greater psychological reactivity of the normals. Another kind of artifact is more systematic. Lacey (1959) has discovered a negative relationship between resting level and amount of increase in a number of physiological measures, including blood pressure. He finds that the higher the resting level, the smaller is the increase during experimental arousal. This effect is evidently so pervasive that Lacey has proposed a regression equation as a statistical means of canceling it. Thus, if an investigator used essential hypertensives whose blood pressures were extremely high, he would have difficulty in demonstrating a differential increase over that of normals. This may account for the discrepancy in findings—some investigators reporting a differential increase and others not—when hypertensives and normals are angered in laboratory situations.

The second difficulty for a dynamic formulation of essential hypertension is the tendency of blood pressure to rise not only in anger but also in fear. There is evidence (Davis & Buchwald, 1957) that a variety of psychological stimuli initiate a blood pressure response, the cardiovascular system being mobile. It is highly probable that maximal blood pressure response to psychological stimuli occurs in the presence of anger and fear. Fear was not included in the dynamic formulation described earlier, yet it is evidently as potent as anger in elevating blood pressure. Any formulation of the dynamics of essential hypertension must explain why fear does not lead to hypertension. The formulation presented earlier must therefore be amended, as follows.

Consider the sequence of events that begin with an anger stimulus. The individual immediately reacts with anger, his blood pressure soaring as part of the general preparation for attack. If the attack occurs, it will dissipate the physiological tension of anger, returning blood pressure to its resting level. Another way of relieving tension is to go through all the motions of attack without attacking anyone—a temper tantrum. Whether the response is a coordinated attack or a violent flailing about, as in a temper tantrum, blood pressure should return to its resting level. What happens if neither of these responses occurs? Once the anger stimulus is removed, the tension state should start to dissipate, but in the absence of a temper or attack response, some time will elapse before resting level is reached. Note that only violent action (temper tantrum) or attack will dissipate the tension state of anger.

Now consider the sequence that is initiated by a fear stimulus. In fear the individual's blood pressure will also be sent skyrocketing, and it will remain high so long as the fear stimulus continues to impinge on the individual. But, like anger stimuli, fear stimuli occur quickly and then are removed. When the fear stimulus ceases to impinge on the individual, his tension level drops quickly to resting level. In the event that the fear stimulus persists, there are two kinds of instrumental responses that serve to reduce tension. The first is aggressive action; eliminate the fear stimulus by destroying it or removing its source from the scene. The second is flight; escape from the noxious stimulus by placing distance between it and the self. These two alternatives represent the familiar flight-or-fight reaction.

Now compare the two sequences. In anger, removal of the anger stimulus does not lead to an immediate diminution of blood pressure; reduction of tension is achieved principally by making one class of instrumental responses, attack. If the attack is not made, considerable time is required for blood pressure to return to normal. In fear, on the other hand, removal of the fear stimulus initiates an immediate diminution of blood pressure. The instrumental response that diminishes fear consists of any action that eliminates the noxious stimulus, and so long as the stimulus is removed *by any means,* blood pressure will start to return to resting level. In contrast, anger is not dissipated by the mere removal of the noxious stimulus. Fear can be reduced by a variety of instrumental escape responses; anger only by aggression or a temper tantrum. Note that when the anger stimulus is removed, it may be impossible for aggression to occur because the object of aggression (source of the anger stimulus) is no longer available. There are many reasons for an aggressive response not to occur: removal of the object of aggression, guilt concerning aggression, fear concerning retaliation, etc. On the other hand, there are few reasons for an escape response's not occurring; not only is it proper to protect oneself from noxious stimuli, but escape does not require the interpersonal situation that aggression does.

In brief, it is easier to make the instrumental responses that diminish fear than it is to make those that diminish anger. Although blood pressure is elevated equally by fear and anger, it should remain elevated longer in anger than in fear. This hypothesis has not been tested, perhaps because investigators are more interested in arousal than in time taken to return to resting state. A comparison of the time taken to return to resting state after fear and after anger stimuli should provide data bearing on the hypothesis. Once the arousing stimuli cease, it follows that blood pressure should return to its resting level faster in fear than in anger, so long as the individual is prevented from attacking.

Clinical Studies

Laboratory studies have indicated that suppressed rage is a major variable in the etiology of essential hypertension. Consequently, essential hypertensives should have more suppressed anger than normals; they should be more hostile and less aggressive than normals. On the basis of psychoanalytic therapy with essential hypertensives, Alexander (1950) and Saul (1939) have described the hypertensive's core conflict as follows. His passive, dependent tendencies are opposed by overcompensatory aggressive tendencies. He can neither accept his passivity nor express his aggression and hostility. Beneath his passive façade the hypertensive is angry and resentful, the unexpressed anger being the cause of chronic high blood pressure.

The problem with this formulation is that it fits many neurotics as well as essential hypertensives. Most neurotics do not express aggression easily because of both guilt and fear of retaliation; they are resentful of others and tend to be both hostile and nonaggressive. Neurotics may attack others in devious ways, but they are not directly aggressive. However, neurotics and essential hypertensives are only superficially similar in their handling of anger and aggression. The neurotic has defenses that help him to avoid anger-arousing situations; once he becomes involved with anger stimuli, he has defenses that prevent him from developing uncontrolled rage. The phobic tends to avoid situations that are fraught with the danger of attack either by himself or others; the compulsive becomes involved with his rituals, thereby avoiding both anger and aggression; the obsessive mulls over the pros and cons of action, displacing his anger and putting sufficient psychological distance between himself and the anger stimulus for him to remain relatively placid.

Unlike the neurotic, the essential hypertensive has no well-developed defenses against becoming enraged. Though he is aware of his burning anger, he tends neither to admit it nor to act it out against the targets of anger. Unable to deal with his aggressive tendencies by either action or by neurotic defenses, the hypertensive must rely on suppression at the last possible moment. After he is worked up with rage and all the physiological preparations for attack have been made, he makes a last-ditch attempt to suppress his anger. The attempt is usually successful, and he remains bottled up in a state of impotent rage. The neurotic does not attain such peaks of prolonged rage because his attempts to cope with anger are made much earlier in the sequence. The hypertensive apparently cannot forestall anger in this fashion and must rely on suppression of aggression at the last possible moment.

These differences between neurotics and hypertensives may become blurred in clinical practice. Neurotic defenses may utterly fail to cope with the conflicts aroused by anger stimuli, and the individual may have to rely on suppression of aggression. He is then caught in the same cycle as the hypertensive, and in clinical situations one sees hypertensives with remnants of earlier, unsuccessful defense mechanisms.

In Chapter 10 a behavioral formulation of the development of aggressiveness was presented, in which such variables as reactivity and impulsiveness were important. These variables are also relevant in the present context. One individual may have a tendency to overreact and to respond quickly, and he requires more defenses against aggression if he is to adjust in present-day society. Neurotic defenses may be insufficient to deal with aggressive conflicts, and he may resort to the kind of suppression seen in hypertensives. Another individual may be slower to react and then react only mildly; yet he may not have developed any defense mechanisms for coping with aggressive conflicts. He too may be forced to suppress aggressive tendencies and become involved in the hypertensive sequence. Thus individuals of divergent temperaments may end up with essential hypertension. The common denominator would seem to be suppressed anger, not impulsivity, reactivity, or any other enduring personality characteristics. With these considerations as background, clinical studies of hypertensives will be reviewed. They may be divided into interview studies and studies employing tests.

Interview studies. These investigations were conducted in clinical settings, and they usually lacked objectivity, controls, and statistical tests. Two studies did employ controls. Saul (1939) reported on hypertensives and neurotic normotensives who were undergoing psychoanalysis. Both groups had essentially the same conflict, passivity versus aggressiveness. Saul suggested that the neurotics avoided high blood pressure by being more accepting of their passivity and also by employing defense mechanisms. Gressel et al. (1949) compared essential hypertensives with two control groups; one consisted of psychiatric outpatients and the other of medical outpatients. The three groups were roughly matched for age, sex, education, and occupation, and all' subjects were rated for six personality variables. The hypertensives were found to differ significantly from the medical patients on all but one of the personality variables, but they differed from the psychiatric patients only on assertiveness and obsessive-compulsiveness. The hypertensives tended to be subnormally assertive and unable to verbalize anger or hostility even to their physicians.

Unlike these first two investigations, most clinical studies have not had control subjects, and there is no way of knowing whether the personality patterns reported are unique to essential hypertension. Therefore, the value of these studies lies in whether they are consistent with the hypothesized hypertensive dynamics: anger and resentment are intense, but there is an inability to express aggression.

Robbins (1948) and Schwartz (1940) reported on hypertensive patients undergoing psychoanalysis, noting the typical pattern of suppressed rage. Suppressed rage was also mentioned by Weiss (1942) in his review of 144 cases of essential hypertension. Engel (1953) followed a case of essential hypertension for 9 years and reported that vasopressor attacks usually occurred in a setting of unexpressed anger accompanied by guilt. Suppression of aggression was also noted by Binger et al. (1945), and Tucker (1949) mentioned that his hypertensive patients kept their hostility to themselves. Wolf & Wolff (1946) reported an appearance of affability in hypertensives that overlay suspicion and strong desires to act out aggressively. Hambling (1951) found suppressed rage directed toward the parental figure whom the hypertensive saw as rejecting. Reiser et al. (1951) concluded that the predominant conflict in hypertensives concerned ambivalence toward parental figures, with hostility being only one source of conflict.

Taken together, these studies offer evidence consistent with the hypothesis that suppressed anger is basic to the development of essential hypertension. Most of the studies mentioned other personality characteristics, and the total number of characteristics ascribed to hypertensives is large. Examination of all the personality variables reported in these studies leads to no consistent finding, with the sole exception of unexpressed anger. Thus there is no "hypertensive personality," but hypertensives tend to suppress rage, however else they differ among themselves.

These studies all used interviews to obtain information. The disadvantages of interviews have already been mentioned, but one advantage should be cited. It is possible in an interview or series of interviews to go beyond the patient's façade, the picture he presents to the world. As a group, hypertensives are rigid and hostile, and they tend not to admit their intense, covert hostility. Interviews are more likely to elicit such information than objective instruments like inventories. Projective techniques should be valuable here, but while they may be better than inventories in discovering covert trends, they are hardly more objective than interviews.

Studies with tests. One of the earliest studies on the personality characteristics of hypertensives used a questionnaire. Ayman (1933) had essential hypertensives and normals fill out a personality inventory and found that hypertensives reported themselves as being more sensitive, quick-tempered, and hyperactive than normals. Storment (1951) compared hypertensives with medical patient controls in a study with the Guilford-Martin inventories. The inventories contained 13 personality factors, and an analysis of variance yielded no significant difference between hypertensives and controls. The only positive trend was for hypertensives and rheumatic heart patients to describe themselves as overcritical and intolerant.

In a large scale, well-controlled investigation, Hamilton (1942) studied three groups of normal subjects: those with high, normal, and low blood pressure (the highs and lows not being pathologically so). Only a few items in a trait rating scale significantly distinguished the highs from the normals, but the differences were sufficiently reliable to appear again on cross validation. The potential hypertensives (highs) were characterized by low dominance, low assertiveness, and susceptibility to anger; the lows were in the opposite direction, being high dominant, high assertive, and unsusceptible to anger in comparison to the normals. The tendency of the lows to have personality characteristics opposite to those of the highs is a striking result, and it corroborates the postulated personality dimensions believed to be crucial in the etiology of essential hypertension: aggressiveness and control of anger.

The remaining studies all attempted to assess personality in hypertensives by means of projective techniques. Saul et al. (1954) employed the unusual technique of analyzing dreams for hostility, comparing normal and hypertensive college students. The dreams were rated for hostility on a six-point scale that ranged from actual or threatened death of people to minor impairment of objects. The hypertensives had dreams that were significantly more hostile than the normals' dreams.

Modell & Potter (1949) analyzed the drawings of hypertension, bronchial asthma, and peptic ulcer patients. They evolved a picture of hypertensives that ostensibly differed from that of the other two groups—inadequate, weak, depleted, and helpless. Anger and aggression did not appear in the hypertensives' drawings.

Two studies used the Rorschach, the first subjectively and the second objectively. Kemple (1945) compared essential hypertensives with several hospitalized groups, presenting her interpretations without any attempt to determine reliability or statistical significance. Hypertensives were described as ambitious for power, consciously hostile, introversive, obsessive-compulsive, and caught in a passive-aggressive conflict with passive trends predominating. Thaler et al. (1957) administered Rorschachs to hypertensives, patients with peptic ulcer, and control groups of medical patients. The DeVos system was used to score the Rorschachs for hostility, but hostile content did not differentiate hypertensives from the control groups.

In the same study another projective technique was used, the Doctor-Patient Projective Stories, which required the subjects to complete and interpret stories of doctor-patient interactions. Responses were scored positive (doctor is helpful, benign), neutral, or negative (doctor is not helpful, hostile). The hypertensives gave significantly more negative responses than the other groups, evidently considering doctor-patient relationships to be unpleasant and unfriendly. This finding is consistent with the observations of physicians, who consider hypertensives to be among the least cooperative and most difficult, negative patients. Thaler et al. attempted to reconcile the positive Doctor-Patient findings with the negative Rorschach findings by suggesting that the hypertensive is not necessarily aggressive but sees his environment as hostile and dangerous. He projects his hostility and aggressive tendencies onto others and is sensitive to slights. Though he tries to avoid close relationships, his hostile attitude provokes anger in others. This is especially true in his relationship with authority figures, the passive role apparently mobilizing considerable anger toward those in dominant positions.

In two studies the TAT was used to detect hostile tendencies. Schweers (1950) rated the TAT protocols of essential hypertensives and found that they were low in aggression and dominance. Hinkle administered four TAT cards and a forced-choice TAT to hypertensives and outpatient controls. The hypertensives told significantly few aggressive stories on the TAT, but there were no significant differences between groups on the forced-choice TAT.

Leary (1957) studied a number of symptom groups, including essential hypertensives and other psychosomatic patients; self-reports, fantasy, and projective techniques were used. The core conflict for hypertensives was between a façade of gentleness and intense inner rage.

In summary, the studies with tests tend to support the notion that hypertensives are caught in an intense approach-avoidance conflict concerning anger. They are covertly resentful and cannot prevent intense bouts of rage, but neither can they act out their aggressive tendencies. When the clinical studies are considered as a whole, the picture is the same, with few exceptions. When the laboratory studies are added, there is further confirming evidence concerning the role of suppressed anger in the etiology of essential hypertension. It may be concluded that a passive-aggressive conflict is the hypertensive's core problem, and it is doubtful that further clinical studies would add to knowledge in this area; rather, more laboratory studies are needed to bridge the gap between diastolic reaction and benign hypertension.

NEURODERMATITIS

Neurodermatitis is a syndrome characterized by reddening and thickening of the skin, exudation of liquid, and intense itching. It tends to be chronic and cannot be ascribed to the action of allergens or specific skin irritants (mechanical, chemical, or thermal). It also goes by the names *atopic dermatitis* and *disseminated neurodermatitis;* together with psychogenic hives and other skin disorders having a large psychological component, it falls under the heading of the *neurodermatoses.*

The psychosomatic aspects of skin disorders have been emphasized only in recent years, and there is considerably less research on neuro-dermatitis than on essential hypertension. The kinds of research in the two areas have followed the same pattern; clinical studies using interviews or tests and laboratory studies in which an attempt is made to exacerbate or ameliorate symptoms by psychological means.

Clinical Studies

The studies vary markedly in controls, quantification, objectivity, and tests of significance. Investigations in which the case study approach was employed are the most qualitative and subjective; these will be reviewed first, followed by studies with tests.

Case studies. Dunkel (1949) reported on a series of neuroderma-titis patients seen in a social casework setting. As a group, they tended to be tense, exhibitionistic in dress or behavior, and nega-tivistic though superficially cooperative. They insisted that they like everyone and bear no one any ill will, but this façade of good will and submission to authority was believed to conceal the most striking characteristic of these patients—intense, covert hostility. An over-strict conscience was prominent, repressing any recognition of resent-ment toward others. It was possible to interview some of the parents of these patients, and, typically, one parent (especially the mother) was domineering and rigid; the impression was that the mother could barely tolerate her child. Dunkel concluded that the major psychological component of neurodermatitis is guilty suppres-sion of hostility.

Grace & Graham (1952) conducted detailed interviews with patients exhibiting several kinds of psychosomatic disorder. They noted that suppressed hostility played a major role in virtually all the syn-dromes, but the special feature of atopic eczema patients was their severe frustration. These patients reported interference from parental figures, with whom there was no reasoning or possibility of change. As a consequence, they tended to develop feelings of chronic frustra-tion and anger, as well as skin reddening and itching.

After examining a large series of neurodermatitis patients, Mc-Laughlin et al. (1953) arrived at the following formulation. Such patients have typically been rejected by their mothers and are over-conforming in an attempt to secure love and attention in the context of a parent-child relationship. Although they tend not to express their emotions, there is an intense underlying resentment concerning their being unloved, such hostility being chronic and intense. In addition, there are sexual conflicts, especially concerning sexual identification.

Lynch et al. (1945) also noted the prominence of intense repressed hatred in their series of neurodermatitis cases. Kepecs et al. (1951) emphasized the importance of sexual conflicts in the development of atopic eczema, but unexpressed anger was also noted. Their patients presented a façade of timidity and shyness, being unable to express their hostility except in dreams and projective techniques. Itching and scratching were interpreted as signs of anger inverted toward the self because it could not be directed toward the frustrating mother-figure or the object of sexual attachment.

Studies with tests. When projective techniques have been em-ployed, they have unfortunately been interpreted qualitatively for the most part. Despite the lack of objectivity inherent in qualitative interpretation, the results of various studies have been consistent enough to suggest at least some reliability. Levy (1952) compared the Rorschach of neurodermatitis patients with control subjects who had skin problems due to external irritants (chemical, mechanical, and thermal). In Levy's opinion, the neurodermatitis patients were characterized by intense repressed hostility. Fiske & Obermayer (1954) administered a battery of tests to atopic eczema patients: Rorschach, TAT, Draw-a-Person, and Shipley-Hartford Scale. On the basis of these tests and biographical information it was con-cluded that the basic personality of the neurodermatitis patient has elements of sadism, paranoia, and aggression; also noted were maso-chism, insecurity, sensitivity, dependency, and marked sexual con-flicts.

Rabin & Kepecs (1954) administered Rorschachs to neuroderma-titis patients, neurotics, and normals. On the basis of both quantita-tive and qualitative analysis of the protocols, they concluded that both sexual conflicts and inability to express resentment are charac-teristics of neurodermatitis patients. Cleveland & Fisher (1956) administered Rorschachs to *neurodermatosis* patients, other psycho-somatic groups, and controls. Since most of the neurodermatosis patients probably had atopic eczema, their finding that such patients had fewer hostile responses may be accepted as consistent with those of other studies also reporting inhibition of hostility.

Several studies employed questionnaires. Allerhand et al. (1950) attempted to construct an empirical "neurodermatitis scale" by means of the usual item analysis techniques, starting out with a 108 item inventory. They found that 25 items significantly differentiated between neurodermatitis patients and other groups. Moldawsky (1953) cross-validated the scale, checking it out on neurodermatitis patients and others with skin disorders, as well as control groups. She found that the scale failed to distinguish between any of the groups, which again emphasizes the need for careful follow-up of any empirically derived instrument.

In one of the earliest studies on the personality characteristics of neurodermatitis patients, Greenhill & Finesinger (1942) compared the inventory responses of neurodermatitis patients, lupus erythematosus patients, neurotics, and normals. The neurodermatitis patients revealed much more hostility toward their parents than any other group. Comparison of interviews with neurodermatitis and lupus erythematosus patients suggested that the former had more suppressed, inwardly directed anger and more depression.

Two recent studies have used the TAT. Gross (1958) compared the TAT protocols of female neurodermatitis patients and matched normal controls. The protocols were scored for themes that ostensibly characterize neurodermatitis patients, such as domination by mother, sexual conflicts, and suppressed anger. There was no significant difference between normals and patients. One reason for this negative finding may have been the pooling of all characteristics into a single score. If sexual conflict and suppressed anger had been isolated and tested separately, the chances for significant findings might have been better.

This suggestion finds support in a study by Klaber (1960). He compared neurodermatitis patients with subjects whose skin disorders were of clearly nonpsychogenic origin. The TAT protocols were scored for hostility, and the neurodermatitis patients had a significantly higher hostility score than the controls. Klaber also attempted to check out the "neurodermatitis scale" of Allerhand et al. and found, as did Moldawsky, that it failed to distinguish between patients and controls.

Klaber's final measure was an operant conditioning task with hostile verbal materials, similar to that described in Chapter 7. Neurodermatitis patients gave significantly *fewer* hostile responses during the free operant period than did the controls, but the conditioning and extinction series yielded no significant difference between groups. In attempting to explain why the neurodermatitis patients had more hostility on the TAT and less on the sentence construction task, Klaber suggested that they are less overtly hostile (sentences) and more covertly hostile (TAT). This suggestion requires the assumption that the TAT is a measure of covert hostility rather than of overt hostility.

Laboratory Studies

The term *laboratory* again includes all experimental studies, whether they were conducted in a laboratory or in a clinic. Only one experiment was conducted in the laboratory with normal subjects, and it is recent (Graham et al., 1960). College men were hypnotized, and two attitudes were suggested. The first was an attitude of "being unfairly treated and not being able to do anything about it," which ostensibly is associated with skin disorders; the second was "being constantly on guard" (containing elements of both hostile suspiciousness and anxiety), which ostensibly is associated with hypertension. It was found that skin temperature rose significantly higher during the "skin disorder attitude" than during the "hypertension attitude," whereas blood pressure rose significantly higher during the suspicious attitude than during the resentful attitude. This represents a striking confirmation not only of the clinical studies just mentioned but also of the formulation of essential hypertension mentioned earlier. Assuming that a rise in skin temperature leads to skin symptoms, it suggests that a key element in the etiology of neurodermatitis is anger that is probably directed toward an authority figure who in some way is blocking the individual. The study is important not only for its results but also for its method; hypnotic suggestion is an excellent technique for investigating the psychosomatic hypotheses that have emerged from clinical studies.

The remaining three studies all took place within the context of psychotherapy. Seitz (1953) attempted brief psychotherapy with neurodermatitis patients, the principal technique being encouragement of angry verbal outbursts. He found that as patients came near to expressing rage, their skin symptoms worsened, causing some of them to quit therapy. Of those who remained, all were able to express aggression and anger in one form or another; shouting, screaming, pounding on the desk, cursing, etc. After continued outbursts and a dawning awareness of their anger, all but one of these patients showed rapid improvement of skin symptoms. Approximately half of those who improved were followed up, and after 6 months all but one were still free of skin symptoms. Another 6-month interval brought about one more relapse, but the majority of those followed had maintained their remission from symptoms. Since the major event that preceded symptom alleviation was the expression of rage, these results lend credence to the hypothesis that suppressed anger underlies neurodermatitis.

Shoemaker et al. (1955) conducted group psychotherapy with neurodermatitis patients, with the therapists keeping their intervention minimal (asking questions about home, job, spouse, etc.) After a number of sessions, some of the patients began to aggress verbally, with most of the aggression directed toward the physicians and medicine in general. Some patients became not only verbally demanding of the therapists but also negativistic, refusing to continue in therapy despite the improvement of their symptoms. Several other patients kept their hostility covert, but they too quit the group. The difference between the two groups who quit therapy was that the aggressive patients showed at least some symptom remission, while those who did not express their anger showed no improvement. Of those who remained in therapy, only the patients who eventually became verbally aggressive manifested any amelioration of the skin disorder, while the others remained unimproved.

Finally, Obermayer (1955) reported a project in which the therapist deliberately mentioned sexual or aggressive conflicts in order to gauge the effect on patients' symptoms. The intrusion of these "loaded" topics tended to exacerbate skin symptoms, but when the patient reacted with an outburst of resentment toward a crucial figure in his life, the skin inflammation subsided.

A Formulation

The clinical studies describe a variety of personality features in neurodermatitis patients, but there are two common threads. The first is sexual conflict, which is seen as hysterical tendencies, exhibitionism, ambivalence concerning sex role, etc.; and the second is the presence of suppressed rage. The laboratory studies are more unequivocal in pointing to suppressed anger as the most crucial determinant in the etiology of neurodermatitis. It has been shown that unexpressed rage is associated with an increase in skin temperature and with the exacerbation of skin symptoms; it has also been demonstrated that skin symptoms tend to subside after an outburst of anger. These facts may be pulled together to make a tentative dynamic formulation of neurodermatitis.

The individual is sensitive to anger stimuli and tends to overreact with more rage than is called for. He feels too weak and childlike to vent his anger against those (authority figures) who thwart him, denying him what he wants. In a world he sees as threatening, he is too fearful of retaliation to strike out even verbally at the targets of his hostility. Because he cannot vent his rage, it dissipates slowly, the state of physiological tension being maintained for some time. In the individual who develops neurodermatitis, the physiological changes in anger are greatest in the skin; a rise in skin temperature as a consequence of dilatation of arterioles. These temporary skin changes tend to be more frequent in such individuals because of their excessive sensitivity to anger stimuli, and they tend to last longer because of an inability to discharge physiological tension by means of an outburst of aggression.

The transition from temporary to chronic skin symptoms is facilitated by scratching. The skin symptom itself often produces an intense itching sensation, and it requires more self-control than most humans possess to refrain from rubbing or scratching an expanse of itchy skin. The scratching further exacerbates the symptom, prolonging its duration and priming the skin for a worse outbreak the next time an anger stimulus impinges.

There is unequivocal evidence that the skin is a labile enough system for it to respond as indicated. Graham et al. (1960) demonstrated that skin temperature could be elevated merely by suggesting an attitude. There have been other hypnotic demonstrations of more striking skin changes, e.g., the development of a blister in a deeply hypnotized subject in response to the suggestion that a burning match was touching the skin.

The skin is a likely site for psychosomatic symptoms. It is responsive to emotional changes and it has usually been primed for symptoms by a variety of nonpsychological irritants. Because the skin shields the body from chemical, mechanical, and thermal stimuli, it receives the full brunt of such stimuli and is often adversely affected by them. Once such irritants are removed, the skin recuperates and symptoms vanish. The sites of such changes, however, often undergo permanent change in that they are hypersensitive to future irritants. Such locales are then primed for future exacerbation of symptoms as a result of suppressed rage. Thus it is not necessary for unexpressed anger to initiate skin symptoms anew but merely to give rise to skin changes at body sites that are already primed for such changes. This may be accomplished in one of two ways. First, the rise in skin temperature may lead immediately to itching and exudation. Second, the heightened physiological tension may render the skin more sensitive to nonpsychological irritants, thus making it more likely that such agents will cause skin eruption.

Earlier it was noted that suppressed anger appears to underlie both essential hypertension and neurodermatitis. Also, it was suggested that the reason for one individual's developing blood pressure symptoms and another's developing skin symptoms probably lies within the realm of physiology. It should be added, however, that there may be a minor psychological component. The prevalence of sexual conflicts and exhibitionism in neurodermatitis patients has been reported in a number of studies. It is also known that most essential hypertensives are men, whereas most neurodermatitis patients are women. It may well be that the additional variable of sexual conflict tips the scale toward skin disorder, the skin symptom being determined not only by suppressed rage but also by a strong need to exhibit oneself.

NOTES

It was mentioned at the beginning of this chapter that only essential hypertension and neurodermatitis would be discussed, the reason for this being their close relationship to suppressed rage. Though no other psychosomatic disorder is as closely linked to problems of aggression and hostility as these two, some investigators have mentioned migraine headache. Because the evidence relating this disorder to aggression and hostility is sparse and by no means consistently positive, it has not been discussed. The interested reader will find migraine discussed in Brenner et al. (1949); Engel et al. (1953); Fromm-Reichmann (1937); Lustman (1951); Marcussen & Wolff (1949); and Van der Linde (1955).

REFERENCES

Allerhand, M. E., Gough, H. G., & Grais, M. C. Personality factors in neurodermatitis: A preliminary report. *Psychosom. Med.*, 1950, 12, 386–390.

Alexander, F. *Psychosomatic Medicine.* New York: Norton, 1950.

Alexander, F. Emotional factors in essential hypertension. *Psychosom. Med.*, 1939, 1, 173–179.

Ax, A. F.   The physiological differentiation between fear and anger in humans. *Psychosom. Med.*, 1953, **15**, 433–442.

Ayman, O.   Personality type of patients with arteriolar essential hypertension. *Amer. J. Med. Sci.*, 1933, **186**, 213–223.

Binger, C. A. L., Ackerman, N. W., Cohn, A. E., Schroeder, H. A., & Steele, J. M.   Personality in arterial hypertension. *Psychosom. Med. Monog.*, 1945, No. 8.

Brenner, C., Friedman, A. P. & Carter, S.   Psychologic factors in the etiology and treatment of chronic headache. *Psychosom. Med.*, 1949, **11**, 55–56.

Cleveland, S. E. & Fisher, S.   Psychological factors in the neurodermatoses. *Psychosom. Med.*, 1956, **18**, 209–220.

Davis, R. C. & Buchwald, A. M.   An exploration of somatic response patterns: stimulus and sex differences. *J. comp. physiol. Psychol.*, 1957, **50**, 44–52.

Dunkel, Mary L.   Casework help for neurodermatitis patients. *J. soc. Casewk.* 1949, **30**, 97–103.

Engel, G. L., Hamburger, W. W., Reiser, M. & Plunkett, Jr.   Electroencephalographic and psychological studies of a case of migraine with severe preheadache phenomena. *Psychosom. Med.*, 1953, **19**, 337–348.

Fiske, C. E., & Obermayer, M. E.   Personality and emotional factors in chronic neurodermatitis. *Arch. derm. & Syph.*, 1954, **70**, 261–268.

Fromm-Reichmann, Frieda.   Contribution to the psycho-genesis of migraine. *Psychoanal. Rev.*, 1937, **24**, 26–33.

Grace, W. J. & Graham, D. T.   Relationship of specific attitudes and emotions to certain bodily diseases. *Psychosom. Med.*, 1952, **14**, 242–251.

Graham, D., Graham, Frances K., & Kabler, J. D.   Experimental production of predicted physiological differences by suggestion of attitude. Paper presented at American Psychosomatic Society meetings, 1960.

Greenhill, M. H. & Finesinger, J. E.   Neurotic symptoms and emotional factors in atopic dermatitis. *Arch. derm. & Syph.*, 1942, **46**, 187–200.

Gressel, G. C., Shobe, F. O., Laslow, G., Dubois, P. H., & Schroeder, H. A.   Personality factors in arterial hypertension. *J.A.M.A.*, 1949, **140**, 265–272.

Gross, D. H.   A test of the personality traits attributed to female atopic eczema patients. Unpublished master's thesis., University of Pittsburgh, 1959.

Hambling, J.   Psychosomatic aspects of arterial hypertension. *Br. J. Med. Psychol,* **25**, 39–47, 1952.

Hambling, J.   Emotions and symptoms in essential hypertension. *Br. J. Med. Psychol.*, **24**, 242–253, 1951.

Hamilton, J. A.   Psychophysiology of blood pressure. *Psychosom. Med.*, 1942, **4**, 125–133.

Harris, R. E., Sokolow, M., Carpenter, W. G., Freedman, M., & Hunt, S. P.   Response to psychological stress in persons who are potentially hypertensive. *Circulation*, 1953, **7**, 874–879.

Kemple, C.   Rorschach method and psychosomatic diagnosis. *Psychosom. Med.*, 1945, **7**, 85–89.

Kepecs, J. C., Rabin, A., & Robin, M.   Atopic dermatitis. *Psychosom. Med.*, 1951, **13**, 1–9.

Klaber, M. M.   Manifestations of hostility in neuro-dermatitis. *J. consult. Psychol.* 1960, **2**, 116–120.

Lacey, J. I.   Psychophysiological approaches to the evaluation of psychotherapeutic process and outcome. In Rubinstein, E. A. & Parloff, M. B.

(Eds.), *Research in Psychotherapy.* Washington, D.C.: American Psychological Assn., 1959.

Lacey, J. I. Individual differences in somatic response patterns. *J. comp. Psychol.* 1950, **43**, 338–350.

Leary, T. *Interpersonal diagnosis of personality.* New York: Ronald Press, 1957.

Levy, Ruth J. The Rorschach pattern in neurodermatitis. *Psychosom. Med.,* 1952, **14**, 41–49.

Lustman, S. L. The headache as an internalized rage reaction. *Psychiatry,* 1951, **14**, 433–438.

Lynch, F. W., Hinckley, R. G., & Cowan, D. W. Psychosomatic studies in dermatology: B. Psychobiologic studies of patients with atopic eczema (disseminated neurodermatitis). *Arch. Derm. Syph.,* 1953, **51**, 251–257.

McLaughlin, J. T., Shoemaker, R. J., & Guy, W. B. Personality factors in adult atopic eczema. *Arch. derm. & Syph.,* 1953, **68**, 506–516.

Marcussen, R. M. & Wolff, H. G. A formulation of the dynamics of the migraine headache. *Psychosom. Med.,* 1949, **11**, 251–256.

Matarazzo, J. O. An experimental study of aggression in the hypertensive patient. *J. Pers.,* 1954, **22**, 423–447.

Miller, M. L. Psychodynamic mechanisms in a case of neurodermatitis. *Psychosom. Med.,* 1948, **10**, 309–316.

Modell, A. H. & Potter, H. W. Human figure drawing of patients with arterial hypertension, peptic ulcer, and bronchial asthma. *Psychosom. Med.,* 1949, **11**, 282–292.

Moldawsky, Patricia. A study of personality variables in patients with skin disorders. Unpublished doctor's dissertation, State University, Iowa, 1953.

Moses, L., Daniels, G. E., & Nickerson, J. L. Psychogenic factors in essential hypertension: methodology and preliminary report. *Psychosom. Med.,* 1956, **28**, 471–485.

Neiberg, N. A. The effects of induced stress on the management of hostility in essential hypertension. Unpublished doctor's dissertation, Boston University, 1957.

Obermayer, M. E. *Psychocutaneous medicine.* Springfield, Ill.: Thomas, 1955.

Rabin, A. I. & Kepecs, J. Personality structure in atopic dermatitis: a Rorschach study. *J. gen. Psychol.,* 1954, **50**, 171–180.

Reiser, M. F., Brust, A. A., & Ferris, E. B. Life situations, emotions, and the course of patients with arterial hypertension. *Psychosom. Med.,* 1951, **13**, 133–139.

Reiser, M. F., Reeves, R. B., & Armington, J. Effect of variation in laboratory procedure and experiments upon the ballisto-cardiogram, blood pressure, and heart rate in healthy young men. *Psychosom. Med.,* 1955, **17**, 185–199.

Reiser, M. F., Rosenbaum, M., & Ferris, E. B., Jr. Psychologic mechanisms in malignant hypertension. *Psychosom. Med.,* 1951, **13**, 147–159.

Robbins, Lewis, L. Psychological factors in essential hypertension. *Bull. Menninger Clin.,* 1948, **12**, 195–202.

Saul, L. J., Sheppard, Edith, Selby, Dorothy, Lhamon, W., Sachs, D., & Master, Regina. The quantification of hostility in dreams with reference to essential hypertension. *Science,* 1954, **119**, 382–383.

Saul, L. J. Hostility in cases of essential hypertension. *Psychosom. Med.*, 1939, **1**, 153–161.

Schachter, J. Pain, fear, and anger in hypertensives and normotensives: a psycho-physiological study. *Psychosom. Med.*, 1957, **29**, 17–29.

Schneider, R. A. & Zangari, Violet, M. Variations in clotting time, relative viscosity, and other physiochemical properties of the blood accompanying physical and emotional stress in the normotensive and hypertensive subject. *Psychosom. Med.*, 1951, **13**, 288–303.

Schnore, M. M. Individual patterns of physiological activity as a function of task differences and degree of arousal. *J. exp. Psychol.*, 1959, **58**, 117–128.

Schwartz, L. A. An analyzed case of essential hypertension. *Psychosom. Med.*, 1940, **2**, 468–486.

Schweers, R. Some personality correlates of essential hypertension. Unpublished master's thesis, University of California, 1950.

Seitz, P. F. Dynamically oriented brief psychotherapy: psychocutaneous exoriation syndromes. *Psychosom. Med.*, 1953, **15**, 200–241.

Shoemaker, R. J., Guy, W. B., & McLaughlin, J. T. The usefulness of group therapy in the management of atopic eczema. *Penn. Med. J.*, 1955, **58**, 603–609.

Storment, C. T. Personality and heart disease. *Psychosom. Med.*, 1951, **13**, 304–313.

Thacker, E. A. A comparative study of normal and abnormal blood pressure among university students, including the cold pressor test. *Amer. Heart J.*, 1940, **20**, 89–97.

Thaler, Margaret, Weiner, H., & Reiser, M. F. Exploration of the doctor-patient relationship through projective techniques. *Psychosom. Med.*, 1957, **19**, 228–239.

Tucker, W. I. Psychiatric factors in essential hypertension. *Dis. Nerv. Syst.* **10**, 273–378, 1949.

Vander, Linde, Jr. Management of hostility in adult males with migraine headaches. Unpublished doctor's dissertation, Boston University, 1955.

Van der Valk, J. M. Blood-pressure changes under emotional influences, in patients with essential hypertension, and control subjects. *J. psychosom. Res.*, 1957, **2**, 134–146.

Weiss, E. Psychosomatic aspects of hypertension. *J.A.M.A.*, 1942, **120**, 1081–1086.

Wittkower, E. & Russell, B. *Emotional factors in skin diseases.* New York: Hoeber, 1953.

Wolf, G. A., Jr. & Wolff, H. G. Studies on the nature of certain symptoms associated with cardio-vascular disorders. *Psychosom. Med.*, 1946, **8**, 293–319.

Wolf, S., Cardon, P. V., Jr., Shepard, E. M., & Wolff, H. G. *Life stress and essential hypertension.* Baltimore: Williams & Wilkins, 1955.

Wolf, S. & Wolff, H. G. A summary of experimental evidence relating life stress to the pathogenesis of essential hypertension in man. In E. T. Bell (Ed.), *Hypertension: a symposium.* Minneapolis: University of Minnesota Press, 1951.

PART THREE

13

Prejudice

Prejudice is defined as hostility or aggression toward individuals on the basis of their group membership. The aggression in prejudice may be physical, as in race riots or lynchings; verbal, as in threats and name calling; or indirect, as in discriminatory practices. The indirect kind of prejudice is most frequent because the aggression is less overt, making it difficult to place blame, e.g., the storekeeper who says that he must keep out Negroes because his customers object to them.

A full treatment of prejudice would require an entire volume, and the interested reader is referred to Allport's *The Nature of Prejudice* (1954). The present account is limited by its focus on the hostile and aggressive aspects of prejudice, a focus that leads to omission of the cognitive aspects of prejudice. Also omitted are historical, political, economic, and sociological variables—in favor of an emphasis on psychological variables. Since the scapegoat hypothesis is the best-known psychological theory of prejudice, it is discussed in detail.

The Scapegoat Hypothesis

Scapegoating refers to the displacement of aggression from an original target to a target less able to retaliate. Its major exponents have been the Yale group:

Frustration is a constant feature of in-group life because of the necessity of interfering with existing goal-responses so that new ones may be learned. Once adult status is attained there is still frustration resulting from the physical nature of man, inadequacies in social techniques in managing the material world, and the inhibition of goal-responses which is necessitated by societal life. Most of the direct aggression which follows upon frustration must be blocked within the peace area. Opportunities for displacement and limited expression are utilized, such as the maintenance of order within the group or attacking some of the sources of frustration as by scientific research. There still remain, however, many instigations to aggressive response which are prohibited within the group and must be either directed toward the self at the price of great discomfort or displaced to groups of persons outside the society. (Dollard et al., 1939, p. 90)

The displacement sequence is as follows. Frustration leads to anger and aggression. If the frustrator is clearly identified, the prejudice (aggression) will be directed against him, unless he is too powerful. If the frustration is impersonal, there is no identifiable target against which to direct aggression, e.g., crops fail because of lack of rain. In either instance (powerful frustrator or no identifiable frustrator) there is a free floating instigation to aggression. This tendency to aggress must somehow be drained, and what is needed is a suitable target, preferably one that cannot retaliate. The anger is therefore displaced from the original source of frustration to a target that is unlikely to strike back, one that is not a part of the ingroup, i.e., a scapegoat.

This sequence does not deal with the justification of prejudice, and to fill this gap the mechanisms of blaming, stereotyping, and projecting have been added to the scapegoat hypothesis. The outgroup selected as a target for aggression is blamed for the original frustration: "The Jews got us into the war." Unacceptable characteristics of the prejudiced person are denied and attributed to the scapegoat group. For example, it has been reported that both German concentration camp guards and Jewish prisoners attributed to each other non-Teutonic traits, both groups being strongly identified as Germans and denying non-German traits (Bettelheim, 1947). Finally, the scapegoat group is labeled with a stereotype or modal personality, which is ostensibly shared by all members of the group.

The scapegoat hypothesis has a strong common sense appeal because most people remember instances of their own anger being displaced from the original source onto a less dangerous target. However, common sense is not a basis for accepting or rejecting a hypothesis; it is necessary to examine both the assumptions and the evidence concerning the scapegoat hypothesis. One distinction needs to be introduced immediately, that between assigning blame and displacing anger. A case report by Bixler (1948) may help to illustrate this distinction. A white truck driver was sufficiently unprejudiced to have a Negro hired as his helper. Subsequently he wished to leave his job for a better paying position in another city, a move that was resisted by his wife who refused to leave her friends and newly decorated home. The truck driver acutely needed the affection and approval of his wife, but he wanted to resign his job and needed a rationale that would be acceptable to her. He chose prejudice, resigning from his job because the contact with his Negro assistant was too close. He claimed that he believed in equal rights but could not go along with eating together, washing together, and so on. He rationalized his move to the assistant by asserting that it was his wife who objected to the association with a Negro.

Note that the truck driver did not become angry with anyone, nor was there any displacement. Rather, he was seeking an excuse for resigning his job and adopted the best excuse available, one that could not be contested in his own subculture. The distinction is an important one. The scapegoat hypothesis suggests that prejudice originates from aggressive tendencies that are displaced from the person who instigated the aggression to members of outgroups; the displacement of anger leads to a prejudice where none existed. In blaming, on the other hand, the prejudice already exists, and there may be no anger involved in assigning blame to another. While scapegoating is a possible explanation of prejudice, blaming is not. The distinction between blaming and scapegoating is important because many of the examples used to support the scapegoat hypothesis, e.g., Bixler's case, illustrate blaming (where prejudice already exists) rather than scapegoating (formation of a new prejudice).

Anger and displacement in scapegoating. According to the Yale group, it is frustration that sets in motion the process that eventually leads to prejudice. The frustration-aggression hypothesis states that aggression is always preceded by frustration, but this was shown to be false in earlier chapters. The antecedents of anger and aggression include not only frustration but also attack and annoyers. Therefore, it is necessary to amend the scapegoat hypothesis to include these antecedents: the sequence that eventually leads to prejudice is set in motion by any stimulus that induces anger, which is then displaced to members of an outgroup.

The concept of displacement includes both stimulus generalization and a lowering of the threshold for aggression. It is doubtful that the displacement occurring in scapegoating involves stimulus generalization. If it did, one would expect that targets similar to the frustrating agent would be attacked, rather than targets dissimilar to the frustrating agent. However, according to the scapegoat hypothesis, the anger is "displaced to groups of persons outside the society." Prejudice is directed toward *dissimilar* individuals, not toward *similar* individuals; therefore, the displacement in scapegoating must involve lowering of the threshold for aggression, not stimulus generalization.

Thus scapegoating does not occur by means of stimulus generalization but, rather, by means of discrimination learning. The aggressor must learn to attack members of the outgroup but not members of the ingroup. Once he has learned this discrimination, he can respond differentially to the stimuli that his culture has deemed important: color of skin, religion, nationality, etc.

The scapegoat hypothesis supplies the motivation for prejudice, but, as Zawadski (1948) has noted, it does not specify the target. Scapegoating involves the displacement of aggression from inside the group to outside the group, but the eventual target is left unspecified; the target might be selected solely on the basis of availability. This failure to specify a target does not negate the hypothesis, but it points to one of its limitations in accounting for prejudice as it is usually manifested. It would seem that the learning of negative stereotypes is antecedent to displacement of anger toward specific outgroups; there must already be prejudice toward a given group before one shifts anger from one's own group to the disliked group.

Studies of displacement. There are two kinds of displacement studies, field investigations and laboratory experiments. The field investigations will be discussed first.

Hovland & Sears (1940) reasoned that economic difficulties would provide sufficient frustration for anger to occur and be displaced onto a scapegoat. In the South scapegoating would be seen most clearly in the form of lynchings, and it was predicted that economic indices would correlate negatively with the number of lynchings. Several different measures of economic well-being were correlated with lynchings in 14 Southern states over a period of 49 years. Since economic indices tended to rise with time and the number of lynchings tended to fall with time, there was a built-in negative correlation. To avoid this spurious correlation, tetrachoric correlations were estimated from the deviations from the linear trends of both economic indices and lynchings. The correlations between lynchings and economic indices were:

Ayres index	− .65
Per acre value of cotton	− .63
Total value of cotton	− .72

Thus when the price of cotton is low, the frustration that ensues leads to aggressive instigations that find an outlet in lynchings, the aggressive tendencies being displaced from a nonspecific source (general conditions) to a specific group that cannot retaliate (Negroes). The findings are clearly in accord with the scapegoat hypothesis, a fact that has not been lost on textbook writers who have made these findings well-known.

What is not so well-known is that the data are suspect, Mintz (1946) having shown that the correlations are spuriously high. The use of deviations from linear trends was inappropriate because neither the economic trends nor the number of lynchings per year are linear functions. Furthermore, the tetrachoric correlations are considerably higher than product-moment correlations for the same data. Therefore, Mintz fitted trend lines to the economic indices and the number of lynchings and then computed product-moment correlations on the basis of deviations from the trends. He used only the Ayres index and total cotton value because per acre value of cotton was almost perfectly related to total cotton value. The lynchings correlated −.34 with the Ayres index and .01 with total cotton value. These correlations are considerably below the ones reported by Hovland & Sears and, taken together, they do not confirm the scapegoat hypothesis. Since the frustration caused by economic difficulties might lead to both more crimes and to other crimes of violence, Mintz also reported some data collected in England. The relationship between economic conditions and violent crime was .06, and between economic conditions and crimes against property it was .04. Thus the frustration engendered by poor economic conditions is unrelated to displaced aggression, either in lynchings or crime.

A study by Crespi (1945) also failed to support the scapegoat hypothesis. During World War II he sent questionnaires to a national sample of respondents, who were queried on their attitudes toward conscientious objectors. The first questionnaire was sent in March, 1944 and the second in April, 1945; in the interim wartime casualties and restrictions increased, suggesting greater frustration.

The scapegoat hypothesis predicts that aggressive tendencies initiated by such frustrations would be displaced onto conscientious objectors. The results were in the opposite direction: the number of respondents approving of conscientious objectors *increased* significantly, and the number of respondents disapproving *decreased* during the interval. It is questionable whether there was more frustration during the 13 month interval; perhaps there was less frustration, which would account for the drop in displaced aggression. Therefore, these findings are not strong evidence against the scapegoat hypothesis.

But Crespi had more data. Respondents were asked if their families were being treated fairly concerning taxes, the draft, food rationing, etc.; the reasonable assumption was made that those answering "unfair" were more frustrated than those answering "fair." The scapegoat hypothesis predicts that the more frustrated respondents would displace more anger onto conscientious objectors, but the results were again in the opposite direction: a higher proportion of the more frustrated respondents reported approval of conscientious objectors than did less frustrated respondents. These data are damaging to the scapegoat hypothesis.

The evidence from field studies is in the main negative, but such investigations suffer from a lack of control. The estimate of frustration in these kinds of studies can only be a surmise, and there is no way of checking it. Nevertheless, the scapegoat hypothesis receives no support from field studies.

Laboratory studies of scapegoating provide sufficient control to test the hypothesis. The ideal paradigm would be to frustrate subjects and determine whether they displace their anger onto members of groups toward whom they are not yet prejudiced. This ideal cannot be met because by the time a child has reached kindergarten age, he has already adopted the prejudices of the important adults in his life (Radke et al., 1949). The substitute paradigm that has been used consists of frustrating a group of adolescents or adults and determining whether such frustration increases their prejudice toward an outgroup. Since the subjects are already prejudiced toward the outgroup, this kind of experiment cannot reveal directly how prejudice originates, but it does yield indirect evidence. If it can be shown that displacement of anger leads to an *increase* in prejudice, displacement might be important in the origin of prejudice.

The best known study in this area is that of Miller & Bugelski (1948). The subjects were young men at a camp, who attended a movie every Friday night. The previous Friday night one of them had won money at "Bank Night," and they were eagerly anticipating the next opportunity to win money at the movie. Instead they were required to take a long series of boring tests, most of which were too difficult. They were frustrated not only by the length and difficulty of the tests but perhaps even more by losing the opportunity to win money. Their comments afterward clearly indicated their anger toward both the experimenters and camp officials.

There were two 20-item check lists, each consisting of 10 favorable traits and 10 unfavorable traits; one referred to Mexicans and the other to Japanese. Half the subjects filled out the Japanese check list before frustration and the Mexican check list after frustration; the other half filled them out in reverse order. There were no systematic differences attributable to sequence, and the two sets of data were combined. The crucial score was the change from pre- to postfrustration. The number of favorable traits decreased significantly, but there was no significant change in the number of unfavorable traits from pre- to postfrustration. These findings were interpreted by the investigators as strongly confirming the scapegoat hypothesis, and most psychologists appear to have accepted their conclusion.

It would be easier to believe that the hypothesis had been confirmed if the *unfavorable* traits had increased because the attribution of unfavorable traits is the essence of prejudice. However, the number of unfavorable traits did not increase in response to frustration; the only change was a decrease of favorable traits. Thus the results are equivocal, and in the absence of replication they cannot be used as evidence for either acceptance or rejection of the scapegoat hypothesis. There has been no replication because of the difficulty in finding such opportune conditions for severe and arbitrary frustration, but there have been several attempts to discover whether frustration leads to displacement of anger onto outgroups, using mild frustration.

Stagner & Congdon (1955) frustrated college men and women by failing them on subtests of an intelligence test. Before and after frustration a rating scale of attiudes toward both ingroups and outgroups was administered. Frustration produced no increase in prejudice, its only effect being a slight increase in favorableness toward both ingroups and outgroups.

In a similar study Cowen et al. (1959) administered two puzzles to college students and gave them insufficient time to complete the puzzles. The experimenter's aloof, skeptical, nonsupporting attitude served as an additional irritant to the subjects. Four scales from *The Authoritarian Personality* (Adorno et al., 1950) were administered:

anti-Negro, F (authoritarianism), anti-minority, and patriotism. Each scale had alternate forms (X and Q); for half the subjects, X was given prefrustration and Q postfrustration, and for the other half the order was reversed.

The results are summarized in Table 13.1. The changes upward

TABLE 13.1. RESULTS FOR PRE- AND POSTFRUSTRATION*
DIRECTION OF CHANGE

Scale	X Pre-, Q Post-Frustration	Q Pre-, X Post-Frustration
Anti-Negro		
Men	Up	Same
Women	Up	Down (slightly)
F		
Men	Down	Down
Women	Down	Down
Anti-minority		
Men	Up (slightly)	Down
Women	Up	Same
Patriotism		
Men	Down	Same
Women	Down	Up

* Cowen et al., 1959.

indicate an increase in prejudice and the changes downward, a decrease in prejudice. The only change that was consistent for men and women and for both sequences of scale administrations was a decrease in prejudice on the F scale, but the change was not significant. The only statistically significant change was the combined change for men and women on the anti-Negro scale. The authors concluded that their results confirm the scapegoat hypothesis, rationalizing the failure of the other scales to show significant changes by assuming that the threshold for anti-Negro prejudice is lower than that for prejudice toward other groups. However, it is difficult to square this conclusion with the results presented in Table 13.1.

The assumption that anti-Negro prejudice has a lower threshold for change than other prejudices tapped by the scales does not account for the consistent *decrease* in F scale scores, nor for the results when the Q form was given before frustration and the X form after frustration (men do not change, and women's prejudice *drops* slightly). Inspection of the table as a whole reveals a conflicting and apparently random pattern of changes in relation to frustration. Therefore, these findings do not support the scapegoat hypothesis.

An experiment by Weiss & Fine (1956) offers evidence for displacement but under restricted conditions. College students were failed at a task and their performance derogated. The insult and criticism continued through the administration of two TAT cards, thereby preventing any possibility of catharsis via the telling of aggressive stories. The TAT protocols were scored for aggression, and subjects were divided into aggressives and nonaggressives. Half the subjects read an article that called for severe punishment of juvenile delinquents and that, in general, was hostile in tone toward delinquents; the other half read no article. Before and after these procedures all subjects filled out a four-item questionnaire tapping attitudes toward delinquents, and the dependent variable was the pre- to postexperimental change in attitude toward delinquents.

Concerning the subjects who read the inflammatory article, the aggressives became significantly more hostile and the nonaggressives showed no change. Concerning the subjects who did not read the article, neither the aggressives nor the nonaggressives showed any change. Thus displacement of anger from the insulting experimenter to the delinquents did occur but only when there was an intense reaction to insult (the aggressives) and only after reading a negative communication. When there was no negative communication or when the anger aroused was not intense, there was no displacement. The scapegoat hypothesis cannot account for the fact that displacement of anger did not occur unless the hostile article was read, but an alternative hypothesis does.

In the Weiss & Fine situation, stimulus generalization was a negligible variable because delinquents are dissimilar to the insulting experimenter. Therefore, the sole mechanism of displacement would be anger's lowering the threshold of an aggressive response toward all targets. In order for an aggressive response to occur, there must be an adequate stimulus. The angry subjects did not make aggressive responses toward delinquents when there was no stimulus to trigger a hostile response. So long as the negative communication was absent, there could be no displacement of anger; but when the negative communication was present, it served as a stimulus for an aggressive response. This stimulus was too weak to elicit an aggressive response when the anger was mild (nonaggressives did not become hostile toward delinquents), but when intense anger lowered the threshold sufficiently (as in the aggressives), the negative stimulus of the article about delinquents elicited an aggressive response toward them.

Thus displacement required *both* intense anger to lower the threshold of aggression and a stimulus for aggression. A hostile attitude toward a group does not develop in angry individuals unless there is a stimulus (a communication) that in some way directs the anger against the group. Hence prejudice is learned first via some channel of communication, and only afterward is there displacement of anger and blame to the minority group. The results of the Weiss & Fine study are consistent with this view.

The displacement paradigm can be altered to yield a test of some implications of the scapegoat hypothesis, e.g., prejudiced individuals are more disturbed by frustration than unprejudiced subjects. The first and best known experiment of this kind was performed by Lindzey (1950). Subjects were severely frustrated by means of failure (see Chapter 3). Several projective techniques were administered before and after frustration, but the TAT was the principal measure. A control group was administered the TAT twice without any intervening frustration. The subjects had been pretested with a questionnaire on attitudes toward minorities, and the experimental subjects consisted of the 20 most prejudiced and the 20 least prejudiced men.

The TAT protocols were scored for aggression, and it was found that for the experimental subjects, frustration tended to increase TAT aggression. There was no significant difference between high and low prejudiced subjects in the amount of TAT aggression. The high and low prejudiced were also compared for intensity of their subjective feelings of frustration (self-report); while the high prejudiced subjects reported being more upset than the low prejudiced subjects, the difference did not attain the accepted level of significance for a two-tailed test. Thus in the face of severe frustration, high prejudiced men did not show any more projective aggression or significantly more intense feelings of frustration than low prejudiced men. Again the scapegoat hypothesis receives no confirmation.

Lindzey's article raises another issue that requires comment. He states that TAT aggression represents displacement of the instigation to aggress from the frustrator to an unspecified target in fantasy. This kind of displacement involves a change in the *mode* of response, in this instance, ostensibly from action to fantasy. The scapegoat hypothesis does not employ this concept of displacement; rather, it employs displacement of *target* as a key concept in the hypothesis. In scapegoating the anger is diverted from a member of the ingroup to an outsider against whom it is safer to aggress; there is no shift from action to fantasy but only a shift in the victim. The definition of displacement, "The energy of the forces behind mental phenomena is displaceable" (Fenichel, 1945, p. 13), includes both a shift in target and a shift in mode of response. The scapegoat hypothesis refers only to a shift in target, and therefore Lindzey did not test the scapegoat hypothesis because he did not assess displacement of target. Nevertheless, his results show no significant difference between high and low prejudiced subjects in either TAT aggression or in feelings of frustration; the failure to find such differences weakens the dynamic assumptions of the scapegoat hypothesis.

The preceding comments do not mean that the TAT cannot be used as a measure of displaced aggression. Since aggression can be scored from TAT protocols, such scores can be used as a measure of displacement of aggression but only if the stimulus figures represent a minority group. Weatherley (1956) adopted this procedure in investigating scapegoating in college students. The subjects were non-Jewish men, who were divided into high and low prejudice groups on the basis of the Levinson Anti-Semitism Scale (Adorno et al., 1950). Half the highs and half the lows were placed in an experimental group, and the remaining high and low prejudiced subjects served as matched controls. The experimental subjects were insulted in a group situation by an experimenter who was nasty and condescending.

All subjects were administered a fantasy test modeled after the TAT. Eight pictures were flashed on a screen for 20 seconds each, and the subjects were given 4 minutes to write a story about each. They were told the age, name, and occupation of a fictional character for each story and told to imagine what was happening to him in the story. There were four fictional characters, two having clearly Jewish names and two having gentile names; two of the characters were described as being similar to the insulting experimenter, and two were of very different status and similarity. The experimental subjects also filled out a questionnaire dealing with their reactions to the arousal situation.

For the Jewish characters, the high prejudice men showed no significant increase in aggression as a function of arousal, whereas the low prejudice subjects showed an inhibition of aggression. Next, the high and low prejudice subjects were compared. There was no significant difference between them in aggression directed toward non-Jewish characters, but the low prejudice subjects manifested significantly less aggression toward Jewish characters than did the high prejudiced subjects. Note that the significant difference is due solely to the low prejudice subjects' being less aggressive toward Jewish characters. When angered and confronted with a Jewish target, very tolerant subjects evidently counter their aggressive tendencies with something akin to reaction formation.

The similarity-dissimilarity dimension of the fantasy characters yielded no significant findings; the high and low prejudice subjects did not differ in the amount of aggression directed toward similar or dissimilar characters. There was no significant difference between highs and lows in impersonal aggression, and in their reports (questionnaires) there was no significant difference between highs and lows in the amount of aggression directed toward the insulting experimenter.

Weatherley's results offer no support for the scapegoat hypothesis. High prejudice men did not become more angered by insult (a finding paralleling Lindzey's results with frustration), and they did not displace more anger onto Jewish characters than non-angered controls. They did not show any less anger toward the insulting experimenter than did the tolerant subjects, nor did they displace any more anger toward characters dissimilar to the insulting experimenter. The only significant difference was the tendency of lows to inhibit aggression toward Jewish characters, which lends no support to the concept that anger is displaced onto minority groups. This finding demonstrates how an experimental treatment may yield results in the opposite direction to that expected; in studying aggression, one-tailed tests of significance are inappropriate.

A more recent study has been reported by Berkowitz (1959), whose subjects were high and low prejudice college women. Half of each group was derogated and insulted by a sarcastic experimenter, and the other half were treated courteously. Subsequently each subject was brought together with another woman to work jointly on a problem. The "other woman," an accomplice, was called by a Jewish name for half the subjects and by a gentile name for the other half. After this joint session all subjects filled out a questionnaire that yielded three measures: annoyance concerning the experiment, liking for the partner (accomplice), and whether the problem solving task was a good measure of their ability.

Contrary to Weatherley's results, labeling with a Jewish or gentile name had no effect on any of the measures. The angered subjects showed more annoyance than the controls, but there was no significant difference on this measure between high and low prejudice women. The liking-for-partner measure did yield a significant difference: an interaction between anger arousal and prejudice. The high prejudice angered subjects tended to dislike their partners more than non-angered controls, but the low prejudice subjects who were angered showed *less* dislike for their partners when angered. Neither of these trends was significant in itself but the interaction was. Thus the low prejudice subjects were similar to those in Weatherley's study, inhibiting dislike when aroused rather than displacing it. The high prejudice women, unlike Weatherley's comparable group of men, tended to dislike their partners more, though the difference was not significant.

On the problem solving task, the interaction between arousal and prejudice was again significant. The decrease for the low prejudice subjects was not significant, but the high prejudice subjects again showed a significant increase. Thus when angered, the high prejudice subjects denied the value of the task significantly more than the low prejudice subjects. There was one more significant finding; high prejudice subjects showed significantly more denial than low prejudice subjects regardless of whether they were aroused.

This study yields two positive findings concerning displacement and prejudice. First, high prejudice subjects tended to like their partners less after being angered, whereas low prejudice subjects liked their partners more. However, there was no significant effect for names, the Jewish-named partner arousing no more dislike than the gentile-named partner. Like the subjects in Weatherley's experiment, these subjects were selected on the basis of the Anti-Semitism Scale (Adorno et al., 1950). Since the high prejudice (anti-semitic) subjects displaced more anger when aroused (disliking their partners more), they should have displaced more anger onto Jewish partners than onto gentile partners. That this did not occur contradicts the finding that high prejudice subjects tend to displace more. When anger is displaced from the instigator to another target, it should be directed more toward a member of a minority group than toward a member of the ingroup. Since this failed to occur, the liking-for-partner measure offers only equivocal support for the scapegoat hypothesis.

The second positive finding was that high prejudice subjects deny more than low prejudice subjects that the task is a good measure of their ability, and anger arousal significantly increases the denial for these high prejudice subjects. This finding suggests that anti-Semitic women tend to use the mechanism of denial more than tolerant women. It is not clear how this result fits the scapegoat hypothesis, but it does indicate that prejudiced individuals may have different personality features from nonprejudiced individuals. The tendency toward denial on the part of high prejudice subjects does not mean that they tend to displace more, only that they tend to avoid blame more. Thus the two positive findings of this study do not necessarily support the scapegoat hypothesis, the first because it is opposed by another finding and the second because it does not concern displacement.

An Alternative Approach

A large part of social development consists of a child's learning the ways of his culture and subculture, and these are passed on to him by his immediate family, teachers, other authority figures, peers, and media of mass communication. He learns a sex role, and he learns to identify as a member of a community; he roots for the local baseball, basketball, and football teams. He acquires a local speech accent and learns local idioms and folklore. He identifies as a member of a religious group, and he learns to take a particular political slant toward current events. Finally, he learns a set of prejudices toward outgroups, groups of people different from his own. The learning appears to take place simply by imitation (Miller & Dollard, 1941), the child mimicking those older than him or those already in the groups that he enters. He may not be aware of the learning as it occurs, nor of the content of the learning until he comes into contact with an individual whose beliefs or accent differ from his.

Local speech inflections provide a good example of such imitative learning. Midwestern, southern, and northeastern accents are demonstrably different; they are learned by the members of these regions simply by imitating those around them. One accent is not better or worse than another, and there is no *specific* reinforcement for using one particular set of inflections or another; nor is there a "dynamic" basis for learning a particular accent.

Prejudice is adopted in much the same way that an accent is, by imitating the negative attitudes of family, community, and media of communication. Until recent years, entertainment media fostered prejudice by portraying Negroes and foreigners in unfavorable and stereotyped roles. In everyday life, ethnic groups have been labeled with uncomplimentary names ("nigger," "kike," "wop," "dago"), which help promulgate negative stereotypes. The compulsory segregation of Negroes, and sometimes of Jews, in ghettoes helps to emphasize group differences and group hierarchies. The fight over school integration further emphasizes to the child that Negroes are different in stereotyped, negative ways.

Studies by Horowitz (1936) and Radke et al. (1949) provide evidence for the early imitation of prejudice. Radke et al. interviewed 250 children from kindergarten, first, and second grades and also administered a Social Episodes Test. It was found that the content of the childrens' learning about colored-white and religious differences mirrored the prejudices of their subcultures. Though many of the children had previous contact with members of minority groups, their beliefs reflected adult values and interpretations rather than the results of such contacts. For many of the children, contact with other groups was not possible because of various kinds of segregation, and they could learn about outgroups only by means of stereotypes and rejection. They inevitably adopted adult prejudices. A large majority of the children were aware of prejudice and accepted it. Since very few of these children could have been maladjusted or subjected to severe frustrations, scapegoating cannot account for their prejudice. Their prejudice was adopted from parents and the subculture.

As the child grows older, his prejudice is reinforced. His peers and parents tend to reward him for associating only with members of his ingroup and for rejecting members of the outgroup. Prejudice against outsiders is often a membership ticket to certain ingroups, and many fraternities, sororities, social, and athletic clubs pride themselves on their exclusiveness and prejudice (Allport, 1954).

There is also the reinforcement of being in a favored position when competing. For example, the white, native-born Protestant has an advantage in attempting to gain admission to a professional school with ethnic quotas. In the mines of South Africa, whites receive more than double the pay of Negroes doing the same work. Because of such strong reinforcement for prejudice, the favored groups resist any change in the social pattern that would lead to surrender of their competitive advantage.

The most potent maintainer of prejudice is habit strength. Throughout childhood and adulthood there are literally thousands of everyday learning situations in which prejudice is stamped in. The habit becomes deeply entrenched, fortified by years of imitation and reinforcement. It is difficult to alter long-standing patterns of thought and action that are familiar and "make sense." It is all the more difficult to alter these patterns when there is strong reinforcement for them. Focusing on habit strength places the emphasis in prejudice where it belongs—on the hard social and economic facts of everyday life.

For most people, habit strength, the rewards of prejudice, and the tendency to blame minority groups are sufficient to account for the maintenance of prejudice. There are extreme individuals, however, for whom prejudice is a more personal matter. The bigot, whose intensity and rigidity of prejudice are marked, has a personal stake in prejudice that goes beyond the variables already cited. Anger and scapegoating are important in both the origin and maintenance of prejudice in bigots, and the examination of this issue falls under the heading of personality and prejudice.

Personality and Prejudice

Psychoanalysts have been the most vocal proponents of a link between prejudice and personality, though it should be stated that some analysts are more cautious than others. One of those advocating caution has been Kris (1949):

> Some authors seem inclined to make the hostile impulses of individuals responsible for the existence of prejudice. This seems a short cut likely to lead to misunderstanding. However, it seems correct to say that the existence of prejudice offers to a large number of individuals an opportunity of relieving their personal conflicts by offering a target for their hostile impulses. (pp. 144–145)

Kris is properly concerned over the tendency of some writers to blame personal conflicts for the origin of all prejudice, and he emphasizes that prejudice, like any other group phenomenon, may be utilized by disturbed individuals in acting out their conflicts.

Besides *Frustration and Aggression,* the major impetus to the "personality" approach to prejudice has been given by three of the volumes in the *Studies in Prejudice* series: *Anti-Semitism and Emotional Disorder* (Ackerman & Jahoda, 1950), *Dynamics of Prejudice* (Bettelheim & Janowitz, 1950), and *The Authoritarian Personality* (Adorno et al., 1950).

Ackerman & Jahoda examined the cases of clients undergoing psychoanalytic therapy. They were attempting to discover an anti-Semitic syndrome and came up with the following picture:

> Such persons suffer, as has been revealed, from a sense of loneliness, emptiness, and privation. Their needs tend to be insatiable; they crave intensely for what they do not possess, and reject whatever is within their grasp. Basically, they reject themselves and envy others. To find a semblance of balance in spite of their frustrations, they mobilize against their anxiety and self-hate a variety of defense mechanisms.
>
> Some of these defenses, such as projection, denial, substitution of aggression for anxiety, and rationalization, are inevitably brought into play, while others, such as avoidance, opposition, displacement, reaction formation,

and compensation, play an auxilliary role and do not constitute a part of the anti-Semitic reaction. (1950, pp. 55–56)

This syndrome immediately raises the question of whether this symptom picture is unique to anti-Semites, and the answer is negative. Ackerman & Jahoda admit that it is not limited to prejudiced individuals, that such symptoms occur in a variety of nonprejudiced neurotics. There is little to add to this admission, except to note the need for control groups. The study of neurotics undergoing therapy who also happen to be prejudiced must inevitably lead to a false personality picture of the prejudiced person because of the contamination of neurosis.

Bettelheim & Janowitz (1950) interviewed veterans in an attempt to relate patterns of hostility and aggression to ethnic intolerance in lower-class men. On the basis of the interview material, the men were assigned to high, medium, and low hostile groups and also into three categories of intolerance. It was found that the most intolerant men were also the most hostile. Unfortunately, these findings may have been contaminated by interviewer bias, because the same interviewer who rated for hostility also rated for degree of intolerance.

Despite the source of possible bias, the results are of considerable interest. It was found that the most intolerant veterans were also the most frustrated, the most aggressive, and the most hostile. This finding fits the scapegoat hypothesis. It does not fit the catharsis aspects of the scapegoat hypothesis because the prejudiced men should have ventilated their aggression by means of prejudice and should then have weaker aggressive tendencies than those who were more tolerant.

An alternative explanation assumes that there is consistency in aggressiveness and hostility, especially in the extremes of the distribution. The extremely hostile individual is less flexible in his hatred than the less hostile individual. The latter may hate some people and not others; the hostile person has a generalized hatred that overflows into ethnic prejudice. Thus it appears reasonable to speak of general traits of aggressiveness and hostilty when referring to the extremes of these dimensions; individuals whose hatred and aggression are so widespread and so intense that they are relatively incapable of making the finer discriminations in intensity of response and in targets of aggression that less hostile people make. The more hostile the individual, the more likely he is to be prejudiced.

The most comprehensive attempt to link personality characteristics with prejudice may be found in *The Authoritarian Personality* (Adorno et al., 1950). The major instrument to emerge from the multiple investigations reported in this volume was the F scale, which taps antidemocratic, authoritarian attitudes, beliefs about strength and weakness, morality, absolutes, etc.   The F scale is highly correlated with the ethnocentrism and anti-Semitism scales.   Thus high scorers on the F scale represent the extreme of prejudice.

There have been hundreds of studies with the F scale, and it is beyond the scope of this chapter to attempt even a limited review. The methodology of the original investigations has come in for severe criticism (e.g., Christie & Jahoda, 1954), and it has become apparent that the "authoritarian personality" is a chapter heading rather than a clearly defined concept.

Most investigators have neglected the clinical approach to high scorers on the F scale, by means of which Adorno delineated six syndromes.   One group was labeled *surface resentment*.   These are people who readily adopt stereotyped, negative attitudes toward minority groups in order to rationalize their own failures or to compete successfully with members of minority groups.   In contrast to the other five groups, they are accessible to rational argument concerning prejudice and can present a reasonable basis for their prejudice, which is often based on overgeneralization from one or two unfortunate encounters.

The two most common groups among the high scorers on the F scale were the *conventional syndrome* and the *authoritarian personality*.   People falling into the conventional syndrome have a strong need to belong to the ingroup and are critical and frightened of outgroups.   They crave orderliness and familarity and are disturbed by strangeness.   Prejudice is accepted as a matter of course because everyone in their ingroup has similar attitudes and because the ways of outgroups are strange and possibly dangerous.

The *authoritarian personality* is the most publicized of the syndromes to emerge from the high scorers.   The authoritarian divides others into two classes, the strong and the weak.   He has a strict, rigid conscience and maintains that something is either good or bad, right or wrong, with nothing in between.   He is afraid of being weak and must prove to himself that he is strong by aggressing against those who cannot retaliate.   Since his morality is strict, it is necessary to rationalize his hatred and aggression toward weaker people by assigning to them traits of wickedness and evil.

The last three syndromes occur less frequently than the first three. The *tough guy* rebels against all authority and revels in excesses of all kinds; prejudice offers an excuse for sadism against members of the outgroup.   The *manipulative* type is so far removed from per-

sonal relationships that he treats people as objects. Once he adopts
the prevailing prejudice of his ingroup, the problem for him is how
to handle or dispose of such matters as the "Jewish question" in an
administrative, depersonalized fashion. The last type involves a
kind of psychopathology often seen in mental hospitals. This is the
crank:

> To them, prejudice is all-important: it is a means to escape acute mental
> diseases by collectivization and by building up a pseudoreality against
> which their aggressiveness can be directed without any overt violation of
> the "reality principle" . . . . Here belong the organized war mothers,
> ham-an-eggers, and regular followers of agitators even in periods when
> racist propaganda is at a low ebb. The often-abused term "lunatic fringe"
> has a certain validity with regard to them: their compulsiveness has
> reached the stage of fanaticism. . . . Ideas of conspiracy play a large
> role: they do not hesitate to attribute to the Jews a quest for world dom-
> ination, and they are likely to swear by the Elders of Zion. (Adorno
> et al., 1950, p. 765)

In light of these differences among people who score high on the
F scale, it would appear futile to attempt to relate the F scale to
any class of personality variables. Since the volume has been criticized for its numerous methodological flaws, there is no need to add
to the critique here. It is perhaps best to regard the three volumes
of the *Studies in Prejudice* series as provocative reports whose clinical features are most worthwhile. They point to the importance of
personality features in prejudice, and there is no doubt that this
thesis holds for extremely prejudiced individuals. However, for
most people, prejudice is generally unrelated to personality variables:

> An examination of the relevant research indicates a sizable negative cor-
> relation between scores on the F scale and various measures related to
> socio-economic status. F scale and ethnocentrism scores also covary
> among face to face groups. These findings are interpreted as running
> counter to the general argument in *The Authoritarian Personality* which
> emphasized the purely personality determinants of potential fascism and
> ethnocentrism and discounted contemporary social influences. (Christie
> & Jahoda, 1954, p. 194)

CONCLUSIONS

The evidence bearing on the scapegoat hypothesis was interpreted
as being equivocal or negative. It may well be that the scapegoat
hypothesis explains so much of prejudice in everyday life because its
terms are fuzzy and imprecise, and they can be applied in many

situations in many different ways. The core concept of displacement was shown earlier to have several different meanings, and scapegoating was shown to have at least two meanings. When a hypothesis is as flexible as the scapegoat hypothesis is, it may appear to have great explanatory power; but the magic is in the words, not the basic concept.

The alternative suggested here is habit strength; prejudice in the normal individual is learned like any other response. It is acquired early in life and receives strong, repeated reinforcement. The normal individual acquires prejudiced behavior from those around him, and he rarely questions his own behavior, which in this instance is only right and proper and familiar—being similar to those around him.

Habit strength is insufficient to account for the vitriolic prejudice of the "lunatic fringe," because for such people prejudice is too much a part of their maladjustment to be explained solely by imitation and reinforcement. Prejudice offers them the possibility of living out their neurotic conflicts concerning aggression and hatred, displacing from the original target to members of minority groups. Thus the scapegoat hypothesis does seem to work but only for a deviant part of the population; the vast majority of people learn their prejudice via imitation and reinforcement.

REFERENCES

Ackerman, N. W. & Jahoda, Marie. *Anti-Semitism and emotional disorder.* New York: Harper, 1950.

Adorno, T. W., Frenkel-Brunswik, Else, Levinson, D. J., & Sanford, R. N. *The authoritarian personality.* New York: Harper, 1950.

Allport, G. W. *The nature of prejudice.* Cambridge, Mass.: Addison-Wesley, 1954.

Berkowitz, L. Anti-Semitism and the displacement of aggression. *J. abnorm. soc. Psychol.,* 1959, **59**, 182–187.

Bettelheim, B. & Janowitz, M. *Dynamics of prejudice.* New York: Harper, 1950.

Bettelheim, B. Dynamics of anti-Semitism in gentile and Jew. *J. abnorm. soc. Psychol.,* 1947, **42**, 153–168.

Bixler, R. H. How G. S. became a scapegoater. *J. abnorm. soc. Psychol.,* 1948, **43**, 230–232.

Christie, R. & Jahoda, Marie (Eds.), *Studies in the scope & method of the "Authoritarian Personality."* Glencoe, Ill.: Free Press, 1954.

Cowen, E. L., Landes, J., & Schaet, O. E. The effects of mild frustration on the expression of prejudiced attitudes. *J. abnorm. soc. Psychol.,* 1959, **58**, 33–38.

Crespi, L. P. Public opinion toward conscientious objectors: V. national tolerance, wartime trends, and the scapegoat hypothesis. *J. Psychol.*, 1945, **20**,
321–346.

Dollard, J., Doob, L. W., Miller, N. E., Mower, O. H., & Sears, R. R. *Frustration and aggression.* New Haven: Yale University Press, 1939.

Fenichel, O. The psychoanalytic theory of neurosis. New York: Norton, 1945.

Horowitz, E. L. Development of attitude toward Negroes. *Arch. Psychol.*,
1936, No. 194.

Hovland, G. I. & Sears, R. R. Minor studies in aggression: VI. correlation
lynchings with economic indices. *J. Psychol.*, 1940, **9**, 301–310.

Kris, E. Roots of hostility and prejudice. In *The family in a democratic
society.* New York: Columbia University Press, 1949.

Lindzey, G. An experimental examination of the scapegoat theory of prejudice.
J. abnorm. soc. Psychol., 1950, **45**, 296–309.

Miller, N. E. & Bugelski, R. Minor studies of aggression: II. the influence of
frustrations by the in-group on attitudes expressed toward outgroups. *J.
Psychol.*, 1948, **25**, 437–442.

Miller, N. E. & Dollard, J. *Social learning and imitation.* New Haven: Yale
University Press, 1941.

Mintz, A. A re-examination of correlations between lynchings and economic
indices. *J. abnorm. soc. Psychol.*, 1946, **41**, 159–160.

Radke, Marian, Trager, Helen G., & Davis, Hadassah. Social perceptions and
attitudes of children. *Genet. Psychol. Monogr.*, 1949, **40**, 327–447.

Stagner, G. & Congdon, D. S. Another failure to demonstrate displacement of
aggression. *J. abnorm. soc. Psychol.*, 1955, **51**, 695–696.

Weatherley, D. A. An investigation of the relationship between anti-Semitism
and displacement, projection, and inhibition of aggression. Unpublished
doctor's dissertation, Stanford University, 1956.

Weiss, W. & Fine, B. J. The effect of induced aggressiveness on opinion
change. *J. abnorm. soc. Psychol.*, 1956, **52**, 109–114.

Zawadzki, B. Limitations of the scapegoat theory of prejudice, *J. abnorm. soc.
Psychol.*, 1948, **43**, 127–141.

14

Aggression in children

Because of the voluminous literature on aggression in children, it was necessary to select major areas of investigation and omit research that does not pertain to these areas. The three areas chosen were method, developmental trends, and psychopathology. There have been numerous methods of investigating aggression in children, and since the information available cannot be understood outside the context of the methods used to obtain it, it is necessary to discuss techniques of investigation. The necessity for a section on developmental trends should be abundantly clear. The reader is warned, however, that the section is briefer than might be expected on the basis of the number of studies in this area. There are three reasons for this. First, most of the studies have focussed on preschool children (who are more available than older children), and little is known of aggressive trends in school age and adolescent children. Second, the older studies (and they are the large majority) investigated sex differences and age differences as the major independent variables, and less is known about the effects of child rearing and methods of control on aggressive tendencies. Third, it is difficult to compare the results of studies that vary widely in characteristics of the subjects, technique of investigation, and methodological sophistication. Thus, while much is known about age and sex differences, especially in preschool children, detailed knowledge about other aspects of aggression in childhood awaits future investigation.

During the last two decades there have been increasing concern and interest in the pathological aspects of aggression in children. It is not surprising that aggression is one of the major problems of disturbed children; this is inevitable in a culture where the most crucial problem in socializing children is the control of aggressive impulses. Pathological aggression is for the most part an exaggeration of normal aggression; it may be placed in proper perspective after reviewing developmental trends in negativism, temper tantrums, and so on.

METHOD

In contrast to adults, children are more direct and more physical in their aggression, and it is easier to observe and record their attacking behavior in realistic, everyday situations. Because children engage in so many play activities and because there is considerable imaginative role playing, symbolic aggression is an excellent source of information about children. It is but a short step from realistic, everyday situations to doll play, which has led a number of investigators to study aggression within the context of doll play. There are also possibilities in the destructive games that children sometimes play.

Observation

It is impractical to record the behavior of children continuously over a long period of time, and it has been necessary to resort to time sampling. The child is watched during a preselected period and at regular intervals, e.g., one minute in every 10 or one 10-minute period during an hour of play. Time sampling has been used for many years in observing a wide range of behaviors in pre-school children. The most efficient procedure involves the use of a check list, the observer merely checking off specific responses that occur during the observing period. A check list requires a standardized list of behaviors. Walters et al. (1957) modified Gewirtz' list (1948), including the following behaviors:

Physical Aggression
  a. Annoys, teases, interferes
  b. Hits, strikes
  c. Competes for status
  d. Threatening gesture
  e. Pursues
  f. Snatches or damages property of others
  g. Negativism
  h. Pushes, pulls, holds
Verbal Aggression
  a. Commands, demands

   b. Conflict over ways of using equipment
   c. Disparages
   d. Entices a child to hit another one
   e. Refuses to comply
   f. Denies privilege to another
   g. Shifts blame
   h. Claims possession
   i. Threatens

In lists like these it is difficult to avoid overlap; for example, *negativism* under Physical Aggression would appear to be no different from *refuses to comply* under Verbal Aggression. Walters et al. (1957) used their check list to record all aggression occurring during a 1-minute interval. The use of such a short interval helps to insure inter-observer reliability, and in their study it ranged between 81 and 86% agreement.

   Young children are a captive group in that they are available in nursery schools or kindergartens. The practical problems involved in studying aggression in the home are much greater. In the home an observer is an intruder who may influence the behavior under investigation; furthermore, the practical and economic problems of having an observer in the home are considerable. One solution has been to use the mother as an observer. Goodenough (1931) had mothers keep a detailed diary of their children's anger outbursts, using the following scheme as a guide:

   Type: undirected energy, resistance, retaliation
   Directed toward:
   Motor: kicking, stamping, jumping, striking, throwing self on floor, holding breath
   Vocal: screaming, threatening, refusing, "calling names," crying
   Behavior following outburst: cheerful, sulky, fretful, continued sobbing, resentful
   Hour:
   Place:
   Duration of outburst:

   Since there were different numbers of children in various age groups, Goodenough was forced to use as a frequency measure the proportion of aggressive responses within a given category to the total number of outbursts of the age group. With a small number of subjects this score is unduly affected by the extreme case, e.g., one child supplies most of the incidents of kicking and screaming, and the mean for the whole age group is thus elevated, yielding an incorrect norm. Goodenough's attempt to deal with the issue of small samples and uncontrolled observation periods is probably as good as can be expected for this method.

Because of the problems of studying aggression in the home, it may be asked whether there is any reason for doing so. The answer is that children vary considerably in the intensity, frequency, and mode of aggression that is manifested at home versus at school or nursery. Some children are remarkably consistent, behaving the same at home or school. Other children show seemingly paradoxical behavior, being active and aggressive at home and model children at school. Knowledge of school or nursery aggression may thus represent a biased sample of children's aggressive behavior, and it is necessary to go into the home for the full picture.

One source of information about aggression is other children. There have been a number of different peer ratings used, but the most comprehensive one is that of the Rip Van Winkle research team (Eron et al., 1956; Walder, 1960). They started out with 1000 items, which dropped to 271 items after screening for clarity and for duplication. The items were then evaluated by judges for pertinence to aggression, and after this selection procedure 106 items remained. These items were administered to third grade children, who used them to assess each other; the 56 items with the highest agreement among the children were retained as the final scale, which consisted of two alternate forms of 28 items each. There are five kinds of items:

Physical—Who starts a fight over nothing?
Verbal—Who says mean things?
Indirect—Who makes up stories and lies to get other children in trouble?
Acquisitive—Who takes the other children's things without asking?
Unclassified—Who does not obey the teacher?

The items have been administered to a large number of children, and they are being factor analyzed and related to other measures of aggression. The technique shows promise of revealing aspects of aggression that are perhaps screened from teachers, observers, and other adults.

Play

Doll play. Doll play is one of the most important techniques for investigating aggression because of the methodological attention it has received and the information it has yielded. There are several doll play kits (Driscoll; Graham & Whitmore, 1954; Lynn, 1955), but these are designed to elicit a variety of behaviors from children. The doll play situation that comes closest to focusing on aggression is that developed by the Iowa group under the direction of R. Sears (e.g., Bach, 1945; P. Sears, 1951, Yarrow, 1948). The furniture is miniature and arranged as the rooms of a house. The dolls are also tiny, and usually a family of mother, father, child, and baby are represented. The experimenter introduces the child to the materials and helps initiate play activity without suggesting a plot or content. The recording of aggression varies from complete running accounts of the child's behavior to systematic time sampling of discrete responses. Generally the investigator is interested in the kind, direction, and intensity of the child's doll play aggression.

The Sears group at Iowa studied a number of methodological variables and established some "constants" of doll play aggression. Phillips (1945) varied the realism of the materials. One set consisted of dolls and furniture complete in all their details, and another set consisted of roughly cut, wooden furniture and dolls without features or clothes. No significant differences in aggression were found in relation to the realism of the materials.

Pintler (1945) found that initial organization of the materials was an important variable. In one set the furniture was organized into the rooms of a house, and in another set the various pieces were laid out like the start of a do-it-yourself kit, without definite organization. The more organized set led to significantly more aggression than the less organized set.

Robinson (1946) compared a standard set of dolls with a set duplicating the family constellation of the child. Preschool children tended to identify more and to direct more aggression toward the mother doll of the duplicated family than toward the standard family dolls.

Phillips (1945) found that the length of the session was unrelated to aggression beyond half-hour periods. After half an hour, preschool children tend to be bored and to become involved in activities tangential to the doll play. Within a given period there seems to be a warm-up effect, aggressive responses not occurring until the child has done some exploring.

The Iowa group assumed that there are similarities in the home, nursery school, and doll play situations sufficient to promote stimulus generalization. Aggression is learned principally in the home, whence it generalizes to the nursery school (the teacher playing a role that in some respects is similar to the mother's). The doll play situation also has elements in common with the home situation (symbolic family figures and furniture) but fewer than the nursery school. Thus aggression would be expected to generalize first to the nursery school and then to doll play.

These three situations also differ in the frequency and intensity of punishment for aggression. The most punishment is usually meted out at home, typically by the mother; there is considerably less punishment for aggression by the nursery school teacher and no punishment in the doll play situation. Thus there is a gradient of anxiety over aggression that decreases from home to preschool nursery to doll play, and the Miller (1948) analysis of conflict is appropriate. The Sears et al. (1953) scheme for generalization of aggression from home to doll play is shown in Figure 14.1. There is a steeper gradient of anxiety (punishment for aggression) than of aggression, and the response that occurs is the net of aggression versus aggression anxiety.

One way of testing this model is to make the doll play situation more similar to the home situation than it usually is and observe whether aggression decreases as expected. This is precisely what Levin & Turgeon (1957) did, with opposite results to those predicted. Preschool children were given two doll play sessions, the first with the standard procedure. In the second session the child's mother was present in addition to the experimenter in one group, and in

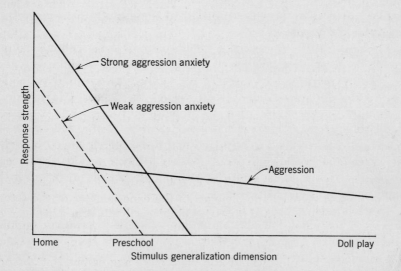

FIG. 14.1. Conflict analysis of doll play (from Sears et al., 1954).

the other group a woman unknown to the child accompanied the experimenter. With the mother present, doll play aggression increased significantly, and with a stranger present there was a nonsignificant decrease in aggression from the first to the second session. Inspection of Figure 14.1 shows that the presence of the mother (which made the doll play more similar to the home) should have raised the level of aggression anxiety, thereby decreasing the amount of aggression manifested.

Several explanations have been offered for the increase in doll play aggression in the mother's presence. Since the mother does not punish the child for his doll play aggression, he may assume that she approves of it; such reinforcement would increase aggression. On the other hand, the child may abdicate responsibility for his behavior when his mother is present, depending on her to inhibit disapproved behavior. In her presence he would tend to engage in more doll play aggression, whereas, with a stranger present, the child himself would remain responsible for controlling aggression and would therefore manifest less doll play aggression.

Support for the second explanation comes from a study by Siegel & Kohn (1959). They did not use doll play (the materials being balloons, clay, a toy clown, rubber daggers, etc.), but the situation appears to be similar to doll play. The major difference was the presence of two children rather than one, as in doll play. For one group of children the experimenter was present, and for the other group the experimenter was absent. There were two such sessions, and the dependent variable was the difference in play aggression from the first to the second session. All the children in the adult-absent group decreased in aggression, and two thirds of those in the adult-present group increased in aggression. These findings are consistent with the hypothesis that in the absence of an adult the child assumes responsibility for his own behavior; since he has been taught to inhibit aggression, he will show a decrease in aggression when left on his own.

Returning to doll play, there is evidence that the adult experimenter may be reinforcing the child for his doll play aggression. It has been found that doll play aggression increases from one session to the next when there are no changes in the experimenter or the setup. P. Sears (1951) suggested that the child gradually loses his fear of punishment in the permissive atmosphere, and with less inhibition there is more aggression in subsequent sessions. If this were true, the absence of an adult would also yield more aggression, but absence of an adult leads to *less* aggression in subsequent sessions (Siegel &

Kohn, 1959). One way of accounting for these various findings is to assume that the adult is a reinforcing agent; play aggression should be reinforced by the presence of any *significant* adult. Thus when either the mother or the experimenter is present, aggression is reinforced and should increase from one session to the next until it reaches an asymptote. When a stranger is introduced, doll play aggression may be inhibited because of the child's learning of "company manners." Children are less aggressive in doll play when the experimenter is new to them than they are later, when she is well-known and therefore a reinforcing agent. They may be expected to revert to a lower level of aggression when a stranger is introduced. Note that in the Levin & Turgeon study with a stranger present there was no significant change in doll play aggression from the first to the second session. In the absence of an adult, the amount of play aggression should not change from one session to the next because there is no reinforcement of it. If another child is present, as in the Siegel & Kohn study, there may be a decrease in aggression because of negative reinforcement from the other child.

Pintler (1945) found that high interaction between experimenter and child yielded significantly more doll play aggression than low interaction. Thus the greater the interaction, the more potent is the experimenter as a reinforcing agent and the more aggression by the child. Hartup & Himeno (1959) divided a 10 minute doll play session into four equal time units and found that aggression increased significantly as the session endured; this is also consistent with a reinforcement interpretation.

Levy's technique. Levy's doll play technique (1936) antedates most of the work in this area. He was interested primarily in sibling rivalry and structured the doll play situation accordingly. The dolls were constant: a brother or sister doll observing a new baby doll nursing at the breast of a mother doll. Reactions of children to this constellation vary: attacking the mother's breast, punishing the self doll, attacking the baby doll, attacking other objects, denial, passivity, and refusal to play. Levy regarded his technique as a clinical tool, and he seems to have used it mainly as an interview aid. The approach to recording aggression was qualitative, with no attempt to establish frequencies or quantitative norms. Thus the technique has little to offer in the systematic investigation of aggression, though it may be helpful in clinical situations. Levy has used his method as a means of "release therapy," the situation providing children with an opportunity to aggress in play without being punished.

Destructive games. Toys and games offer myraid possibilities for the child to aggress or to attempt harm or destruction of objects. In "cowboys and Indians" and "cops and robbers" the child may indulge in stylized aggression in the context of a clearly delineated role. Towers may be pushed over, clowns attacked, and constructions demolished—all in play. In an effort to promote such symbolic aggression, several investigators have designed situations that encourage the child to destroy objects or attack toys. These situations are promising in that the child may aggress without fear of retaliation, in a situation whose stimulus is known, and in which frequency and intensity of aggression can be measured.

BALLOONS. Stone (1956) chose balloon breaking as a practical situation in which children's destructive and inhibitory tendencies might be investigated. If the child does not spontaneously break the balloons, he is urged to do so, first directly and then indirectly by experimenter's breaking them. The child's behavior is recorded by an observer, and the following aspects receive special attention: strength of impulse to destroy and strength of inhibitions (fear, conscience, fondness for balloons as toys). The outcome is a subjective evaluation of the child's tendencies to aggress and to inhibit aggression. One problem that arises is that it is difficult to distinguish between a weak tendency to destroy and a strong tendency to inhibit destructive behavior. Breaking balloons would seem to be an interesting context for the study of aggression, but it needs quantification.

TOWER OF PANS. When a balloon is pricked, it is destroyed; a much milder aggressive response is to knock down a play construction. Beller & Haeberle (1959) were interested in mild aggression, and they had children knock down a tower of pans. The child is exposed to toys that are placed behind apertures. When the aperture is opened, the child is told that he can get to the toy only by knocking over the tower and that the tower will fall if it is merely touched. Thus making this mildly destructive response is the only way to reach the desired toy. The measure used is the number of seconds required to knock down the tower, this measure being an index of inhibition against making an aggressive response. The question may be raised whether knocking over a tower of tin pans should be classified as a destructive response because the destruction is so minimal.

BOBO CLOWN. Most children like nothing better than to pummel a soft toy, and there are "Joe Palooka" clowns which may be used for just this purpose. Walters[1] has adapted a "Bobo clown" so that

[1] Personal communication, 1959.

children can be reinforced with marbles or candy for striking the clown. The apparatus is set up for automatic dispensing of the reinforcer whenever the clown is struck in the face; in addition to candy and marbles, lighting up of the clown's eyes may be used as a reinforcer. The apparatus records frequency and latency of response. The child is allowed to aggress in a situation where aggression is not punished but reinforced; there are none of the problems associated with having observers or with ratings because recording of aggression is automatic. More techniques like this are needed, in which a play situation intrinsically interesting to children is combined with adequate laboratory control and recording.

DAVITZ'S GAMES. Davitz (1952) utilized three aggressive nursery games in an attempt to train children to be aggressive. Though he did not use the games as measuring devices, they could easily be converted to measures of aggression:

Cover the Spot: At the center of a mat placed on the floor was a small x marked in black chalk. Each S was instructed to cover the spot with some part of his body, and that person covering the spot at the end of the game was the winner. Only one person could cover the spot at one time, and it was emphasized to the Ss that there were no rules limiting their aggressive behavior during the game.

Scalp: A piece of cloth was tied around the arm of each subject and he was informed that this was his scalp. The object of the game was to tear the scalps from the other S's arm while protecting one's own scalp.

Break the Ball: Each S was provided with a ping pong ball which was placed on the floor and could not be touched by hand. The object of the game was to break every one else's ping pong ball while protecting one's own ball. (p. 311)

Projective Techniques

The Rorschach and TAT may be used to assess aggressiveness in children as well as adults, and various children's projective techniques (Children's Apperception Test, Blacky Pictures, Children's Form of the Picture-Frustration Study) are also available. But this section deals only with techniques that focus directly on aggression.

Pictures. Kagan (1956) developed a series of 13 pictures, which were mentioned in Chapter 8. Four of the pictures depict boys fighting, and these four were the most successful in distinguishing between boys who were behaviorally aggressive versus nonaggressive. He also found that the differences between boys differing in behavioral aggression were greatest on the cards that unambiguously depicted fighting.

Lesser (1957) used a series of 10 pictures that vary in degree of aggression portrayed, some pictures showing more violence than others. An attempt was made to scale the pictures, and seven of the ten were found to line up in order of frequency of aggressive response. Since these seven pictures comprise a set of aggressive pictorial stimuli that are scaled for intensity of aggression, they should prove useful in studying aggression in school age children.

One limitation of Kagan's and Lesser's stimuli is that they both depict boys fighting and are thus best used for boys. Their use with girls would seem to be limited, and what is needed is an alternate series of pictures designed for assessing aggression in girls. Perhaps techniques designed especially for girls should depict quite different activities (more arguing and negativism than violence) than those used for boys.

Stories. Korner (1949) devised incomplete stories for young children to complete verbally or in play. The children are supplied with dolls and doll furniture in order for them to complete the story in play. The episodes deal with everyday occurrences that might anger children, e.g., a boy in the bath who loves to splash but hates to have his ears washed, gets his ears washed by his mother; a boy has been fighting with friends, and his father scolds him; a boy has been having fun and making a mess, but his mother makes him clean it up before his father comes home. After each incomplete story the child is urged to tell what the boy feels like doing and what he does do. It can be seen that this technique is a mixture of thematic apperception and doll play tasks, especially adapted for use with children who cannot read (the stories are read to them). The aggression score is simply the frequency of aggressive incidents occurring in the story protocols. Korner demonstrated high agreement between raters but found little agreement between aggression in the stories and behavioral aggression.

The notion of using incomplete stories was taken over and adapted for adolescent boys by the group of investigators under the direction of Miller & Swanson (1959). In Allinsmith's doctoral dissertation (1954) there were six incomplete story episodes, all dealing with situations that should incite anger; an aunt cleans up a room and destroys a ticket to a big football game; a boy's father dies, and his mother remarries a man the boy hates. Since the subjects were boys, all the stories have boys as the main figure, and in each story the boy is frustrated or angered by an adult figure he likes.

Cartoons. Cartoons have considerable appeal to children, and Patterson (1958) took advantage of this in devising a test of aggressive and other reactions to attack and frustration. The child is presented with four cartoons arranged from left to right, and, like those in the "comics" section of newspapers, they tell a story, e.g., a boy is being attacked. The child is then presented with six response cards and must choose the two that depict what the boy might do in response to the attack. The six alternatives are as follows:

Uncontrolled counter-aggression—the boy overreacts to the attack
Controlled counter-aggression—the boy attacks the frustrator or attacker
Displacement—destroying the property of the attacker
Passivity—flight from the scene
Dependency—a parental figure gives support or resolves the issue
Reaction formation—denial of attack and a friendly gesture toward the attacker

There are nine sets of stimulus cards, each with its set of six response cards. Three sets of stimulus cards depict a boy being attacked, three show rejection by peers, and three show difficulties with siblings or parents. In addition to these nine sets, there are three more sets of stimulus cards that show a boy engaged in aggressive behavior, and the response cards portray different degrees of punishment (boy loses fight, boy gets scolded, boy is physically punished, etc.), which are weighed for severity.

The technique yields quantitative data about several kinds of aggression and other reactions to attack and frustration, and, in addition, provides information about the expected consequences of aggression. The use of a choice rather than a free response by the subject makes the scoring completely objective. With these advantages, the technique should be a useful one in studying aggression in children.

Morgan & Gaier (1956) devised a Punishment Situations Index, modeled after the children's form of the Picture-Frustration Study. There are two sets of cartoons, 10 each for boys and girls. In the cartoons, children and mothers are depicted in situations that commonly lead to punishment of the children, e.g., boys fighting, destruction of property, bad report card. There are blank "balloons" in the cartoons, which the child (or mother) completes, and the responses are scored like the Rosenzweig Picture-Frustration responses: extrapunitive, impunitive, and intropunitive. This technique is best used for investigating punishment after aggression rather than investigating aggression itself.

Experimental Frustration

The last method of investigating aggression in children is to frustrate them under laboratory conditions and then attempt to recover whatever aggressive responses occur. The best known technique is that of Barker, Dembo, & Lewin (1941), who allowed nursery school children to play with very desirable toys and then brought them to another part of the playroom where there were less interesting toys. A wire mesh screen was dropped into place, preventing the children from getting back to the better toys but not preventing them from seeing them. There were various reactions by the children, including aggression, but, unfortunately, the method of recording was crude and qualitative. Wright (1943) adapted the situation for studying the behavior of children in pairs. He found that there was considerably more aggression (both verbal and physical) against the experimenter when there were two children than when there was a single child; furthermore, there was more aggression when the children in the pair were friends than when they were not.

Haner & Brown (1955) varied the degree of frustration of their child subjects. The task was to place marbles in holes until all the holes were filled with marbles, at which point there was a reward. Children were failed at varying distances from the goal. The response measure was pressure exerted on a plunger, which is not a good measure of aggression. This task could be converted into an excellent technique for assessing aggressive reactions to frustration; all that is needed is a means of allowing children to aggress. The means might be any of those mentioned in the section of destructive games: breaking balloons, knocking over constructions, or stomping on other's ping pong balls.

Comment

Most of the techniques reviewed here are intended for use with young children. Direct observation has been used almost exclusively with preschool children, as have doll play and destructive games. Projective techniques and experimental frustration may be used with children of all ages, the sole limitation being ability to verbalize. The older the child, the more his aggressive behavior is tempered by the sanctions of society and the more devious and covert it becomes. Overt, direct aggression is best seen in young children, who are at the beginning of the socializing process.

Aside from their intended use with younger or older children, the techniques vary in four different ways. First, the aggression may be behavioral or symbolic (as in play); in experimental frustration the child may attack the experimenter, whereas in doll play the aggression is symbolic. Second, the aggression may be against people, as in experimental frustration or as observed in nursery play; or it may be against objects, as in destructive games. Third, the responses may be verbal, as in projective techniques; or it may be nonverbal, as in destructive games. Fourth, there may be no stimulus for aggression, as in doll play or nursery play; or there may be incitement to aggression, as in experimental frustration. With techniques varying in four different ways, the investigator of aggression in children has considerable lattitude in choosing an appropriate measuring instrument.

At present the technique that has the most to offer is doll play because it has received much methodological attention. Other techniques show considerable promise. The destructive games are interesting, especially Walter's "Bobo clown" because of its combination of intrinsic interest to children with laboratory control.

DEVELOPMENTAL TRENDS

Age

The findings concerning developmental trends of aggression in children, especially preschool children, are contradictory. In children aged two to five inclusive, the frequency and variety of aggressive behaviors increase. Must & Sharpe (1947) reported a correlation of .54 between age and frequency of aggression in a preschool nursery sample. Walters et al. (1957) noted that in nursery school, three-year-olds aggress more frequently than two-year-olds, and four-year-olds show still more aggression; but the curve levels off, and there is no increase in aggression in five-year-olds. Appel (1942) found that four-year-olds tend to have aggressive episodes of longer duration than two-year-olds. Goodenough (1931) reported that the after-effects of anger (sulkiness and resentment) increased steadily with advancing age in a sample of children from 1 to 8 years. Ammons & Ammons (1953) discovered a peak of doll play aggression at 3 years, with decreases from this maximum at 4 and 5 years.

While the above studies agree in finding that aggression increases with age, the following studies are contrary. Jersild & Markey (1935) noted that nursery school aggression declines with age, a finding that is seconded by Dawe (1934). Roff & Roff (1940) and McKee & Leader (1955) found no age differences in the aggression of preschool children. P. Sears (1951) reported a slight and non-significant increase in doll play aggression from 3 to 4 years but no appreciable difference between 4 and 5 years of age.

These contradictory trends suggest two possibilities. First, perhaps there are no developmental trends in aggression, no waxing or waning as children grow older. Second, perhaps there are developmental trends, but they are obscured in some fashion. The second alternative appears to be more correct. In many investigations of aggression in young children, various aggressive responses have been lumped into a single summary score, which assumes that all aggressive responses develop at the same rate. It is doubtful that this is true. Physical aggression occurs before verbal aggression simply because the child can make striking responses before he has sufficient command of speech to use it in attack. Temper outbursts occur before coordinated attacking responses, again because the child cannot attack with any precision until he has mastered his gross musculature. The pooling of diverse aggressive responses and the lumping together of anger and aggression may well obscure developmental trends. Since the behaviors included under the heading of aggression vary from one study to the next, the presence and direction of developmental trends should also vary. If the focus is on temper tantrums, it is found that aggression decreases with advancing age; if the focus is on retaliation and counteraggression, it is found that aggression increases with advancing age. If both kinds of behavior were included in a single study, no developmental trends would emerge. Thus it seems likely that the studies mentioned above, when taken as a whole, have tended to cancel out developmental trends in aggression.

One of the rare studies with a comprehensive breakdown of aggression is that of Goodenough (1931), who had mothers keep a diary of their children's aggressive outbursts. Kicking, screaming, and holding the breadth were found to be frequent at 1 and 2 years but drop out thereafter. Verbal threats do not occur until 2 years and then increase throughout the preschool period. Retaliative behavior is seen as early as 1 year, when it is rare, but it increases in frequency throughout childhood. These findings must be accepted only tentatively because of the faults of the study mentioned earlier in the chapter, but these facts are consistent with the notion that various aggressive responses develop at different times and with different rates. Thus undirected anger is most frequent in infancy and decreases in frequency thereafter, probably because of both parental punishment and improved emotional control. Physical aggression starts relatively early and increases steadily as the child: (1) acquires greater control over motility, (2) acquires a greater range of attacking responses, and (3) is reinforced for the physical attacks by acquisition of reinforcers. Verbal aggression appears on the scene later, and, like physical aggression, it increases in frequency throughout childhood.

Goodenough's data show a drop in anger outbursts as the child matures, but there is nothing in her book about aggression in the presence of strangers or in situations outside the home. One of the tasks of childhood is to learn the fine discriminations required by our civilization: when to aggress and against whom. As the child grows older, he becomes increasingly aware of the need to inhibit aggression unless it is "safe." This has the consequence of making his aggressive tendencies both more covert and more uneven. When aggression is assessed in situations in which an adult is present, e.g., doll play, its frequency should increase only until the child reaches the age of making necessary discriminations; subsequently, frequency of aggression might diminish. On the other hand, when aggression is assessed in the absence of adults, it should increase in frequency with advancing age. Thus there are two major sources of divergent results in developmental studies of aggression: the particular aggressive responses studied and the presence-absence of stimuli (such as adults) that are cues for inhibition of aggressive tendencies.

Throughout childhood the child is called upon to enter new situations: nursery, kindergarten, grammar school, various peer groups. What is the course of aggression upon entry into a group and upon later acceptance in the group? The answer given by observational and doll play studies is clear. Initially the child's level of aggression is low, being inhibited by at least mild anxiety in a new and unstructured situation. As the child becomes accustomed to the new setting, aggression increases. There are session to session increases in doll play; there are increases in nursery school aggression as the child learns that aggression may be necessary in order to acquire toys, to defend his use of toys, and to retaliate against aggression from others. In a peer group, aggression declines after an initial increase because the child learns his place in the pecking order; once the order is established, less aggression is required than during the process of establishing the order.

The emphasis in this discussion has been on the preschool period, and less is known about aggression in later childhood and adoles-

cence. Older children and adolescents are not readily available as
subjects, and they have been less studied. The few studies available
suggest the following age trends. Aggression continues at a steady
frequency from the peak attained at 4 years until 6 to 8 years of age.
Subsequently, aggression in school and with peers tends to increase
in frequency, the increase continuing until adolescence. Aggression
in the home against parents and siblings tends to decrease until
adolescence, at which time it jumps markedly (Kepler, 1933). The
increase in self-control that occurs between 6 and 12 years is demonstrated by Patterson's finding (1958) that children in the 6 to 9 year
range manifest significantly more uncontrolled aggression on his test
than children in the 10 to 12 year range.

The one type of aggression on which there is general agreement
concerning developmental trends is negativism. The period varies
with the individual child, but between the ages of $1\frac{1}{2}$ and 4 years
there is an era of resistive behavior, involving the child's refusal to go
along, stubborn insistence on having his own way and of blocking
the efforts of others. This negativism is familiar to parents, and it
has been corroborated by observational studies. Ausubel has attempted to formulate a rationale for such behavior, as follows:

Threatened by the complete loss of an ego status he is loath to relinquish,
despite its untenability, he asserts its dominant characteristics even more
aggressively and vigorously than before. In the face of greater threat,
tolerance to restraint and frustration reaches a new low. Uncompromising
and petulant assertiveness, frequent temper tantrums, tyrannical ordering
about, and insistence upon "baby ways," become familiar response patterns in the daily behavior routine, reaching a peak and then declining
as the new ego organization begins to take root. (1950, p. 802)

Ausubel's hypothesis, which implies that negativism is inevitable,
fails to give appropriate weight to the training the child is undergoing. During the second year of life the child begins the long process of learning the proper responses in his culture. The crucial adults
in his life teach him the necessary responses in areas of eating,
elimination, relations with siblings, etc. Most of the new learning
is strange and arbitrary to the young child, who is forced to bend to
the ways of his parents. If the training process is handled efficiently
and with the use of appropriate techniques for inducing new responses, the child should manifest little negativism. New learning
occurs all the time; and each time the individual acquires new responses, he does not necessarily respond with obstinacy. On the
other hand, when the training process is inefficient, the child is reluctant to give up his old response modes; and the tendency to op-

pose the adult who is pressuring him often generalizes to a variety of situations. The present formulation differs from Ausubel's in its emphasis on the training process rather than on ego organization. Thus the occurrence of negativism is regarded not as an inevitable consequence of maturation but as a consequence of inadequate training procedures. Techniques that involve coercion, that fail to regard the socialization of the child as a training process (utilizing learning principles) do lead to negativism. However, a child who receives minimal pressure to conform and who is lead to conformity by reinforcement rather than punishment should manifest little negativism.

Sex Differences

The presence of sex differences in aggression is widely accepted on the basis of everyday observations and empirical evidence. Almost without exception, the studies that compare aggression in boys and girls have found that boys are more aggressive, especially more physically aggressive.

The important variable appears to be sex role. The male role is active, assertive, dominant, and competitive, with an accent on physical aggression. A boy must be able to defend himself in a fight, and he must establish himself within the peer group by manifesting at least a modicum of combativeness. Boys who refuse to fight are labeled "sissies," whereas boys who like to fight are "real boys." On the other hand, a girl's role is relatively nonaggressive, with fighting strictly taboo. Girls must resort to the more verbal forms of aggression, especially to the more indirect types of attack, e.g., tattling, spiteful rejection. Girls who violate their role expectations are not so negatively labeled as boys, but they are still called "tomboys."

The acquisition of sex roles is accomplished in a number of ways, but the two greatest influences are the peer group and the parents. The peer group becomes more important in older children and adolescents, and once the individual passes puberty, the parents cease to be a strong influence with respect to both role models and discipline. For the young child, however, the most important influence in the acquisition of sex role is the parents. In the normal course of events the child should take as a model the same-sexed parent. Boys tend to identify with their fathers and girls with their mothers. It has been contended (Levin & Sears, 1956) that the process of identification is more difficult for boys. Usually the father is away from the home most of the day, and the only adult available as a model and as a disciplinarian is the mother. Thus girls find it easier to identify because the mother is around, and boys identify more slowly because the father is not available. It follows that if the father were completely absent, the boy should be less aggressive than if the father were present. Two studies have attempted to verify this prediction by means of doll play. Bach (1946) showed that boys and girls whose fathers were absent from the home were less aggressive (in doll play) than those whose fathers were present. P. Sears (1951) repeated these findings for boys only; for girls, presence or absence of the father made no difference. Sears' findings are more in line with the hypothesis because boys would be expected to show less aggression in the absence of an aggressive role model (father), while girls would not show a drop because the father is not their role model.

Levin & Sears (1956) attempted to assess the effect of identification on aggression in children whose parents were both in the home. They interviewed mothers and then rated both degree of identification (by the child) and severity of punishment; aggression was assessed by means of doll play. For boys, the high identifiers manifested significantly more aggression than the low identifiers, especially when fathers were the punishing agents. For girls, the high identifiers manifested more aggression only when mothers were severe punitive agents. Levin & Sears account for their findings as follows. It may be assumed that because the mother is the crucial adult during early childhood, girls learn their identification earlier than boys, whose role model (father) is not seen as much. By the age of 5 (the age of the subjects), girls have achieved a stable identification with their mothers; therefore, whether they are high or low identifiers should have no effect on their aggression. If the mother is unusually punitive, she stands out as an aggressive model for her daughter; as a result, her daughter should be more aggressive than the daughter of a mother who is only mildly punitive. It may be assumed that boys are still in the process of identifying with their fathers at the age of 5 years; therefore, those who identify more with this aggressive model should be more aggressive. Since the model is already aggressive, the additional aggressiveness of a punitive father can add little to the aggressiveness of his son; consequently, the sons of punitive fathers are not more aggressive than the sons of nonpunitive fathers.

This formulation fits the data not only of the Levin & Sears study but also of studies of the effect of father absence on aggression. The assumption that girls identify earlier than boys is reasonable, but it has yet to be empirically verified. One aspect of the account may be questioned. Levin & Sears assume that a punishing parent will produce an aggressive child; it may be assumed with equal or greater rationale that an initially aggressive child will result in the parent's being more punitive. This point will be discussed more fully in the next section.

Methods of Control

The struggle to keep children's aggression within bounds is never ending, and parental attempts to control aggression have taken many forms. Goodenough (1931) listed the following methods:

Scolding	Appeal to self-esteem or humor
Reasoning	Spanking or slapping
Threatening	Other corporal punishment
Frightening	Deprival of privileges
Coaxing	Putting in a chair
Bribery	Putting to bed
Praise	Deprival of food
Soothing	Isolation
Ridicule	Ignoring attitude
Appeal to the emotions	Diversion of child's attention
Social approval or disapproval	Removal of source of trouble

She found that with advancing age of the children, there was a decrease in the use of physical punishment, coaxing, ignoring, and diverting and a shift to the use of scolding, threatening, and isolation. Boys received more spanking, threatening, bribery, and isolation than girls, who received more ignoring than boys. While there were differences in the effectiveness of these various methods of control, the differences were overshadowed by the manner in which they were used. Goodenough found that virtually any method is effective in controlling aggression when used by some parents, but other parents had little success no matter what the method. This point is important in attempting to evaluate the relative effectiveness of parental discipline; there may be more variance attributable to parents than to method.

Nursery school teachers are called on to keep the aggression of their charges within bounds, and Appel (1942) investigated the effectiveness of various techniques. The successful techniques included diverting, separating, interpreting the wishes of one child to another, explaining property rights, and suggesting a solution to the conflict. Disapproval and moralizing were usually unsuccessful in settling quarrels, but it is not clear whether this was so because of the techniques or because teachers tend to show considerable irritation when using these two techniques. The teacher's self-control and nonrejection of the child may be more important than the particular method used to control aggression.

Punishment inhibits responses it follows, including aggressive responses. Hollenberg & Sperry (1951) demonstrated the effects of verbal punishment on doll play aggression, their punished group decreasing in doll play aggression and their permissive group increasing in doll play aggression. The mothers of the children were interviewed and rated for severity of punishment meted out to their children. Severe punishment was associated with more doll play aggression than was mild punishment, but the difference did not attain significance. One interpretation of these two sets of findings is that, while punishment inhibits the immediate aggressive response, it elicits more aggression in other contexts because punishment is in itself an attack and, therefore, an antecedent of aggression.

The long term effect of punishment on various aggressive responses would seem to depend on how much generalization occurs. The negative reinforcement of an attacking response lowers the probability of its occurring subsequently, but there is also a spread of inhibition to responses similar to the one punished. The closer the response resembles the one that is punished, the more likely its habit strength will be diminished. An analogous situation may be assumed to occur with the stimuli involved. Thus a child may be punished for attacking a parent, and the resulting inhibition of aggression may generalize to all adults in his environment; but the less like his parent the stimulus object is, the less likely the inhibition is to affect aggression, e.g., punishment for aggression toward the parent may have little inhibiting effect on aggression toward siblings.

It is known that differential reinforcement leads to a steep generalization gradient, i.e., very little generalization. One child may be punished severely for aggression toward his parents but reinforced for aggression toward his siblings. Aggression toward parents should decline and aggression toward siblings rise; and the total frequency of aggression would remain the same. Another child may be punished severely for aggression toward parents but not reinforced for aggression toward siblings (either because of parental nonpermissiveness or because of the failure of aggression to achieve the sought-after rewards). Inhibition of aggression should generalize to most stimuli, and his total frequency of aggression should decrease.

Permissiveness is not necessarily incompatible with punishment, as

Sears et al. (1957) have pointed out. A permissive parent may allow the child to aggress and then punish him afterward, though there is some association between allowing the aggression to continue and punishing it subsequently. Extreme permissiveness constitutes a kind of reinforcement because the child realizes that aggression is entirely acceptable to the parent. Thus permissiveness may be expected to encourage aggressive behavior, and in the doll play studies this is precisely what occurs. Doll play aggression rises steadily within a session and from session to session when the experimenter is permissive, in contrast to decreases in doll play aggression when the experimenter is punitive. However, permissiveness and punishment probably have different effects on aggression in general than they do on the specific aggressive responses that occurred in the doll play situation.

Sears, Maccoby, & Levin (1957) interviewed mothers and obtained information on their children's aggressive behavior and methods of dealing with such behavior. Permissiveness and severity of punishment correlated —.46, suggesting that permissive mothers were less punitive. The correlation between the child's aggression (as reported by the mother) and permissiveness was .23, and between aggressiveness and punishment it was .16. Although both correlations are significantly above zero, the relationships are weak. When permissiveness and punishment are considered together, a stronger relationship appears. Low permissiveness and low punishment were associated with low aggression in the child; low permissiveness and high punishment were associated with medium aggression, as were high permissiveness and low punishment; high permissiveness and high punishment were associated with high aggression. The mother who allowed her child to aggress and then punished severely had the most aggressive child, but the mother who stopped aggression quickly but did not punish it severely had the least aggressive child.

As Sears et al. are careful to note, perhaps it is not maternal punishment that causes aggression but rather the child's aggression that leads to punishment. Sears et al. prefer the interpretation that has punishment as an antecedent of aggression because permissiveness is also related to aggression and the child's aggression obviously does not lead to maternal permissiveness. This interpretation is reasonable, but so is the alternative assumption. Assume that there are differences in irritability among the children of the parents in the Sears et al. study. The nonpermissive mother would tend to curb her child's aggression, which would diminish the tendency to attack in both the initially aggressive and the initially less aggressive child.

The mother of the more aggressive child would have to cope with more aggressive responses and, therefore, resort to punishment more often than the mother of the less aggressive child. With time, punishment might diminish the tendency to aggress; the need for punishment would then decrease. Thus punishment and aggression would continue to covary whether aggression were high or low.

It is not necessary to choose between the alternative assumptions. Rather, it seems better to accept both and to posit the influence of three variables: permissiveness, punishment, and irritability. Permissiveness increases aggression because of the implicit reinforcement it offers. Punishment decreases aggression in the immediate situation but probably increases the probability of aggression in other contexts. Irritability is associated with more frequent aggression simply in terms of a lower threshold of anger stimulus being necessary to trigger off an aggressive response.

So far the discussion has centered on punishment for any attacking response made by the child, but, as Sears et al. (1957) have made clear, punishment varies with the victim of the aggression. They found that mothers tolerate very little aggression directed against themselves but are more permissive of attacks against the child's siblings and playmates. Some mothers encourage aggression against children in the neighborhood, believing that a child must learn to "take care of himself." The child learns that it is dangerous to attack authority figures, and his aggression becomes limited to peers and those weaker than himself. If the child does not learn to inhibit aggression toward his mother (as the first of a succession of authority figures), there is a danger of acting out against authority.

The connection between antisocial behavior and parental control over aggression is demonstrated in a study by Bandura & Walters (1959). They interviewed aggressive, antisocial adolescent boys from an area with a low-delinquency rate and obtained from their parents a description of methods used to control aggression. A control group was matched for most of the pertinent variables. The mothers of the aggressive boys were found to be significantly more permissive of aggression toward themselves than mothers of the controls, and the aggressive boys, not surprisingly, were found to direct significantly more physical aggression toward their mothers than did the controls. Both mothers and fathers of aggressive boys were significantly more punitive of aggression toward other adults than the parents of the control group. There were no appreciable differences between parents of the two groups of boys in their punishment of aggression directed toward siblings or peers. These findings are similar to those of Sears et al. (1957) with mothers of an unselected population of children. The interaction of permissiveness, punishment, and the child's own aggressiveness is evident. The mother's permissiveness for aggression against herself encourages such attacks. When the boy attacks the mother or other authority figures, he is punished (more frequently than control boys because he aggresses more frequently), and the punishment acts as incitement to further aggression. The vicious cycle starts with a combination of excessive irritability on the part of the child and excessive permissiveness on the part of the mother.

The type of punishment for aggression that predominates in a family would seem to be related to the social class of the family. Lower-class parents would use physical punishment and middle-class parents psychological punishment (Davis, 1943). Furthermore, middle-class parents, having been made more aware of the dangers of various child rearing practices and having been taught self-control, would tend not to lose control when punishing their children; in contrast, lower-class parents tend to become angry and use more severe and more physical punishments. These variables have been studied by Allinsmith (1954). Parents and children were interviewed, and the children's aggression was assessed by means of a story completion test. Allinsmith divided families into middle or lower class on the basis of the father's occupation and income level. The parental interviews determined the predominant mode of discipline of aggression, whether the parent lost control of himself when disciplining the child, and how severe the physical punishment was. The story completions yielded measures of how much aggression was manifested and whether it was direct or indirect.

Lower-class children manifested no more aggression on the story completions than middle-class children. Rather, class differences showed up in child rearing, and the child rearing variables were related to story completion aggression. The middle-class parents typically used psychological punishment, while the punishment of lower-class parents was predominantly physical. Physical punishment resulted in more aggression than psychological punishment; furthermore, physical aggression led to direct aggression against authority, while psychological punishment led to indirect aggression against authority.

On the basis of the interviews, mothers were rated for how much emotional control they exercised when punishing their children, and it was found, as expected, that middle-class mothers had better control over themselves than lower-class mothers. The more emotional the mother was when punishing, the more the punishment tended to be physical rather than psychological and the more aggression the child displayed on the story completion test. Punishment delivered in a calm manner is likely to be less severe and to act less as an anger stimulus to the child. When the mother loses control and becomes angry, the anger intensifies her punishing behavior, making it more severe and more physical. Her punishment then becomes a strong attack, inciting the child to further aggression.

Loss of control by the parent is perhaps a more crucial variable than severity of punishment. The parent is not only a source of differential reinforcement for the child but also a model whose behavior is closely imitated. When the parent loses control, the effect of punishing aggression is counteracted by the presentation to the child of angry, aggressive behavior to be copied. If this analysis is correct, punishment is best accomplished in a detached manner. Particularly with physical punishment, it is important for the parent to provide a ritualistic, adult quality to the act (such as in spanking) so that the child can differentiate between such disciplinary aggression and aggression that the child might copy.

Allinsmith also attempted to relate rewards to social class and to children's aggression. She found that lower-class parents tended to employ concrete, tangible rewards (money, gifts), while middle-class parents relied more on psychological rewards (child's own feeling of worth and of being good). However, neither the kind of reward nor the amount of reward was related to the directness or the amount of the children's aggression on the story completion test. It is not surprising that the system of reinforcement typically used is unrelated to aggression because parents rarely reinforce their children's aggressive behavior. Attacks and anger outbursts by children tend to be reinforced by the acquisition of other reinforcers (toys, prestige, dominance, etc.) or by internal reinforcement (relief of physiological tension).

Beardslee (1955) used the same instrument as Allinsmith in studying modes of parental discipline and defenses against aggression. Adolescent boys were angered in an experimental situation and their defenses against aggression (in stories) were measured before and after arousal. There was no relationship between increases in defenses against aggression and methods of parental discipline (psychological versus physical punishment). The only significant results involved social class and demands for obedience; middle-class parents who made the strictest demands for obedience had children who showed the greatest increases in defenses against expressing aggression in the story completion task. Thus Beardslee's findings with the same instrument (although used differently) and the same population as Allinsmith's, yielded different results.

Earlier there was mention of the problem of assessment of children's aggression by means of their mothers' reports. Now the issue is parent's reports of their own disciplinary practices. Middle-class parents are aware of what is considered desirable in disciplining children. Parents have been exhorted to remain calm when punishing children, and they may be less ready to admit emotional upset because of its current social undesirability.

Many years ago Goodenough (1931) demonstrated that there is a discrepancy between parents' recollection of their typical practices in punishing aggression and their day-to-day practices. She had mothers state the approximate frequency with which they used a number of methods of controlling aggression. There was a tendency to report high frequency for methods like praise, appeal to self-esteem, and appeal to reason; threatening, ridiculing, and deprival of privileges were denied. Then the mothers kept day-to-day diaries of their children's outbursts and the methods used to handle them, and they did not have access to their answers to the questionnaire. There was little relationship between the questionnaire answers and the frequencies that were reported in the daily diaries. Goodenough pointed out that most adults cannot give an accurate account of their own procedures in discipline unless they are alerted in advance to focus on these aspects. This is a serious problem in studying the effect of child rearing practices on children's aggression because virtually all investigations have used the parent's recollections.

PSYCHOPATHOLOGY

Aggression is a major issue in the psychological problems found in children. It has been found (Kepler, 1933) that in children referred to clinics, the major source of difficulty is rebelliousness, with temper tantrums noted less often. Aggression is equally important as a problem area in children who are not referred to clinics. Conrad (1948) checked the frequency of complaints in children who were brought into a "well-baby" health hygiene clinic, the age range being 1 month to 6 years. He found that half the children were regarded by their mothers as having a problem concerning temper tantrums (screaming, kicking, stamping of feet, or other violent psychomotor outbursts when thwarted); another one quarter of the children tended to hold their breath, becoming immobile and cyanotic.

During the developmental sequence, different kinds of aggression are prominent, and aggression occurs in different contexts. Bender (1943) outlined a developmental scheme for the aggression displayed by children referred to clinics. Children as young as a year and a half are referred for dangerous head banging, persistent screaming, refusing food, and biting themselves and others. The usual background for such violent and rebellious aggression is desertion by the parents, following a period of gross neglect. The previous severe physical restrictions, privations, and lack of emotional contacts all contribute to massive frustration, and the child rebels against *any* adult who attempts to interact with him.

Children of 3 to 4 years who are seen in a clinic have often been raised in institutions, and they have had no close contact with a single adult figure. They are aggressive without anxiety or guilt, evidently never having identified with an adult sufficiently for a conscience to start developing. Their destruction is aimless and uncontrolled, and they have no real idea of the value of the objects they destroy or of the consequences of their destructiveness.

In children from 3 to 8 years, Oedipal rivalry is often an important variable in their excessive aggression, and this is especially true for boys. Children who are excessively stimulated sexually come to hate the rival parent, and eventually they hate the opposite-sexed parent on learning that this parent rejects them for the rival. Primal scenes lead to impotent rage directed against both parents, leading to generalized rebellion and destructiveness.

During the period of 6 to 12 years, the frustrations of school often lead to excessive aggressiveness. The child who finds he cannot compete in the school situation, and who is frustrated by an inability to read or to master arithmetic, may develop destructive tendencies.

Finally, there is a group of children who are usually seen as inpatients in hospitals; they are continually running back to aggressively rejecting mothers and meeting rejection each time. These children want only to go home to their mothers, but the basic problem is a refusal to leave the world of childhood for adolescence. Any attempt at directing their behavior is met with massive defiance: throwing chairs, butting heads, kicking, screaming, homicidal and suicidal threats.

There have been several attempts to classify children with milder psychopathology on the basis of symptom picture, background, and treatment method. Such classifications may be essentially psychoanalytic or nonpsychoanalytic; an example of each will be discussed.

Rambert (1949) used a psychoanalytic approach, dividing aggression into primary and secondary aggression. Primary aggression, such as is seen in delinquents who have no conscience and are not susceptible to psychoanalysis, develops during the pregenital period. Secondary aggression, which is more frequent and is amenable to psychoanalysis, develops after the Oedipal stage. There are four types of post-Oedipal aggression. The first stems from the Oedipal situation directly, the aggression being caused by revived fears of abandonment. The second is the result of a badly liquidated Oedipus, the child continuing to hate the rival, same-sexed parent. The third concerns aggression that is linked to guilt and fear of castration over loving the opposite-sexed parent. The fourth is sibling rivalry, which antedates the Oedipal situation but which is fixated by it.

Slavson (1943) is more eclectic in outlining nine types of aggression seen in problem children and methods for dealing with each type.

1. *Aggression from prolonged infancy.* The child has been overprotected and has not been required to control his anger. He is demanding, provocative, immature, and in non-home situations he is insecure.

2. *Aggression as attention getting.* The child feels inferior, and though he expects an unfavorable response from the objects of his aggression, negative attention is better than no attention.

3. *Aggression as a release of organic tension.* The child is overactive and is so free-wheeling that he is bound to intrude on others in his social interactions. Since energy level is not subject to change, the child's activity must be diverted into free play and into constructive and nonaggressive channels, e.g., building with toys rather than charging around knocking them down.

4. *Aggression as the acting out of a neurosis.* The child's hatred is distorted and shows up in bizarre ways, e.g., sadism, masochism. What is needed is release therapy.

5. *Aggression from maturity fantasies.* The child attempts to assume a role that is too mature for his peers, reflecting his exaggerated need to grow up fast. He dominates his peers, assuming an adult's role as the conscience for the group; this role thinly disguises his self-righteous tyranny over his peers, and he is typically hostile and aggressive in condemning the "childish" and "wrong" practices of his

peers. The solution to this problem is to get the child to identify with peers rather than adults.

6. *Aggression from effeminacy.* There are too many women in the family, and the boy learns a feminine role. Under a submissive façade he tends to be extremely hostile, and there may be sadism toward weaker, younger children. The goal in therapy is to switch to a masculine identification by means of boys' games, e.g., wrestling, manual games; a male therapist is essential.

7. *Deflective aggression.* The child fears an attack, in order to forestall it, he attacks a weaker child, inducing several children to gang up. The goal in therapy is to build up security and self-reliance, obviating the need to forestall possible attacks.

8. *Oral aggression.* The child engages in continued verbal attacks on others, with screaming and cursing prominent. The child is usually a plump and seemingly good-natured girl who is a voracious eater; there is no known therapy for this kind of problem.

9. *Aggression from hostility.* Disturbed children act out their sadistic impulses, and they cannot be treated in outpatient settings. They constitute a separate group for which there must be special treatment methods.

The most extensive exposition about children whose aggression is so intense and distorted that they must be hospitalized is that of Redl & Wineman (1957), the volume being a combination of two earlier books. They present in detail the everyday behaviors of aggressive, disturbed children and the methods used to modify and ameliorate uncontrolled aggression. Their account leans heavily on the concept of ego strength, as follows. Because of weak egos the children are incapable of mastering and controlling their intense hatred. The hostility is expressed in aggression that goes far beyond reaction to frustration or the acquisition of wanted objects; it is aggression for its own sake. Anxiety, insecurity, and guilt all lead to distorted, disorganized aggressive outbursts. There is so little tolerance for tension that even mild frustrations trigger destructive responses, which go beyond the stimulus for the aggression.

Despite the ego's being essentially weak, it can be strong defensively in four different ways. First, the ego successfully defends itself against the superego, leaving the ego free to express unlimited aggression. Second, the ego may rationalize the destructiveness to itself and others by admitting the bad temper but also admitting that nothing can be done about it. Third, the ego stoutly maintains that it should not be changed, and any attempts at change are met with more violence. Finally, the ego is used to goad others, especially adults, knowing how long it is safe to continue to be annoying. Thus the ego can use all its intelligence in defending aggression, e.g., being very sharp concerning rules of evidence—"You can't prove that I broke it because nobody was around."

Raush et al. (1959) reported considerable improvement in such children as a result of intensive and varied treatment procedures. Using time sampling and careful observation, they demonstrated that during the course of a year and a half there was a significant decrease in hostile-dominant behavior and a significant increase in friendly-passive behavior. Their approach constitutes a large step toward the objective evaluation of changes in aggressiveness in disturbed children.

Wolberg (1944) has also described the aggression seen in disturbed children and methods for dealing with them. He noted that the child has failed to develop a repressive mechanism and is neither respectful toward nor fearful of authority. Aggression is used coercively, and there is no guilt. Retaliation not only may fail to stem the aggression but also may incite further aggression. The therapeutic goal is to build a conscience. This is initiated by discipline and the setting of limits, with punishment restricted to mild disapproval. After the first violent reaction to limits, the child becomes adjusted to them and tends to respect them. The next step is to have the child prescribe his own punishment, which helps him to set his own limitations and begin to have responsibility for his own behavior. As time passes, the child begins to like the therapist and will attempt self-control in order to win approval and praise. Eventually it is hoped that the child will inhibit his destructive tendencies for a positive goal rather than the negative goal of avoiding punishment.

Of all the children seen in clinics and hospitals, the aggressive, disturbed child is probably the most resistant to change, and there is a low rate of therapeutic change. Morris et al. (1956) followed up children who were originally seen when they were in the 4 to 15-year range. Their IQ was greater than 80; there was no brain damage, and there was no psychosis when they were originally seen. They manifested at least four of the following seven features: (1) repeated truancy from home or school; (2) stealing or purposeful lying; (3) cruelty, teasing, or bullying; (4) disobedience, defiance of authority; (5) marked restlessness or distractibility; (6) wanton destruction; and (7) severe tantrums when crossed. They were followed until the age of 18, and in the few followed beyond 18 there was little change. Of the 66 children who were followed, only 14 were reported as doing well. Of the remainder, 34 had never adjusted, 12 were psychotic, 7 had a criminal record, and 10 were "borderline." The prognosis for aggressive girls was much worse than that for aggressive boys, but, as can be seen from the figures, the prognosis for the entire group is appalling.

REFERENCES

Allinsmith, B. B. Parental discipline and children's aggression in two social classes. Unpublished doctor's dissertation, University of Michigan, 1954.

Ammons, Carol H. & Ammons, R. B. Aggression in doll play: interviews of two- to six-year-old white males. *J. genet. Psychol.*, 1953, **82**, 205–213.

Appel, M. H. Aggressive behavior of nursery school children and adult procedures in dealing with such behavior. *J. exp. Educ.*, 1942, **11**, 185–199.

Ausubel, D. P. Negativism as a phase of ego development. *Amer. J. Orthopsychiat.*, 1950, **20**, 796–805.

Bach, G. R. Young children's play fantasies. *Psychol. Monogr.*, 1945, **59**, No. 2 (Whole No. 272).

Bach, G. R. Father-fantasies and father-typing in father-separated children. *Child Develpm.*, 1946, **17**, 63–80.

Bandura, A. & Walters, R. H. *Adolescent aggression.* New York: Ronald Press, 1959.

Barker, R. G., Dembo, Tamara, & Lewin, K. Frustration and regression: an experiment with young children. *Univ. Iowa Stud. Child Welf.*, 1941, **18**, No. 1.

Beardslee, Betty A. J. The learning of two mechanisms of defense. Unpublished doctor's dissertation, University of Michigan, 1955.

Beller, E. K. & Haeberle, Ann. Dependency and the frustration-aggression hypothesis. Paper read at American Psychological Assn. meetings, 1959.

Bender, Lauretta. The treatment of aggression: III. aggression in childhood. *Amer. J. Orthopsychiat.*, 1943, **13**, 392–399.

Conrad, S. J. A study of preschool children. *Amer. J. Orthopsychiat.*, 1948, **181**, 340–344.

Davis, A. Child training and social class. In R. G. Barker et al. (Eds.), *Child behavior and development.* New York: McGraw-Hill, 1943.

Davitz, Joel R. The effects of previous training on postfrustration behavior. *J. abnorm. soc. Psychol.*, 1952, **47**, 309–315.

Dawe, H. C. An analysis of two hundred quarrels of preschool children. *Child Develpm.* 1934, **5**, 139–157.

Driscoll, Gertrude P. *The Driscoll Play Kit.* New York: Psychological Corporation.

Eron, L. O., Laulicht, J. H., & Walder, L. O. Psychosocial development of aggressive behavior. *Proc. Rip Van Winkle Clin.*, 1956, **7**, 3–23.

Gewirtz, J. L. Succorance in young children. Unpublished doctor's dissertation, State University, Iowa, 1948.

Goodenough, Florence. *Anger in young children.* Minneapolis: University of Minnesota Press, 1931.

Graham, E. E. & Whitmore, Lillian E. *The use of dramatic play for diagnosis and therapy.* Denver: Whitmore Drama Kits, 1954.

Haner, C. F. & Brown, Patricia A. Clarification of the instigation to action concept in the frustration-aggression hypothesis. *J. abnorm. soc. Psychol.,* 1955, **51**, 204–206.

Hartup, W. W. & Himeno, Y. Social isolation vs. interaction with adults in relation to aggression in preschool children. *J. abnorm. soc. Psychol.* 1959, **59**, 17–22.

Hollenberg, Eleanor & Sperry, Margaret. Some antecedents of aggression and effects of frustration in doll play. *Personality,* 1951, **1**, 32–43.

Jersild, A. T. & Markey, F. V. Conflicts between preschool children. *Child Develpm. Monogr.,* 1935, No. 21.

Kagan, J. The measurement of overt aggression from fantasy. *J. abnorm. soc. Psychol.,* 1956, **52**, 390–393.

Kepler, Helen. Distribution of aggressive and submissive behavior among 200 problem children. *Smith Coll. Stud. Soc. Wk.,* 1933–34, **4**, 167–168.

Korner, Anneliese F. *Some aspects of hostility in young children.* New York: Grune & Stratton, 1949.

Lesser, G. S. The relationship between overt and fantasy aggression as a function of maternal response to aggression. *J. abnorm. soc. Psychol.,* 1957, **55**, 218–221.

Levin, H. & Sears, R. R. Identification with parents as a determinant of doll play aggression. *Child Develpm.,* 1956, **27**, 135–153.

Levin, H. & Turgeon, Valerie. The influence of the mother's pressures on children's doll play aggression. *J. abnorm. soc. Psychol.,* 1957, **55**, 304–308.

Levy, D. M. Hostility patterns in sibling rivalry experiments. *Amer. J. Orthopsychiat.,* 1936, **6**, 183–257.

Lynn, D. B. An investigation of hypotheses basic to a concept of relative intensity of interaction. Unpublished doctor's dissertation, Purdue University, 1955.

McKee, J. P. & Leader, Florence B. The relationship of socio-economic status & aggression to the competitive behavior of school children. *Child Develpm.* 1955, **26**, 135–142.

Miller, D. R. & Swanson, G. E. *Inner conflict and defense.* New York: Dryden, 1959.

Miller, N. E. Theory and experiment relating psychoanalytic displacement to stimulus-response generalization. *J. abnorm. soc. Psychol.,* 1948, **43**, 155–178.

Morgan, Patricia & Gaier, E. L. Direction of aggression in the mother-child punishment situation. *Child Develpm.* 1956, **27**, 447–457.

Morris, H. H., Jr., Escoll, P. J., & Wexler, R. Aggressive behavior disorders in childhood: a follow-up study. *Amer. J. Psychiat.,* 1956, **112**, 991–997.

Muste, M. J. & Sharp, D. F. Some influential factors in the determination of aggressive behavior in preschool children. *Child Develpm.,* 1947, **18**, 11–28.

Patterson, G. A nonverbal technique for the assessment of aggression in children. Unpublished paper, 1958.

Phillips, Ruth. Doll play as a function of the realism of the materials and the length of the experimental session. *Child Develpm.*, 1945, **16**, 123–143.

Pintler, Margaret H.　Doll play as a function of experimenter-child interaction and initial organization of materials. *Child Develpm.*, 1945, **16**, 145–166.

Rambert, Madeline L.　*Children in conflict.*　New York: International University Press, 1949.

Raush, H. L., Dittman, A. T., & Taylor, T. J.　The interpersonal behavior of children in residential treatment. *J. abnorm. soc. Psychol.*, 1959, **58**, 9–26.

Redl, F. & Wineman, D.　*The aggressive child.*　Glencoe, Ill.: Free Press, 1957.

Robinson, Elizabeth F.　Doll play as a function of the doll family constellation. *Child Develpm.*, 1946, **17**, 99–120.

Roff, M. & Roff, L.　An analysis of the variance of conflict behavior in preschool children. *Child Develpm.*, 1940, **11**, 43–60.

Sears, Pauline S.　Doll play aggression in normal young children: influence of sex, age, sibling status, father's absence. *Psychol. Monogr.*, 1951, **65**, No. 6.

Sears, R. R., Maccoby, Eleanor E., & Levin, H.　*Patterns of child rearing.*　Evanston, Ill.: Row, Peterson, 1957.

Sears, R. R., Whiting, J. W. M., Nowlis, V., & Sears, P. S.　Some child-rearing antecedents of aggression and dependency in young children. *Genet. Psychol. Monogr.*, 1953, **47**, 135–234.

Siegel, Alberta E. & Kohn, Lynnett G.　Permissiveness, permission, & aggression: the effect of adult presence or absence on aggression in children's play. *Child Develpm.*, 1959, **30**, 131–141.

Slavson, S. R.　The treatment of aggression: VII. through group therapy. *Amer. J. Orthopsychiat.*, 1943, **13**, 419–426.

Stone, L. J.　Aggression and destruction games: balloons.　In Lois B. Murphy (Ed.), *Personality in young children.* vol. 1.　New York: Basic Books, 1956.

Walder, L. O.　Validating a sociometric measure of aggression.　Paper read at American Psychological Assn. meetings, 1960.

Walters, J. & Pearce, Doris, & Dahms, Lucille.　Affectional and aggressive behavior of preschool children. *Child Develpm.*, 1957, **28**, 15–26.

Wolberg, L. R.　A note on the treatment of aggression in emotionally disturbed children. *Psychiat. Quart.*, 1944, **18**, 667–673.

Wright, M. E.　The influence of frustration upon the social relations of young children. *Char. & Pers.*, 1943, **12**, 111–122.

Yarrow, L. J.　The effect of antecedent frustration on projective play. *Psychol. Monogr.*, 1948, **62**, No. 6.　(Whole No. 293).

Author Index

Subject Index